SEVEN STEPS IN THE DARK

SEVEN STEPS IN THE DARK

By

Bob Smith

Luath Press Ltd.
Barr, Ayrshire.

First Edition 1991

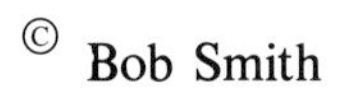

The publisher acknowledges subsidy from the Scottish Arts Council towards the publication of this volume.

FOREWORD

By Martin O'Neill, M.P.

I am pleased to be able to write a foreword to Bob Smith's autobiography. Not only is this a most important document of social history, but also a compulsive "good read".

Bob started work in the mines when it was "every man for himself", right down to buying and using your own gelignite. If you were lucky your father took you down the pit and taught you all he knew about safe working practices. Bob worked in seven pits, starting with the most primitive pick and shovel work and pit ponies dragging out the coal, and ending with modern automatic cutters and hydraulic safety props.

A fearless man, both in the face of the physical dangers of the pit and in verbal combat with mine owners and managers who sought to risk men's lives for the sake of profit, Bob has worked all his life for improved wages and conditions and above all for safe working in the mines. When accidents did occur he spent long hours in paper work to obtain the maximum in compensation for his colleagues.

Bob came to my office with some queries and saw my assistant. Sadly, we were not able to help much with the problem, but she got Bob talking to see if there was any other kind of help that could be offered. So it came out that he was writing his life history and Ann saw for the first time the hundreds of close covered, hand-written foolscap pages where his story flowed freely and virtually unedited, moving effortlessly between dialogue in the vernacular and vivid descriptive passages. These range from romantic evocations of the wildlife and countryside as viewed by the boy exploring with his mates, to a compelling description of the life and characters in the old Miners Rows. Then on to tell of each of the mines, both detailing the changing techniques of winning the coal and evoking the fearful claustrophobic dangers of the pit. Throughout the account, his good humour shows through, and many problems are solved with wit rather than force.

A phone call to the People's Palace gave the name of a possible publisher. At this point Bob was introduced to a local Mining History Group run by Andy Gallagher, and they took over liaison with the publisher, and you here see the result.

Bob Smith is one of those working men who clearly could have achieved a great deal in other walks of life had he not gone down the pit. In doing so, however, he contributed so much to the welfare of his fellow workers that it is doubly important we have such a vivid record of what he gave, and for that we have to be grateful.

I am proud that Bob's story first came to light in my office, and look forward to reading more of the stories that are still flowing with enviable ease from his pen.

Martin O'Neill

Martin O'Neill

CONTENTS

Introduction I

Every Day Summer 1

The First Step — Ferniegair 35

The Second Step — Bothwell 105

The Third Step — Burghlea 137

The Fourth Step — Tower Mine 153

The Fifth Step — Shotts 166

The Sixth Step — Alloa 181

The Seventh Step — Bogside 206

Postscript 312

DEDICATION

I dedicate this book to my Mother, Father and the family I was born into, to my Wife, a patient, caring woman of high moral values, and a loving Mother.

This book should give the reader an insight into the lives of miners. It is an authentic account of my own experiences, and typical of the lives of many others.

In this book I have written of the atrocious conditions in that unnatural environment, those wet and dangerous places, the gases and other noxious fumes that burn men's lungs, the many injuries and deaths. But above all, I have written of the comradeship that prevails, the unity and the struggle for a reasonable living wage, the generous support for other workers in industry, the unfailing support and help to charities.

I also try to pay tribute to the wives and mothers who stand by their men in the struggle for a better and brighter future for all.

This is their story.

My special thanks go to Andy Gallagher and Ann Henty, and the other members of our local history group, whose unfailing support and assistance made my task of writing possible.

Frontispiece by courtesy of *New Caledonian Mercury*

INTRODUCTION

THIS COLLIERY
IS NOW MANAGED BY
THE NATIONAL COAL BOARD
ON BEHALF OF THE PEOPLE

On Vesting Day, 2nd January, 1947, that sign was unveiled on every colliery, and the coal mines became the first nationalised industry in the country. It was a great day, a proud day, the culmination of generations of effort to remove the coal industry from the grasping and inefficient hand of private ownership.

As long ago as 1892 Scottish miners were demanding nationalisation as the only solution to the problems of the industry and the miners. They won the support of the T.U.C., and from then onwards, nationalisation of the mines was a central demand of the Trades Union movement.

In 1919, the Royal Commission chaired by Lord Sankey roundly condemned the coalowners and recommended nationalisation as the only remedy for the industry. The Government had undertaken that it would implement the findings of the Commission, but when the central finding was that particular "extreme measure", the devious Welsh Wizard, Lloyd George, premier of a coalition Government, declined to keep the promise. Instead, the industry was left in private hands, a decision which led directly to the General Strike of 1926, a traumatic experience, which reverberated down the years, and whose effects can still be felt today.

There can be no doubt that the leaders of the miners in Scotland always regarded nationalisation of the industry as a political step towards the socialism they espoused so strongly. That was by no means the case with the rank and file, who regarded that form of pit ownership in purely econonomic and social terms — a means to better conditions, better wages and more security.

In the event, both leaders and men have been disappointed. Far from leading towards the socialism of which the leaders are still convinced advocates, nationalisation led only to a different degree of capitalism, state capitalism, which proved just as intractable, just as inexorable, as the private owners ever were. As for the men, after a short period of comparative goodwill, they found they had to battle again, but this time to preserve their industry. They failed. Today there is only one deep coal production centre left in Scotland, and that is under constant threat.

Coal is still being produced, but most of it, about 3 million tons each year, is dug from open-cast mines, thirteen of them worked by the Coal Board and forty-seven by private operators. Open-cast does not need colliers. The workers use great diggers and bulldozers in vast holes in the ground. Generally, they are not Unionised and have not got the long tradition of organisation and militancy that made the miners special. They present no threat to the political climate of the day.

So deep coal mining in Scotland is dead. Or is it? There are many, and Bob Smith is one, who argue that sooner or later it will have to be revived, and when that day comes, Scotland will have to start all over again, learning how to mine coal, learning how to exploit the estimated 700 million tons of coal left in deep seams. When the oil runs out, as it most certainly will, then coal will again be the only source of fossil fuel, Scotland's last natural resource.

Bob Smith has written his life story, and it enthralls. But it is nothing unusual, except in so far as he has written about it. Hundreds of men, over hundreds of years, have devoted their life and their strength to the betterment and the welfare of their mining comrades. Bob spent his life and his strength working through his beloved Union for the improvement of conditions in the collieries. Not just for more wages and increased production, but also for improved safety, for treatment of industrial diseases, for compensation for injuries. He devoted his life to his comrades, and no man can do more. This is a side of Trades Unionism that is little noted. Co-operation with management, not conflict. Adaptation to new methods, not Luddism. Self-sacrifice, not self-interest.

Bob was the proud bearer of a long tradition. Again and again, he refers to the lessons he learned from his father, lessons not just about how to work safely and well, but lessons on how to deal with people, how to be a miner, with all that implies in terms of readiness to sacrifice yourself for a brother miner.

Bob's father, with his love of the country and farming, and the small holding which he ran, was a direct link with an older, kinder sort of mining. In the middle of the 19th century, Larkhall, where Bob was born, was a village of 2453 people, and they were weavers, colliers, smallholders and farmers. Many of the colliers had smallholdings, and many smallholders worked in the collieries Some even owned their own small pits, worked by family labour. Coal mining was a cottage industry, just like weaving. Writing about Larkhall in 1893, one miner, Thomas Stewart, described his childhood. He grew up in *'A little thatched cottage, beyond the door was an orchard, and beyond that a wee burnie.'* He worked in a small mine owned by his father, along with an aunt and his brother. Even the families which worked only as colliers frequently had a cow or two in a little byre, and a paddock for grass and crops, often worked by one of the women, while the men and other women worked the coal.

It sounds idyllic, and perhaps it was, but, just like their neighbours the handweavers, the colliers' was a way of life doomed by the inexorable march of industrialisation.

Such primitive methods of production could not serve the growing industries. Coal was needed in vast quantities by the ironworks and other industries so rapidly developing. Deeper pits, bigger pits, expensive pits with expensive machinery were required, and only those with capital to invest, and large amounts of capital, too, could establish them. The days of the coal owners had dawned.

But even in the new conditions, the character of those old colliers, handed on from generation to generation, remained the same. They were proud and self-assertive, forming unions, striking, demanding — and winning — control over their working conditions. They rejected and were contemptuous of the incomers, mostly Irish, brought in to work alongside them, and who were seen as pliable tools of the bosses and as diluting the fine militant tradition of the old colliers. And of course they brought their Roman Catholic religion with them, and that, for many years, introduced new social strains. Sometimes those strains were no more important than rivalry between football teams, but occasionally they erupted into riot and mayhem.

Just a little further back in history, of course, Bob Smith's collier ancestors would have been serfs, bound for life to the coalmines, bought and sold with the coal seams, flogged if they were judged to not be working hard enough. Men, women and children were thirled to the coal owners. At their very baptism babies were bound to a life-long serfdom in the pits. That was not so long ago, and it ended only in 1799. For almost two centuries, Scottish coal had been won by serf labour, in conditions of brutality and inhumanity almost incomprehensible.

Children as young as six years old were put to work. Girls were considered better than boys at their work, because they were more amenable. At first they stood for fourteen hours a day in the blackness of the pit, opening and closing doors to direct the airflow. Then as soon as they were strong enough, they were put to coalbearing, dragging sledges of coal from the face to the ladders leading to the surface, or climbing the ladders with over a hundred-weight of coal in baskets on their backs, supported by a leather strap round their foreheads.

Injury and death, pain and exhaustion, were their constant companions. They did not go willingly into that hell — the law compelled them to do it. None escaped the chains. If a collier married, then his wife and their children were bound to work in the pit.

Of course, like that other Peculiar Institution of slavery which it resembled in so many ways, it was an inefficient method of production. No-one willingly entered into servitude: only those born to it and compelled by law did so. Even when the coalowners were given the right to impress "Vagabonds" and orphans, coal production was limited by a shortage of labour. Consequently, when the demand for coal increased so enormously with the Industrial Revolution, the two centuries of serfdom ended, and labour became free. The immediate effect of that, naturally, was that those previously bound left the mines, and the labour shortage increased, as did the price of coal. In Glasgow, coal doubled in price in five years. Wages in the pits also increased, as the coalowners attempted to attract the labour they neeeded.

As the production of coal increased, though, demand also leaped ahead. The large cities of Glasgow and Edinburgh were powered by coal, of course, and the population was increasing. The great deposits of exploitable Lowland peat were exhausted, and the revolution in agriculture meant a greatly increased demand for lime, which was produced in coal-fired kilns. In those circumstances of growing demand and of production limited by labour shortage, the coalowners again turned to imported labour, again mostly Irish, although some miners were brought from as far as Lithuania. These were collectively known as "Poles", and they long preserved their national identity and culture.

The first records of coal production in Scotland indicate that the monks of Newbattle began the industry in the twelfth century. By the seventeenth century London and the other great cities of England depended on coal, for the English woodlands were exhausted. This presented a great opportunity for those who owned coal mines on or near navigable water, and the mines along the Forth flourished. Landowners drove pits, and found coal everywhere. By 1690 half the ships leaving Scottish ports were carrying coal to the English markets. Three big new ports were developed to meet the demand — Methil, Port Seton and Saltcoats.

The name "Saltcoats" draws attention to another vital trade of the day, the production of salt. Salt, then, was not just something to sprinkle liberally on fish suppers. It was a necessity for preserving food, and the demand round all the European coast line, and in the vast Dutch salt herring industry was enormous. Scotland, in a sense, was lucky. Virtually surrounded by salt water, she also had easily available coal which could be used to evaporate the sea water in great iron pans.

Lucky, yes, but the workers were not so lucky. Serfdom was imposed on both the colliers and salt workers to ensure, it was hoped, enough labour for those two vastly profitable industries. The power of the State was used, at the behest of the owners, to enforce labour.

It was not enough. Shortage of labour was strangling the coal industry by the mid-eighteenth century, and in 1775, there was the first half-hearted attempt to free miners. An Act was passed to make all new recruits to the pits free workers. That, too, failed in its objectives, and it was noted that *"There are not a sufficient number of colliers, coalbearers and salters in Scotland for working the quantities of coal and salt necessarily wanted, and many newly discovered coals remain unwrought....."*

So the coalowners had to think again. In 1799, after almost 200 years of serfdom, the colliers were finally free. Once again, the medicine did not provide a cure, and the shortage of labour intensified, rather than eased, as colliers took their first opportunity of getting out of the mines to which they and their ancestors had been bound. There was an acute shortage of labour, which of course left the remaining colliers in a strong bargaining position to win higher wages and better conditions. Again the demand for cheap (and pliable) labour was met by importing it, mainly from Ireland.

Coal fired the Industrial Revolution, and it changed the face of the coalfields. What had been a rural industry became the centre, the very powerhouse, of industrialisation. Lanarkshire, for example, became "The Land of Fire" as the Neilston Hot Blast process of smelting took the Scottish iron industry into the very forefront of the industrialised nations of the world. From being an idyllic place of rural peace and tranquillity, Lanarkshire became a place where there was:

A hunnert funnels bleezin, reekin,
Coal an iron stane, charrin, smeekin,
Navvies, miners, keepers, fillers,
Puddlers, rollers, iron millers.
Reested, reekit raggit laddies,
Firemen, enginemen, and Paddies.

That was how Janet Hamilton saw it. She was a poet of the early nineteenth century, and previously had extolled the loveliness of the countryside, but later, as that countryside disappeared beneath the Dark Satanic Mills, she went on to describe the effects of industrialisation, in the vivid words of her own Scots tongue.

A growing social conscience in the country began to protest about the employment of women and children in the mines. Characteristically, the protest was based largely on the moral danger they were alleged to be facing, rather than on the inhumanity of their conditions. Lightly dressed women and girls were dragging hutches of coal in the mines, and carrying baskets up steep ladders. Who was to know what immoral thoughts and acts such sights might engender in the minds of the men? However, and for whatever reasons, the campaign was successful, and in 1842 a Mines Act forbade women and children from working underground. So ponies took the place of the women, and mechanical hoists the place of the ladders.

Gradually as King Coal became more firmly ensconsed on the industrial system, skilled colliers became the aristocrats of labour. With that thrawn independence which marked them always, they embarked upon struggles to improve their lot. As early as 1871, the miners of Fife won the eight-hour day, after a long stay-down strike, and, as Bob Smith makes clear, an attack on one miner was an attack on all.

As time passed the older and shallower seams in Ayrshire and Lanarkshire became exhausted and production moved to thicker but deeper seams in the Lothians and Fife. In 1913, Ayrshire and Lanarkshire produced two-thirds of Scottish coal, but by 1937 the production was only 7 million tons, down from the seventeen and a half million tons of 1913. That meant a mass movement of men to the east, as they followed the work. It also meant that some of the sectarian troubles of the western coalfield migrated to the east.

Scottish mining was efficient, producing one eighth more per man than the U.K. average. Scottish pits were also in the forefront of mechanisation, with machine-cut coal amounting to 80% of production by 1938.

Miners themselves did not always benefit from increased product-ion. Indeed, real wages in the pits actually fell nearly 5% between 1913 and 1938. The coalowners, faced with a declining market and the necessity of increased capital investment, struggled to hold down costs: the colliers struggled to maintain their standard of life. Out of that conflict there came the 1926 General Strike, the sharpest example of social and economic struggle Britain had seen.

The coalowners were intent on wage cuts: the miners were intent on resisting: the Government (shades of 1984!) saw an opportunity of breaking the power of the Miners Union, perhaps the strongest and (as they saw it) most threatening Union in the country. In 1925 the Government agreed to give a temporary subsidy to the coalowners to keep wages at their existing level, and meanwhile Government and industry stockpiled coal.

A year later, in 1926, they were ready, and in early May they ended the subsidy. The coal owners cut wages, and the men went on strike. The T.U.C. declared a General Strike in support of the miners, and for nine days the country came to a standstill. But only for nine days, and then the General Strike ended, and the miners were left to stand alone.

They fought on, facing incredible hardship and deprivation, until November, and then had to go back, with reduced wages and worsened conditions, which left them living standards hardly above those of the unemployed. The coalowners won, and the Government won, and they showed no magnanimity in victory.

All those who had been prominent in the strike were blacklisted, and many were unable ever to find work again. '*Do you remember 1926?* asks Idris Davies, a Welsh poet.

Do you remember 1926? That summer of soups and speeches,
The sunlight on the idle wheels and the deserted crossings,
And the laughter and the cursing in the moonlit street?
....
Do you remember 1926? The great dream and the swift disaster?

At the end, a group of Welsh miners, blacklisted and destitute, are singing for coppers in the London streets.

'Ay, ay, we remember 1926,' said Dai to Shinkin,
As they stood on the kerb in Charing Cross Road.
'And we shall remember 1926 until our blood is dry.'

The coalowners and their managers became dictators, controlling every aspect of life and death, especially in the isolated mining villages. The miners lived in company houses, bought their goods in the company store, traveled in company buses. The word of the manager could deprive a miner and his family of their work, their livelihood, their house and everything they possessed. It was not enough for the miner himself to acquiesce to the whims of the manager, but the whole family, even unto uncles and cousins and nieces had to acquiesce, or else it could be be, and often was: 'Get down the road, and leave the keys of your houses at the office tomorrow morning.'

Gradually, of course, things changed, and miners, especially in Fife, began to reassert their old individualism and organisation. The industry was sick, and that was plain enough to see, but diagnosis and prescription were not so easy. The coalowners struggled to hold down costs while the miners struggled to maintain some standard of life and dignity. Some coalowners took swollen profits and reinvested in the industry; others invested their profits elsewhere, or squandered them. Certainly the financial world of the day regarded coal mining as a sound investment. Mining shares rose in price 300% between 1913 and 1938, while real wages for the miners continued to fall

As industrialists always do when faced with intractable troubles, the coalowners turned to Government for assistance, and in 1938, mining royalties were nationalised. Royalties were the sums paid by the coalowners to the actual owners of the land on which the collieries stood. They had amounted to one shilling or one shilling and sixpence for every ton of coal extracted, and of course were a considerable burden on the industry, with a vast sum being paid to landowners who contributed nothing to the industry.

Again, in 1942, at the height of the last war, Government intervened, and the Coal Commission took total control of all pits. It served as a trial period for the nationalisation of 1947.

Unquestionably nationalisation was an initial success. The industry expanded in the following ten years, and as Bob Smith makes clear, there was often a good spirit of co-operation between management and men. Conditions improved. A five day week was introduced. By 1960, though, the N.C.B., then under Lord Robens, had begun its programme of pit closures, arguing that oil was cheaper than coal, and that only the most efficient pits could, and should, compete. Also, coal was being imported, cheap coal from Poland, China and Australia. The destruction of the mining community was under way, and the seven hundred years saga of Scotland's coal was drawing to its close — or its intermission.

The miners, as one would expect, did not accept this without a struggle. National strikes in 1972 and 1974 delayed the process and even led to some temporary progress. In 1972 the strike lasted seven weeks, and in 1974, four weeks, and the latter led directly to the fall of the Tory Heath Government.

In 1972 especiallly, the immediate results for the miners were good. Their wages had sunk below the industrial average for the country, and that was remedied. Increased pensions were negotiated, and a reduced retiral age. Adult wages were paid at eighteen. Beyond doubt, the public supported the miners in 1972. Engine drivers, for example, refused to move coal. There was also public support, and a lot of it, during the four-weeks strike of 1974, and that support was shown by the election of the Harold Wilson Labour Government, when Ted Heath, the Tory Prime Minister of the day, decided to go to the electorate in what became virtually a referendum on the justice of the miners' strike.

1984 was a different story. The people involved were different, public perception had been changed, and the whole political climate had been manipulated. The miners were drawn into a battle on the issues chosen by the other side, at a time chosen by the other side, and at places decided by the other side.

The miners struck in 1984 to prevent pit closures. They failed, and the result of their failure was a series of pit closures that has left only the tattered rump of an industry. Equally important, it left a mining community split and divided.

In 1914 it was estimated that one fifth of Scotland's population was directly concerned with coalwinning. Today, perhaps 2000 people are so involved. Not so long ago, the Scottish Miner's Gala, held in Edinburgh every June, saw tens of thousands marching with proud banners through the streets of the capital. Now, about 1000 people march, and the miners are seeking to change their own gala into a general Trades Union Gala, in order somehow to preserve the tradition. That is a fair measure of the importance of mining in the industrial structure of the country today.

It may be that deep coal mining really has ended, and that its skills and traditions will soon be no more than a memory, rose-tinted and nostalgic. If that is so, then something very valuable will have gone from Scotland. The mining communities were special, and certainly irreplaceable.

The whole nation is the loser by the loss of the mining community. Both men and women in that community needed qualities of courage special even in industry, where courage is always essential.

There were very few miners who ever encouraged their sons to go into the pit, but there were almost no sons of miners who did not want to emulate their fathers, even if in fact their lives took them in other directions. It was a mans' world, and even those who had gone elsewhere looked back with nostalgia and envy and a peculiar sense of inferiority at the life they had left.

And yet it is common to hear old miners today say that the pit closures were the best thing that ever happened, that they should have happened years ago, and that the pit was no place for a human being.

It is hard to say just what made the mining community so special, but one factor is obvious. Collieries are dangerous places. Men are killed and injured in them, sometimes many men. The awareness of shared danger and the awareness of willing and immediate self-sacrifice was a constant.

It was a tradition, and not only amongst older women, that the wife always saw her husband and sons off to work, at whatever ungodly hour that might be. Unspoken always, but always present, was the fear that the man might not come back frcm the pit, or might not come back whole.

It was the women who waited at the pithead when the horn sounded to signal an accident. One of Bob Smith's earliest memories is of the dead pitman being carried home on a coal cart.

Joe Corrie was a pitman. He was also a poet and a playright, and a man who gives us a better picture of mining than all the pages of official reports and dry statistics. Read Joe Corrie to learn what it was like to be a collier, or a miner's wife. (Much of his work has recently been reprinted by the 7:84 Group.)

We have borne good sons to broken men,
Nurtured them on our hungry breasts,
And given them to our masters when
Their day of life was at its best.

....

We have stood through the naked night to watch
The silent wheels that raised the dead,
We have have gone before to raise the latch,
And lay the pillow beneath their head.

As for the miners themselves, Joe Corrie injected a note of peculiar bitterness:

Crawlin aboot like a snail in the mud,
Covered wi clammie blae,
Me, made after the image o God —
Jings! but it's laughable, tae.

....

Howkin awa neath a mountain o stane
Gaspin for want o air,
The sweat makin streams doon my bare back-bane,
An my knees a hauckit and sair

Of course, everything passes: nothing is eternal. If indeed what we see today is the death throes of coalmining in Scotland, if the industry and the mining communities are to go into the mists of history along with the saltworkers and the kelpburners and the charcoal makers, at least Bob Smith's *Seven Steps In The Dark* will ensure that some aspects of that life are not lost altogether.

TOM ATKINSON

EVERY DAY SUMMER

I was born at Larkhall, Lanarkshire, in 1920. In those days, Larkhall was a mining village set amid a farming community. Once it had been a village of weavers, working in their own houses, and those old houses remained. There were other industries at Larkhall, a foundry, a silkweavers and a bleachfield amongst others. The village was attractively situated between the rivers Avon and Clyde.

I was the youngest of my very loving family, and was affectionately called the Babe. There was Father, Mother, Grandmother, two sisters and two brothers living upstairs in that two-storied building. We had one living room and another room we called the bedroom, and there were also two 'sitting-in' beds in the living room, masked by heavy curtains.

Cooking was done on the coal-fired grate, which had an oven and a swee — a long arm that swivelled pots into position over the fire. There was a smoke board, a sheet of tin plate which could be moved up and down two rods, and was used to ensure that all the smoke went up the chimney, and not into the room. The mantlepiece above the fireplace held various oddments and ornaments, and there was a swan-necked copper gas pipe above the mantlepiece. This gas lamp was fascinating to me, and I chuckled with delight when Father lifted me up to light the lamp with a wax taper, warning me to be very careful and not to touch the flimsy mantle. He turned on the tap, said, 'Right, noo', and as the gas hissed through the pipe I delighted in the soft sound of the flame lighting and the room filling with the yellow light.

There was a large shelf above the door into the back room, stretching the length of the wall. This held many things — jugs, kettles, teapots, vases and a set of three pans used mainly for making the assortment of wines and jams in which my mother and grandmother took such pride. Just above the door there was huge set of cow horns which also fascinated me, and in my innocence I often enquired how and why the coo's horns were up there. At the front of the kitchen was the earthenware sink, with a single cold water tap. On the floor there were home-made rugs designed and made by Mother and Grandmother from strips of woollen rags. This was done on what they called the Tent: a wooden framework about four feet high, with T shaped ends. It was mounted on small wheels, and there were rollers around which the canvas backing was wound — old flour or potato sacks usually. The patterns were drawn with chalk on this canvas, and then they would start making the rug. A long strip of rag was held underneath the canvas and pulled through to the front with a specially made steel hook. There were many hours of work in each rug, and the task of cutting each loop was especially tedious, but the result was fine, a thick and warm new rug to be laid out with pride on the floor. I often fell asleep on the rugs when they were new and thick, and found them comfortable and comforting.

A door to the left of the front window led into the wooden porch, shared by the next door neighbours. There were wash tubs, coal scuttles and a huge mangle used for wringing out the clothes in this porch.

From there a door opened out on to the steps, which were of stone, with an iron railing on each side. The steps themselves were well worn by the constant traffic up and down over the years. Several steps led down to a landing, and then further again to the earthen road passing the building and through the close on to the main road. That earthen road was rutted by carts, and when it rained was a quagmire in which one sank to the ankles. We children enjoyed squelching through the mud, much to the annoyance of our mothers. Ashes from the coal fires were spread there in an unavailing effort to dry it up, for once it had rained again, and a heavy cart had passed, the ruts were as bad as ever. Alongside this roadway was an open drain in which my pal, Charlie Downey, or 'Cha', and I played at sailing our boats. They were really only pieces of wood, although in our imagination were lovely sailing boats, and we had fun.

One day the sewer clogged, and the flood spread over the road. Cha and I were delighted, splashing around at the edges, when suddenly I tripped and fell headlong into that huge pool that stank horribly. Cha, like a good friend, sprang to my rescue, pulling me to my feet coughing and spluttering, soaked from head to foot, with water dripping from me. I ran up the stairs, Cha following, shouting to my mother that I had fallen into the big puddle. Mother rushed out, took one look at my bedraggled figure and said: 'Oh my, what a mess! Scourie dookie fur ye, and ye'll no git oot the nicht agin.' So it was the tub for me and a good scrubbing, though once washed and with dry clothes, Cha and I were allowed to play marbles, or plunkie, as we called it, on the rug.

Charlie and I were inseparable, and were nicknamed the Terrible Twins. Not that we were troublesome: we were fun-loving and a bit mischievous.

It was our delight to stray across the road into a place we called the Buffy. This was a collection of Miners' Rows — tiny, miserable houses owned by the coal company, and let to miners. The people there lived in dreadful conditions, with the houses smoky and bug-ridden. The folks living there were rough and tough, but formed a close-knit community. We often ventured over to play there, and were sometimes invited into the houses by the children we played with, and the mother or Big Sister would usually ask 'Who's this: what's yer name. Dae ye want a jeely piece?' and cut a thick slice of bread, spead a large dollop of jam or jelly on it, double it over and hand it to us. This was a treat, although my mother would have said it was greed, for we were fortunate, and I was well fed with plenty of soup and porridge, and always had a good dinner — so different from some of our mates.

One pal of ours was ill and Cha and I went to visit him. When we knocked at the door a huge figure appeared. It was his Big Sister. 'Whit dae you twa want?' she shouted, rather than asked. 'Is Midge in?' enquired Charlie. 'Of course he's in: in his bloody bed. Dae ye want tae see him? Weel, cam in.' She turned, leaving the door open for us to follow, but we were shy and bewildered by her gruffness. 'Are ye comin in or are ye no?' she called from the back of the house. We entered rather sheepishly, and found Midge in a sit-in bed with chairs arranged at the front of it. He was very pale and could only whisper. 'Whit's wrang with you?' I enquired. 'I've goat a beelin throat,' he croaked. 'That's sair,' I said, 'I had that and ye canna eat onything at all, it's that sair.' 'Aye, yer right there,' replied Midge with difficulty.

Cha spoke up, telling him everything we had been doing, while I looked round the smoke-laden house, with a table in the middle of the room with the remains of their dinner still on it, dirty plates and all. The floor had a few rag rugs covering parts of the stone slabs. An oil lamp hung from the ceiling and there were big armchairs on either side of the blazing fireplace. A pile of clothes lay on one chair, and Midge's mongrel dog on the other, fast asleep. A rope was strung across the mantlepiece carrying socks and shirts, rather tattered, and shabby-looking womens' dresses. The door opened, and Midge's father came in, a scraggy looking man. 'Ahm hame, is ma denner ready, how's the boy the day, is he ony better?' he said, all in one sentence. 'And who might you be?' he asked of us. 'Twa of Midge's wee pals in to see him: yer soup is oot, better tack it the noo when its warm,' shouted Midge's Big Sister, who seemed to be able to speak only in a shout.

Midge's father, Pate, drew a chair into the table, pushed a pile of dirty dishes to one side and started on his soup. 'Hey, Jessie, is there ony breed?' he demanded. The father was in from the pit, and his clothes stank with sweat. Unwashed and filthy, he gobbled his soup hungrily. 'Gae me anither plate o soup, hen, that wis guid, and by God I wis ready for it.' Big Sister filled his plate and he dipped a slice of bread into the soup. 'Whaur dae ye twa cam fie? Ye dinna stie aboot here.' Cha told him where we lived. 'I socht that ye dinna luck like ony buddy aroon here. Whit brings ye ower here?' 'We come oor to see Midge: he's oor pal,' I said, rather sheepishly, taken aback by this rough looking man who sat supping and slurping over his soup. Finished, he wiped his mouth on his sleeve. 'That was guid, Hen, ony left for the dug?' 'Naw, naw, that wis the lot,' replied Big Sister. 'Weel, gie him the bloody bone oat the soap.' She rushed to get the bone which he took from her and called to the dog. 'Come oan, Scamp, ye auld flea-bag, here's yer bane.' Scamp leaped from the chair and snatched the bone and went under the table with it.

'Better noo gae near him when he's eatin his bane ur he'll eat you tae,' laughed Pate. 'Is ma watter ready?' Jean told him it was, and brought in a large tin bath which she put before the fire. A large pot of boiling water from the fire went into it, and another of cold. Pate stripped to the waist, taking his pit boots off and tossing them to one side. Jean hastily picked them up and took them outside to brush the mud from them, while Pate washed the dirt and grime from his body. 'Wull ah wash yer back the day?' Jean asked from the doorway. 'Naw, naw, ye ken it wakens the back washing it too often: it wull dae the day, Hen.' Pate dried himself with a coarse sacking towel, then pulled on a heavy striped shirt that came down below his knees, and changed his pit trousers for a pair of long johns. He sat down on the chair where Scamp had been sleeping, and sighed contentedly. Lighting his pipe, he stretched his feet on to the fender before the fire. He was a man well fed and at rest after labour.

It is strange how that cameo of pit life has stayed with me all these years: I remember it all very clearly, and even remember how poor little Midge asked all kinds of questions, as we chatted, about what was going on outside. I also clearly remember that as we left Midge's house, promising to come back soon, there was quite a commotion in the lane, with various voices calling to one another that the Pack Wife was here. Women rushed out of their houses, down the earthen road, and made a ring round the Pack Wife. She was a fat, stumpy woman, carrying a huge tarpaulin-wrapped pack on her back, supported by a strap round her forehead. She carried a selection of secondhand clothes, shoes, hats and boots. When she stopped at her selected spot, she gave a great 'Hup', as she heaved the pack down on to the road, then shouted in a loud voice 'Noo, here, Wives, staun clear till ah get ma pack opened!' The women, eager to be the first to snatch whatever bargains might be disclosed, jostled for the best position in the ring around the pack and the Pack Wife.

She was puffing and out of breath as she untied the big sheet, exposing the contents. As she leaned over, she let off a fart. 'Aam aa oot of pech this morning,' she cried, and farted again, much to the shrill amusement of the women. 'That's no pechin, that's a fart,' shouted one, 'Better watch its no a shite, ur we will awe be stunk oot and noo git anythin.'

'Right,' called the Pack Wife, undisturbed by the laughter and shouts and the remarks, 'Let's git started. Dae ye see onything you would like the day?' And so the women got down to the job of sorting out what they wanted or needed from the big pile of used clothes. They held dresses aloft, and trousers for the men folk, and clothes for the kids, asking advice from their neighbours. 'Dae ye think that wad fit oor Wull or Tam? Wad this dae oor Betty or Jeannie?' They argued and squabbled over the poor bits of clothing, buying them for a few pence, and leaving some almost in tears as they turned away. 'Na, na, ah canna afford that: ah hive na tuppence tae ma name.'

It was on our next visit to Midge, still in his bed, that Cha and I witnessed one of the major tragedies of pit life. As we turned into the Miners' Row, we heard shouts and saw people running out of the top close. A crowd gathered, whispering amongst themselves. There had been a serious accident in the pit. As we stood on the outskirts of the crowd, we saw a horse-drawn cart, the type used to deliver coal, being led along by a grim-faced carter, followed by tired, black-faced miners, all solemn and sad. 'Is he hurt bad, Rab?' called one of the women. 'He'll noo get hurt again: he's deid,' came the curt reply.

The women began their lamentations. 'Oh my,' they wailed, 'An that puir Jessie wi ah they puir weans. Whit wull she dae noo!' 'Onybody else hurt?' cried another voice. 'Aye, your Johnnie has his leg brokken and wee Rab an arm brokken and yin or twa more hiv got some cuts and bruises,' one of the tired miners replied. The procession of the dead man in the coal cart went on, with some of the women scurrying ahead to make his bed for him and to do whatever they could for his new widow and their children. Not that they could do much, but they would do what they could, as they had done so often before, and would do again.

As the nights grew darker, it became time again to play marbles. My brother and his pal would take Cha and me over to where a squad of lads were playing Muggie or Ringie at the old school dyke, where there was a convenient lamp post. Muggie was a game played with bools, small balls of brightly coloured hard clay. We bought them, when we could, at a halfpenny for a box of twentyfive. A small bug hole was dug out at the base of the dyke, then the players called a number, perhaps three or six, and then the two of them stood side by side, about six feet away from the hole on the mark. The first player threw his handful of bools towards the mug hole. If an even number went in, he was the winner and won the lot, but if an odd number went in, then the other player won the lot.

Ringie was a game several players took part in. A small square was drawn on the hard earth with the heel of the boot, and each player put into the square the number of bools agreed on. The first player had a steelie, a big ball bearing, and he knuckled the steelie into the square to knock out as many bools as he could. He won those he knocked out, and the next player had his turn, till all the bools had been won.

Plunkie was a game where four stonies, small stone balls, were stamped into the earth in an area about ten feet square. Each player, fist on the ground, stonie between thumb and forefinger, would plunk the stonie towards the first hole to try to put it into the hole. The second and third players would try. The one nearest the hole would try again, knocking the first player's stonie out of the way, which gave you another try.

Winter and its hard frosts brought sliding down the brae. Usually we had to make the slide, carrying buckets and washtubs of water and pouring them down the frost-hardened earth until we had a fine long slide. Then we could play coorie dookie or shoot the craw as we slid down the slope. In coorie dookie you crouched down at the top of the slide, holding your knees, and slid down until you decided to stop, simply by sitting down on the ice. In shoot the craw, you crouched down on one foot, with the other leg sticking out forward, and slid down on one foot, until either you tipped over, or a friend caught you by the leg.

Another winter game was hunch cuddie hunch, in which two teams competed. The leader of the first team stood against the wall and the rest of the lads bent down, in a long line, head between the legs of the lad in front, with the front lad leaning against the leader. The other team then took running jumps onto the backs of the bending boys and when they were all in place, the first team, the cuddies, began to shake and heave, trying to dislodge their riders.

High Spy, or ben gee lum also needed two teams. A den was marked out, usually near the school wall beneath the lamp post and the first team went off to hide. There were plenty of nooks and crannies for this, washhouses, coal houses and even dustbins were used. The second team searched for the lads in the first team, patting their heads three times when they were found. Those lads then had to go to the den and stay there until they were released by one of their number bravely creeping or racing up to the den without being seen and shouting 'Ben Gee Lum'. This released all the prisoners.

Kick the can was rather similar, except that the rescuer released all the prisoners by kicking an old tin can out of the den.

Then of course there was school. I quite enjoyed the primary school; there were lots of friends and lots of games, and two very fine teachers. My first teacher was the headmistress, Miss Percy. She looked huge to me, being both tall and stout, and with a loud and commanding voice. When dealing with children she was very gentle, though strict enough, demanding and receiving respect and attention. In the higher classes we had Miss Raesbet. We all loved, almost idolised, her. In our eyes she was beautiful, very kind and gentle and very caring. We knew that she had taken some boys who had no boots for school up to the Co-op and bought boots for them. She had also bought dresses for some of the girls. She had a great flair for teaching and could hold our attention all day, and still find time to help those who were in difficulties, either with their lessons or at home.

The boys and girls sat next to each other in class, and I was seated next to a lassie from the Miners' Rows. Jean Bent was a pretty wee thing, and I enjoyed her company. She treated me like a brother. One day she was in tears when the school bully was ragging her about her name. I found her crying, and tried to comfort her. Tam, the bully, found us both, and began to rib me, singing the weans' song 'Lawd and Lass, kiss the lass.' 'Go on, wee yin, gie her a kiss,' he sneered. It was too much for me. Dropping my slate I rushed at him with flailing tiny fists. Down he went, with me on top, still hitting whatever I could find. Suddenly I was dragged away, still struggling to be at him. 'You little devil. Stop this at once,' ordered the voice, very stern now, of Miss Percy. She shook me like a rag doll. 'Go to my room at once, and you too,' she added to the dejected and battered Tam. We both slunk away, sure we would be punished for fighting in the playground. Miss Percy pushed me into the empty class room and I staggered across the floor. 'That was disgraceful: two of my boys fighting.' She began her lecture, while at the same time trying to stem Tam's nosebleed, holding his head back and pressing between his eyes, an operation I watched with interest. I was a bit sorry for Tam by this time, although I had no regrets for the action I had taken in defence of Jean.

When Miss Percy had unravelled the whole story of why we were fighting, I expected that we would both have a taste of the belt right then. Instead she told us to come back to her room after school. She made us shake hands, and sent us back to our classes.

After school, in her quiet class room, we were told to write out twenty times, on our slates 'We must not, will not, fight in school again.' It seemed to take an age, with the slate pencils squeaking loudly in the unaccustomed silence of the classroom. When we had finished, she checked our writing, which we had copied from the blackboard, and then gave us a lecture on the evils of fighting, and exacted a promise that we would not transgress again, otherwise we could expect a much more severe punishment. In fact, Tam and I never did fight again, and we became good friends.

It was about this time that my father arrived home one day with some of his workmates, talking in serious tones about an impending strike. Mother looked worried. 'Is this true? Is it tae be a strike,' she asked. 'Aye, aye,' replied Father, 'there's nae other alternative. The hale o the country will be oot this time. It's tae be a General Strike.' 'How lang will it last? Mother enquired. 'Naebuddy kens that,' Father replied, 'As lang as it takes.' The other men laughed, but there was no humour in their laughter. I had heard my father say that a strike is a good weapon to threaten with, but a bad weapon to use, and clearly he and the rest of his mates were concerned about what was facing them. They began discussing what could be done if there was a long dispute, when every one would suffer the effects and the misery. I heard my father say again that this time there was no alternative, and that he for one was out until there was a settlement. It all seemed remote and unimportant to me, more grown-ups' business, and I slipped out to play footie with my mates.

At school the rooms buzzed with talk of the strike. There was talk of fighting, riots, scabs, and blacklegs, although we younger children did not really understand much of it. We were soon to learn, though, and discover for ourselves the misery and the anguish of a long-drawn-out struggle. We saw the poverty, and the hunger and the ragged clothes, and the struggle of the ordinary, decent folk to feed and clothe the children, and we saw those children and their parents gradually ground down and defeated.

One day about mid-day Miss Raesbet called us all together in the school and told us that we were to have a half-holiday for the rest of the day. There were whoops of delight. 'Now, children, when you leave the school, I want you all to go straight home. You are not to play or hang about in the streets. I don't want to see any of you in the street when I come out. Now off you go, and straight home.'

We all dashed out, screaming with delight at the unusual occurence, and all, obeying the instructions, ran straight home. I told my mother about it, and she nodded understandingly, although she said nothing as I sat down to a plate of soup, which had become the standby, often the only meal.

I was thinking of the joys of playing all the hours of that free afternoon when my mother told me that I would have to stay at home, and at most just play round at the back of the house. 'Ye have nae tae go roon the front,' she insisted. 'There ull be a lot of trouble and maybe fighting, and you stay back and no git hurt.' She was serious and looked very worried. 'Noo, dae ye hear me?' I nodded sheepishly, not understanding. 'If ye gae roon the front I'll skelp yer backside!' she added, menacingly.

I promised, although I was full of curiosity. I would bide my time and see what developed in this strange situation.

That afternoon our usual gang gathered to play football, and we had just selected sides and kicked off the ball to start the game when we saw men and women hurrying towards the close mouth. Willie Douglas, the biggest lad of our gang, picked up the ball. 'Come doon and see whits gaun on. Ah doot there's ganna be some trouble.' We rushed to the close, to find a crowd of neighbours, men and women, blocking the entrance. There was excited talk. 'Aye, they'll stop the blacklegs alright,' shouted one woman. 'Whaur aboots hae ah these men cam fae?' asked another. 'Bloody hell, here's the bloody police, merchin down the street.' 'Hell, it wull be murder. Polis noo! If they start there wull be a bloody riot. The colliers ill noo staun fur that.'

Cha and I tried to worm our way through the crowd, and finally got right up to the front, but our success did us no good. Mrs. Davidson spotted us. 'Hai, Davie, catch they twa wee buggers!' Davie caught me by the right ear and Cha by the backside of his trousers, and we were pushed and shoved back through the crowd out of harm's way. There was some laughter from the men and women, but we were angry at our unceremonious treatment. The gang laughed at us when we were once more at the back of the crowd, but questioned us eagerly about what was going on. We told them that the road was packed with people, but that the police were coming. 'There'll be a battle noo,' said Rab, 'and we'll not be able to see it.'

'Aye we wull,' I cried. 'If we gang ower the dyke inti Walker's building and oot the close at the tap we kin see it awe.' This was a good idea, and we whooped with joy. We raced to the dyke that separated the two buildings and clambered over, heedless of the shouts of some women who had spotted us, and knew what we were doing. We cleared the obstacle and ran through the open space that served as a drying green, ducking under the clothes that hung on the lines, with more shouts from the angry women. 'Watch ma claes, ye wee devils!' We reached the mouth of the close, to find only a few people there, watching what was happening further down the road. Men were coming out of the Miners' Rows and marching down towards the Drygate, past the two-storey building and stopping at the Tally shop we knew as Angelo's. The crowd grew by the minute, jostling for a position where each man could see down the Drygate, the route the blacklegs must come.

We stood by the mouth of the close, not knowing what to expect, but sensing trouble. There was a shout: 'Here they come, the blackleg bastards!' There were screams of hatred, obscenities yelled and a surge forward as the scabs approached, with their police escort. 'Git the bastards,' and there was a rush forward. As the two sides clashed, punches were thrown on both sides, and the police escort was broken up. There were several fights taking place at the same time, and more men were rushing forward out of the Rows and closes. Suddenly a mass of blue uniforms appeared from what seemed nowhere as police reinforcements charged into the fighting mass, truncheons flying. There were bloody heads and faces, but this seemed to enrage the miners even more, and they tore into the attack with boots and fists. Gradually, as more police appeared, the battle, which had been swaying backwards and forwards, swayed in favour of the police and the blacklegs, who had suffered the brunt of the attack. The miners began to retreat down into the closes, chased by the police. It seemed that the police had lost any semblance of self-control, and were lashing out furiously with their batons at anyone who stood in their way. I saw one young lad struck viciously across the head. Others saw that, too, and one big miner, retreating into the safety of the close, turned and raced back to where two policemen were standing over the bleeding form of the young lad. 'You bastard! You've killed him!' Incensed with rage at seeing this obvious child struck down so senselessly, the miner struck out at the policeman, once, twice, and he went down across the body of the unconscious boy. The miner went down with him, still punching wildly. The other raced across and laid into the miner with his baton. He groaned, and slumped unconscious across the unconscious boy. Other miners had by now appeared, and so had other policemen. The struggle was short and furious, but it ended by the miners retreating again into the closes, and the first man, the avenger of the young boy, being dragged away, still unconscious, to face whatever happened to him later. The injured police were led and carried away, leaving the lad still lying on the ground, and still unconscious. He was carried into the nearest house, and the blood washed off his face and body, while a very angry crowd stood by the door, waiting to hear about his condition. He was a well-liked lad called Lance Barr, and although still at school worked in the butchers' shop at weekends, and so was known by everybody. He had not been seriously injured by that totally unprovoked attack, but he carried a large scar across his forehead for the rest of his life — a memento of which he was very proud.

There were other skirmishes that day, and for several days following, as the police tried to escort their little handfuls of blacklegs to the mines. It all ended quite suddenly when the few blacklegging families did a moonlight flit and left the area. They were never forgotten, and ever afterwards, wherever they were, carried the brand of 'Blackleg', like the mark of Cain.

The strike dragged on, from days to weeks, and then to months. There was a terrible struggle in every family to keep food on the table, and to keep the family together. There was not just poverty: that we all knew, and our parents knew how to cope with it. Now we faced real hunger and starvation. Still the men and women fought on. There were soup kitchens, and the local butcher and grocer helped as much as they could, but what they could do was little enough. At school we were given porridge, soup and cups of cocoa. This was cooked up in the schoolyard, and we thought it was a wonderful novelty. Our parents and teachers did everything they could to shield us from the worst hardship, but they could not shield us from some understanding of the misery our elders were undergoing.

After school we often followed the men down into the woods, where they would saw down a tree and cut it into lengths, and then men and women together would carry it back and cut it again into logs. Everyone got their share, and the waste wood was then gathered into a heap for a bonfire, into which potatoes were placed for roasting. I remember them being pulled out of the embers with long pieces of wire, and shared out among the children. I remember, too, how they tasted. Often enough the bonfire was also the scene for a bit of entertainment, unusual enough in those bitter days to be recalled even today. A man called Nicol had an accordion, and he would bring it out and sit on the steps of the Buildings, near the bonfire, and play jigs and reels and the music hall songs of the day. Men and women and children gathered around, and there was some dancing and singing, and for an hour or two the utter misery and increasing hopelessness was banished from the minds of those struggling people.

The winter came on, and the men were still out. It was no longer a General Strike, of course. That had lasted only a few days, and then been betrayed by leaders — not miners' leaders — who had never sought it in the first place, and were terrified of it when it happened. The miners were alone in their struggle, and were feeling the pinch. The houses were cold and damp. There was no coal now to fuel that big constant kitchen fire which was the very heart of the household. The Pack Woman came no more: there was no money now to buy her second-hand clothes and shoes. Winter was biting deepest when the men found an outcrop of coal down in the Milburn area. It was not very thick, but at least it was coal. The bings had been raked over again and again for every scrap of coal that could be recovered from them, and the fires were burning low in every house. The outcrop could be the saviour.

And so it was. Except for two young girls, who were buried in a cave-in. They had been working there, and had dug too deep. The men working the outcrop dug with desperation to get the lassies out, but it was too late. One was dead when they reached her. They carried her body home, wrapped in an old sack, without even the dignity of the carter and his old horse, and in procession went to her home and laid her down, another martyr, another unsung victim. Cha and I watched the sad little procession, and saw men and women weep as it passed.

Somehow the long months of the strike wore over. We children were sheltered from its worst effects. We were never really hungry and never really in want, although our parents suffered deep and genuine hardship. We did not really understand what was going on, but we did feel the increasing tensions and frustrations and deprivations of our parents. Finally, the men went back to work, those who were allowed to, beaten and bitter, but certainly still proud and undefeated.

The end of the strike seemed to mark a whole series of changes.

Midge and McGuire moved away. The Miners' Rows were to be pulled down, and the families rehoused in a new scheme on the other side of the village. Of course, we swore undying friendship, and were sure that we would meet just as before, but it did not happen like that.

I began to get a series of sore throats, and finally my mother took me to the doctor, who diagnosed infected tonsils, and said that they had to be taken out. Arrangements were made for this, and my father was livid with rage. He had little time for doctors or hospitals. 'Damned doctors! If nature had not wanted they organs tae be there they wadnae be there. Aw doctors ken nooadays is cut, cut them oot.'

In spite of father's objections, mother took me off to the hospital on a cold, wet morning. There were lots of children waiting there, for cutting out tonsils was a very popular thing at that time. There seemed to be very little compassion about the process, and my memories are of being lifted like a bundle onto a big white table by a big man dressed all in white with a white mask. A black funnel was put over my face and I was told to count. I remember nothing after "four", until I woke up, alone in a darkened room, with a very sore throat and a bitter-tasting mouth.

Eventually I crawled out of the bed and wandered off down a long corridor until I was found by a motherly and sympathetic nurse, and carried off to where my mother was waiting with all the other mothers and the children who had been operated on that morning. We left the hospital into a day of pouring rain, and waited for a bus to take us back to the village, where I was assured my father would be waiting for us. Indeed he was, still black from the pit, and soaked with rain. He swept me up onto his shoulders and carried me back to the warmth and security of home.

Things did not go well, though, and I got some kind of infection that kept me in bed for two weeks, sick and sorry, with a sore throat far worse than any I had had before.

My usual morning treat before then had been the top off father's boiled egg every morning, but during the weeks of my illness I was given a whole soft boiled egg to myself. Unfortunately my poor sore throat would hardly let me enjoy even that, and certainly I must have been poor company for Cha and Midge when they came visiting. It was weeks before I was fit enough to be allowed up and out, to resume the old ways of play and wandering. Even worse, the illness left me with a speech impediment, a stammer that seemed to change my nature. I was happy enough with my own friends, who seemed to understand and sympathise, but with strangers, who seemed to annoy and taunt me, I became agressive and quick tempered. My love for the woods and their wild life was unchanged, but I became very withdrawn, shying away from any large company and avoiding conversation.

It was strange that when I was with my own friends I hardly stammered at all, and when I did they ignored it. So it was doubly unfortunate that just at that time several friends moved away. Midge went off to another part of the village, and the Douglas family emigrated to Canada, where Mr. Douglas had found work in the emigration scheme known as The Harvesters. Many other families, desperate to avoid the Depression and the misery of unemployment left for Canada at that time.

My stammer became worse, and I began using it as an excuse for not working in school. If there was reading aloud to be done, or a poem to be said, I would start by stammering, and the teacher would tell me to sit down, saying that she knew I knew the piece. I certainly used the stammer as an excuse to avoid working, although at the same time I hated it as an embarrassment, something which kept me separate and different from the rest.

My teacher thought I was bright enough, and certainly I won some book prizes. There was one prize, a medal which was kept by the winner for a fortnight, until the next examination, and this eluded me until one day my Granny lectured me about the importance of learning — a lecture I had heard before, but Granny gave it a new twist. When she asked why I never won the medal, I told her it was just for sissies, a term of particular abuse amongst us boys. 'If you want to get anywhere, you must learn your lessons and read books and be clever. You should always try, try your best. I'll tell you, if you win the medal, I'll gie you a penny.'

A penny would have been wealth indeed. So I did try for the medal, and I won it three times, and it cost granny three pennies. I really did like school, although I seemed to be always getting into trouble and fights. Most of them were caused by lads ragging me about my stammer. I developed a fiery temper and would flare up at the slightest slur, much to the alarm and dismay of my parents. They lectured me repeatedly about this, but it made no difference. Indeed, it was years before I overcame that speech impediment, and equally years before my temper settled down. Even today, if I hear a boy struggling against a stammer, I cringe and realise again some of the agony that lad is suffering.

My Granny helped me very much at this time. She was a devout Christian, and would take me through to the back room and have me read to her from her big Bible. I did not stammer then, except when I came across a word I had not met before. She told me stories about her life, which had been a hard one. My grandfather had died from lung disease contracted from White Damp (★) in the pit. He was one of the Rescue Team who carried out the dead and injured after an explosion. The Team were engulfed in White Damp, and grandfather's lungs destroyed.

Granny nursed him for a long time before he died, a slow and agonising death. There was no compensation or pension. Granny was left to bring up her family as best she could. So she struggled. She worked long hours carting coal. She kept pigs and collected food for them where she could. She worked at anything that would bring in a few pennies to help in raising her children, and she still found time and energy to help others in worse need than herself. She was a remarkable woman, and a true Christian. She lectured me about my fiery temper, saying I should be kind and helpful to others. 'Stand up for what you believe is right,' she told me, and I have never forgotten. I told her that I never started any fights, but I finished them if they started on me. Granny smiled and told me I was a guid wee lad. There was often a reward for me after those sessions with granny, perhaps a large red apple, or there would be a poke of sweeties in her big black handbag, and I would get a Cinnamon Ball or an Imperial.

I went to church with Granny, and to Sunday School twice every Sunday. The best thing about the Sunday Schools were the annual trips. I seem to remember that we always went by train, either to the seaside or out into the country. The train journey itself was a tremendous thrill, and we delighted in watching the cattle and horses scattering across the fields as the train, belching smoke, clattered past.

There were always races on these trips, and I always won one or two. The prizes were small enough, but I was proud to win them. My mother was persuaded once to run in a Mothers' Race. She was embarrassed, and had to be coaxed to run, but she did run, and she won. I was cheering as she flashed past the post, leaving the others well behind. Mr. Lawrie, the Pastor, presented her with the prize, a large cake, and asked her how she had managed to beat all the younger women. She was breathless, and I answered for her. 'She gets a lot of practice every day chasing me to do her messages.' This brought laughter from the crowd, and I was very proud of my mother that day.

★ *White Damp:* Most gases in the pits were called 'damp'. White damp was carbon monoxide.

My father was still in work, so we were amongst those lucky enough to be well fed and clothed. There was still porridge for breakfast, and I still had the top of father's egg every morning. It was my job to take a cup of tea into Granny every morning, and I usually found her already awake and reading her Bible. She often took this opportunity to teach me some sort of lesson. 'Aye, we're the lucky yins. Luck oor there, at the Miners' Rows.' There would be lots of activity there, with those men still in work leaving their houses, the women doing their house work, children playing and dogs chasing around. Smoke from the coal fires would be pouring from every chimney. 'It's gonna be anither guid day, ye can see auld Tinto's tap is clear, but luck at all that reek, it's nae wonder thurs sae much folk wae consumption and bronchitis and rickets and fevers and awe that. Nae gettin fed richt and livin in they hovels. Ah wadnae hae kept ma pigs in them. It's a guid job fur they folk the hovels ur comin doon and they puir folk ur movin tae better hooses. It's nae afore time.' Granny had always been concerned about the folk in the hovels, many of whom went to her Church. 'Eh, oor porridge will be ready. I'll get the pig oot o ma bed and git ma face washed.' The pig was an earthenware hot water bottle that comforted Granny every night, and she used the still warm water every morning to wash herself. The rest of us used the cold water from the tap, unless, on some exceptionally cold days, mother provided a kettle of hot water as a treat.

There had been a short, one-week strike about this time, and some of the men had amused themselves by fixing up a sort of slide across the burn. They used a length of old wire rope, fixing it high up a tree on one side, and running it across the burn to a tree on the other. The idea was to climb up the tree on the high side, put an old horseshoe or a hooked gabbie from an old hutch discarded at the pit, across the wire, hang on, and slide down the steeply sloping wire rope across the burn, leaving go before crashing into the lower tree, and rolling into the soft grass on the bank of the burn. This was great fun, and we lads made full use of it when the men went back to work. We hardly thought of its dangers: in the middle of the burn the rope was a good twenty feet above the water and rocks below.

It only lasted about a week, though, until there was almost a tragedy. One lad got stuck about the middle of the burn. As he shouted for help, his pal started the slide behind him, crashed into him, and they both fell, fortunately not on to the rocks, but bad enough to give one of the lads a broken arm and leg, and the other a broken leg. After that, the police came along and made the men take down the slide, and insisted that it never be replaced.

When the Miners' Rows were being demolished, all the lads thought they had found a great source of wood for making swords and other things we coveted for playing with. However, we found that the hovels were absolutely infested with bugs, and were forbidden to go near. We did recover the smoke hoods from the old fire places, though, and they provided the means of a new adventure.

This was to slide down the pit bing on the curved metal hoods. The slope was very steep, and you reached a high speed on the small stones before getting near the bottom where the bigger stones had come to rest. It was highly dangerous, because there was no real way of controlling the sledges, and no way of stopping except rolling off on to the stones. But it was very exciting, and somehow no-one came to any harm. That seems to be so often the way with the things that lads get up to.

It was also during the time of the bing-sliding that we organised the Great Rat Hunt. At the bottom of the bing there was the burn, only at that point it was no longer really a burn, but a stinking sewer, coming out of a tunnel. It was a rats' heaven, and we saw many of them as we played on the bing and waited for our turn on the sledges.

We decided to hunt them. There were some bigger lads with us, and they seemed to know how it should be done. Perhaps they had done it before, or had watched bigger brothers at it. Anyway, the materials we needed were at hand, right there on the bing.

There was plenty of strum lying about. This was the fuse the miners used for shot-firing, and it gave off a thick black smoke when lit. We needed torches, both to light the strum and to give us light in the tunnel, for it was proposed to hunt the rats there. Again, there was plenty of wire haulage rope lying around, and we soon learned how to strip the wire off the central core of this, and were left with a thick tarry rope, which burned well. Puggies, or catapults were needed for the kill, and some of the lads produced these. Fine puggies they were, too, and we had a contest to determine who would have these and act as marksmen. I was a good shot with a puggie, and so was chosen as one of them.

When we were fully equipped, we climbed down to the stinking burn, torches lit ready, and into the tunnel, which was no more than the outfall of the sewer. The lads with the torches kept them alight by occasionally whirling them round their heads. There were rats there alright; we could see them, and they could see us.

We used divots to stop up the holes we found, and stuffed a length of strum into others. Then the strum was lit from the torches, and the thick black smoke poured down into the rat holes. In a very short time we marksmen were busy. In all, six rats ran out of holes and up the bank. We accounted for three of them, and thought that a very good total. But it was a filthy and rather frightening experience, especially for the lads who had gone up the tunnel to block the holes, and although we said we would return the next day, we never did, and the rats continued to thrive.

Although our gang of lads was certainly a rough little bunch, equally certainly there was no harm in us. Of course we got up to many kinds of mischief, like sliding down the pit bing and being chased off by the police, and hunting rats in the village sewer, but there was no harm in it, and I know now how we were watched over by the grown ups, who made certain that we never stepped over any of the lines which were necessary in that community, where poverty was general, and real hardship not uncommon.

It wasn't just the youngsters who had to be guarded by the people of the village. There were some others who needed protection, people who perhaps had cracked under the strain of living, or who had suffered more than they could bear. There was Harry Dawson, a simpleton. He was a grown man who spent his days running round the roads and streets with girr and cleek. This was a round hoop, about two feet in diameter, of thin iron rod, and a long-handled crook. Many of us had them, and got a lot of pleasure racing them along, keeping them going and guided in the right direction by cunning touches of the hook to the spinning hoop. But Harry Dawson was a man, and dresssed always in a long coat that flopped open as he ran along, with his girr whirling and singing (as they did) at his side. We always knew when Harry was about, for he carried an old bulb motor horn, and honked it constantly as he ran. He was absolutely harmless, but rather terrifying to the kids, who ran and hid when they heard the hoarse sound of his old horn.

Poor harmless Harry died tragically a few years later when he was knocked down and killed by a bus.

I think perhaps it was those visits to the wood to cut down trees during the General Strike that first led me to a deep and abiding love of woodlands and the birds and animals that live there.

That long and hard winter passed, and summer came again. There were school holidays, and long summer days. It was the delight of we children to go barefoot, although my mother did not like that. I would protest that the others were all barefoot, while I had to wear my boots and socks. Often enough the boots and socks were left in the wooden porch, and I slipped quietly off down the steps to join my barefooted mates in visits to the woods.

We scoured those woods, seeking birds' nests, and learned the names and habitats of them all. We watched the nest building, then saw the eggs and the hatching and the feeding of the young, and then the first flights of the youngsters. Miss Raesbet, our teacher, helped us a great deal in this. She would bring pictures of birds and insects and animals and pin them up in the classroom. Cha and I in particular became very skilful at finding nests, slipping silently through the grass on our bare feet and being extra careful to make no noise or sudden movement to frighten the birds.

Our interest in wildlife led us to Midge's pal, a lad called McGuire. He was an expert, and we learned a lot from him. At first I did not like him very much. He was a scruffy lad, a bit taller than me, and very dark skinned. I thought he needed a good wash. His ragged trousers and shirt made him look like a little tough, but in reality he was gentle enough, although he could handle himself well in a fight. He was happy to show his skills in the woods, and could talk with endless enthusiasm about how to find the different kinds of nests, and about the butterflies. He had a large collection of eggs, and was delighted to take us home with him and show his collection, telling us the name of each bird, and where he had found the nest.

I almost had a fight with him when I told him that he had no right to be taking eggs. He gave me a baleful scowl and threatened to punch my face in. He said that he never destroyed any nest, and took an egg only if there were four or five of them in the nest. He was a very angry boy, and it was easy to believe him. Anyway, he certainly taught us a great deal, especially when he agreed to lead us through the woods to some of the sites he knew.

It was about this time that I experienced the first great sorrow of my life when Granny died. I had been very close to her, and was often her companion when she went to church. She always slipped me a couple of mint sweeties before the sermon began, and we listened to the Pastor expounding the word of God in an atmosphere of peppermint and piety.

I was inconsolable when she died, and when the funeral took place. This was on a very cold morning, and great plumes of steam rose from the nostrils of the funeral horses as they stood by the door, waiting for their sad burden. The hearse was drawn by two great black horses, each with a large black plume attached to the headband. I noticed that even their hooves had been painted shiny black. We walked in silence behind the hearse, a long procession, with most of the village attending to pay their last respects to this good woman. Our feet crunched over the red whin stone chips of the cemetery path until we stood by the grave side. Mr. Lawrie, the Pastor, took the service, speaking warmly of my Granny and of her good life.

Mr. Lawrie had been extremely attentive to Granny during the time she was ill, visiting often, and comforting her as she grew worse. The full realisation of my loss hit me as the coffin was slowly lowered down, and I cried bitterly, holding on to my oldest brother, and pressing my head into his chest. He put his arms around me, and rocked me slowly to and fro.

We walked slowly home, and found the house full of friends and relations, with the women busy making tea and preparing food. All the grown ups seemed to be talking at once, and ignoring me, so I went over to the fireplace and sat on a footstool. Mr. Lawrie saw me, though, and came over and squatted down beside me. I noticed that he wore pin-striped black trousers with spats over his shoes. He told me again what a good woman my Granny had been, and how he hoped I would still continue to come to the meetings and Sunday School.

Shortly after this I had to change schools, going to the Big School from the primary. I still had my stammer, and again found I had to face a lot of problems with lads who made fun of me. So I again gained the reputation of being a 'fichter an a wee devil'.

For the first term at the Big School we were lucky in that our old teacher, Miss Raesbet, had also changed, so that not everything seemed so strange. It was a mixed school, with mixed classes, and I was seated next to a very pretty little girl with long hair, called Barbara Allan. We knew the song, and it seemed strange that there should be a real girl, sitting next to me, called that. My friendship with Barbara caused my first fight at the school, and indeed led to my reputation of being a fighter, and to some very painful interviews with the Headmaster.

There was one particular bullying lad in the class, and he had taken Barbara's scarf, leaving her in tears. I went to her rescue, and the two of us got into a right good scrap, until we were pulled apart by the school janitor, a big, very strong, military sort of man. He led us off to the Headmaster, who gave us each a severe lecture about fighting, and then three clouts from the belt on our crossed hands. He knew how to use that belt, and our hands were swollen and sore, but at least I had faced up to the class bully, and Barbara was very grateful.

It was not finished, though, for the next day the bully and his particular friend cornered me in the school yard and I had to face the pair of them. The friend was quite easily seen off, but the bully lad and I got into a real battle, and I was on top of him, hammering away at his head and face when one of the teachers came up and separated us. Again it was us for the Headmaster, and this time, as well as a lecture even more severe it was six with the belt. This was a really heavy punishment, and brought our hands and wrists up in big red marks. The other lad snivelled and cried, but in spite of the pain I refused to cry, at least in front of anybody, and tucked my hands under my armpits, and went back to the classroom, where the teacher looked at me with sympathy and understanding. She thought I was very pale, and she was probably right, for that Headmaster was a strong man, and he had used his strength with his belt.

Barbara was her usual kind little self, and slipped me a wee poke of sweeties as a comfort. I certainly hoped that there would be no more conflicts with that lad, and no more interviews with the Headmaster. I was not going to duck out of anything, but the Headmaster had said that he would double the punishment every time I was brought in to him for fighting, and I was sure he would. It was just a few days later that I was going home after school with a lad called Andy Craw when we saw a gang of lads, led by the bully, waiting for us down at the crossroads. There were six or seven of them, and we hesitated. Finally I said: 'Come oan, they'll no tak us', and I walked on. Andy came too, but I knew it was me they were after. I could feel the tension build up as we approached.

The wee bully was there, and his pal, and a gang of lads from another school. I could feel the tension building up as we approached. They began to taunt me. "Teacher's Pet," they yelled, and a lot of other things. I dropped my school bag and challenged them to come on, that I would take them all on one at a time.

The challenges and counter-challenges flew thick and fast as they formed a ring round Andy and me, with occasionally one of them rushing forward a few steps and then retreating.

'Come oan, wha's furst? Yur awe guid whin thurs a gang! Wha's furst?', but there were butterflies in my stomach. To his credit, it was the wee bully who made the first attack, and he came at me, fists flying. I screamed 'I'll ca yur heid oaf,' and we went at it. It was not going too badly for me, when suddenly another of the gang jumped on my back, and I went down, hitting my head on the road. Andy pulled the lad off my back and allowed me to scramble to my feet. We were now closely surrounded by the gang, and fists were flying in all directions. It looked as though we were in for a bad beating.

By this time a crowd from our school had gathered round, enjoying the fracas, but there seemed to be none of our friends among them. Suddenly there was a shrill whistle and cries of 'Charge!' Midge and Big Tam and a few others were coming to the rescue. This was too much for the wee bully and his gang: they turned and ran off, leaving the field to us and our rescuers.

'We sorted that lot oot. They aa scooted awa like big feirty lassies.' That was Midge. Andy and I inspected and showed off our cuts and bruises — a split lip, one nose bleed and my knees were skinned.

'Whe telt ye there was a ficht gaun oan?' I asked Tam. It was Barbara. She and some of the other girls had heard it being planned, and she had told Midge. The little girl I sat beside in school, and liked so much, had saved us from a bad beating up.

We were often at the pit gate when the shift changed, and asked the tired and grimy men if they had any pit pieces left. 'Aye, here ye ur,' they would say, and opened their tin piece boxes and gave us any bread they had left. This was usually double slices of bread with cheese or dripping or even "Carluke steak", which was what we called jam, after the jam factories at Carluke. Somehow those pieces of bread always had a dank and musty smell after being down the pit in the tin piece boxes. Most of the men had something left at lousing or finishing time. This was a habit in those days, and the idea was that if the men were trapped underground by a roof fall, which was not unknown, they would have at least something to eat. If the men didn't feed their piece to the ponies, they would usually feed it to the birds on the surface, or give it to us if we were waiting for them.

This was a bonus for us, and although I was always well enough fed at home, those pit pieces, with the curious musty smell were always enjoyed. If we had a good collection, we would take what we could not eat and feed it to some pit ponies in the field by the bing. Of course, we were not supposed to be there, and we had to wait till all the miners had gone away, and until the bing pickers had left. They had scratched and scraped around the bing all day, searching for odd bits of coal, putting it into a sack, and then finally carrying it away in a home-made barrow or across an old bike. They were poor souls, desperate and hungry, living somehow on handouts from what we called The Parish. To my shame now, we tended to look down on those folk, condemned to be at the very bottom of the social heap.

When the last of the bing gatherers had gone, we would climb through a hole in the fence into the field where the ponies were. They were happy grazing, although many of them were blind or half-blind from the years of darkness underground. They all got to know us well enough, and would gather round when we called, eager to have their share of the pit pieces. Perhaps they were reminded of their days underground, which would start again soon for them, once their "holiday" was over, and they went back to their arduous and dangerous work. They were quite happy for us to ride on their backs, with only a piece of rope for a rein. We knew the commands used by the pony drivers underground, such as *Ven* or *Hap*, which meant "left" or "right". We had a lot of fun with those ponies, and of course would never abuse them. Often enough we would be chased by the pithead Gaffer, but that was no problem, for he could never catch us, and we would be back another day.

I had learned something about ponies and other animals from my father, who had been raised on a farm, and still went working on the farms round about in his spare time. He sometimes took me with him, and we both enjoyed feeding the animals and cleaning out their sheds on those farms, and my father told me repeatedly to respect the animals and never to abuse them. 'You be guid tae them, an they'll be guid tae you,' he often said, and I have never forgotten.

My family was lucky, because father was in regular work. There were many others whose lives were desperate with want, with the father either out of work or perhaps black-listed at the pits for striking. Although my father would always be on strike with the rest of the men, he was never prominent in the strikes, and always managed to stay in work. As a result, our family was invariably well enough clothed and warm and fed. Indeed, we were lucky enough to have the occasional treat, and even to share some of our good fortune with others.

For birthdays, Mother always made a cloutie dumpling, stuffed with fruit, and containing little silver trinkets and, best of all, paper-wrapped threepenny pieces. This was a great treat, for Mother was a grand cook, and it was made even better by the prospect of finding a threepenny piece or a tiny silver horshoe or bell or thimble in one's helping. We children were always impatient for Mother to decide that the cloutie was ready, and watched as she stuck a long steel knitting pin into the great linen-wrapped bundle boiling away in its big pan on the fire. When she decided it was ready, the pan was lifted carefully onto a pile of newspapers on the table, and the cloutie taken out and put on an ashet. The cloth was carefully removed, and the dumpling put by the fire to dry off. I think I can still smell the wonderful steam that came off it then, and certainly we could hardly wait for Mother to cut the first slices, and warn us to be careful, because it was still very hot, and to be careful, also, not to swallow any of the trinkets or coins it contained. I remember that on one of Willy's birthdays I found two threepenny pieces, a bell and a horseshoe in my helpings. Of course, I know now that the helpings were carefully arranged so that we children got the little gifts, and so that no-one was left out or disappointed.

Mother, and Granny when she was still alive, used to make a lot of jams and jellies and wines from all the fruits we could find growing around in the woods and hedges. It seemed that our kitchen was always in a turmoil of cooking and baking and boiling. It was my regular job to go down to the corner and get the sour dook (buttermilk) from the sour dook man when we heard his bell. I did not have many domestic chores to do, not like Cha, who had to get in the coal every day, and clean and dubbin the pit boots of his father and brothers. But even the job of getting the buttermilk for mother's baking, or bringing up the occasional scuttle of coal was often resented. It seemed to me that every time Mother asked me to do these things, I had just got started on one of the more interesting bits of one of the weekly magazines which were my chief reading at that time — *The Rover, The Wizard* or *Adventure*. These cost two pence each, and of course I could not afford more than one of them, and nor could my friends. So there was a regular network of swaps, and that way we all managed to read all the magazines every week. It was usually a grumbling small boy who went down the dark stairs with a big jug and a few coppers to buy the soor dook from auld Tam.

Auld Tam and his auld horse came round once a week, and most of the wives were waiting for him, because buttermilk and skim milk were essential in baking. Also, Tam sold butter, and very good butter it was. His cart was different from all the others we saw. It was lightly built, with two big wheels, and had large churns with brass taps fitted at the back. Tam was a character, and seemed to know the business of every one of the women who bought from him. He would happily give credit when money was tight, but always let everyone else know that he was doing so, and would comment loudly about the shortcomings of the husband who had not yet brought his wages home, but was still in the pub. I was always thankful when it was my turn, and I got my jug full, with a pat of butter balanced on top, so that I could get back to my reading, and Mother could get on with her scones and cakes and oatcakes.

Another chore that I disliked was going off with Mother to help her carry jams and wines to her friends the Fells. Mr. Fell was a farm labourer, and his tied cottage, which went with the job, was a disgraceful place, cold, damp and gloomy. They lived about three miles away from us, up wet and muddy paths, and it was no easy task for Mother and me to carry the heavy baskets of full jars and bottles all that way. But it was done year by year, and the Fell family, who must have been really in extreme poverty, were always welcoming and kind, so far as they could be. I was never at ease in their house, though. It was small and dark, with tiny windows, and a lamp burning night and day. The floor was of flags, cold and noisy, and always seeming to be damp. Indeed, it probably was.

It was while I was still seated beside Barbara at school that the epidemic of yuck hit the children. This was the itch, a nasty skin disease that spread all over the body, with sores that itched terribly and oozed an unpleasant white pus.

We had already had our heads inspected for lice several times, a procedure that puzzled me, because I had never seen or heard of lice before then. My mother ensured that we were clean, and soap and water was the order of the day in our house. Often enough I was inspected carefully after washing, and sent back to wash again behind my ears, where, Mother said, there was enough dirt to grow tatties. If the teacher found lice in anybody's hair, they were sent off to the headmaster, and treated. Yuck was something else, though, and it spread rapidly through the school. Cha's brother was one of the first to get it, and then Cha. We were rarely apart, and so it was perhaps inevitable that I should get it, too. It really was most unpleasant, and the itching intolerable, but when you scratched, you spread the disease to other parts of the body.

Mother tried all kinds of remedies, various ointments and salves and lotions, but nothing did much good until she discovered a particular sort of black soap, with a horrible smell. That seemed to work, and she also made up a bottle of tonic from an old recipe she had got from Granny. This was a clear liquid, with a pink tinge to it. Unfortunately, I never did find out what it was, but it was pleasant to drink, and seemed to help in getting rid of the itch. 'This wull purify yer blood,' she said. Father laughed and asked for a taste. He nodded his head, and said 'Tae hae guid health ye hae tae hae guid blud, so here's tae yer bloody guid health,' and emptied the glass. When she saw that her cures were working with me, Mother shared her knowledge with Cha's mother, and so he and I were cured much more quickly than the others, and it was a great relief to be rid of that awful itching.

There were few enough celebrations in those days, and little money to celebrate with, but Christmas and New Year were always looked forward to for weeks before they happened. Christmas was a working day for my Father, of course, but the children always had their stockings, filled with little gifts. For long after we knew the secret of Santa Claus we kept up the pretence, and there were shouts of delight each Christmas morning when we were called out of our inset beds into the warmth of the kitchen where Mother had a fine blazing fire going, and had prepared Father's breakfast and pit piece. Our stockings were hanging on the mantleshelf, stuffed with little presents — an apple and an orange, a box of marbles, a small box of sweets, and once a small red tin engine that wound up and would run along the table.

The days between Christmas and New Year were busy for Mother, because New Year was a real celebration. The elderberry and potato wines would have been made long ago, and well matured. There was all the baking to be done, the currant buns, scones and pancakes to be made. For some reason she always had the shortbread made by Lee, the baker. The butter for this was sent round to Lee's shop, and we had several rounds of his wonderful shortbread in return. The dumpling left over from Christmas was already to hand, and there was a big pot of soup. After all the baking and cooking was done for Hogmanay, the house was thoroughly cleaned, the brasses polished and the furniture waxed. Then she could sit back and wait for midnight and the bringing in of the New Year.

Mother hated strong drink and loathed the sight of drunken men, but on this one occasion she accepted that Father would be over at the pub, the *Ranch* or the *Aggie Reid,* with his workmates, getting wound up, or getting in a guid tid, as he said. He always arrived home just ten minutes after the pubs closed at nine o'clock, carrying the traditional whisky and screw tops of beer, to be lined up on the dresser, with a warning against any of the young ones going near it.

'Ah hive jist had a wee dram, Maggie,' he would say, 'Hive ye onything fur a hungry man?' Mother would lay him out his supper, with perhaps a bit of word abut his 'boozy, drunken cronies.' But she accepted that he would be exceptionally cheery and jovial, for this was Hogmanay. Father would hand out bars of tablet for us children, and chocolate for Mother and my sister. 'Eat jist a wee bit noo, and keep the rest for the morn. Noo, awa to yur beds, and ah'll wake ye whin the bells ring.' So we were tucked in for a while, until Father shook us awake a few minutes before midnight. It was a delight to hear the first of the bells, and then loud bangs as some of the men let off shots to mark the New Year. And then all the bells burst out together, clashing their message of a Happy New Year, and men fired off shot guns, and some fired off explosives from the pit. All the hooters and horns from every pit and the steelworks and even the silk factory joined in, and there was a positive Bedlam of noise. In the distance would be the sound of bagpipes, and nearer at hand a bugle blast and someone blowing at a trumpet. Father filled his first dram of the New Year. 'Here's tae ye, an a Happy New Year tae ye, may it be better than the last, an lang may yur lum reek!' and he swallowed off his whisky. The bun and shortbread were already on the table, and tea was prepared. We could hear people singing and shouting in the street. Then there would be footsteps on the stairs, our First Foot. 'It'll be Jock Stewart, tae be share,' said Father, and indeed it would, for Jock had First Footed our family for twenty years. He was usually a bit unsteady on his feet, and glad to be given a seat, but would produce his bottle and give Father a dram, and have another himself, while the lovely old warm expressions of hope for a better future were exchanged.

Jock, however foo he might be, always gave us his favourite song. We all knew it well from the past, and joined in the chorus. 'Eat whan ye ur hungry and drink when ye ur dry. Dinnae stop breathing or else ye wull die.' We all thought this was very funny, and laughed about it, and laughed also when Father gave his song, which was always *Rothesay Bay.* Soon enough the room would be crammed with people, friends and neighbours and relatives. There were more songs and crack and jokes, but by this time my head was nodding, and Mother would lead me off to the little back room, where I was to sleep that night, in the bed already warmed by the "pig", away from all the happy noise and good fellowship. I was too young then to take part, but not too young to remember it all.

I remember once when big Tam Barnes broke down in the middle of his song. His wife had died during the year, and Tam was struggling alone to bring up his children. He had a fine voice, but it broke and strangled when he was in the middle of *Ae fond kiss*. There was no embarrassed silence in the crowded room, although everyone knew why Tam had broken down. There were rough jokes and advice to get some axle grease for his throat, and half a dozen hands pushing drams at him, and very soon Big Tam was on his feet again, with another lovely Burns song, sung in his clear voice, but he did not try *Ae Fond Kiss* again.

The beginning of each summer was marked by the May Day March. When we were children, we did not understand the significance of May Day. To us it was just a grand day out, with a march led by pipe bands, and the pit banners carried by proud men. There were speeches, which meant nothing to us then, for we were interested only in the food and the races. There were little prizes to be won — two pence for first, a penny for second and a halfpenny for third, and sometimes boxes of marbles or pencils. The money prizes were promptly spent on sweeties, or perhaps on chips or fritters from Angelo's fish shop. These were a great treat, and somehow, however much we might have spent there, we were always ready for our food at home.

It seems to me now that quite a lot of our time was spent in doing things that brought in a few coppers, all of which went either to the sweet shop or Angelo's. One of the regular, although rare, sources of a few coppers was any local wedding. We knew when there was to be a wedding because it was the custom for some young man to hoist a flag on to the chimney of the house where it was to take place. The flag stayed there until the bridegroom paid his ransom of a bottle of whisky to have it removed. It was the custom to scatter copper coins to the waiting children after the ceremony, and we gained many a poke of sweeties or fritters from that source. There was one occasion, though, when at a rather superior sort of wedding, there was quite a big crowd of children gathered outside the house, calling for the money to be thrown out. Eventually it was, but it had been heated in a pan of boiling water first, and there were some burned fingers that day. There was also a fusilade of stones thrown at the house, and at least one window broken, and I can't say even today that I think the broken window was not deserved.

Helping farmers with their sheep or cattle also produced the odd penny, although the usual reward for that was a good tea in the farmhouse. We would never refuse it, and indeed enjoyed all the scones and home baking, but somehow it never tasted as good as my own Mother's baking. Certainly, however big a tea we might have had elsewhere, we were always ready for whatever might be on the table at home.

It was always good fun to work in the hay fields, along with the men and women from the farm, and with others, such as my Father, who delighted in getting away from the pit and into the fields for the sort of work they had done in their youth. In those days, the harvest was a time of hard and communal labour, but also a time of pleasure at working together, of enjoying the picnic atmosphere of baskets of food and drink carried by the women out into the hay fields and consumed under a hay cock just built.

We got as much as sixpence each for the day's work when it came time to shift the hay rucks out of the fields and into the hay loft. It was a day we enjoyed, not just for the reward, but because we were working with the men, and also we were allowed to ride the empty ruck lifter back from the farm yard to the fields. We were even allowed to drive the old horses sometimes, although, truth to tell, they knew better than us where to go and how to do it.

The ruck lifter was a low flat cart, on small wheels. It was tilted, then backed up to the base of each ruck of dry hay. There was a windlass at the front, and ropes were put round the ruck and attached to the windlass. Then two of us, usually one man and a boy, turned the handles, and the ruck was pulled up on to the sloping bed of the cart. When it had been pulled up, the bed of the cart was drawn down level again and fastened, and we were ready to go off to the hay loft with another load. We did not ride when the ruck lifter was full, for one ruck was a fair load for the horse. It was our job to pack the hay into the loft as it was forked up by a man down below. It was hard and dusty work, and often there were lots of thistles in the hay, which stuck in our hands and bare arms, but it was work we all enjoyed and looked forward to.

Sometimes there would be a spontaneous sort of picnic out of the village to the banks of the Clyde, when everyone who could, men, women and children, would go off for the day, well equipped with baskets of food. They were good days out, especially if the river was low and there were banks of sand where the children could run and play at the water's edge while the grown-ups built fires to make tea, and we all enjoyed whatever food we fancied from all the baskets. Usually someone would have brought along an accordion, and the day ended with dancing and singing before we all walked back home to the village.

There was always adventure and entertainment to be had in the country round about. If we wanted a change from the banks of the Clyde, we would walk round by Millheugh. The way led up Raploch Street, which was the home of some of our local heroes. They were the footballers who played in the junior team, and we younger children were pleased and proud if those lads spoke to us. The local pawn shop was in Raploch Street, and it did a good trade in those days when hardship was the constant state of most people, and when poverty, real, biting poverty, the state of many. Monday morning was the big day for the pawn shop, and it was common to see women on their way there, with some clothes or household item wrapped up in a cloth, to be "popped" at the pawn shop until the end of the week. There was a public house right next to the pawn shop, and I suppose what came out of one door only too often went into the next door. The pawn shop really was the last refuge of the poor and desperate, though, and it is a measure of change, perhaps of progress, that you rarely see one today, whereas not so long ago there was one in every village and several in every town.

The game of quoits was very popular with the men of the village, and we always delighted to squeeze in amongst them and watch them play. There were small cash prizes for the winners, but there was also a lot of side bets, and a good deal of money changed hands there. The quoits were heavy iron rings, about nine inches in diameter, bevelled on one side, and polished bright from constant handling. A pitch was laid out for the game behind the old houses, with a heading, or patch of clay at each end, and about ten yards apart. There was a pin, an iron rod, hammered into each heading so that about two inches stuck up above the ground, and this was marked with white paper so that the players could see it clearly. The idea was to throw the heavy quoits with an underarm swing towards the pin. The one nearest, or even over the pin was the winner. It was a bit like bowls, in a way, with much skill shown in knocking other quoits away from the pin. It was more exciting than bowls, though, with the heavy clang of the quoits as they struck each other, with sparks flying, and with no inhibitions about cheering good shots or shouting encouragement.

So the years drew on, and it seemed that the long summer days were endless, and the long winter nights too. My memories of those days and nights are clear and sharp, even though nothing of moment happened. I remember the year we built the biggest bonfire yet for Guy Fawkes night, and how the grown-ups came out and lit it themselves, "to keep us safe", and how they danced round it till the embers glowed in the winter darkness and we children roasted potatoes and burned our fingers and tongues eating them.

I remember my father especially constantly encouraging me to work hard, and "stick in" at school. He himself had had only one year of schooling before going off to work on farms in conditions of great hardship, and yet his handwriting was a thing of beauty, and he could add up columns of figures in his head faster than anyone else I knew could do it on paper. And he never had a moment of idleness without a book in his hand. He loved books, and respected them, and he strove to instill that love and respect into his children. He knew a great deal about the countryside and about farming, and was often asked by local farmers to help at harvest or ploughing. I helped him once when he was ploughing a field. I realise now that he did not really need my help, but he asked me to do it, and I was proud. We walked from home very early that morning, and the dew on the hedgerows was a delight to see.

When we got to the farm, Father showed me how to groom the horses for their day's work — although my task was to muck out the stables. The horses, big Clydesdales, were given their food and drink, and then the plough harness put on them. We walked them out to the field where the plough was waiting for us, and then Father carefully cut long sticks from the hedgerow and pushed them into the ground, two at each end of the field. These were his sighting sticks, and he took the greatest care to get them placed correctly.

Then the horses were hitched to the plough, and I was instructed to lead them very carefully to the top of the field, keeping a very straight line to the first of the sighting sticks. This was the most important furrow of all, my Father explained, this first one, because if it was out of the straight, every other furrow in the field would be wrong. So I stepped out very deliberately indeed, and never took my eye off that distant stick until Father called for a stop. Together we looked back over that first furrow, and he expressed his satisfaction. He told me about the parts of the plough, the coulter and the share, and of how they worked together to produce that lovely wave motion as the furrow was turned. He told me that some ploughs had landwheels to help the ploughman control them, but said that he could not be bothered with such things.

Then the plough was turned, and we went back again, with me again leading the horses, and keeping a fixed eye on the distant sighting stick. When we had finished that furrow, Father said that he could manage on his own now, and that I should go back home. I had been a great help, he said, and without me he would never have been able to get such good first furrows. He had managed often enough before, and did so often enough afterwards, but his praise and thanks meant a great deal to me. I watched for a while as he guided his plough backwards and forwards, with the two big horses pulling quietly and evenly, requiring only a word now and again, more as an act of companionship than as an instruction, for they were experienced beasts. I watched, and wondered about, the hundreds of seagulls that gathered in that field. There had not been a seagull in sight when we started work, yet as soon as the plough bit into the soil, there they were in their hundreds. I wondered then about how they knew we were ploughing, and I wonder the same thing today. Anyway, they had a field day, fighting and squawking over the worms and insects turned up by the plough, and ignoring the heavy hoofs of the horses as they passed up the next furrow.

Another job my father had every year was walking the Clydesdale stallion. This stallion was taken to all the farms to serve the mares as they came into season, and, of course, he and his attendant had to walk from place to place. This job took my father away from home sometimes for weeks at a time, but he always tried to get back on a Saturday night, very weary and literally foot sore after a week spent tramping many miles. Of course, the whole family looked forward to his return, and he was always in a very jovial mood when he came into the house. Often enough my Mother's lips pursed when she saw him, for he would have a pint and a dram with his mates before coming home. He always brought bars of tablet for the children, and always his first job was to get off his boots and thick socks and get his sore feet into a dish of warm water. There was a tin of Johnson's Baby Powder kept specially for Father's feet, and it was used liberally when he came back from his stallion walking.

There was one occasion when I was sent out with a parcel to a distant farm to meet my father there. I had to take the bus, and then walk along unfamiliar roads for a long way to this farm, but the welcome when I got there was warm and sincere. I was taken through to the kitchen, where Father and the farmer were sitting talking about farming, and horses in particular. Father was always listened to with respect on such occasions, because he certainly knew a lot about all aspects of farming, and had read and thought about it, even though he no longer worked full time on the land. I was given milk and fresh baked scones, and was then sent off to look over the farm with the farmer's children, while Father and the farmer went off to see that the stallion did his work properly.

Faralton was a big horse, standing seventeen hands high, but he was a quiet and gentle beast. I was a proud laddie as we set off down the farm lane to the road, with Father leading Faralton, and me walking beside him. The stallion was a grand sight to see, for Father kept him groomed and polished and brushed to perfection, and his great muscles rippled under his silken skin. When we got to the road, my happiness was complete when Father told me to lead the stallion while he got his pipe going. 'Here, thin, tack a haud o the helter wa yer richt haun and the kyle in tha ither haun,' he said. I gripped the rope halter and the coil of rope, and Faralton looked down at me. He gave a little prance sideways across the road, but I kept a firm hold of the halter. There was no evil in Faralton: he was only having his little joke, and he plodded on gently again when I spoke to him. It was a grand feeling to be leading that big stallion, with my father, pipe going well, walking beside me, and talking about all the things we were passing, all the crops and the hedgerows and the animals.

My parents were already about forty when I was born, but they had long lives ahead of them still. Orphaned when he was six years old, my father went to live on a farm, and worked for his keep from that day on.

He was still working on the farm, near Carnwarth, when he met my mother, and they married. It was then that he went to work in the pits, where the money was better, but still spent every moment he could spare working on farms. He was as good a pitman as he would have been a farmer, and he worked as a faceman till he was sixty-eight. He then had the job of ostler in the pit, looking after the pit ponies, and held that job until the Damp (gas) began to affect him.

So finally he went up the pit for the last time, but he did not finish work. He went back to his first love, the land, and rented a smallholding, which he and my mother worked until he was eighty-eight, when he finally gave up. Not that he was finished then. He lived another five years, reading constantly until his eyes failed just weeks before he died.

He was a man, and I was as proud of him when I was a small boy as I am today.

About this time there was a domestic crisis when my sister Lizzie got a poisoned hand from her work in the silk factory. This was a noisy, dusty place. We often gathered at the door on summer days and peered into the roar of the weaving shed, trying to see our sisters or their friends. We were chased away from there often enough by one of the men. Anyway, somehow, and I don't know how, Lizzie injured herself at work, and the cut went poisoned. In those days before antibiotics this was not uncommon, and it was always potentially dangerous. In Lizzie's case, the poison started to spread up her arm, and she was in great pain. It was Auld Joe who treated her. He was an old sailor, with tales of every port in the world, and a reputation for being a good man with poisoned wounds.

The treatment was simple enough — clean cloths soaked in boiling water and put onto the girl's poisoned arm — but it must have been hellishly painful, and poor Lizzie's moans were difficult to bear. We younger children were sent out of the house while the treatment was being given, and that was several times each day. But at night, when we lay in bed in the back room, where we had been banished for the duration of the crisis, while Lizzie lay in our bed in the kitchen, we could hear the cries and moans, and we pulled the blankets over our heads. Still, the treatment worked, and after several days Auld Joe pronounced himself satisfied, and not too long after that, Lizzie was back at work.

As we lads grew a little older, it was possible to earn a few shillings during the school holidays by working on the local farms. Berry picking was a favourite, partly because the pay was quite good, and partly because we worked in gangs, and could joke and have some fun while working.

There were strawberries to pick, then raspberries and black currants and red currants, and we could be kept busy through most of the summer holidays. The money was very welcome to our mothers, and, of course, we were allowed to keep some for ourselves, and that meant extra sweeties or fritters, or visits to the cinema. Most of the picking gangs were women, and a tough crew they were, but kind hearted and more than able to look after themselves and their own. They knew their worth, and they knew that the farmers needed them to get the perishable crops gathered. They took no nonsense from anyone.

There was one occasion when a small gang of us were working away from the main group. We were picking red currants, working our way up the long rows of bushes, glad to have a bit of shade, for it was a very hot day. Cha and I were working in adjoining rows, when we heard a lassie shouting and crying some distance away. We recognised the voice: it was one of our gang, a bonny, long-haired lass of about seventeen. Cha and I pushed through the bushes to where the noise was coming from, and found the lassie on the ground, with the gaffer, a sleekit wee man, on top of her and with his hand up her blouse. We did not hesitate, although I am not sure we knew what was happening. We rushed forward and challenged him, and it must have been a shock to have two half-grown but fighting-mad lads appear at that moment. Anyway, he slunk off, and we comforted the lass as she arranged her clothing. She was distraught, and weeping, but insisted that we tell no-one of what had happened. We promised, but in fact our gang of women did learn of it, for the lassie herself, when she got back to the gang, was still greetin, and Big Aggie, the gang leader, got the story out of her.

It was the next day that the gaffer paid for his sins. Out of nowhere a big clod of clay sailed over the rows of bushes and caught him fair on the head. He went down, and his roars of distress brought the farmer himself running to the scene. We all gathered round, and were threatened with instant dismissal for this affront to the person of the Gaffer. Of course, nobody could say where the clod had come from, and as Big Aggie pointed out, if the farmer sent us out of the gate, his berries would still be on the bushes that night. So we were warned that there must be no more of it, and we went back to our picking, and the Gaffer went off to another field, but not before Big Aggie had a quiet word with him.

By this time I had left the primary school and was in the Academy. I had passed the exams, and was enjoying all the new sorts of lessons and experiences of the new school. There was a more serious atmosphere about the Academy: lessons were taken seriously, and the scholars were expected to respond seriously. Most us did, and generally my reports were good, although there were some things on which I just could not seem to get a grasp.

I had my troubles there at the Academy, and my brushes with authority. These were not concerned with work or lessons, for I got on well enough with them, but were mostly revolts against discipline, or, again, for fighting. Generally speaking, I enjoyed my years at school, and am grateful for what I was taught there. Just the same, it was certainly my own father who had the greatest influence on me, and who taught me most. It was not only that he knew so much about the ways of the countryside, and was so skilful with animals and the work of the farms. Rather, it was his determination to do the best at any job he tackled, and the way he went about things. Time and again I heard him say 'If a thing is worth daen, it's worth daen weel', and he did all things well — not least bringing up his family in times of hardship and sometimes want.

The time was fast approaching when my school days would end. Perhaps I could have stayed on at school, and gone on to some higher education, but that was not an alternative. There was money to be earned, and a job of some sort to be done. The few shillings a week that I could bring into the household were sorely needed, and I had to go out into the world of manhood and learn to be a man.

FERNIEGAIR COLLIERY

The First Step.

My father brought home the news I had longed for. I had a job, in the pit alongside him. I had already refused offers of three apprenticeships to different trades, and that was a disappointment to my parents. Although still so young, I was already stubborn and strong-willed, and I had stuck out for what I wanted, and now I had what I wanted.

Father curtly told me 'You start with me tomorrow as a collier. Your brother Jim goes on the backshift to accomodate you.' I tingled with excitement. This was to be a new life, a sort of adventure, I was to be a man! I heard Mother gasp with dismay. 'Oh no, Wull, He's no gaun doon a pit.' 'Wheesh, wuman,' retorted Father, 'He starts tomorrow.'(★)

My mother was distraught at the idea of her youngest child going down the pit, but I could hardly restrain my excitement. 'Am I gaun tae the coal-face?' I enquired. 'Aye, tae the coal-face, an ah'll mak a man o ye,' replied Father. My mother still lamented the fate of her last-born. 'Oh no, he's surely not gaun doon the pit!' 'Aye, he is, an that's the end ont. Say nae mair,' ordered Father.

I now know that Father had also been reluctant to have me go down the pit, and had thought that after a few days I would realise my mistake "once the novelty has worn off." He told my mother that, although perhaps he secretly hoped that I would make a collier. After all, he was a collier himself, and rightly proud of his skill and strength and craftsmanship.

★ *Pit, mine, colliery:* Generally speaking, these terms are interchangeable, although colliers will always refer to a 'pit' when they mean a colliery entered by a shaft, and to a 'mine' when they mean a colliery entered by an incline or tunnel. You were wound down the shaft or shank in cages, and walked into a mine, although in modern times there were often manriding bogies or carriages. 'Colliery' is the generic term for all pits and mines.

I was rigged out with appropriate clothing. It was all done in a rush. The pit boots were a spare pair of my brother's — too big, but a couple of pairs of heavy socks would take care of that. A jacket, again from my brother, and also too big, but that could be adjusted. A pair of Father's Long Johns, taken in at the waist to fit my small frame. A heavy vest and a dark blue shirt appeared, and then a pair of moleskin trousers. These at least were new, and buying them had been a struggle for Mother, because this was the middle of the week, and there was little left in her purse. And the trousers had to be moleskin, for that was traditional in those days for all colliers. A carbide lamp was made up from spare parts, and I was assured that it was a good lamp, and that I must take great care of it, for my safety depended on it.

I dressed in my pit clothes, and grumbled that the trousers were too long. So I was shown how to tie strings round the knees to sort out that problem. The new trousers gave off a heavy musky smell, and I commented about it. 'Oh, ye'll get used to it. Ye'll find a bigger guff than that when yer doon the pit,' Father told me.

So I was all ready to start my new life, and I could hardly sleep for excitement that night. I woke up when Mother lit the lamp and started her chores of preparing breakfasts and pieces. She spoke softly to me, telling me it was not time yet, and that I should try to go off to sleep again.

Soon enough I heard her call out 'Come on, Wull, come on, son,' and she gave me a little shake. It was 5 a.m. on a Wednesday morning, and I was ready for my first shift. Father and I stepped out into frosty darkness, and went up the road together to catch the first bus to the pit.

When we got there I was taken into the office. 'Mornin, Wull, so this is the man himself,' the clerk greeted us. 'How dae ye feel, son?' 'Gae me a chance tae find oot!' I replied. 'Ha, we've got a perky wee lad here, Wull. Come oor here an ah'll sign ye on. This is only a formality, but all new starts have to sign these forms to show that you are fit, nae diseases, nae glenny blink — that's nystagmus(★). Just sign these and yer a collier.' So I signed, and I was a collier, as I had long wanted.

We made our way up the rickety stairs to the gantry on the pithead, to wait a turn on the cage to take us down to the depths of the pit.

'So this is the young un,' an old miner said. 'Aye, this is his first shift,' Father told him. 'Dinna be daft, laddie, don't go doon,' the old

★ *Nystagmus:* Spadmodic eye movements once very common amongst miners. Caused by working for so long in very bad light.

miner advised me, but I only smiled, and said that I would see how I got on.

The men gathered to wait for the cage. 'Who's last?' they asked as they came up the stairs, and someone would reply 'Follow me.' Mostly they stood quietly, with just a bit of soft banter, but more than one advised me to turn round and go home while I could. 'Ye'll find it's a different world doon there, son,' said old Joe Bartley, pointing his thumb at the open shaft. 'Mak this the first an last shift. This is a life for naebody. Git oot a it while ye can.' I wondered about his words as we waited for the cage, and indeed I still wonder about them today. Should I have turned round and gone home that morning? Should I have become an apprentice in some trade on the surface? If I had done, I would certainly have had an easier life, and a more prosperous one, without all the hazards and the dangers and the fight for better conditions and a decent wage. But looking back now I am glad that I stayed there on the gantry, waiting for the cage, waiting to enter that strange black world of sweat and toil and comradeship and shared danger and responsibility. I am proud to have been a collier, and to have worked with and for colliers.

As we waited, we prepared and lit our lamps. There was no inflamable gas in Ferniegair: it was not a "gassy pit", so we used lamps with an open flame. Had there been gas, we would have had to use safety lamps. Carbide (grey pieces of calcium carbide, which gives off inflammable acetylene gas when it is wetted) went into the bottom container of the small, cylindrical lamp, water into the top. Spit into the carbide and be sure it was giving off gas, then screw the two containers together and rub the flint wheel smartly. There was a fine white flame, ready to be adjusted, and the water drip to be adjusted also. I was watched carefully as I lit and adjusted my lamp. My own safety certainly depended on it, but so might the safety of others, and getting your lamp right was the first lesson all youngsters had to learn.

It was a noisy place where we stood, with signal bells ringing out. The onsetter, who controlled the cages, was a busy man, with an important job. He sent signals and instructions to the bottom of the shaft and to the winding engine man who sat, solitary and silent, in the engine house, and controlled the movements of the cages. There were two cages and two shafts, working in tandem. As one cage went down one shaft, the other cage was drawn up the other. The onsetter sent an empty hutch down the shaft, and a few minutes later drew a full hutch from the other cage. The full hutch was sent along the rails to the tumblers and the picking table, all to the accompaniment of loud bangs, hissing of air and signal bells. As the hutch was turned upside down by the tumbler and the coal it contained slid down to the picking table, a cloud of dust enveloped us. 'That's the lot,' the onsetter shouted, and signalled "Man Riding" to the winding engine man.

We stepped forward ready to enter the cage. I was excited, but also fearful. It was a practice that members of the same family did not ride together in the cage, so that my father hung back, waiting for a later ride. My knees were shaking with a mixture of fear and anticipation as a group of us entered that cage. 'Haud tight on that bar,' advised old Joe, and I grabbed the iron bar he indicated. There was a shout of 'Right', and more signals jangled between the onsetter and the engineman. Safety gates crashed into place, and then the six of us imprisoned in that steel cage waited for a second before there was a whoosh, and the surface disappeared as we dropped into the shaft. The cage rattled and rocked from side to side in the darkness, at what seemed an alarming speed, and for an eternity. No-one spoke, for this, I learned, was always a tense moment as the daylight disappeared, and we went down the mine for the long hours of the shift. The cage shook as it hammered its way down, banging against the wooden sides of the shaft. Water splashed over us, and our lights flickered over the slimy straps of wood lining the walls of the shaft. Suddenly I could see a light through the bottom of the cage, and there was a jerk as we slowed down and then eased further to stop with a jolt at the bottom. My cap lamp slid down over my face, and I had to struggle to put it straight as everyone started talking and we emerged into the brightly lit pit bottom.

As well as being brightly lit, the bottom was high, and the floor laid with steel plates, which made it easier for the bottomers to run the hutches into the cages. The damp air smelled foul, and there was a constant drip of water.

My father came down, and we set off together along a tunnel and up an incline with two sets of rails running along the bottom. This was the Cuddy Brae, and a steel rope ran along its length and round a huge terminal wheel. The rakes of full tubs ran down on that rope, and the empty tubs were pulled up. Nearby there was a lighted manhole, which was the Deputy or Fireman's post(★). My father called out 'Alright,' as we passed, and the deputy responded 'Right. O.K. Wull, I see the laddie's there.' We were still on the Main Road, and

---

★ *Deputy: Fireman:* The lowest grade of officials in the pits. They were safety men, and tested for gases. They ensured that supplies of material, props, etc. were available, and that the men worked safely according to the rules of the Coal Mines Act.

travelled it for about a mile. I was silent, listening to the banter of the others as we walked along. There was an occasional 'Watch the heid' as we came to a low girder and had to duck under it. Most of the time there was not enough height even for me to walk upright, and it was a relief when we came to a place where it was possible to straighten up. Already my back was aching with the stooping.

It seemed a long way to our road, where we parted company with the others. My father called 'See you at lousin time,' and we entered a roadway even lower than the Main Road. I looked at the wooden trees or props above our heads, and thought about the tremendous weight of the earth above them. My father saw me looking, and explained that those props supported the roof and sides of the road. They were squeezed and tightened by the weight on them, and quite safe, he assured me. Eventually we reached the road head, and I sat down, thankfully, for a moment. 'That's quite a hike, Pop,' I said. 'Aye, but there's a lot worse than that.' I thought of how we had had to walk for so long bent almost double, and wondered how any place could be worse. I was soon to learn.

I could now see the coal face where we would be working. It glistened in the light of our lamps. This was the end of our road, the road head, and it looked rather like a small room. It was about five feet high, and the coal seam about four feet thick. There were many wooden props supporting the roof, and I noticed my father looking at them keenly as we undressed to singlet and trousers. I shivered a bit as the cold, damp air hit my body. Pop laughed. 'Ye'll no be long in warming up,' he said, and he was right. 'The first job you always do when starting a shift is test your roof, always mind your head, make sure your roof is safe.' He tapped all over the roof with the head of his pick, listening carefully to the sound it made. He called me over to one place, and pointed to a curious shape in the roof, and told me it was called a "pat arse". 'Watch out for them. Many a man has been killed by them.' He told me to stand back, and gave the rock several hard blows with his mash, a heavy hammer. 'It's coming!' he shouted, and jumped out of the way as the heavy rock slid out of the roof and crashed to the floor. It was a large rock, conical, black and shiny, and probably weighed two or three hundredweight. 'Aye, watch they buggers,' he said, 'and always make sure your props are always tight.' This was Pop's way, I found, always to lecture a lad on every job they were doing, and to instil the first lesson in pit work — the safety of yourself and your mates is the first priority.

The seam in our heading was the Main Coal, and it had different layers in it, and different shades of colour. Some were soft, and others, like the Splint, very hard. The Splint was about a foot thick. Pop carefully tapped at the coal face to ensure nothing was loose, and then pointed to a layer about three inches thick at the bottom of the seam. 'This is where you pick,' he said, and got down on his side and began picking away at that thin layer. The coal sparked and burst out of its bed as the weight came on it. I shovelled the coal away as it came out of the seam under his skilful pickwork. He hacked out coal to about two feet high and to a length of perhaps ten feet. Quite soon he was under the head coal to a depth of three or four feet, and he put up supports, gibs or stells to hold the headcoal as he worked underneath it.

I had my turn at the picking. 'Tak a guid grip at the top. Let it slip through yer other hond,' he told me. 'Let the pick do the work.' I soon got the idea, and was swept into the rythm of the work.

It certainly wasn't easy, and to me it felt as though the pick was striking solid stone. I was soon sweating heavily. Pop noticed, and told me I should change my pick blade. I looked at it. It was sharp and needle-pointed. He tossed me over a new blade, which was square at the edge. That was certainly easier to work with, and I had learned another lesson. 'Keep yer graith in good order. It maks the work a lot easier.'(★)

I was glad to stop the picking and start shovelling the coal into the hutch that was waiting, and when that was full I had a short break and a drink from my flask. There was the rumble of a tub coming into the road, and a jangle of chains as the pony appeared in the dim light. Davy was the driver, and the pony was Sharp. He *was* sharp, too, as he listened to Davy's orders, and responded immediately. Davy unhooked the tail chain from the gabbie of the empty hutch he had brought in, grabbed the side of the hutch and overturned it clear of the road. To cries of 'Ven up: Steady: Hap Hap,' Sharp turned and stood ready by the hutch I had filled. He knew better than I did that "Ven up" meant Turn Left and "Hap Hap" meant Turn Right. He was a bonny wee pony, a jet-black Shetland, with a white blaze on his forehead, and he was delighted when I went up to speak to him, rub his nose and give him a bit of bread from my piece box. Davy warned me, jokingly, that Sharp would kick my head off, but I knew better. 'Yer just like the Auld Yin, a chip off the auld block, aye fond o horses,' Davy said. He was right; I could never be near those pit ponies without giving them a word and a caress.

★ *Graith:* Tools and other hand equipment used by miners in the pits.

Davy hooked the tail chain of Sharp's harness to the gabbie of the hutch I had filled, and then went over to look under the head coal to where my father was lying on his side well under the coal by this time. He had carefully set short wooden props to take the weight of the coal as he worked under it.

'How's it goin, Auld Yin?' Davy called. 'Not too bad, Davy. Pass me those wedges.' Davy threw him two wedges. 'Aye, an that splitter.' The wedges, I knew, were to bring down more coal, and the splitter was a smaller wedge used to split stones. 'Are ye no going to bore an fire it,' asked Davy. 'Na, Na. Gelignite costs money. We'll get it this way.'

He drove his splitter into a hole at the top of the seam, then replaced it with the bigger wedge. He went along the length of the headcoal doing this, and a crack appeared between the coal and the stone along the length he had undermined. He had already pulled out all but one of the stells he had carefully placed while he was working under the coal. Pop warned us to stand clear, then struck out the last stell with one heavy blow from his mash. He leaped nimbly to one side as the head coal came crashing down and a pall of dust enveloped us.

Father and I broke up the bigger lumps of the coal with our picks, and then he cleared a space and began to place props under the roof where the coal had fallen. Again he warned me that I must always attend to the roof and make sure that the head was safe. Davie helped me to shovel some of the coal into the empty hutch, and promised that he would be back later to help again, whenever he could spare the time. Then with a 'Gee, Sharp' to his patient pony, he rattled off down the road, leaving me to finish filling the hutch he had left.

It was piece time when I had finished it, and I was glad to sit down for a few minutes and eat some bread and cheese, and have a drink of almost cold tea from the tin flask covered with an old sock. Meanwhile my father had undercut another length of the coal, and we were ready to repeat the process. Davie was as good as his word, and each time he brought us an empty hutch he helped me to shovel the coal my father was cutting so tirelessly and skilfully. By the end of the shift we had filled six hutches, each of about fifteen hundredweights. When the time came — and it was a long time in coming — Pop carefully checked all his props, then we collected all our graith and put them in a safe place out bye in the road. I had finished my first shift as a miner, and I was pleased and proud when Pop said that I had done well.

We then had the long walk back to the pit bottom, being joined as we went by other men and boys from other headings. My back ached, and I was very tired. It was not the tiredness I knew after a game of football or a long day roaming in the woods. This was a bone-aching weariness, the weariness of a body stretched to its utmost in unnatural conditions of dirt and danger. It was the total weariness of a miner after his shift. All the men felt the same, and it was a feeling I too was to know well in all the subsequent years.

At the pit bottom, as we waited our turn for the cage, I was asked how I had got on, and my father again said I had done real well. 'Aye, son, nae blisters yet?' Joe Bartley enquired. I glanced at my hands, black on the backs and with red palms, with fingers a mass of small cuts and scratches. There were no blisters, but my hands, were sore and stiff, as indeed was my whole body. As we rode the cage upwards, Joe said 'Tek my advice, Son, this was yer first shift, an mek it yer last. If yer as smart as yer luk, get oot noo.' I smiled, and shook my head. I was a collier laddie, and I was going to be a collier, like my father.

It was then on to the bus and off home, to get into the wash tub and get all the grime off and have a well-earned dinner. Mother had made a special effort that day, and we had a fine meal, but although I ate everything put before me, and could have eaten more, my head was drooping with tiredness. I heard Father say that in two or three days the worst would be over, but all I wanted then was my bed, and I was asleep as soon as I pulled the covers over myself. So ended my first day as a miner.

My mother had to waken me the next morning, shaking me gently and speaking quietly so as not to disturb my brother Wullie. I had been sleeping so soundly that I had not known he had joined me in the bed. 'Is it that time already,' I asked, drowsily. 'I could sleep for a week.' And surely I felt as though I could, but it was another day, and I was a collier, and had to be up and away. My breakfast was waiting, and Father was sitting by the fire lighting his pipe. 'Coom on, Son, dinna be late or we'll miss the bus,' was his greeting. 'Ah could sleep for a week, an ahm sore,' I told him. 'Aye,' he replied, 'Ye will be, but the soreness will go in a day or twa. Hurry up an git yer claes on.'

Mother had put my pit clothes down by the fire to warm, for it was a day of hard frost. Already the clothes had that musty smell of the pit about them, and my boots, brushed cleaned and dubbined by Mother, felt as hard as blocks of wood. "Tackety bits", we called them, and they were heavy and strong, for they had to protect our feet, but they took some getting used to.

Father was ready to go, and called me to hurry. I suppose I was still sleepy, and certainly my dreams of that first shift were still with me. In fact, this was a decisive moment for me. I could have said that the mine was not for me, and gone back to my bed. That was what some of the older men had hinted yesterday, and that was what my Mother, at least, hoped would happen. Was I really going to be a miner? Was I really going to spend all my working days down a pit? Was I going to join those hunched, crouching figures as they hurried down the underground roads to their working places? Was I going to spend years in that awful atmosphere of stench and dampness and the acrid reek of explosives? Was there to be always that hellish noise of the haulage ropes hauling their rakes of hutches along the main road? Were my days to be divided into sections by the rattle of the pony chains as a new hutch was brought along, another one to be filled, another one in an endless succession of them? I stamped my feet more firmly into my boots, picked up my piece tin and flask, my lamp and carbide tin, and went out of the door after my father. I was going to be a miner, like him.

It was still dark when we reached the pit head, and the few lights showed the way up the rickety steps to the gantry. It was a stark scene in black and white, with a few columns of steam rising into the frosty air from leaky joints and valves on various pipes. There was no colour, nothing natural, nothing growing there. This was industry, the business of wrenching coal from its ancient bed, and it was very far removed from the village and the woods I knew so well. This was where my father and all the men I knew spent a lot of their lives, and I was now one of them.

My father sent me off to the checkweighman's hut to pick up our pins. The checkweighman was a very important person. He was elected and paid by the men themselves, and it was his job to check the weight of every hutch that came up the shaft. Of course, the management also weighed the hutches, but in the past it had been clear that the men were not always paid for the coal they had won. So the system of appointing checkweighmen was set up, and he ensured that the men were credited with all the coal they sent up. Each man had a set of pins, metal discs stamped with their individual number, and a pin was put on every hutch before it left the work place. At pit head each pin was removed, and the number noted, and so every man was properly credited with the work he had done. At least, he was now that the checkweighman was present. I went up to the bolthole in the checkweigh hut and called out '88' — that was Pop's number, and it appeared on all his pins. McLean, the checkweighman, put his head out of the bolthole. 'Hello, Son, an hoo dae yer like the pits?' I told him that I thought it not so bad, and he replied that it was a hard life I was letting myself in for. 'I ken yer faither, an he's a guid man. If yer as guid as him ye'll dae,' and he passed out the pins. I went back to the men waiting their turn to go underground. 'Wha's last?' I called for the first time, again with a feeling of pride that I was a man amongst men.

There was thick black smoke with a strange smell hanging around the pit head, and I enquired what it was. 'What's aa the reek?' I said. 'That? That's the pit heedman pittin his sweety pitsocks on the brazier,' replied Big Tam jokingly, and explained that braziers had been kept burning all night round the pit head to keep the shank (shaft) free of ice. 'It's been a gae hard frost through the nicht, an the cage'll be like an ice-box this mornin. Mind an watch yer feet,' said Big Tam, and explained that the cages had been kept running up and down the shaft all night to keep it free from ice. If that had not been done, and there had been icing up of the shaft, we could not have gone down that frosty morning.

I was near the front of the line by now, and waiting my turn. The winding engineman's signals rang out loudly, and a cage dropped from sight down the gaping hole of the shaft. The wire rope hummed, and then hissed through the cold air as the winding engineman opened his valve. Shortly there was a low rumble and then a crash as the other cage came into view and stopped. The onsetter leaped forward, opened the gates, and grabbed the rings of the full hutch. He kicked off the guard that held it in place, and pulled the hutch forward, then jumped to one side as it went off to the tumbler. He rang "Man Riding", and we entered the cage. It was full of reek from the braziers that were burning at the pit bottom, and today seemed even more like the entry into Hell. There was thick ice, two or three inches of it, coating most of the cage, and we had to tread carefully over the angle irons that served as rails for the hutches. The hand rail was also covered in ice, and wee Charlie Fisher took off his scarf and wrapped it round the rail before taking hold. 'Canna get cauld hands. The wife disnae like them at aal.' There was laughter at his joke, but most of the men followed his example. I simply pulled down the sleeves of my over-size jacket and grasped the rail like that.

The onsetter gave the signal to go, and it felt as though the bottom had dropped out of the cage. I gasped for breath and felt real fear. Charlie noticed and laughed. 'Dinna worry, lad, there's a rope haudin on tae the cage, Ah hope. If it broke we'd git tae oor wark all the quicker.'

'Shut yer face, ye daft bastard,' shouted Big Tam. 'Don't scare the wits oot o the laddie. He's no used tae this, so shut that daft gob o your's or ah'll shut it for yer.'

There was no more talking amongst us. The cage was shuddering and jerking, and everyone, including the experienced men, was uneasy. Lumps of ice rattled down onto the roof of the cage and we huddled closer, covering our faces with a free hand. 'Gees,' someone said, 'Ah wish we were oot o here.' 'It'll no be long noo, Son,' Big Tam said to me, as the lights of the pit bottom appeared. 'Anybody hurt?' he enquired, as the cage gave a final lurch and stopped at the bottom. 'Thank Christ we're doon,' he added quietly to me. 'Were ye feart?' 'Na, na, Tam,' I replied, although my white face told another story. 'Weel, ye'll get mony a feart in the pit,' he said.

There was a shout of 'Haud on, we hive an injured man.' Charlie was leading Rab, who was holding his hand over his face, with blood seeping through his fingers. 'Auch, it's no sae bad. Ye ken ah hardly felt it,' said Rab, unwilling to make a fuss. 'Ah thocht it was a splash o watter as we passed thon wet bit.' Sandy, the pit bottomer, lifted Rab's hand away from his face and examined the wound.

'Christ,' he said 'Ye've given yersel a right nasty yin. There's a big cut doon the side o yer face. Haud on and ah'll git a rag and stoap that bleedin. Ah'll fix up Rab,' he added to the rest of the men, 'an ye can get oan to yer wark.'

We left Rab to the rough ministrations of the bottomer and made our way to the fireman's cabin. Father was waiting for me there, and I told him about Rab's accident, that a lump of ice had fallen down the shaft and cut his face open. 'Damn it,' said Pop, 'there's always something,' and went on to shout 'Right, Jock,' to the fireman. Jock marked his book, recording Father's presence down the pit, without even lifting his head, but when I also called 'Right, Jock,' he looked up and smiled. 'Yer place is richt, Wull. Aye, richt, Son, hae yer nae sare banes or blistered hands this mornin? Aye, richt, Son, oan ye go,' and I followed my father down the road for my second shift.

'Ah, weel, here we are agin,' said Pop when we reached our roadhead after another journey mostly crouched double under the low roof. We stripped to singlet and trousers, and I could not help noticing how powerful he looked compared to me. He must have felt this, too, for he said 'Aye, ah'll no be long in buildin up some big muscles on ye. But sit doon an rest for a minute while ah check this roof. Ye'll be tired efter that walk.' He ducked under the roadhead, and I could hear him tapping his way along the roof with the head of his pick, listening carefully to the various sounds which told him so much about the condition of the rock above his work place. There were broken props here and there, and I was surprised to see them, for we had left all the props well in place the previous day. The roof had been working, and the terrible pressures had splintered some of the props. 'Could ye saw some trees an put them up alongside they brokken yins?' I was glad to try and eager to prove I could do another job efficiently. I measured the height with my pick and a piece of wood, sawed off the tree (as we sometimes called props) and erected it, tightening it into place with a short strap across the top, and hammered into position, making sure it was straight, so that the pressure came down true on it.

Pop came over and inspected my first prop. 'Aye,' he said, 'That's fine. Noo always mind an mak sure yer trees are up tight. Always watch yer heid. Just carry oan noo and replace all they broken trees, while ah try an get some coal for ye to shovel.' He went under the head, and I could hear his pick as he began, it seemed tirelessly, to cut under the coal.

As I worked away at replacing the broken props, there was the rattle of iron wheels on the rails and the jingle of the harness as Davie brought up the first hutch of the day. He greeted me, and I left my work to have a word with Sharp, who stood patiently awaiting the next command. He nuzzled at my bare chest, and I gave him a piece of bread from my tin. He seemed grateful for it, and I stood a moment rubbing at his soft muzzle. He gave a little snort of pleasure, and stamped with his back hoof. 'Doan't ye be spoiling ma pownie,' Davie called, but I knew well enough that he did not mind anybody paying attention to his companion.

'How's it goin, Wull,' Davie called to my father. 'Auch, there's been a bit o weight on the place last nicht,' Pop replied, 'There's a lot o wood brokken.' Davie took a pick and went under the place to help my father for a while, and I took up the shovel to turn back the coal they were winning. Then I began filling the hutch, while Davie and Pop turned out the coal to the roadhead. Davie left with the full hutch, and promised that he would be back whenever he could to help with the pick work. I took up the pick he had been using and went under the coal myself, lying on my side, picking away at the hard surface, and turning back what I had loosened.

I was well under the head coal when Pop came across and warned me that it was time I had some stells up. 'Ye dinna want that lot to come doon on top of ye, dae ye?' he said, and helped me to put up the stells. He looked at the place, tapped it, and told me to hit the coal hard with the pick 'till it speaks back to ye'. This was an expression used when the weight of the head coal caused the bottom coal to burst out in flying fragments when struck by the pick. This was a dangerous time, and you had to be careful about your eyes, for those fragments burst out with a lot of force. The bottom coal I was howking was two or three inches thick, and then there was a layer of perhaps a foot of splint, a greyish, almost stone-like coal, and above that again was the head coal. We worked away, burrowing into the seam, lying on our sides by the flickering light of our lamps, our very lives depending on the stells we set. There was my father, an old miner, and his son, me, a lad of fourteen, deep under the earth, digging away at the very foundations of the world, winning coal, earning money literally by the sweat of our brows and the muscles of our bodies. It was a man's life.

At last Pop called a halt. 'Ah think that'll dae. Get me a splitter an a couple o wedges.' I went for them, and took the opportunity of having a long swig of water to ease my parched throat before taking them over to him. 'Richt,' he said, 'Now we drop the heid coal. Just watch.'

He hammered the splitter in between the top of the coal and the stone at one end of the section we had undercut. Before quite burying it, he worked it loose again, and hammered a thicker wedge into its place. Then he knocked the stells free from underneath the coal, and repeated the process along the whole line of undercut coal. 'Staun clear!' he warned me as the coal began to split away from the stone roof. The crack he had made was widening. 'Staun weel clear!' he shouted again, as the last wedge went in. 'Here it comes!'

He leaped clear as the head coal came down with a roar and a great cloud of dust. We were enveloped in that coal dust, and I got a mouthful. I was coughing and spluttering and spitting to clear my mouth when the dust settled, and Pop saw what had happened. He laughed. 'That'll teach ye tae keep yer mooth shut. Away an get a drink o watter an rinse yer mooth oot,' he said, and I was glad to do so. We had cut a lot of coal in that one stretch, enough to keep me filling for most of the day, and I took my pick and began to break up the biggest lumps. Father went back to the face and began putting props under the roof where the coal had fallen. Davie arrived with Sharp and another empty hutch just then, and he looked at the coal. 'Ye'll manage to fill a day's daurk oot o that lot,' he said, and picked up a shovel to help me fill the hutch.

Davie showed me how to "build up a heedin oan the hutch". That is, to place the larger lumps of coal in a sort of wall above the edges of the hutch, and fill in the middle with the smaller stuff. That was to give us extra weight in the hutch, and it worked so long as the hutch stayed on the rails and did not overturn and spill its contents. If it did that, we would be losers.

So the day wore on, and my second shift was coming to an end. Davie had helped as much as he could all week, and my father was glad enough to give him five shillings (twenty-five pence today) as a tip. That was in fact a very good tip, for a day's wage for a collier like my father was ten shillings, and Davie would have been earning four or five shillings a day. But, as Pop said, Davie had earned his corn that week by helping so much whenever he could.

It was a great relief when we loused that day, and I was a very stiff and sore laddie as we stood waiting for the bus to take us back to the village. Still, I felt like a man amongst men, standing there in our sweat-soaked clothes, weary to the bone, black from the pit, and smelling of the pit's mustiness. 'Let's see yer hauns the day,' demanded Big Tam. 'Ah, they're aaricht,' I answered, rather untruthfully, for my hands were very sore and blistered. 'Come oan,' he insisted, 'let's see they hauns.' I held out one hand for inspection. 'Oh, hell,' Tam said when he saw the red and blistered palms, 'Ye've bin haudin the pick oor ticht. They'll be gae sair, ur they noo?' I admitted that they were indeed very sore. 'Tell ye what tae dae,' Tam went on, 'Ye'll hae to pish oan them, that wull harden them up,' he said quite seriously. 'That's the auld cure for blistered hauns.' If so, it was a cure I did not use, and in a few days my hands were calloused and hard, although already marked with the ineradicable blue marks of my trade, where coal dust had got into the innumerable cuts and scratches.

'Aye, yur a gran wee worker.' That was my father's comment after we had been together for a week or two, and I was becoming more used to the job, with my hands hardening and my muscles beginning to build up, and my body becoming more accustomed to the unnatural strains and stresses of the colliers' life. We got along together very well at work, and he never ceased his watchfulness as I learned new aspects of the job. Sometimes at home I thought he was an auld crab, but not when we were together in the pit, and I was always pleased when one man or the other commented that I was a chip off the old block. It was not only Pop's attitude to the job that I was absorbing, but also his approach to all the problems of life in the pit and amongst the miners. He was a man respected and popular, and I was proud that, under his teaching, I was becoming accepted as one of them.

After a few weeks the stoop of coal we had been working was finished. A "stoop" is an area of coal that is left when a seam is being developed. Roads are driven through the seam up to the end of the march, where either the seam ends or the end has been been reached of the particular stretch being worked. Other roads are driven off those roads, leaving large square areas of coal to be worked later. It was those areas we had been working on, and we had come to the end of them, and broke into the waste, an old road that had collapsed. It was the brushers' work to drive another road into the next stoop, and Pop and I were given another section. This suited us, since it was not so far from the pit bottom, and we did not have such a long and tiring walk to get into it.

There were other roads nearby our place, and so we could all meet at piece time and have a blether, instead of sitting alone at our place. My piece box was never big enough for me, and Pop used to carry extra food in his box for me. And even then I was always ready for anything extra that might be going. It was usually Carluke steak, of course — jelly pieces, that is — but sometimes it would be Poe Toast, that is bread allegedly toasted by the fire while the maker sat on the chanty (chamber pot) by the fire. Often enough, just before pay day, there would be nothing but bread and dripping. But for me, at least, it was the quantity, rather than the quality, that counted, and everything was equally welcome.

'Ah wudnae sit there, Son,' Old Jock Baxter warned me the first day at our new place as we gathered together at piece time. 'That side is no verra guid. It could lunge o'er on tap o yer. That stain yer sittin oan is the stain that killed big Jock Rundle.' I froze for a moment, then leaped up and went to a safer place. I was shaken, for I had known Big Jock. It was a few years earlier that he had been killed, but I remembered him well. He had often carried me on his shoulders, and we had played football together many a time on the drying green. And I had been sitting on the very stone that had killed him. It was a shock, and I always looked at that stone with some horror whenever work took me to that place.

It was always a delight to me listening to the old miners blethering at piece time. The talk was nearly always of the pits and pitmen, and there was humour and tragedy and tales of bad places and good men, of prices and strikes and struggles. It was not a question of being educated by those old miners, for they were just blethering together at piece time, but it was impossible to listen to them and not learn a great deal, not only about mining and its skills, but also about what had forged them into the men they were.

The new place Pop and I were working was strange, and was the subject of much discussion amongst the men. None of them had seen anything like it before. The coal was hard, and it came off the face in layers of about two feet. Behind each layer was a band of clay two or three inches thick, and this we had to dig off the coal and throw to one side before starting on another layer of the coal. The Manager, Jimmy Lawrie, and the fireman, Jock Clarke, examined this strange formation, and theorised that at some time there had been an inrush of water in this area, and that the water, carrying clay with it, had seeped into every crack in the seam, which was under great pressure. As the water drained away, the clay was left behind, and hardened until it was almost like a rock under the great pressures. This was possible, because we were in fact in old pit workings that had been closed many years ago after flooding which had caused the deaths of several men. Whatever the explanation, it was not an easy place to work, and the clay intrusions meant a lot of time was spent just digging out that clay, and not in winning coal. Of course, we were not paid for working the clay.

There was a lot of black damp in that place, too. This was a gas in which the oxygen in the air has been replaced by carbon dioxide. It was a menace, and sometimes a lethal one. It seeped through from old workings, and you knew it was about when the temperature dropped suddenly. It made you very tired and drowsy.

When we struck the black damp, the older men recalled the loss of a man called McKechnie, who had worked in the Ross pit. He had simply disappeared one day from his place in the pit, and was never found, although every known corner had been searched. It was believed that he had been overcome by black damp, and had wandered off into old workings.

It was said, and many believed it, that McKechnie still haunted that pit.

We continued working that stoop, with its strange intrusive bands of clay, and one day my father called to me when he was well under the head coal. 'Come ere an see this. We ur through intae an auld road.' I joined him, and he picked more coal away to enlarge the hole he had made. We both squirmed our way through. The air was foul, stinking and damp. It was quiet and eerie, a place from the past. 'The men that worked in here will no hae a sore heid the day,' Pop said. I was anxious to explore this old road, but Pop wanted to get back to his work. He warned me to be careful and stay in earshot, and then crawled back through the hole he had made.

What would I find? Maybe a skeleton, or some old tools. I tripped over a stone, and the noise startled me. As I went along the roadway I had to brush aside long tentacles of fungus and cobwebs. The fungus was wet and slimy, like seaweed. In a few yards I was clear of the obstructions and was amazed to find the old roadway in good condition, although dust lay thick on the ground. At a crossing there was a full hutch still standing on the angle irons that served for rails. Nearby there were various tools, such as round-mouthed shovels and picks, much bigger than the ones we used. Some coats hung from a wooden beam, strange and old-fashioned. They fell into dust when I touched them. There were also some green glass bottles with long necks.

Clearly, we had broken into the old workings that had been abandoned when the pit flooded, and those jackets and bottles belonged to the men who had fled for their lives that day. Not all of them would have won their way to the surface, and even those who had were long dead. This was no place to linger, and I turned back, with some fear in my mind, because this was a tomb of miners, and I wanted to be back to the companionship of my father.

I had wandered far out of earshot of Pop, in spite of his warnings. So I turned back to find the hole through which I had crawled. But I could not find it. Had I passed it already? I had worked my way back through the hanging fungus and cobwebs. Surely it must be somewhere just about here?

Suddenly I was very frightened indeed. After all, I was still just a small boy, and had been working in the pit only a few weeks. I was aware of the absolute blackness of everything around me, and the feeble light of my little carbide cap lamp. I was aware of the total silence. I thought, too, of the hundreds of feet of rock above my head, and of the old wooden props carrying that immense weight. I wanted, desperately, to be out of that old working and back to the familiar sights and sounds of our work place, and to be with my father. Where was that hole?

I knew that I could not really be lost in the old workings, because I had carefully kept to the one road, ignoring the few side roads I had passed. But still I could not see the hole. Suddenly I was aware of a sort of rustling noise. I stood very still and listened. Yes, there it was again. It was nothing I could recognise, and I could see nothing, but certainly there had been some sort of noise in that total silence. My lamp flickered in the current of damp and mouldy air, and the shadows moved. Where in hell was that hole?

Then a voice spoke, and literally my bowels loosened. I had to fight hard to keep control. 'Hello. Who are you? I am McKechnie.' *McKechnie!* Christ! He was the man who had been lost in these very workings so many years ago!

'I am lost. I am McKechnie.' I spun round, peering hard into the darkness, fearful of what I might see. A piece of coal landed at my feet from somewhere, and then I saw it. A stick was poking out of a small hole in the coal face, and the voice was coming from there. I picked up a stone and flung it as hard as I could at that hole, and it shattered as it struck the coal face. There was loud laughter from the other side of the hole, and then I knew. McKechnie be damned! That was Davie's voice, and he had been taking the mickey! By God, I swore to myself, I would fix him for that! I had been very frightened indeed. I had almost messed myself in fright. And it was only the bloody pony driver having his fun!

Still, what I had seen had been very exciting, and I wanted to share it, so I called to Davie to join me. He scrambled through the hole that I had come through — it was a yard or two back from where I stood, and I had missed it when I passed. He was astonished when he got into the old roadway. 'Jees, Ah niver expected to see an auld place like this still standin up sae weel. Ye wud think that men were still workin here,' he said, as I led him off to see the old hutches and the graith lying about. He looked at the big picks and the shovels, and commented that the men must have been very strong to have used such tools. I showed him the old jackets and the bottles. 'The men must have left in a damnable hurry to have left all their gear behind,' I said. 'Aye,' he replied, 'an ye would be in a damnnable hurry yersel if ye knew the watter was comin in ahint ye!'

He was right, of course. There would have been no time in that moment of desperate danger to worry about old jackets and tea bottles. There would have been a life-saving rush to get to the pit bottom and safety.

We turned back and scrambled through the hole to where Pop was still working away. He had not troubled to come and look at the old roadway. Perhaps he had seen that sort of thing before, or perhaps, more likely, he was just intent on getting out the coal and making sure of a full paypacket. In fact, he was not too pleased with Davie and me when we got back, and warned us that going into such old workings was dangerous. He told me that I must never do it again, but in fact I did go once more into that old roadway, a few days later, and found that others had been there, and all the old graith and bottles had been taken. A couple of days after that, as Pop and I finished off that particular stoop, we must have weakened the roof of the old road, for it collapsed and was closed up for ever.

We were glad to see that particular stoop finished, for it had been a difficult and awkward place. However, our new stoop was no great improvement. It was an old place, and the roof had squeezed badly and was very low. There was a lot of weight on the roof, and we had to be particularly careful with the props, and had to use a lot of them. It was a low road into the place, too, and the pony driver had a lot of trouble.

It was a new pony driver, and a new pony. The driver was Tam, a red-faced lad, always cheery and with a smile. His jet-black pony was Spot, named because he had one white spot on his forehead. I kept all my crusts for Spot, and Pop seemed to have a particular affection for the wee thing, too, for he took to bringing down an extra slice of bread specially for the pony. Tam called to me one day 'Come an see this.' I went over to him, and we watched Spot nuzzling at Pop's jacket. He knew where that piece of bread came from every day. He actually succeeded in getting the piece tin out of the jacket pocket and was nosing it along the ground, trying hard to get it open, before Tam decided he had better rescue it before Pop lost all his piece, which would not have been a joke for any of us.

The road into our place was long, and had several turnings. It was an old road, and had been squeezed badly. Not only was it a low roof, but the sides also had squeezed in, and Tam often had trouble getting his hutches through. It meant that he and I spent a lot of time picking at the sides of the road to make room for the hutches, and this was a nuisance, because it meant that our regular work was held up. 'It's a guid job Spot is nae verra big,' Tam said one day. 'He was chosen fur this road because he's the wee-est in the stable. Just the same, he has a sore on his back,' and he pointed out a place where indeed the pony's back had been rubbed raw against the roof. It was red, and obviously must have been giving the pony hell every time it was dragged across the low places in the roof.

'Ah noticed it yesterday when ah was brushing him, and ah showed it tae the ostler in the stables, but he said it would be alright,' Tam explained, rather nervously. He had some reason to be nervous, too, because he knew how my father felt about this pony, and indeed all the ponies. I think perhaps Tam had showed me the sore because he hoped that Pop would do something about it, either dress it, or ensure that the ostler did. People would ignore Tam, but would certainly listen to Pop.

'Hey, Faither,' I called, 'Come ere tae see this.' Pop crawled out from under the head coal and came over to where we stood. 'See this pownie's back, it's aw raw flesh an the bloody ostler says it's awricht.' 'When did this happen,' he asked Tam, as he examined the sore place. 'I saw it yesterday when ah wus cleanin him,' Tam replied, rather defensively.

'Well,' said Pop, 'I'll tell ye, yer're just aboot finished here the day. Ye'll hae to git this hutch oot, and yin mair'll dae us. You tell the fireman ah want to see him. Gae on. If this road is no repaired tae let a pownie get in it, it can stay in the stable tull it is sorted, ah'll mak share o that!'

'O.K., Wull, ah'll tell him,' said Tam, glad that something was to be done. Pop took another look at the sore place. 'Nah, better still,' he said, 'ah had better see baith they buggers masel. Just ye finish up. Niver mind that other hutch, just git that pownie back tae the stable.' Tam went off with the full hutch, while I filled the empty one, which would be left on the roadhead until the next shift.

We finished for the day, and as we were walking out Pop marked the places where the hutches were rubbing the roadside and also the roof where it was so low that the pony had to squeeze through. My father was a very angry man. Any ill-treatment of animals angered him, and he always showed compassion for the ponies he worked with. Some of the conditions they had to face could not be changed, and he accepted that, but anything that caused them unnecessary trouble or pain or made their work harder than it had to be always upset him. 'Ah niver thocht it was that bad,' he said, as he marked another low spot. 'We'll git the repairers in tae dae something afore we come back.'

We met Jock Clark the fireman, and told him about the pony's back and what we intended to do about it. There was bedlam, and I walked on, certain that my father could deal with it without any help from me. But I could hear the shouts and curses and I turned back to give my moral support. Jock was really roaring at the top of his voice, trying to intimidate Pop, and I stood back and smiled. Nobody could do that when my father was determined, and he was determined then. Pop dropped his voice to a conversational level. 'Jock, ah want that road repaired so that a beast can git in an oot withoot tearin it's back off. It's bloody cruelty, an ah'm no stannin fur that.' 'But ah hae nae men,' Jock cried, clearly beginning to wilt under the onslaught. 'Then git men,' retorted Pop, 'Fur if ye don't the road ill staun tull ye dae!'

'Alright,' Jock finally said, in submission, 'Ah'll see whit ah can dae.' We left him, and went off in search of the ostler. He was due a more forceful meeting than even Jock had.

The stables were just off the pit bottom, and I waited there while Pop went off for his interview. After a few minutes Tam came towards me, grinning widely. 'Ah, here,' he said, 'Ye should hae heard that! Yer faither fair tore intae that ba-heided nunk an left him in ribbons. Wull is sortin oot Spot's back, and the pownie's no to wark till it's back's hale again. Yer faither jist waded intae that git. Jist what the eedjit needed, because he kens fuck all aboot hosses. Ah've tae tack a new pownie the morn.' Tam was obviously delighted with the outcome.

The fireman found men enough to repair the road, and the spots Pop had marked were widened and the roof repaired. Even then, it was a low and bad road, and we were glad when that stoop was finished and we could move to a better place.

As that winter drew to its close there was a sudden thaw after the long spell of bitter hard frosts. This was fine, but it brought new hazards in the pit. There was a lot more water about, and a lot of black damp. This was always a threat, but with the sudden change of temperature much more of it came into the workings. If the concentration grew too high, the men had to be withdrawn, and of course there was no payment in those days for lost time. We were always on the edge of poverty, anyway, even when working, and any idle time caused real financial hardship.

There was one morning in the early spring of the year when we had just reached our place and I had started filling the first hutch. We heard our mates in the next place calling to us that there was a louse oot — we were to go home. 'Whit the hell's up noo?' Father enquired. He was upset about losing more time, because the black damp had lost us more than enough already. 'There's a wreck in the shank (shaft),' Tam told us. 'We hiv tae gang an mak oor way tae number yin shank.' He turned to me. 'Ah hope tae hell that yin's no wrecked tae. Ah hiv a date oan the nicht. Ah wouldnae like tae be stuck doon here aa weekend.' I didn't have a date (at that age I had never had one) but like Tam, I had no wish to be stuck down any longer than necessary. The very idea of being down the pit without the shaft and the cage standing ready to take me back to the surface was rather frightening. Tam warned us to be as quick as we could in getting to Number One Shaft, and then went off to see to his pony, who had to be stabled and fed at the pit bottom before Tam himself could leave.

The shafts at Ferniegair had been driven through various strata of rocks, some of them hard, like whin, and others, like sandstone, comparatively soft and porous. The sudden thaw that year weakened those soft layers, which were full of water and had frozen hard during the winter, and in freezing had fractured the rock, which tended to flake away and fall now that the thaw had come. When the shafts collapsed in this way, it was inevitable that we had closures.

We all hurried to the pit bottom, and were directed through a small trapdoor, about three feet square, which was normally used to control the ventilation. Beyond that was a low companion road that would eventually lead us to Number One shaft. It was a matter of crawling along that road for some distance, but eventually it led us into the Pump House, a place I had not seen before, and which astonished me. It was big, very big, and filled with machinery and pumps pounding away deafeningly in a steady rhythm. The fireman, Jock Clark, who was leading us, noticed my amazement at this place. 'These is what keeps the pit dry an us workin,' he explained, and went on to say that the pumps were not full on, and that when they were they could pump the whole Clyde dry even if it was in spate. I looked at those huge machines with great interest. They shone like new coins, with not a speck of dust to be seen, and with huge pipes leading off in all directions. The noise was deafening, and the whole Pump House seemed to vibrate with a steady rhythmic pounding. 'Aye,' Jock said, 'They never stop, twentyfour hours every day. Ah reckon they could pump the Clyde *and* the Avon dry.' I was sure this was an exaggeration, but said nothing, for clearly Jock was very proud of those pumps. When I thought about it, I was proud of them, too. So long as they kept on working there would be no repetition of that flooding which had driven out the men from the old road I had found, and which had killed some of them.

Jock led us on, over and under various pipes till we came to another low tunnel, with a pipe running along its length. We had to crawl on top of that for some distance, with the roof bearing down on our backs as we went. It wasn't too far, though, before we came to a higher road and went along that to the shaft. The men formed up in single file and I joined them, but I was puzzled by the whole procedure. I could see the shaft, but there were no ropes or cages, or even gates there.

The man in front of me must have seen my bewilderment, for he said 'Ye'll noo hae saw oanny thing like this afore. This is whit we caa a blin pit. There's nae cages, just ladders ye sclim up. At the top there's a wee road that taks ye to Number One pit. This is the escape shaft in case ony o the shanks close.' That was fine with me, but I had to ask the one question. 'What if they baith closed at the same time?' It was Jock who answered. 'That wud be too bad. We'd hae to wait till they dug us oot.' So I had my answer, and it was not much comfort.

'Has this happened before, then?' I asked of the man in front, as we moved slowly towards the mouth of the shaft.' 'Aye,' he replied, 'Plenty o times, but we always get oot, you'll see.' I think he realised how nervous I was, and was doing his best to encourage me as we moved slowly towards the Blind Pit.

Wullie Moffat, another firemen, stood at the entrance to the shaft, giving instructions and controlling the entrance. 'So it's you next, Son,' he told me, with a reassuring grin. 'Now don't be feart. Tak yer time an go easy. Mak sure to tak a guid grip on the ladders, but above all, don't luck doon.' I swung out into the shaft and grasped the first ladder, which stood on a wooden platform projecting over the darkness below. I began climbing steadily upwards towards the next platform, grasping the ladder firmly and trying not to think about the great depths below. I wanted out of that shaft, and the only way was to climb the ladders. So I climbed the ladders.

There was water dripping down the shaft, and that helped to cool me down, but it also made the sides and rungs of the ladders slimy. It was necessary to grip tightly and be careful how the feet were placed. Looking up, I could see the men climbing, some distance apart. There was no talking or joking now: everybody concentrated on the climb, and we all knew that one slip could be fatal.

I was glad to reach the first platform, and stood for a moment till the man I was following had got some distance up the next ladder before I swung out onto it. This was an older ladder, and the rungs creaked as weight went on them. It was also vertical, and had to be climbed with great care. I reached the second platform, and went on again, and then again and again, and eventually reached the roadway where the men stepped off the ladders and began moving along to Number One shaft. It had been a strenuous climb, and my legs were shaking with fatigue, even though I considered myself to be very fit. I was sweating heavily and out of breath, and glad to feel the draft of air sweeping along towards the shaft. Number One shaft was the upcast, the shaft up which the ventilation for all the pit was driven. We had climbed up a long way, and were at mid-shaft, and could hear air whistling up the shaft from the workings far below.

'Ur ye faggot an oot o puff ur wabbit, young yin,' laughed Sandy, our pit bottomer who would now take charge of the winding of men up this shaft. 'Wis ye oot wi the lassies last nicht?'

I scowled, and said nothing. I hadn't been out with the lassies, although that was a matter that was beginning to assume some importance with me. But it was my business, not his. 'So ye were oot wi the girls last night!' Sandy taunted. 'Go tae hell, ba-heid,' I snapped, 'An git the men up the pit. That's yer bloody job.' Sandy was going on 'Ah, the young un's angry,' when Joe Bartley intervened. 'Let the laddie alone. Come ower here beside me, Son, and dinna let that big gowk annoy ye. He's a big eedjit, a knuckle-heid. An what did ye think o that sclim, Son?' I admitted that it had indeed been some climb. 'I don't know how they auld yins did it,' I said. Joe laughed. 'We're tough auld buggers, dae ye no think.' I laughed, and agreed with him. They were indeed tough, and that hard climb up those near-vertical, slippery and unsafe ladders did not seem to have upset them.

'Hoo lang dae ye think it will tak tae get us up the pit?' I enquired. Joe shrugged and reached for his pipe, and sat down to wait his ben (turn). 'Oh, it will take a guid while yet. An some of they ladders ur no tae guid. They ur a bit shaky. They need new yins puttin in, an mair tie-bolts tae haud them tae the shank. Hell, ye could feel them shuggly, and they was bluidy greasy, tae wi aw them dreepers. Ah felt twa or three wee stones hit me as we went up, aye, an some daft bugger wis shoutin tae get a move oan because we hadnae aw day. Ah wis glad when big Tam helped me oot at the tap,' Joe concluded. He was one of the older men, and that climb had been as much as I could manage. It must have been very tough indeed for the older ones.

The roadway in which we waited was about six or seven feet high, and thick with dust, which rose in clouds as the men moved about waiting for the cages to come. Jock Clark was to organise the men, and Sandy was in charge of the signals. Jock was on the blower, and we could hear him giving instructions to the pit head onsetter. 'Aye, aal the men are about up. Tell the engineman we're mid-shank. He'll ken the signals.' Jock turned to us. 'It'll be a wee while afore we can git up. They hive tae dug oan that rake that's in Number One bottom, then we'll git up. There was a groan from the men. 'Hoo lang will that tek?' someone shouted. 'Keep the heid,' retorted Jock. 'They'll not be too long. Jist content yersels.'

After a while there was a signal at our level. 'An aboot bloody time,' someone called as Sandy gave the reply signal on the long handle at the side of the shaft. The rope began to whine, and we soon heard the cage coming. It stopped abruptly, then inched down in a series of bounces and jerks. Finally it came to rest, swaying gently, about two feet above the level of the road, leaving a dangerous gap between the floor of the cage and the mouth of the shaft. The engineman was not used to stopping at mid-shank. 'Nae doot he'll git his mark. But that's nae bad,' said Jock. 'Richt, Sandy, git these men up the pit.' Sandy pressed his long signal handle three times, and the reply came back. The winding engine man now knew he had "Men Riding". The first four men stepped forward, looking uneasily at the big gap they had to negotiate to board the cage. 'Come oan, then,' shouted the first man as he scrambled up. 'If ye fall doon there we'll ken where ye are!' They helped each other to climb up, and Sandy belled them away. The cage was whisked up, and there was silence for a while till the next cage slid into view. 'Thank Christ,' shouted some wag. 'Ah thocht it had got lost.' 'Ah, shut up, Geordie,' Sandy called. 'Yer mooth's as big as that cage. Watch ye dinna swallow it, or nane o us wull git up the pit.' The tension amongst the men was easing now, after the effort of that long climb up the ladders, and their natural humour and good temper was restored.

It was soon my turn, and I looked with a bit of apprehension at the big gap under the floor of the cage. 'Richt, Son,' said Sandy, 'Tek yer time an watch yer feet,' and he held out a hand to help me climb up. I was quickly on board, then turned to help the others up. 'Richt, Sandy,' the last man called. 'We're aw aboard, noo bell awa!' Sandy did so, and we rose swiftly up towards the surface. There was a loud bang and a crash as we struck the gates on the surface and stopped. We had arrived, and I was very relieved. That was my first experience of an emergency exit from a pit, and it wasn't an experience I wanted to repeat. That climb up the ladders, with the knowledge that a slip would have meant a fall of several hundred feet, was not enjoyable.

We made our way to the Baths. I had just got a locker, and this had made a great difference. No more tin tubs on the kitchen floor, and no more dirty pit clothes and boots for my mother to take care of. 'That was a quick shift this mornin,' said Tam McGuire. 'Aye, it was that, Tam,' I replied, 'But that'll no feed the stomach or pay the rent.' We would not be paid for that shift, and it was another idle day. I went over to the big revolving brushes that took the mud off our boots. 'Aye, that's true,' said Tam, 'But we'll nae doubt survive. We've had aw this afore. It's a haun to mooth existence at the best o times. Nae money, hard wark, and plenty o laughs.' We went into the Dirty Clothes section and stripped off our wet and smelly pit clothes before going through into the showers. It was a short day, but at least we would be going home clean.

We were idle for several days following the wreck in the shaft, while the Shankers (Shaftmen) repaired the damage. They were courageous and skilful miners, working there in the shafts, in the most dangerous situations, clinging to the walls, and with certain death waiting if they fell. There was no way I would have volunteered for that work, and I could only admire their courage and skill.

It was only a few days after we got back to work that a friend of mine was involved in a serious accident. His name was Taylor, and he was helping the pony driver to get a hutch back on to the rails. There was a bad turn in the road where he had been working, and the driver had been having a lot of problems with the hutches coming off the rails there. Taylor was a strong lad, and willing. The driver and he had partly lifted the full hutch, and were packing straps under the wheels before trying another lift to get it back on the rails. For some unexplained reason the pony moved forward. It was a good pony, well-trained and intelligent, but when it moved off it dragged the hutch forward on to Taylor, who was trapped. We had just finished work and were moving out into the roadway when we heard the scream, and the driver shouting 'Whoa, Whoa!' We knew there was trouble and raced to the scene. Taylor was trapped by the legs under the hutch, and had a head wound from which blood was trickling down his face. He was semi-conscious, moaning, and clearly in great pain. Jimmy, the driver, had unhooked the chains from the hutch, and the pony stood quietly, looking round with his head down at the scene. Jock and Ernie, Taylors' two brothers, with whom he worked, rushed up, and Jock, being the oldest there, and the most experienced, took charge. 'You tek the rings,' he shouted to the driver, 'An you two get straps below the buffers. When ah say "Richt" you all lift an Ernie an me will pull him clear.' We heaved at the hutch, but it was tightly jammed against the side wall. We had to ease it away and lift again, with every muscle straining and blood pounding. We succeeded in lifting that full hutch enough for Jock and Ernie to drag their brother clear.

Other men were arriving now, and they rammed packing under the wheels. The fireman was very quickly on the scene, and he was giving first aid to Taylor. The lad was in a bad way, and it was essential to get him to the surface as quickly as possible. Two men were sent racing off for a stretcher, and we made a bed with our jackets and eased the injured lad on to it. The stretcher was very soon there, and the fireman used the splints that came with it to tie Taylor's legs, which were obviously broken. He also cleaned and bandaged the wounds on his head and chest. There was no hesitation about that fireman. He rapped out his instructions. He selected the strongest men to carry the stretcher, and named others as their reliefs. It was essential to get to the pit bottom as quickly as possible. We set off, leaving only one man behind to help the driver get the hutch back on to the rails. It was a long journey, and a very arduous one for the stretcher bearers, and of course for Taylor also. The road was low in places, and they had to stoop and struggle to get through with their burden, testing their strength to the limit, but doing it without even thinking. As the first bearers began to tire and flag, others took over, as all possible speed was made to get to the pit bottom and up the shaft to the First Aid room. We got to the bottom finally, and the injured man — or boy, rather — was very gently put in the cage, which was waiting, and sent up to the surface.

Later, I learned that both of Taylor's legs had been broken in several places and his pelvis crushed. We were told that he would never walk again. It was several years later that I saw him again, quite by chance, when I was standing at a bus stop in Hamilton, and recognised him also waiting there. We exchanged greetings, and he told me that in fact he had learned to walk again, although with a severe limp. He had not worked again, though, and never would. There had been several operations on his legs, and the convalescence had been long. He was in constant pain even those years after the accident. His had been a hard life, and a poverty-stricken one, all because of an accident in the pit. He had been a big strong lad, and he was still big, and his arms were strong, as I felt for myself when we shook hands on parting. But he was one of the sacrifices we had made to coal, and he had virtually given his life to it.

There is so much of my early days in the pit that I still remember vividly. They were exciting, a challenge, and I was responding. It was the exuberance of youth, according to old Hugh Love, who, with his son Jimmy, worked the next place to us once. We had our pieces together, and Hugh loved to reminisce and philosophise about mining and miners.

To him, miners were a strange breed of men. We lived and worked hard in an unreal world; we fought the elemental forces of nature in a hostile environment. We worked in hellish conditions of blood, sweat and muck. We breathed foul air, and at the end of the day we had not very much for it. We were exploited, he maintained, and I began to see that he was right. We experienced it ourselves. In a reasonable place, where the coal came out well, and we looked like earning a reasonable wage, the Manager would come along and knock a few pence off the ton rate. It was no good cursing the Manager, old

Hugh argued. He was just as much a victim as we were. The fault lay with the owners. It was those distant and mysterious beings who cut the rate and broke agreements. Usually we would be getting two shillings and three pence or two shillings and six pence (twenty three or twenty five new pence) for a ton of coal cut. If we were getting too much out, and taking home a decent wage, the rate would be cut by a few coppers. So there was a strike, and the owners would then set on extra shifts in other pits to make up for the shortage in output. And the strikers would be forced back to work, simply by hardship and by refusing to have their wives and families suffer any longer. They had to go back at the reduced ton rate, and accept that again the owners had won. In those days, in the mid 1930's, a faceman, like my father, would be earning about nine shillings a day. A fireman, or deputy, would be getting eight shillings and sixpence and pony drivers three shillings and sixpence. Repairers and roadsmen got five or six shillings, while surface workers took home only three shillings. So even the aristocrat of pitmen, the faceman, was earning less than fifty pence, in today's money, for each shift he worked. Miserable wages for a job that used every ounce of a strong man's strength, every vestige of his skill, and only too often killed or maimed him.

But at least we had some work, although it was intermittent. We were the lucky ones. Others, thousands of others, had nothing to do all day but hang around street corners, waiting for something to turn up, and it never did. Boys hung on aimlessly at school, for want of anything better to do and for want of a job to go to. Girls served in shops for five shillings a week, and were glad to have the job. Children could never remember a time when their father was in work, and a sense of hopelessness hung about like smoke. Houses cracked and broke from neglect and the few public buildings, like schools, were half falling down. Old Age Pensioners clung on to what was left of their lives, and spent their ten shillings a week frugally. They had to be frugal, if they were to survive.

But we were in work, and I was learning to be a miner. There was a great deal to be learned. Mining was certainly not just a matter of brute strength and stamina. It was a craft, almost an art, and one that had to be studied and learned thoroughly. It was more than our livelihood that depended on our skills. Our very lives did, and so did the lives of our mates. Amongst much else, I was taught to use explosives. It was "Gelly" — gelignite — made by John Nobel, and it was the miners' friend. Detonators were given out by the fireman, who carried them in a leather case filled with sawdust. The fuse, strum, (which was what we had used to smoke out the rats when I was a small boy) came in large coils. We had to cut off the length required, making sure that the end was cut clean and square. This was inserted into a hole in the detonator, after making sure there was no sawdust in the hole. You then crimped the detonator tight down over the strum. But first you had to bore the shot hole into the coal or rock. This was done with a hand boring machine which worked by jamming the end of the machine against a carefully positioned prop and then working a ratchet handle backwards and forwards, which both turned the drill bit against the rock and advanced it as the hole grew deeper. It was hard work, sometimes very hard work indeed if you were drilling into rock. And sometime you met what we called pyrites, a sort of hard metal intrusion in the coal or rock that the drill would not penetrate. When that happened, you had to pull the drill out and start all over again. When the hole was deep enough to take the cylindrical packet of gelly, it was carefully pushed into place and the detonator after it. This had to be done with brass or copper tools, not steel, since steel could have struck a spark from the rock and caused a premature explosion. When all was ready, everybody was cleared from the place, and the end of the strum ignited from a cap lamp. Seconds later there would be an explosion and billowing clouds of dust filled the air. It was crude, but effective, and if done properly brought down a lot of coal. Of course, we could only use such methods in certain places, depending on the condition of the roof and the coal, and if the pit had been gassy (containing inflammable gas), we could not have used it at all.

I was still working with my father, and glad of it, for he was a careful miner, and took care to explain everything and teach me as we worked. Most of the time we were working on stoops, those big square pillars of coal left behind as the roads advanced. Some of them were good to work, and some bad. There was one which we had worked only for a few days when we broke through into another old road, only this one was blocked solid with hard sand, embedded with large pebbles. We could make no impression on it with our picks and had to abandon that place. It was there that I found a couple of fossils, one a fish, which unfortunately broke, and another a fern. I was very interested in these, and even more interested when Willie Moffat, the fireman, explained how they had been formed, and loaned me some books about geology.

So it was another road and another place. This one looked good. The coal was much softer there, because there was considerable roof pressure bearing down on it. My father was delighted, although the roof was dangerous. He warned me to take extra care and never take a chance. We did well for several days, but one morning found water dripping fast into the place. 'Damn it,' said Pop. 'There's aye somethin tae crop up an hinder us. If it's not hard coal then its watter. An they trees (props) are no verra guid, neither.' The props we had were Scotch pine, soft and unseasoned. Usually the props were of Russian pine, strong and well seasoned, and fit to be trusted.

The water inflow became heavier each day, and we had to put up berges, corrugated iron sheeting, to direct it away from where we were working. That helped, but even so the water was coming through every break in the berges as though from a tap. We had cleared away the loose coal one day when Pop called me. He had been inspecting the roof. 'Come here a meenit an gie me a haun wi this. That's a gey bad stane abune ye.' I looked at the stone he indicated. It was indeed a bad one, big and loose and threatening. 'Pit yer fit at the bottom o this tree and pull the heid tae ye when ah hit it. It'll hae to be tight.' I did as he said, pulling the wet and slimy tree towards me with all my strength. Pop aimed a blow at the prop with his mash hammer, and it bounced back off the soft bark of the unseasoned wood. Bits of wood and bark flew off and splattered around me. 'Again,' Pop said, and struck another blow as I pulled back with all my strength. The heavy hammer squelched in the sodden bark, then slipped off and struck me fair in the mouth.

There was a searing pain and a blinding flash as I was knocked off my feet, with blood spurting from my mouth. My lips were split, and my front teeth, of which I was very proud, all slackened. I could feel them move backwards and forwards as I put up my hand to staunch the blood.

Pop was at my side in an instant, but I pushed him away and staggered out to the roadway, carrying my cap with the lamp still lit. I was like a drunken man. I couldn't speak, but spat out mouthfuls of blood. Pop, of course, was very agitated, blaming himself for the accident. He put his arm round my shoulders, and there was a look of desperation and concern on his face. I swigged at my water bottle, once and then again. It seemed to help. 'Hell,' said Pop, 'That was my fault. Dae ye want to go hame?' My split lips were sore and hot, and I felt at them gingerly. 'No,' I said, 'Ah'm no goin hame. Ah'll finish the shift. Don't worry. It might improve ma luks.'

After a short rest, we went back and tightened that prop, and finished the shift. I had recovered quite well by lousing time, and was able to give as good as I got in the way of remarks when we got to pit bottom. 'Whit the hell hae ye done to yersel? Ye'll no be able to kiss the lassies the nicht wi a mou like that,' came from Sandy the Bottomer. 'Ye'll be able tae gie us plenty o lip noo. It looks as though you hae foor o them,' someone else said. 'Bloody funny,' I replied. 'Pity it wasnae you that got it. It would shut ye up for a while.' 'Coom on, lad, we ken it's gae sore,' someone else said, and indeed he was right. It was sore, but fortunately it all healed up quickly, although I had difficulty in eating for a few days, until the lips healed and the teeth bedded back down, and I had a nasty scar for a long time to come.

The weeks passed, and I was becoming more confident in my work, and more useful as my strength grew. My father continued to be an excellent teacher, and took the greatest care to introduce me to more and more aspects of the miners' skills. It was summer by this time, and he was planning to go off walking the stallion, as he did every year. In fact, he had done that job for over forty years, and he could proudly relate the name and characteristics of every stallion he had handled during that time. He loved walking the roads with those big Clydesdale stallions, and meeting and talking with farmers. Of course, he should have been a farmer himself, and a fine one he would have been, but there was no money to start up, and so it was the pits for him. His love of animals, and his gentleness and knowledge had to be shown only in those few weeks each year when he walked the stallion for the farmer from Kirkmuirhill. It was only in his later years that he had the chance of being the ostler in the pit, and working all the time with animals.

He made arrangements for me to work with two brothers, Wull and Charlie Fisher. I always got on well enough with Wull, but found Charlie a wee nark, always complaining and grumbling. Wull was just the opposite, a cheery chap, usually with a grin on his face, who treated me like a son. I was paid half stuff, that is, half of what a man got, and I didn't take too kindly to that, since I felt I was doing a man's shift, and was equal to them in ability, even if they had a lot more experience than I had.

I argued about the wages, but Charlie was adamant, insisting that this was the arrangement they had made with my father. Charlie would concede nothing, although I felt that Wull would have been more flexible. Finally, Wull was prepared to give me a bit extra, but Charlie flatly refused, and the two began quarrelling. It was a bitter quarrel, and I stood back and listened, until finally Wull shrugged his shoulders and walked away. Charlie turned to me, smirking, and poked my chest with his fingers. 'See you, you'll tak what ah gie ye and be pleased. That's aa ye're gettin frae me.' I was furious, with the sort of blind anger I used to feel sometimes at school, when I got myself into so much trouble for fighting. It was the same thing, and I remember calling him a louse bag and a snivvle-eyed bastard as I swung at him. Charlie went down, and I was about to leap on him when I was caught and held very firmly and dragged back by Wull and Davie. They calmed me down, and Wull went to help his brother, who was not much hurt. 'By Christ,' he said, 'He's goat sum punch. He gae near caud ma heid aff!' I might have "caud his heid aff", too, had I not been pulled off by the others.

The upshot of it was that later, when everybody had cooled down, Wull came over and slipped another pound note into my hand. 'Ah think ye're a guid worker, and ye deserve this. It'll mek up a bit fur the time ye've been wi us. But dinnae say oot tae the wee yin, mind noo,' he said. I was surprised and pleased. 'Aye, richt, Wull,' I replied. 'We'll say nae mair aboot it,' Wull went on. 'See ye enjoy yersel the nicht. This is the nicht the Bear dances,' he said, and walked away. That was an expression we used when men intended to go out on the booze.

The bear might have danced in the village that night, but not for me. I had other ideas. Get home, and then have a game of football. There would still be time after that to go to the pictures. That was my idea of a night out, and I looked forward to every Saturday, when we started work an hour earlier, and finished earlier.

Other interests than football and the pictures were beginning to creep into my life, though. I had started to learn to dance, with my sister Lizzie as teacher. She was a very good teacher, and I soon picked up the basic steps, and started to go to the village dances. These were usually on Saturday nights, and it was becoming a bit of a rush to get in a game of football, then the pictures, and then a dance. Something was going to have to be dropped, and I suspected that it would not be the dancing, because with the dancing there was the wonderful combination of being out with the boys and yet also being with the girls, and holding them. It would be great, I thought, when I could dance properly and didn't have to think of my feet all the time. So I was very keen on my lessons with Lizzie.

It was on the Sunday following my fight in the pit with Charlie that a group of us were out for our usual Sunday walk. This was a very common thing to do, especially in the long summer evenings. It was always a great pleasure to be out then, in the woods, with the air fresh with wildflowers, or sweet with new-mown hay. We were lucky in the village, for there was a good choice of walks to take. We could go along the Avon, or, for a change, along the Clyde. It wasn't always a matter of luck which way we went. There was the question of which way the girls had decided to go that night. We were at that age when any contact with girls was desirable, and all girls were desirable. Not that we really knew what desire was: it was just that being with girls, close to them, talking with them, joking and playing with them, was important to us. It was the upsurge of youth, and those long summer evenings in the woods and fields were replete with vague longings.

This particular evening we had gone along past Garron Bridge towards Rosebank. The road was edged with mature trees which arched and met overhead. The birds were in good voice, and the westering sun was still warm. It was a whole different universe from that in which my working days were spent, and I savoured every moment of it. Where the arches of trees ended, we came onto the Maulslie Castle gatehouse. There was a high stone wall, and closed wrought iron gates, through which we could see the drive sweeping up to the castle, and the bridge over the Clyde. There was a crest carved in the stonework of the gates, a small dog, and a motto, badly weathered, which we tried to decipher. As we stood there, a motor bike and side car drew up along side, and I recognised the rider as my work mate, Wull.

As usual, he was grinning. 'Whit ur you lot daen?' he asked. 'Jist enjoyin a walk, or ur ye lookin fur the lassies?'

'Hello, Wull,' I said, 'This is a surprise. Whit are ye daein away oot here?' 'Ah could ask ye the same,' he laughed. 'Are ye jist tackin in the scenery, or are ye lookin fur lassies?'

'We were jist lookin at that wee dug up there,' I replied, pointing to the motto. Wull looked at it. 'Aye, it's been there a lang time. It says "Wha's like us", an it was the family motto. Ye'll find sich things on a lot of places like this. Ah'm off fur a run up tae Lanark. I've goat a chap tae see up there. There's a big statue of Wallace in Lanark, would ye like to see it?'

I looked at Harry and Davie, and their faces lit up in expectation. 'Can ye tak the three of us?' I asked, thrilled at the prospect of a ride on the motor bike. 'Yes,' Wull replied. 'Twa of ye in the sidecar and the other up ahint me.' Harry and Davie immediately squeezed into the sidecar and I mounted the pillion, and off we went. I had never experienced anything like that. The sense of speed was tremendous, although I suppose it was not really all that fast, and the wind whistled round my ears and through my hair. I clung on to Wull, and enjoyed every moment as we roared through Crossford and Kirkfieldbank and then slowed down as we approached the brig across the Clyde. There was a steep brae there, and the engine note changed as Wull selected a lower gear. It was even more exciting as we raced up the hill with the engine roaring. I looked back at the scene, to see Kirkfieldbank in the valley below, with the Clyde ribbon-like and glistening. I remember thinking that the people who lived there were very lucky, and that I would love to be able to paint a scene like that. But that I could not do, and would have to be content with my memory of it.

We soon arrived in Lanark, and Wull showed us the Wallace statue, and spoke about the life and death of that Scottish patriot. He told us that every year there was a celebration in Lanark, and that there had been for generations. He had attended several of them, and described the streets decorated with bunting and flags, and bands leading a procession. He made it sound very attractive, and I determined that I would do my best to attend the next one.

We then went on to the old part of town, and Wull drew up beside a short flight of stone steps with iron railings leading up to a doorway. 'Ah'll no be lang,' he said, as he went up the steps, but before he got to the top, the door opened to reveal a short, very fat, red-faced woman with a happy smile on her face. She greeted Wull warmly, and then called to the rest of us to join them in the house. She was very welcoming, and made us tea immediately. But that wasn't enough for her. 'You laddies must be gae hungry,' she said, 'Ah'll mak somethin to fill ye up!', and laid plates and spoons out on the table. A big iron pot was by the fire, and she proceeded to heat up the soup. As she ladled it out into the plates, she said 'This was made yisterday, bit tattie soup is fur better the second day. Noo come on, wire in, there's plenty mair soup if ye want it. Ah ken young bucks like ye are aye starvin, so come on noo, jist make yersels at hame!'

It was good soup indeed, and we did not really need urging to have second helpings, and it was only good manners that prevented us asking for thirds. While we were eating, Wull's friend came in, a tall, gangly man, whose dark-tanned face suggested that he worked out of doors, not down the mine. Wull and he discussed their business, while Sadie plied us with more soup and questions. She was a very friendly woman indeed, and proud of her house. Everything there was shining clean, with very old dark furniture. There were china dogs and china cats and china jugs, as well as brass pots, all highly burnished, used for making jams and wines. There were several oil lamps, with glass chimneys and brass bases. And everything shone. Sadie, it was clear, was a very hard-working woman, and proud of her home.

We chatted for a good long time while Wull and Jimmy completed their business, and then Sadie made more tea, 'jist fur the road; jist tae keep ye goin till ye git hame.' Jimmy told us about Lanark, and about the mills. He knew a lot about the town and its history, and about Robert Owen, the great reforming mill owner, who built decent houses for his workers and educated their children and saw that they shared in the prosperity of the industry. He talked about the principles by which Robert Owen lived, and which he applied in his factories. He talked about co-operatives and profit-sharing and the ways in which the burdens of life could be eased if only the ideas of those such as Robert Owen were carried into effect.

I was enthralled by all of this. It was putting a completely new light on to a lot of things that had been in the back of my mind. I had felt that the system of work into which I had so recently been introduced was really very unfair. However hard we laboured, somehow at the end of the week there was just sufficient money in the wage packet to keep alive till the next pay day. It wasn't a matter of good luck or bad luck in the getting of a work place where the coal came easy. If we had a good place, then the price was cut, and at the end of the week, the result was just the same, although we had sent up a lot more hutches. I can't honestly say that Jimmy's conversation in itself had a very strong effect on me and my thinking, but it is certainly true that he made me think. And how was it that I had gone through all those years at school and had never heard of Robert Owen, even though he lived and worked so close to where I lived?

We had several other trips with Wull and his motor bike, although I was no longer working with him. My father had come back from his annual stallion walking, and we were working together again. I was glad of this, because I found working with him more satisfying than with others. He also taught me more, and I felt he was more careful in his work and about his safety and the safety of his mates. I had filled out and grown a great deal in the past few months, and now felt able to tackle any jobs I was given. Father commented on this, and made me proud, because a compliment from him was praise indeed.

It was about this time that steel props were introduced into the Main Coal, the part of the pit we were working. The new props were simply straight girders, cut into various lengths to suit the height of the seam. They were heavy and cumbersome to erect, and you had to be absolutely sure they were erected properly, because if they were not, then they had a tendency to spring out when the weight came on them. Several men had been injured in that way. There had to be a good wooden "lid" on the prop, made to fit the roof exactly, and the props had to be erected at specified distances from each other, in order to comply with the regulations of the Coal Mines Act. I had a bad experience with steel props myself, and was taught a severe lesson, although it was one which I should have learned anyway, from the example and teachings of my father.

We had worked out the bottom coal of the stoop this particular morning, and had cleared the full length of the stoop. This had taken a full day, and although not many hutches had been filled that day, we now had all the headcoal to get, and that should more than make up for the shortfall of the previous day. We had carefully stelled up the headcoal as we worked underneath it, and could now hear the weight coming on to it.

'It's beginning to cheep now,' called Pop. 'Aye,' I said, 'Ah hear it.' 'Right,' he went on, 'Get all the graith back out the road.'

Davie, the pony driver, had been helping us by filling some of the coal we had turned out. He crawled under the headcoal with us to look at the work we had done. 'Ye'll git a guid few hutches oot o that, should ye no?' he said to Pop. 'Aye, Davie,' Pop replied, 'We will that.' He gave me my orders. 'We hiv to draw all the stells. You start drawin them at yon end.' I took my mash hammer and started knocking out the short props holding up the head coal. Father started doing the same at the other end, and we would meet in the middle to knock out the final stell. I could hear the head coal creak, and the creaking got louder as the stells came free under the blows of our hammers. Tension mounted, for this was always a dangerous moment. How long did we stay, and how many stells did we knock out? When was the weight of the coal going to overcome the support of the stells remaining? Quite literally, our lives depended on our judgement of this.

The creaking over my head got louder still. 'Pop,' I called, 'it's coming.' 'Right,' he shouted, 'You get yerself clear and ah'll finish it off.' I got back to the roadhead where it should be safe, and turned to watch my miner father exercising his craft. He was in danger, and knew it, but was still calmly knocking out the stells. This was always an exciting moment. We had worked long and hard to undercut that coal: now it was about to fall, and we could harvest it. I stood and watched, in a place I thought was safe enough. Pop was out from underneath now, and standing clear, listening to the creaking and waiting for the moment of collapse. He glanced round at me. 'Get oot the road!' he shouted. I heard the last two stells snap and crack, and then the headcoal collapsed with a thunderous roar. I was too close, and the falling coal threatened to fall on me. I leaped back, but caught my foot on a shovel I had left lying, and fell flat on my back. Large lumps of coal were falling around me, but I was not touched. One lump, bigger than the rest, flew across and struck a steel prop just above my head. The prop was dislodged and began falling directly across me. It was a big and heavy prop, and surely would have injured me badly had I not somehow, instinctively, rolled clear. That prop fell exactly where I had been lying a moment earlier. I was shaken, but unscathed as Davie rushed across and I got to my feet. 'Ah thocht ye were gonna be killed!' he cried, 'Are ye alricht?' 'Aye, Davie,' I replied, 'Ah'm alricht. Ah was born lucky.'

In fact, I was shaking, and had had a severe fright. I was scared, and my white face told the story. It was a narrow escape, and one I would long remember.

I would also long remember the tongue lashing I got from my father. 'Ah've telt ye afore: alwys put yer graith out the road. Don't leave it among your feet. Mak sure there's naethin to trip you up. Mak sure ye hev a clear road to run. Ye were lucky this time, but ye micht not be sae lucky next time.' That, and much more, I got, and I could say not a word, for he was right. I had been careless, and there was no room nor time for that in a pit. Whatever he said was quite justified.

It was just the following week after that incident that we were told the section we were working was to be closed. There was no work for us: we were out of jobs.

This was a severe blow, especially to the married men with families. They knew the degradation and deprivation of being out of work, of living like paupers at near starvation level, unable to provide for their families. They knew the bitterness of it, and the sense of failure and the problems it posed for their families and their family life. They felt all the familiar confusion about the system that had them working so hard for a pittance one week, and then thrown out to the scrapyard the next. And this while the coal owners, those distant, mysterious beings who controlled our lives and destinies, continued to live in wealth and luxury. It was no use turning to the Union. There was nothing the Union could do. It was not yet strong enough, indeed in some places it hardly existed. It was growing, though, through the efforts of such men as my father, who was a strong Union member, and had been a Delegate at one time. No, the men were on their own, and had only their own individual strength to fight with, not the collective strength of the Union.

Once again, though, we were lucky. We had only been out of

work a week, and it might only have been my imagination that the soup was not as thick as usual, and there were not quite as many tatties on the plate at dinner time. Pop came in, with a big happy smile on his face. 'Richt, Maggie,' he called, 'Git ready. It's pit claethes and parridge on Monday. We hive tae start on the back shift, baith o us.' My mother was delighted, although in her kindness she first asked whether all the others had also got a start. They hadn't: that was where our luck was.

So we started on the backshift, that is, from noon to ten at night. We had previously been working only foreshift, from seven in the morning until three in the afternoon, so the new hours were a novelty to me, and took some getting used to, but I soon settled into the new pattern of living. We had worked three days, and had just started our fourth shift when the fireman came into our place with a message for my father. I could see Pop was angry, and went over to find out what the trouble was now. 'Git yer jacket on, Son, the Manager wants to see ye. It's aboot yer age. It seems ye're too young.'

'Too young!' I said. 'It's taken them a bloody lang time tae find oot ah'me too young! Too young ma arse! This is bloody ridiculous!'

'Just git yer jacket on and go an find oot whit the Manager wants,' he said. 'Ah'll jist wark away till ye settle up. Jist watch yer temper. It'll turn oot alricht. There's been a mistake somewhere.'

I could not understand what was going on. The pit had my records. I had signed on when I first started work, and again when we had started on the backshift. There had to be a mistake somewhere. I went off to the pit bottom, answering questions from other men as I went. Sandy was surprised to see me. 'Hello, cock,' he roared in his usual loud voice. Whit's up, son. Are ye alricht?' 'Aye, Sandy,' I said, 'Ah'm alricht. The Manager wants to see me. Jist git me up the pit.' He pulled an empty hutch out of the cage, and signalled "Man riding" to the engine man on the surface. The acknowledgement came, and I entered the cage. Sandy belled it away, and the cage jerked upwards as I held on to the safety bar. It was a strange experience to be riding the cage alone, the first time I had done it.

At the surface, the onsetter also enquired where I was going and whether I was alright. Everybody seemed to be concerned lest I was ill or had been hurt. I knocked at the Manager's office door and walked in. Jimmy Lawrie, the Manager, was sitting behind a big desk piled high with papers and books. 'Sit down, son,' he said.

'You'll be wondering why I sent for you. I've got bad news for you, and I'm sorry about it, because all the reports say you are working very well. But it's been drawn to my attention that under the law you are underage to be working the backshift. I'm sorry, but that's the law, and you'll have to go. I know how you feel. It's not your fault or mine, but there's nothing I can do about it.'

'In other words,' I said, 'you're sacking me.' 'No, son,' he said, 'It's not me, it's the law.

He went on to say that he didn't like what he had to do to me any more than I did, but that he had no alternative. I was furious, and felt anger beginning to wash over me in the old familiar way. I had to keep a grip, but had to express something of what I felt. 'Richt,' I said, getting to my feet, 'I'll git a job somewhere else. Ye can stuff yer job!' and I stamped out of the office, slamming the door as I went.

Of course, as I learned later, the Manager was quite right. The regulations forebade anyone under sixteen from working at night, and our backshift, finishing at ten o'clock, was legally night work for the one hour from nine to ten. I was just fifteen at the time, and so could not work that shift. I resented that bitterly, chiefly, I think, because I did not consider myself a child.

When I left the Manager's office I was livid, and shaking with anger and frustration. I had suffered a blow to my pride. It all seemed like nonsense to me, absolute rubbish, but if that was the law, there was nothing I could do about it. I went back over to the pit head, and met the onsetter on the steps. He stretched out his arms, blocking my passage. 'Whoa, there,' he said, 'Whit's aa the rush? Haud oan a bit!'

'Git oot aw ma way,' I snapped. 'Ah want to use yer phone.' He realised that there was something seriously wrong. 'Coam oan, son, tell me whit's wrang an ah'll see if ah can help.' I told him that I wanted to use his phone to get word to my father, and told him what the Manager had said.

'Oh, hell,' he said, 'They canna dae that!' 'Aye they can!' I replied, 'An they hev. Ah'm sacked fur being oor young.'

'Jist calm doon, son. Away an get washed. Ah'll git word tae yer faither. Ah'll tell him whit's happened and ye ur awa hame. Ah'll mack sure he gits the word. Noo oan ye go and dinna worry. Ah'll go an phone doon the pit and yer faither wull git the message.'

I did as he said, and Tam went off to send the message to my father. When I went into the house, my mother was startled at seeing me arrive home so early. She was afraid that something had happened to my father, a constant fear, always in the minds of the womenfolk when their men were down the pit. I reassured her, and explained what had happened. Like me, she was angry. 'Yer faither should ha went wi ye. He knows whit Manager's are like!' she said. 'Aye, well,' I replied, 'Nae doot he'll be seein the Manager when he comes up the pit, and ah can imagine whit he'll hae to say.' And I could imagine it, for my father was a fearsome man when he was roused. But it seemed that what had happened was the law, and I could not really see what could be done, although I still hoped that my father would find an answer somehow.

When Father came home at the end of his shift I was sitting waiting, and after he had eaten he asked me to tell him exactly what was said between the Manager and me. I gave him a detailed account of everything, and he sighed when I had finished. 'And is that all that was said?' he asked. 'Aye, that was all. He just said he was sorry, it had been an oversight on his part, but that was the law, and he could do nothing to change it,' I told him.

'Aye, aye,' Pop said in reply. "Ah've heard all that guff afore. Ah'll see aboot this. Ah'll see that bugger the morn afore Ah go down pit.' He laughed. 'You know you almost caused a strike. When the men heard they almost downed tools. Ah managed to stop them. Ah gave them the story an told them Ah would hear your side first and deal wi the Manager after that. If there was no satisfaction Ah would put it tae them. Aye, they were angry, but dinna worry, Ah'll git things sorted oot when Ah see Jimmy Lawrie the morn's afternin.'

I went to bed easier in my mind. I had been very angry and disturbed by this. Getting the sack for being too young seemed quite ludicrous. But I had every confidence in my father, and was sure he would be able to resolve the problem. Next morning Pop again took me over the interview I had had with the Manager, wanting to be quite clear in his mind about what had happened. 'Aye, well,' he said, 'Ye'll git another wee holiday. It'll dae ye nae harm,' and went off to the pit.

I was anxiously waiting for him when he came off his shift, and knew by his expression as soon as he came into the house that he had been satisfied by his meeting with the Manager. 'Well,' he said, 'Ye can start back again tomorrow.' I was delighted, and showed it. 'Aye,' he went on, 'Ah saw Jimmy Lawrie an he told me aa aboot his meeting with you. It was much the same as you telt me. He was sorry aboot it, an after you left he made further enquiries an foond a loophole in the law. It seems a boy can work backshift, but, an here's the "but", he has to be up the pit afore nine o'clock. That means you only work a short shift. Well, hoo does that suit ye?'

'That's great,' I told him, 'An ah can start wi you the morn!' I was excited and delighted. Not only had my Father solved the problem, but he had again showed that he was capable of dealing with any problems that arose. 'Ah'll tell ye something else,' Pop added. 'The men were goin to strike if ye didn't get yer job back. They think a hell of a lot of you, ye ken.'

I was greeted very warmly by the men the next day. 'So yer back, wee yin. Ye wee snout, ye nearly had us on strike!' someone called. It was pleasing to be welcomed so warmly, and to realise that those men I liked and admired so much had accepted me as one of their own, and were prepared to make big sacrifices for me. Of course, I would gladly have done the same for them, and it was out of that incident that I first developed the sense of comradeship and solidarity which has meant so much to me all my working days.

We were walking down the road into the workings when I became aware of a horrible stink which fouled the air even above the usual smells. 'Whit the hell is that guff?' I enquired. Big Jim was walking beside me. He laughed. 'That's Tammy,' he explained. 'His carbide lamp is buggered up and he canna buy another yin. He's usin an auld ile (oil) lamp. Wait till ye see it!' Tammy was approaching, with on his head something that gave out a tiny flickering yellow flame and a lot of smoke and reek. I had seen those oil lamps before, but had never known anybody to use one. It was like a little tin teapot, with a cotton wick running down the spout into the container of "pit ile". The wick burned away quite quickly, and the man using it had to carry a pin or a long nail to pull up the wick when it burned too low. The oil kept spurting up out of the container, and dripping on to the head of the user. Altogether, what with the yellow flame and the plumes of smoke, it was a pretty poor sort of contraption, especially when compared with the carbide lamps we used. It was hard to imagine how, just a few years earlier, those primitive little oil lamps were the only ones miners used. It must have been hellish dangerous working with them, and hellish hard on the eyes, too. And of course the ventilation would have been a lot worse than we had, so the smoke from those little oil lamps would have lingered around every work place like a constant pea soup fog. Tammy passed us, on his way to the pit bottom. 'Jist luk at him go. Wi aal that reek he's like a train gannin intae a tunnel!' someone said, and we all laughed. It can't have been much of a joke for poor Tammy, though. He simply could not afford to buy a new lamp, and certainly not one of the latest American ones we were using. These were called "Guys Droppers", and they were very good, with a grand clear flame.

My father and I worked the backshift for about a month, with me leaving each day in time to be up the pit before nine o'clock, and thus obeying the law. I did not resent this, although I did not exactly like being treated as a child. I was doing a man's work, and thought I should be treated as a man. Somebody had explained to me how the regulations about boy's hours had come about, and once I understood this, I did not feel half as bad about it. The regulations had developed out of the great battles of the previous century, battles to humanise and ameliorate the conditions in the pits. Men, women and children had been working in conditions unfit for animals. They were virtually serfs to the coal owners, bound to the pit and with no means of achieving even reasonable conditions of work and life. After many great struggles, regulations of various kinds were introduced to make the miner's life more reasonable. Hours of work were limited, and women no longer permitted to work underground, where previously they had been used for the hardest work of all, dragging hutches or sledges along the worst roads, where even ponies could not travel. Boys were still permitted to work underground, but the hours they could work were strictly controlled, and the Manager had been quite right in his interpretation of the Regulations. When all this had been explained to me, and I understood it, I then felt much better about what had happened.

My father and I worked the backshift together for some months. Neither of us was very happy about it, because the hours of work meant that there was virtually no time left for any sort of social life. Of course, for me, a "social life" consisted mainly of a game of football in the evenings, although lassies and dancing were beginning to loom quite large. I don't know whether at that age I went to the dancing in order to be with the lassies, or whether I went with the lassies in order to get to the dancing. Anyway, that was a question that answered itself soon enough.

It was while we were still on the backshift that I acquired one of my most precious mementoes of that period of my life as a young collier.

One of the men working near us was old Archie. He was unique because he always wore a leather cap on which his lamp was fixed. He maintained, and I have no doubt he was right, that the leather cap had saved him from many a cut and knock on the head. We always got those, from falling stones and from low roofs in the roads, and of course in those days there were no safety helmets. He met me one night as I was coming out on to the main haulage road. My head was all bloody from a rather bad cut I had just received from a falling stone as I was filling the last hutch of the day. It was quite a bad cut, and I was feeling sickened by it, and my face was still covered in blood. Old Archie expressed his concern when I lifted my cap to show the wound. 'Oh hell,' he said, 'Ye've given yerself a sair un. Ah'll tell ye, Ah'll mak ye a leather bunnet jist like mine. It might save yer heid a bit in future an it'll no cost ye a penny. Juist a wee present frae me to ye.'

I thanked him, and was really grateful, not only because he was to give me a present, but also because it showed that he liked me. He took my old cloth bunnet with him after we had been through the baths, and next morning, good as his word, he was waiting for me to arrive at the pit head. 'Hello, ma son,' he greeted me, 'An hoos the heid the day?' I told him it was not so bad, a bit tender still, and with a big lump, but that I would survive. 'Ah, weel,' he said, 'Ye'll git oor that. Here's yer leather cap. Ah juist goat it finished afore ah cam tae wark. Try it on for size.' He handed me my new cap, and I examined it with delight. The workmanship was fine, and he must have spent a long time making it. He had shaped soft leather into panels and then stitched double layers of that soft leather on to them to make the crown. He had taken the tin plate from my old cap and riveted it on to the new leather one so that my lamp could be mounted. I was delighted with it, and tried it on for size. It fitted perfectly. 'Ye've made a richt guid job o this, Archie,' I told him, 'My faither will no ken me wi this oan.' Archie beamed with pride. 'It's perfect, Archie, jist perfect. Noo, hoo much dae Ah owe ye?' 'For you, son, naethin at all. It'll remind ye o auld Archie,' and he patted me on the back. I kept and used that cap for years, until the introduction of safety helmets some years later. It did all that old Archie promised, and saved my head from many a cut and bruise. I still keep it by me as a reminder of those days, and of old Archie and his kindness.

The months passed, and we were returned to the foreshift, and I was glad of it. The weather, though, had taken a turn for the worse. There was a lot of rain and high winds, and I could not take much advantage of my free evenings to play football. More important than that, though, was the effect the weather had on working conditions in the pit. Bad weather brought with it a lot of Black Damp. Often enough we arrived for work in the morning only to be told "Ye're Damped oot this mornin", and we had to go home, with the loss of a shift, and a shift's wages. It was the changes in temperature that caused the inflow of the Black Damp. It was an insidious thing, and had really bad effects. It didn't kill you, at least not directly, but your eyes became heavy, limbs ached, and you became tired and sleepy. Of course, if you stayed in conditions of bad Black Damp for a long time, then it would be fatal.

Our carbide lamps told us when there was Damp, and we always watched the flame carefully when conditions favoured the gas. Instead of a clear bright flame, it turned yellowish, and if conditions were really bad, there would be a twirl of black smoke spiralling up from the flame. If you were foolish enough to stay there long enough, the flame would be snuffed out. Many men, including myself, have often gone home after working for a while in Damp, thinking that the conditions were not too bad, and then found ourselves incredibly sleepy and weary. You could fall asleep over your dinner. More than once I have decided to have a short nap after my meal, and asked Mother to waken me at a certain time, only to fall into such a deep sleep that she could not rouse me, and the next thing I knew it would be morning, and time for work again. Even then it was hard to believe that the night had passed, and that Pop was already up and ready to go. 'It's no that time yit!' I exclaimed, not believing that I had slept so long. 'Aye, Son,' Mother would say, 'Come on, ye'll be late. Yer faither's just goin.' He always liked to be away early, and be amongst the first men at the pithead. He had to go alone on those mornings, though, for it really took some time to rouse me, and it was only the shock of the ice cold water in the sink when I washed my face that really persuaded me that this was another day.

Even as he got older, Pop followed the habits of a lifetime. He was amongst the first to arrive at the pit, and he always kept his work place tidy and safe, a lesson he never ceased to impress on the youngsters he taught their craft. But he was getting on in years, and although he never failed to do his stint, and more, it was becoming a greater effort for him. When he was sixty-eight, it was no surprise when one day the Manager called him into the office.

However, it was not to get his cards. Jimmy Lawrie knew Pop well, and understood his value. So Pop was offered the job of ostler. His love of horses and his knowledge of them fitted him perfectly for that job, and the Manager knew it. However, Pop being Pop, although he was glad enough to have the chance of giving up the hard graft at the coal face, he had to make his own conditions.

I could imagine him saying to the Manager, 'Aye, Jimmy, but it'll be on my own terms an conditions. Ah dinna want you or any Paper Eleck (his term for the pen-pushers in the Office) tellin me whit tae dae. Ah'll be in complete charge, an whin ah want onythin fur the beasts Ah'll git it straight away and no hae tae come tae ye tae git it. An another thing, Ah'll be sayin whin a pony is gaein oot tae wark. Ah'me no gaun to hae onybody tack oot a beast that's no fit or his already worked a shift. Nane o this pownies warkin double shifts. That'll be stopped, and Ah'll be watchin all the drivers, that they wash an groom the beasts tae ma satisfaction. If they don't, it'll be on their heids. Ah'll be standin nae nonsense frae they young buggers.'

I was not there at the interview with the Manager, of course, but I am quite sure it must have gone something like that. In any case, the Manager agreed that Pop would be in complete charge of the ponies. Jimmy Lawrie knew well that my father would take great care of them, and that they could only benefit from being in his charge.

Indeed, it was not long after Pop became the ostler that we could see the difference. He determined what road a pony would work in, and he always checked every road for height before selecting the pony to work there. He insisted that some roads had to be back-brushed and heightened to give the pony head-room. This made the job of both pony and driver much easier, and Pop soon gained the respect of all the drivers for his care and attention to the ponies.

After he had taken over his new job, I was detailed to work with two other men. This was the rule, since I was still considered too young to have a place of my own. But I was learning, and could look forward soon to having my own place, and being a fully-qualified face worker.

The men I was with were Bobby Nutt and Tam McGuire. Bobby was a wiry wee man, and a hard worker, although I thought he took too many risks in order to get out that extra hutch. This was against everything my Father had taught me, and I was not happy about it. Tam was an entirely different sort of person. He was more methodical, and looked a bit slow and sluggish compared to Bobby, who was always rushing things. "A bloody wee gitter" I used to call him when he irked me. Tam, on the other hand, worked away slow and steady, and still got the coal out.

The seam we were working was called the Pyotshaw. It varied in height from about fourteen inches to two feet, and working there was the first time I had experience of machine coal cutting. This was another sign of the times: steel props replacing the old wooden ones, and now a mechanical coal cutter.

Not that that rather primitive machine took any of the hard work out of the job. Perhaps it was the reverse, because we had to work at a pace dictated by the machine, and in a pattern that its limitations decided.

When we started the shift, my first job was to secure the roadhead, and ensure that the roof was sound. Tam and Bobby turned out the gum (small coal from the machine, which had undercut the seam). When that was done, Tam took the low side and Bobby the high, while I worked the roadhead, filling the coal they turned out. To burst into the coal, that is, bring down what had been undercut by the machine, we fired shots, and the next job after clearing away and filling the gum was to drill the shotholes and stem them up with explosive.

There were six shots to be fired, and of course they were all done at the one time. We were on a corner road, the end road of our section, and so we had only to warn the men below us when the shots were ready. That was Tam's side, and he would warn the men as soon as he had lit the last of his fuses. Bobby and I timed our shots to give him time to crawl down to the next road. There were six shots to be fired, and three of us working, so we each had the job of lighting two fuses. Tam was off fast, crawling away to the safety of the next road, while Bobby and I made off to a refuge hole a safe distance from the shots, and settled down to wait for the strum to burn down and fire the shots. Well, that was how it was in theory, but on one occasion the theory did not work out in practice.

Bobby and I were in the refuge hole, having lit our strum, and were awaiting the explosions, and then for the reek to clear. The first explosion came in good time, and it sounded fine. I counted as each shot went off. Five? Had there really been only five? Did we have a misfire? Could I have miscounted, or had two shots been so close together that they sounded as one?

A misfire was one of the things we dreaded most. If a shot failed to explode, somebody had to go in and find out why. The explosive had to be pulled out of the shot hole, complete with the very sensitive detonator, and then replaced after the fault had been cleared. It was nerve-wracking, because we knew that if the shot went off when we were near, or actually handling it, we could be injured, or worse.

I sat and strained my ears. Perhaps I really had miscounted. Suddenly I received a hearty poke in the ribs. It was Bobby. 'Come oan, you, time we wur in. Ur ye gonna sit aa day?' 'Hold on,' I told him, 'There's only five off,' angered by the dig in the ribs.

'They're aw off by this time. Come oan, get off yur arse. There's work to do. Git into the face,' Bobby said. 'Bobby,' I told him, 'You take a fuck at yerself. Ah'm not goin in there yet. There's only five off.' He went off into the face, still muttering to himself, while I sat still, wondering what to do. Finally, I convinced myself that I had either miscounted the shots or that there had been two close together. After all, Bobby, an experienced miner, was in there. Finally I decided to go in, still dubious and uncertain. Bobby was already at work, turning coal out from his side. I got down on my knees and began to crawl along to where I had left off clearing away the gum. Then I froze.

There was the danger call: 'Fire! Fire! Git tae fuck oot o there!' It was Tam, screaming his head off. So there *had* only been five shots, and there was one more to go. I began to crawl backwards towards the roadhead, but it was too late. There was a fearful roar and a white flash as I dropped my head into the gum. I could feel my shoulders, head and arms being ripped and pitted by the bits of coal. My ears felt shattered and my head ached. I cried out in pain as the coal smothered me and stung my body. But I was still conscious as the noise died away, and I dragged myself back to the roadhead. I could hear myself cursing and swearing, but I was shaking with shock, numb and befuddled. There was a voice in the distance saying over and over again 'Are ye alricht?' It sounded a bit hysterical. Well, I was alright. There was nothing broken, and I was not seriously injured, but my whole body ached and stung and my ears were still ringing. I staggered off to my jacket, and took a swig of water from my bottle. The singlet I was wearing was in tatters. I struggled to concentrate through the roaring in my ears and the throbbing of my head. A hand touched my shoulder. 'Are ye alricht?' the voice asked again. Through my bewilderment I saw this head near me, and the lips moving, but nothing was making sense. Then I knew. It was Bobby. A wave of anger and hatred swept through me.

'You bastard, you stupid lousy bastard,' I screamed, 'It was all your fault.' I struck out at him, a backhanded blow that knocked him over, and I jumped on top of him, wild and furious, still not in control of my senses. I hammered his head against the hard road, but fortunately it was cushioned by my jacket that had fallen from its nail. Then someone grasped me and threw me roughly to one side. It was Tam.

He was gasping for breath after crawling as fast as he could to reach us. 'Steady, lad, steady on. Simmer doon,' he commanded, as he held me. He looked at my body, peppered and wounded by the blast, with some cuts bleeding profusely. 'Oh, hell, we'll hae tae git yer cleaned up. Is it sair, son?' I muttered something in reply, and he went off for a moment to return with a cloth and a bottle of water. Gently he sponged the worst of the coal off my body. 'Cor, ye're a mess, but tak it easy,' he said, as he worked away, gently and quietly. I was beginning to recover, although my body still shook and my head was ringing. My new leather cap had without doubt saved me from head injuries, but all the rest of my body was cut and lacerated.

'Did ye not hear me shouting "Fire" '? Tam asked. I could see the worried look on his face. 'Aye, Tam, Ah heard ye,' I answered. 'A guid thing for me that ah did. Ah would hae been richt in front o the blast when it went off. Ah was crawling back oor the gum when the shot fired. Guid thing that gum was there or ah would hae had the full blast on top o me!'

'Ah, well,' he said, 'ye're not too bad. Ah'll git yer cleaned up. Ah'll hive tae dig out the wee bits o coal, bit ah'll be canny an try not to hurt ye. Jist ye tell me if ah hurt.' He was gentle and kindly, but just the same I did a bit of yelping as he dug some of the larger bits of coal out of the various wounds. Bobby looked on silently as Tam worked away, occasionally passing the water bottle as Tam asked for it. There was blood trickling from his mouth from the skelp I had given him, but I felt no sympathy. 'Ah'm sorry, son,' he said, 'It wis ma fault. Ah should ha listened to you an waited.' He looked pathetic, and was blaming himself for the accident. But I was in no mood to offer forgiveness. 'Jist shut up, ye greedy little snivel-eyed bastard,' I snapped, 'Ye canna dae onything aboot it noo. It could hae been a lot worse, so just forget it. Ah'll be alricht.' Indeed, I was feeling better by the minute, as Tam continued to pick bits of coal out of my wounds. The pony driver came along at that moment. He couped the empty hutch at a wider part of the roadway, and then came in for the full hutch. We had to explain what had happened, and Bobby repeated his moaning apologies. I insisted that Davie, the driver, say nothing about what had happened, and told the others also not to say anything to anybody. I did not want a lot more sympathy or regrets.

Tam dug out a particularly painful lump, and I winced. 'Whit are ye daein. That's bloody sair,' I told him. 'Oh, be quiet,' Tam retorted. 'Ah'll no be lang noo an ye'll be as guid as new. In fact, it micht be an improvement.' I was not amused, although I certainly did appreciate the way in which he helped me, and tended my wounds.

He had picked most of the coal out of my body and cleaned the cuts as well as he could. 'There ye go, noo. Hoo dae ye feel?' he asked. 'A lot better noo, Tam,' I replied. 'Ah've got oor the shock. Ah got a richt bloody fright there.' 'An sae did ah,' Tam said. 'Ah saw yer licht just as the shot went off. Ma hert nearly stopped.'

Bobby offered me a pullover to wear, since my singlet was in rags, and I gladly accepted it. I was much calmer now, and apart from a hissing in my ears, that I knew would go away, felt reasonably fit again. We had an early piece break, and then went back to work. Nothing too serious had happened, and indeed we had been lucky. I cannot speak about the others, but beyond any doubt that accident taught me a lesson I have never forgotten. I would always be careful when firing shots, and take no chances. If I ever had forgotten, one glance at my body, with all the blue scars where the coal dust had settled in the wounds would have reminded me.

That accident with the shot made a changed man of Bobby. He had been inclined to be bossy, and nothing I did seemed to please him. Now he knew that I would take no nonsense from him, that, having clouted him once, I might do it again. Working with him became much more pleasant.

It was about a week later that we were reporting for work one day when the fireman warned us that we would have to be very careful because the crush had come on to the place where we were working. This usually happened when a place or a road had been worked for a time, and the weight came on to it. You could hear the rock moving and creaking. The tremendous overhead weight snapped the wooden props like matchsticks, and you had to replace them immediately to prevent a closure. All the broken props were collected and built into wooden fillers to support and strengthen the roof. It was a dangerous period when your place was on the move, and you had to be extra careful and take all precautions to ensure the roof was safe before stripping the coal.

The Pyotshaw, the seam we were working, was directly above the Main Coal. There was only a thin rib of rock, possibly two feet thick, separating the two seams. The Main Coal had been all but worked out, and obviously the rock post between the two seams weakened. When we turned into our roadway we could already see the telltale signs of the crush. The stone walls built at the side of the roadway had been spilling out under the weight, and stones were scattered over the hutch rails. The roadside breakers had snapped and stuck out dangerously into the road. These had to be removed and the rails cleared so that the pony driver could get in with his hutches.

'Cor,' Tam said, 'The Wee Man has been busy last nicht. Ye would think a bomb had struck the bluddy place.' To me it looked more as though an earthquake had struck it, and indeed in essence that was just what it was — an earth tremor which had crushed the height of our road so that we no longer had plenty of headroom. We cleared the damage as we went along. Bobby was in front and suddenly he stumbled and fell into a crack in the pavement. There was a volley of oaths and curses, and Tam and I laughed, for it was unusual to hear that sort of thing from Bobby, who was a church-goer. There were a lot of cracks and fissures in the pavement, at various distances from each other. This was dangerous enough for us, but impossible for the pony.

Bobby had an idea of how we could overcome that problem. He had the pony driver bring in a load of straps, which we laid across the cracks for the pony to walk on. Then we had to re-lay the rails and sleepers. It all took time, but at least it made it possible for the pony to get into the work place. The driver, Dougie, was surprised to find the rails relaid on top of the straps. 'That's great,' he said, 'It's jist like walkin across a brig noo. The only thing wrang is that if the road gits ony lower aal no git in wi a hutch, far less wi a pownie, and he's jist aboot the wee-est in the stable.'

We worked that place for a week, with the squeeze getting worse by the day, before the Manager decided to abandon it. Not only was the roof working constantly, but the rock post between us and the Main Coal was getting thinner all the time. Eventually the two would meet, but in the meantime the cracks in our pavement were getting deeper and more frequent. We were not sorry to leave there, and move to another place in the Pyotshaw.

This was a very different place. It was lower by several inches, for one thing, which meant that we had to lie on our sides while stripping the cut coal. Also, the seam was so low that the coal cutting machine had to cut into the stone pavement to give us a little height. The stone dust was hellish, white and thick. While you were shovelling the stour (dust) into the waste, you were enveloped in a cloud of dust that clogged your eyes, nose and throat. It was almost a pleasure to get that job done and start on the coal stripping.

We found that a number of men in this section were troubled by what we called Beat Knees. Of course, we worked on our knees, or our sides, or our backs, all the time, and the hours we spent like that, with bare flesh being ground into that mixture of stone dust and small coal caused all kinds of skin complaints and poisons. The Beat Knee was a large swelling, very painful till it came to a head and burst, ejecting a thick slimy pus, mixed with blood. We called that noxious grey fluid "beeling".

Tam was the first of our team to suffer, and I watched day by day as the swelling at his knee grew bigger. Obviously it was hellish painful, but Tam kept on working. Then he was off for one day, and came back looking and feeling much better. The swelling had burst, and he had got rid of a lot of pus. He had to nurse his knee a bit, and try to keep it clean, because the wound was still open, but that was not easy to do down the pit.

It was only a few days after Tam's return that I began to feel my own right knee getting a bit sore and swollen. I mentioned it to Tam, who examined it and told me that it was the beginning of a Beat Knee. He advised me to plot it (bathe it) with hot water and vinegar or epsom salts. That was supposed to bring it to a head more quickly. He also advised me to try and keep off my knee as much as possible. I was rather bemused by that. How the hell could I keep off my knees when nearly all my work was done on my knees? 'If ye canna go doon on yer knee ye'll jist hiv tae shovel off yer arse, that's whit ah had tae dae,' Tam said. He offered to give me a hand whenever he could, and was full of encouragement and advice.

When I got home Mother noticed my glum face, and asked how I had got on that day. 'Ye shouldn't be warkin wi a knee like that,' she said when I showed her. 'Ah'm no a wee laddie,' I replied (although, really, I was not much more), 'So stop tellin me whit tae dae.' I followed Tam's advice, and bathed the kneee, but the swelling got steadily worse, and there was no doubt that I had a bad Beat Knee.

The pain of it got steadily worse, and working became more and more difficult. I was tired and miserable. My brother Jim was waiting for me one day when I got home. He offered to look at the knee after I had eaten, and I was glad to let him do so, for he was a qualified First Aider, a member of the pit First Aid Squad, and had experience of these things.

My knee was badly swollen by this time. It felt like a balloon. The swelling was soft, with a cone shaped, fiery-red top with a couple of holes in it, from which pus was beginning to ooze. 'Aye,' Jim said, 'It's ready to burst. That's the beel coming.' Mother had a large pot of water boiling on the stove, and had brought through the bine, the large tub we had used for washing ourselves before the pithead baths were installed. There was a big bottle of vinegar waiting, and some clean white cloths. The boiling water was poured into the tub, and vinegar added to it. I slung my leg across the tub, and waited for Jim to begin.

Jim warned me that it would be hot, but that it was necessary to be cruel to be kind. He rolled up his sleeves, swished a cloth around in the boiling water and then, with a quick flick, slapped it across my knee.

It was hot alright, and I nearly howled. I bit my lip and hissed to myself. Jim took off the cloth, and repeated the process. Sweat was pouring off my face. Time and again the cloth went into the water and then onto my knee, and I winced each time. I asked him to go easy, but he ignored me. He knew well enough what the suffering was — he had had Beat Knee himself. He was gentle and compassionate, but determined. Eventually he examined the swelling again, and was satisfied with what he saw.

Now came the worst part. He had to squeeze that fiery-red cone to try to burst it. Two thumbs and all his strength went into that squeeze, and I yelled with the pain of it. He continued to press. 'It's coming,' he said, and I looked down. Greyish pus, thick and mixed with blood, was being squeezed out. I thought it looked like a volcano, and certainly it felt like one. Jim continued to press around the base of the cone, and more pus flowed out, more easily now. Jim decided that was enough for the moment, and dressed the knee with lint and a clean bandage. He was pleased with the job, and told me he would be back that night to repeat the treatment. He said it would be easier the next time, and that with the pus out the knee would not be so sore. He was right, and with his treatment the swelling began to go down. Of course, I could not kneel on that leg, and had to sit when shovelling the coal. Tam and Bobby were both very good, and would not let me go under the coal face, where I would have had to kneel. They turned out the coal for me, and I only had to fill the hutches.

Then, to my dismay, my other knee began to swell. I had a second Beat Knee. Jim examined this, and looked worried. He assured me that this one would not be as bad as the first, but still it had to be treated. So it was more boiling water and scalding hot cloths. He was treating both knees at once now. The first one had begun to clear up, with the open wound looking clean and red. The other knee had no red cone on the top, although it was very swollen. When Jim pressed it, the imprint of his finger was left for a moment. He thought it had been caught in time, but decided to keep on plotting it till all the swelling had gone. He insisted that I take a couple of days off work, and, truth to tell, I was glad enough to do that, for work was just about impossible with two Beat Knees.

My mother had taken the opportunity of washing all my pit clothes, and then she made two pads of soft flannel and sewed them into the knees of my moleskin trousers. This was much more comfortable, and took a lot of the misery out of kneeling when I went back to work. We did not have kneeling pads in those days, and the soft flannel in the knees of my trousers certainly helped.

I went back to work, but Jim warned me that I must be careful to clean out the wounds every day when I finished work. On the first day back I asked the Bath Attendant, a rather surly man called Black, for some cotton wool to clean out the pus that still oozed from my knees. He was a First Aider, and examined my knees, and offered to dress them every day after I had bathed. I was a bit surprised about this, for generally he was a dour and secretive man, but I found him kind and considerate. Later on, he was very helpful when I got several boils on my back through working wet, when the inevitable scratches and cuts turned into big, and very sore boils. Black was gentle and sympathetic, cleaning them out and dressing them each day.

When I went back to work after my couple of days off, I was greeted with a lot of good wishes and questions about the knees. Nearly everybody said that I should have taken more time off, and told me to take it easy. There's not much chance of doing that in the pit, though. If you are there, you have to work.

Tam greeted me with the news that Bobby was off work. He, too, had a Beat Knee. I was not sorry at his absence, although I sympathised with anybody who had the same as I had just suffered. Still, it would be peaceful without Bobby for a while. He was always yelping on about something, especially to Dougie, the pony driver. I told Tam I thought Bobby a carnaptious little git, and that I would belt him if he spoke to me the way he spoke to Dougie. Tam laughed. 'Aye, he kens ye wid. He kens ye're a quick tempered little bugger, that's why he sooks in wi yer at times, especially after that last skelp ye giv him.' We went into the road, and Tam warned me that we would be working wet. Water had come into the place. It was heavy in the low side, but not too bad in the high. Tam warned me that we were in for a drooking.

Sure enough, the place was wet. The gum from the bottom of the seam was wet, and stuck to your shovel as you tried to turn it out into the roadhead. As you lay on your side stripping coal, water was constantly dripping from the roof on top of you. It was icecold water, and you felt pretty miserable. There were no oilskins or any other sort of protection: we simply worked in our trousers and singlets, lying in the wet mud and wielding shovels to which the coal stuck as we tried to shovel it out behind us. We were paid an extra shilling a day for working wet, and that was the only recognition we got from the owners. It was different with the men. They all knew just how miserable work of that kind was, and did their best to make it bearable. When we finally put on our jackets and hurried to the pit bottom at the end of the shift, everybody made way for the wet men, and they rode the cages first. They were first into the bathhouse, and the first to get warmed up under the showers and into warm dry clothes.

With the constant wetness and perhaps also because there was some lingering infection in my body after the two Beat Knees, I developed boils on my body at that time. One particularly troublesome one was on my back, just where my belt rubbed. There was another on the back of my head, where it was caught by my cap. They were large and ugly, and very painful, so that it was a great relief when they finally burst and released their loads of sickly, greyish pus, again mixed with blood. It was then that the baths attendant, Black, was very helpful and gentle with me, dressing and cleaning the boils each day.

The wetness finally began to ease off in our place, and the seam began to get a bit thicker. From fourteen inches it went up to eighteen or twenty inches. Work was much easier in those conditions, and I was back to my usual bouncy self. Nobody enjoyed working wet, although we welcomed the bob a day extra that it brought in "Wet Money". The results of too much wet work was rheuumatics, Beat Elbows and Knees, and boils, and of course the work was much harder as the wet coal had to be handled in those cramped conditions. Constantly lying on your side in several inches of gritty mud, while trying to turn out coal into the roadhead was no joke.

With the dry conditions and the increased height of the seam, we were able to win more coal, and the driver was kept busier bringing in the empty hutches and taking away the ones we had filled. As a result, he did not have so much time to help me, and so I had to work harder. The driver, Dougie, was a good lad, always willing, and a hard worker. We usually tipped him a couple of packets of fags or five or six shillings at the end of the week. He would help me erect props at the roadhead when I had stripped the coal. He wanted to be a faceman himself, and considered it good practice to help whenever he could.

There was one occasion when Dougie was laid off work for a few days after some injury. His place was taken by another driver, called Pate, a surly, sleekit-looking chap. I took an instant dislike to Pate, especially as I could see that his pony, a small white beast, was terrified of him. I caught him kicking the beast in the belly one day, and once again that old familiar black anger washed over me. I smashed him full in the mouth with my fist, and, screaming with rage, would have continued going for him had not Tam shoved me off to one side, so that I fell heavily against the roadside. He was furiously angry. 'Whit the hell's gaein oan? Dae ye daft buggers no ken ye can baith be sacked for fichtin doon the pit?' Bobby had also appeared, and lifted Pate up. His mouth was bleeding, and two teeth were missing, and I didn't care a damn. I explained that Pate had been kicking Snowy, and, struggling to get loose from Tam's grip, screamed that no-one was going to illtreat a pony when I was around. Pate spat out more blood. 'It's a daft beast, onyway. It'll nae dae whit it's telt,' he said. 'Of course it won't,' I shouted, 'Ye've got it terrified.'

Pate pointed a rather shaky finger at me. 'Ye've got it comin. Naebody punches me an gits away wi it, ye bastard. Ah'll git ye!' Tam snapped at us both. 'There'll be nae mair fichtin doon here, and nae kickin pownies, either. If there's ony mair o that I'll deal wi ye, nae the laddie!' I walked away, rubbing a sore elbow that had hit the wall hard when Tam had thrown me off. I was shaken, but the black anger had left me. We found Snowy, a quiet, patient and intelligent pony, waiting for us. He had gone off by himself to where the full hutch was, and stood ready for someone to hitch his tail chain to the hutch. 'Ye see,' I said to Bobby, 'He's got mair sense than his bluidy driver,' and rubbed his nose and patted his neck. 'Aye,' Bobby replied, 'Ye can say that agin. But ye'd better watch oot fur that yin. He'd smash yer face in when ye weren't lookin.' I hitched the chain to the hutch, and slapped the pony on the side. He went off happily enough, and I stood to one side to let the hutch pass. Pate went off, still spitting blood, and scowling at me as he passed. Tam joined us. 'Ye'll need to watch him, son,' he said. 'He's a fichtin man, that. He'd put the heid in as fast as look at ye. Watch him, son, he's a bad yin, an comes frae a bad lot. They're always in trouble. Hit yin, and ye hit the lot.' He warned me to stay away from the Old Town, where Pate's family lived. It wasn't a place I visited, anyway, but I certainly listened to Tam.

I was still angry about the ill-treatment of Snowy. He was an old pony, really beginning to show signs of the wear and tear of his hard life. He should have been happily grazing and gambolling somewhere in a sunny pasture, but I knew that ponies were worked until they dropped dead in those days.

The next day we had a pleasant surprise when we heard someone yodelling and the rattle of an empty hutch. It was Jimmy, the Singing Cowboy. He had replaced Pate as our driver. I learned later that Bobby had been the cause of Pate's removal, reporting that he was unsuitable and incompetent driving hutches in to us, over a low and tricky road. It was good to see Jimmy, a bright and cheerful lad, with an excellent singing voice. He always sang cowboy songs, hence his name. He told me that Pate had been transferred to the Main Coal, 'an guid riddance tae him.' I agreed, and helped him to throw the empty hutch on its side off the rails, to allow the full hutch to pass.

It was true that the rails in to our place were difficult. Tam described them as being like 'a dug pishing in the snaw' and he was right. There were lots of twists and turns, and it took a really skilful driver to negotiate them. With Jimmy we were never kept waiting for empty hutches, and had the added pleasure of his singing as he worked. Jimmy was also a cheerful companion on the road out of the pit at shift end. It was a long walk along the Main Haulage Road, but Jimmy would enliven it with his songs, as he walked along holding Blackie's collar. *I'm heading for the last round up*, he would start, and then it would be *Git along, little dogie, git along,* and then *Old Faithful*. It certainly helped to shorten that road when we could all join in a verse or two.

It was 1939, and I was nineteen years old. More important, it was September, and there was war between Britain and Germany. That came as no surprise, and we had been waiting anxiously for it. We did not know then of the real horrors of Nazi Germany, but we knew enough to realise that it had to be stopped. All the intricacies of diplomacy and negotiation meant nothing: we just knew we were opposed to Hitler and all his works. There was a blackout and rationing began. Picture halls were closed, football matches and greyhound meetings ended. We carried gasmasks and identity cards and air raid shelters were built. People joined the A.R.P. (Air Raid Precautions) service, and, eventually, the Home Guard. As miners, we were exempt from military service, but many of my friends had been in the Territorial Army, and they were called up for full-time service. That was the time of the Phoney War, and gradually, as the holocaust we half expected failed to appear, conditions resumed a strange sort of normality.

Picture halls re-opened, and so did the football grounds and the dog racing tracks. We listened to the radio playing the same songs over and over: *Run rabbit, run: Roll Out The Barrel: We'll Hang Out The Washing On The Seigfreid Line: We'll Meet Again.* The Government exhorted us to *Dig For Victory,* and (it seems incredible today) *Be like Dad: keep Mum.*

But then came the terrible defeat of the Allied Armies in France, and the retreat of the British, what was left of them, to Dunkirk. By a stupendous effort of improvisation and bravery, many thousands of soldiers were plucked off the beaches and returned to Britain. The whole nation waited with anxiety and fear for what came next. We were, in fact, defenceless. The soldiers returned from France were without weapons. The L.D.V. (Local Defence Volunteers, precursors of the Home Guard) drilled and practiced with broomsticks and sickles and carving knives stuck into belts. And nothing happened. There was no invasion. In the air, young boys no older than myself fought Homeric battles over southern England, and the whole nation girded itself for a stupendous effort in producing whatever was required to fight the war.

There was a tremendous unity of purpose then, with hard work and some hardship, but little complaint. In the pits we worked overtime and earned a few extra bob that way. Women went out to work, many of them in munition factories where they earned very high wages for the very long hours they worked. I had a girl friend at the time working in a munition factory, and one night she showed me her wage slip. *Thirty-eight Pounds*. I could hardly believe it: it would have taken me a couple of months to earn that amount. It seemed somehow wrong that a munition worker should earn that much, and that I should earn so much less. But then I thought of the servicemen, for whom we were working, who received even less than I did.

Because of the war effort, we worked in some conditions that previously would have been considered unsafe. In particular, we tended to ignore Black Damp. Our section was bad. There was one day Bobby asked Tam if he did not think the air a bit sluggish and heavy. 'Aye, ah think it is,' Tam replied, and took the lamp off his cap to study the flame. 'Ah thocht ah wis needin a new jet,' he said, as he looked at the yellow flame. The flame of my lamp was also yellowish, instead of the usual clear white. I lowered the lamp to the pavement, and a thin plume of black smoke came off it. I began to feel a tightness around the chest, and breathing was difficult. Tam looked again at the flames and the plume of smoke. 'Git tae hell oot o here,' he ordered. 'Leave yer graith. Come on, son, but dinna run whitever ye dae.' I began to stagger, and my eyes were getting heavy and my head woozy. Someone gripped my arm. It was Jimmy, our driver. He led me further out into the road, where the air was somewhat clearer, and I found I could breath more easily. It was obvious that we could not work in that place that morning. Bobby thought it might clear in a while, but Tam snapped at him. 'Clear, my arse. It'll no clear the day. It's gaein richt doon the face.' Jimmy agreed. 'Ah'm no workin in that, an neither is ma auld pal Blackie.' He slapped his pony on the rump. 'Gee up, Old Faithful, head for the Old Corral,' and we went off towards the pit bottom, not hurrying, for in Black Damp you must take your time and not become breathless.

The management put in a bigger ventilation fan, and conditions improved for a while, but deteriorated again as we worked further in. We were not often stopped, but the Damp was always there, and we finished our shifts very weary indeed. There was one day we were going along the Main Haulage Road after the shift, very tired, and glad to get into the fresher air, when we heard the rattle of a rake of hutches coming along behind us. We were a bit surprised, because normally the haulage was stopped when men were walking the road. We stood to one side to let the rake pass, and then heard whoops of laughter and singing. A lot of men were riding the rake. This was very much against regulations, but the chance of a ride to the pit bottom was too much to resist, and a lot of men were riding the full hutches. They shouted to us to jump on. I was a bit reluctant, but as an empty hutch approached, I jumped aboard, and landed on something soft. My cap fell off, and the lamp went out. Time and again I flicked at the flint, and cursed as it failed to ignite. When eventually it did light, I found to my horror that I was sitting on a dead pony. Its eyes were open, and it seemed to gaze pathetically at me. It was on its side, with its legs twisted to fit into the empty hutch, and a small round wound on its forehead still oozed blood, and blood trickled from its half open mouth. I recognised it. *Spot*, or *Old Faithful*. It had been a strong, gentle, intelligent beast, a favourite with everyone. People brought tit-bits for him, and he had learned to drink tea from their tin flasks. Now here he was dead, and I was riding with him. I patted his head for the last time, and jumped off the rake. I was alone in the quietness of the roadway as the rake went on, and very sad as I walked to the pit bottom. I learned later that old Spot had broken a leg, and had been shot. Like all real miners, I had a great affection for the ponies we worked with, and a great pity for them. At least we went up the shaft at the end of the shift, and felt the wind on our faces and saw daylight and colours. They didn't. Their lives were spent in the pit, working hard in conditions unnatural and cruel. They worked until they went blind, and then worked again until they died in harness. It was a terrible existence for them, and we knew it.

As I walked along, sad and thoughtful that day, I met Spot's driver, Tam. He was slouching along, head down and tears still in his eyes. He told me what had happened, and sobbed as he told the story. 'Ah'm leavin the pit,' he said, 'Ah'll niver drive a pit pownie agin.' He meant it, and did indeed leave the pit, and got a job on a farm, where he worked with horses. I met him some time later, and he told me he thought it was the best thing he had ever done. He was happy and content, without the pale face that went with working in the pits. He was brown and deeply tanned. The money he got was not as good as in the pit, but he worked in the open air. 'There's naethin noo tae faa oan ma heid. Nae mair big stanes. The oanly thing tae faa is the sky, an that's been up fur a lang time.' We were talking over a pint in the pub. I couldn't stay long, because I had a date with a lovely girl, and two tickets for the late night dance. Tam encouraged me. 'Aye, gan oan, Lad. Remember how we used tae talk aboot Edmundo Ros an his sang *It's later than you think'?* So away ye go, enjoy yourself, it's later than you think!' I went off, and did enjoy myself.

There were changes at work about this time. My brother had come back to the Ferniegair after working for a time at a small local drift mine. We arranged that he and I would work together with our own place. Jim was a big chap, and a skilled miner. I always looked puny compared with him, but just the same I was a wiry wee man, and always managed to do my share, and more, of any work that was going. I was glad to have the chance of working with Jim, although sorry enough to be parted from Tam and Bobby. Tam I liked well, and got on with him, and Bobby I had learned to put up with.

Those two went off to a new Pan Run Section in the Main Coal. This was a new development, with Pan Run Conveyors. The conveyors were also new to us, and yet another sign of the changing times in mining. They were troughs, each about seven feet long, mounted on rollers and overlapping. They were set on a slope along the length of the face, and were shaken back and forth lengthwise by the Pan Engine. That made the coal travel down their length, and at the end it was loaded into the hutches. It was a deafening operation, and very dusty. None of the men liked it, even if it did make the work somewhat easier. We had been used to the comparative quietness of working only with pick and shovel, so that we could hear the movement and creaking of the roof. We felt a lot safer when the place was quiet enough for that, because we judged the condition of the roof and the sides by the sounds they made. In the deafening din of the Pan Run, you could hear nothing else but the incessant roar of the machinery, and felt very defenceless. Of course we adapted to the new conditions, just as we had to the introduction of steel props. It was just as well that we were able to adapt, because we were just at the very beginning of a real revolution in mining methods. The old days when men lay on their sides to hew coal out of the solid face with their picks, and then with shovels turned it back, still lying on their sides, when it was again shovelled up into pony-drawn hutches — those days were going, and going fast. There would soon be scrapers and belt conveyors, Dobson Props and Gullick supports and new ventilation. They were in the future, though, and Jim and I were still working in the old way. It might perhaps have been harder work, the way we were doing it, but we were free of the terrible dust and stour and noise of the new sections.

There was one morning of gales and heavy rain as we went down the pit. This was always a bad sign, because it usually meant that Black Damp got into the workings. Jim and I both checked carefully as we went along, and sure enough our cap lamps soon showed the dirty yellow flame that indicated Damp. Jim cursed under his breath, and asked me what I thought. It did not seem too bad to me, and perhaps it would be clearer in the road. Jim considered the flame for a moment, and then moved further into our road. He tested carefully as he went, and indeed it did seem to be better the further we went in. When we reached the face, the lamps tested clear, so we started working.

About an hour later we were both out at the roadhead, and when we tested there, found signs of damp again. Jim tested up and down, and decided that it was not too bad just then, but that if it got any worse, we would get out. Jim went back underneath, and I filled the empty hutch with the gum we had turned out, and then built up a heading on the hutch with the larger pieces of coal. Meanwhile Jim was busy turning out more gum. When he came out again from underneath he was accompanied by Wullie Moffat, the fireman, who had crawled the whole faceline from the place below. We began to discuss the conditions. Both of them were concerned about the Black Damp, even though the concentration was still not heavy. Then we saw a light bobbing along in the road, obviously somebody in a hurry.

It was Jimmy, our driver, and he was out of breath and exhausted by the speed he had made along the road. He sank to his knees, sweating heavily, and between gasps of air managed to tell us that the big fan had stopped, and that we were to get out quick.

Wullie took quick action. He told Jimmy to tell all the drivers to stand by in the lye and warn everybody. He went crawling off up the wall to warn the men up there, and just a few minutes later we heard a cry from the next place that we were to louse out and pass the word along. Jim gave the call, and we went off to the lye, (★) where the men were waiting to make sure everyone was safe before moving off up the pit. Everybody *was* safe, and when Wullie Moffat came out, we all went off together, feeling heavy and weary from the Damp, and depressed at the thought of losing another day's wages. However, the fan was repaired by the next shift, and we were able to start work again.

That was an incident that has stuck in my mind all these years. Not that there was anything special or dramatic about it, but it demonstrated the comradeship and readiness to self-scrifice of the miners. They all waited in the lye until every man was out. Nobody moved off to the fresh air and the pit bottom. Nobody told them to wait, but they all did, to be sure that no-one had been left behind and overcome by the Damp. As it happened, no-one had been overcome, but if any man had been missing from that gathering, the men would have gone back into the gas without a moment's hesitation, and brought the man to safety. There were no respirators, no protection, just their willingness to do it. When I thought of it later, and indeed, when I think of it now, I am immensely proud to have been part of that group.

Only a few days after that we got to the pit to find that the pony drivers were in dispute, and there was a possibility that they would strike. We started work and before long were being held up because there were no empty hutches. Then there was the rattle of a pony and hutch approaching. I was in the road, and stepped to one side to let it pass. To my surprise, the driver was not our regular, but instead a chap called Agnew. I called out 'Hello, what's going on here, then. Whoa, boy,' and the pony obediently stopped. Agnew told me that the drivers were on strike, and that he was to work with us instead.

★ *Lye:* A higher and wider place, away from the coalface, where the hutch rails ended, and where there was space for both empty and full hutches to stand.

I had known Agnew for a while. He had been in the Territorial Army before the war, and had often advised me that I should join, saying that it was a great life, especially at the camps, and that you got paid for it. It never appealed to me, though. He had been called up at the beginning of the war, but had then returned to the pit when it was realised how vital coal was. Many miners had chosen to stay in the forces, but he had volunteered to return.

I was angry. 'See you, ye've nae richt tae be driving. Ye're naethin but a low down bastard, a scab, a blackleg. Ye should hiv stayed in the army!' He protested that he had been in the army, and had sworn allegiance to the King! I failed to see the relevance of that, and told him he should also think about his allegiance to his fellow men. I warned him that he would not draw a single hutch out of the place, and went off to tell Jim. He was as angry as I was. 'Richt,' he said it's home we go. Ah'm not workin wi blacklegs. Put the graith past.' We cleared our place and went out into the lye. The other face men felt the same as we did, and we gathered there. Agnew meanwhile had gone into our road and hitched up the full hutch. There was a bad jink in the rail where our road turned into the lye, and as we walked past I kicked the rail. As I expected, it sprung out of place. A few minutes later we heard the rattle of the hutch as Agnew drew near. There was no danger for the pony, or the driver, for that matter, but we knew what to expect for the full hutch. There was a loud crash as it left the rail and tipped its contents. The pony stopped, and looked round, while Agnew stood and cursed beside the half-empty hutch. I knew from the sound it had made that the hutch was off in the nineties, as we said when all four wheels were off the rails. 'Ah think that scab is off the road,' Jock Taylor said, 'Well, he'll be needin a haund,' 'Aye, a haund across the mouth,' I replied, 'He can stay off the road as far as ah'm concerned.'

Jock and I went back to see what was happening, while Jim and the others just sat where they were. We found Agnew on his knees, looking at the problem, and figuring how to get the hutch back on the rails. 'Gaun tae gi me a lift?' he asked, expectantly. 'Aye,' I replied, 'Ah'll gie ye a lift wi the toe o ma bit, ye bluidy scab.'

Jock laughed. 'Auch, man,' he said, 'Ye should hae nae bother whin the hutch is half empty.' Agnew pleaded 'Ah, come oan boys, gie us a haund.' 'A haund, is it,' I snapped back, 'That'll be richt. Git that man ye swore allegiance to tae gi ye a haund. Nane o us wull,' and turned to walk away. 'Come oan,' said Jock, 'We cannae leave a man like this. We'll gie him a haund.'

Agnew was much relieved, and said that when he got the hutch back on the rails he was taking the pony back to the stables. 'Guid,' said Jock, 'Naebody would wark wi a blackleg.' So we helped him, and off he went, with a lesson learned.

The strike was settled by the next day, and the drivers won their case. The Manager accepted that they had a genuine grievance, but it was sad that the whole pit had to come to a standstill before that was recognised. It would have been much better to have had talks and consultation earlier, and avoided the dispute. As my father used to say, the strike is a good weapon to threaten, and a bad weapon to use. He was right then, and he would be right now, although there are times when there is no alternative to using the weapon.

Ventilation in our section continued to give trouble, and we lost a lot of time. It seemed that the fan, even when it was working, just could not cope, especially when the weather was wet and changeable. We checked the air very carefully every day before starting work, and often had a debate with ourselves over whether or not it was safe to work.

On one occasion both Jim and I were dubious. The lamps showed signs of gas, but not very bad. We had already lost shifts that week, and could ill afford to lose more. Jim decided that he would start, and went under the headcoal to turn out the gum, leaving me in the road. He had only been working for a few minutes when I heard him shouting for a light. The gas had got so bad that his lamp had gone out. My lamp was still fairly bright, and I had just recharged it with carbide and water, so I dropped down to my knees and began crawling along the face to Jim. Almost immediately my lamp flame spluttered and went out. The Damp must have been very thick. I felt my way out to the road, crawling along in the utter blackness, and with fear making my heart pound. Time and again I flicked at the flint lighter, trying it as high up as I could, and in different places, but the lamp refused to light. When it finally did, the flame was weak and yellow. We had to get out of there, and bloody quick.

Jim was able to crawl out from under the headcoal in the very weak light from my lamp, and we began to travel along the road, staggering and badly affected by the gas. We knew the others were also leaving their places because we had heard their shouts, but there was almost no-one in the road. We learned that several men had been overcome, and were being carried out to pit bottom. Hurrying as best we could, and that was no more than a slow walk, we overtook the stretcher bearers. But there were more casualities than there were stretchers available, and two men were being carried along in a Fireman's

Lift. We took our share of the carrying, and it was far from easy. Not only were we all badly gassed, but the roof was low and the pavement broken. Carrying a man in a Fireman's Lift in such conditions was not easy, but they had to be taken out to fresher air. We learned that the men who had collapsed had been found by the pony driver. If he had not happened to go into the place just then, the men would almost certainly have died.

When we reached the lye, where the air was much fresher, the men who had collapsed began to recover, and we all began to discuss what should be done. It was plain that the places were unsafe, and that the fans were not doing their job. The ventilation was inadequate, and unless conditions were improved, there was every chance that we would lose a whole section of men. Action was needed, because our lives were in danger every time the fan broke down. We decided to strike.

When we reached the surface, there was word waiting for us that the Manager would see a delegation, so after we had bathed and changed, a team of six was chosen by the men to discuss and settle this grievance. Jim and I were amongst those selected, and that was my first opportunity of being a member of a delegation negotiating on grievances and conditions. I learned a lot from that first experience, but the most important lesson was that I had a lot to learn.

We met in the Manager's Office, and he opened the proceedings by asking how we all felt, whether we were dizzy or feeling sick. 'I understand how you all feel, and I don't disagree with the action you have taken. I'm glad you got those men out safely, and I should tell you that they will be alright in a couple of days.'

Jock Taylor spoke first for us. 'Listen, Manager, instead of those few men being carried out, it could have been a whole section of men. What we want to know is what you intend to do about the ventilation. This is not going to happen again. That whole section of men could have been killed down there today.'

The Manager listened politely, and said that he was as much concerned about what had happened as we were, perhaps more so. Jim intervened. 'Come off it, Manager,' he snapped, 'What we are in here for is: what's to be done about that section? How can we overcome this problem, for I tell you right now we are not going back into that section as it stands at the moment.'

The Manager had his answer ready, and unrolled a big sketch of the underground workings on his desk. 'I want some of you men to work that new section that's developed, the Humph Coal. It's a bit wet at the moment, but as its opened out it will be dry. I've stopped the

Pyotshaw meanwhile, and intend to drive a new airway from the Main Coal section. That should give us a good air current and better ventilation, and keep the Damp out.' He showed us the plans, where the new aircourse was to be driven, and a new driveage to shorten the existing roads. It all looked very well on paper. We continued the discussion, and it was decided that Jim and I, together with Jock Taylor and Ernie would work the new section, while the others would go to different parts of the pit until the new workings were ready. We left the office, discussing the prospects. We had made our case, and the grievance had been resolved. The men would no longer be working in the Pyotshaw, with its very bad Black Damp problem, until the new ventilation was ready. Jock remarked that he thought we had got a bad deal. The Humph Coal, he said, was a hell hole, very wet, and with a roof you couldn't hold up. We were soon to find out how right he was.

When we started our next shift, we first collected our graith from the old section, and made our way to the Humph Coal. It was bad. Jim and I had been allocated the straight down road, while Jock and Ernie were to work on the left side of us. We stopped at the entrance to this road and looked at it. The wooden crowns supporting the roof were broken and splintered, with jagged slivers of wood jutting menacingly into the roadway. 'Gawd, that's no verra healthy,' said Jock, 'They bluidy crowns could poke the eye oot yer heid.' Jim agreed with him, but said that the repairers were coming in to sort it out. This was a new section, but yet it was in a terrible, unsafe condition. If this was the state of the road, we wondered what our places would be like. They were terrible. Ice-cold water dripped on us as we went in over the muddy and slippery road. A hutch stood at the end of the rails, anchored there by two snibbles or drags on the wheels, and resting on a short length of rail jammed across to the road to prevent it from running away into the face.

My heart sank as we looked around. The road head was about eight feet high and six feet wide. The seam was supposed to be two feet thick, but we could only see a thin line of coal standing up above the water. 'Well, whit dae ye think o this place, Jim,' I asked. He looked round again. 'Not very much,' he replied, 'We'll hae to dae some repair work afore we start at the face.' I was angry. 'Jim,' I said, 'It's a bluddy shite house. Hoo dae they expect men tae wark in that?'

Jim wanted to keep our spirits up. 'Auch, it micht nae be sae bad yince we git that wattter oot and some wood up tae save the heid.'

As we stood there looking around at everything that needed to be done before we could start getting coal, we heard the approach of a pony driver with an empty hutch. It was Andy Strain, a strong, well-built lad whom I knew well. He looked round, and whistled in surprise at the state of things. 'This is a hell o a place! They werena kiddin when they telt me it was a hell o a mess. Luk at aa that muck an glaur! Ah'm glad it's no me workin this! Ah'll hae tae tak awa that full hutch an bring an empty yin tae bile (bale) oot that watter.' 'Aye,' Jim said, 'An bring in some crowns and some straps whin ye're at it. We need them to mak this roof safe.'

Andy hooked the pony's tail chain to the full hutch and cried 'Gee, boy, come oan, Gee!' His pony, Darkie, tried hard to get the hutch started up the road, but slipped and slid on the wet mud. The hutch was heavy and overloaded, and sodden with water, and the pony couldn't move it. 'Hoo the hell dae ye expect a beast tae haul that?' Jim shouted, 'It's far ower much fer the beast. Imagine some daft bastard fillin a hutch as fu as that. Some men hae aw their brains in their arses!'

We began to empty some of the weight out of the hutch, and then Andy tried the pony again. 'Coam oan, Darkie, wee pal,' he encouraged it, and we put our shoulders to the hutch and pushed. Andy snatched the snibbles from the wheels as it began rolling. There was a loud sucking noise from the glaur, and the hutch shot forward, with Andy whooping and yelling like a banshee.

He was soon back with an empty hutch, a good one with no holes in it, and he had found an old bucket for us to use in bailing the water out of the work place. But he had forgotten the crowns and straps, and Jim was not pleased. Still, we had plenty of work to do, and began the job of bailing, Andy with the old bucket and me with my shovel, while Jim went to work on the roof. We half filled the hutch with water, and decided that was as much as the pony could manage, and then took it out to an old end. Andy unhooked the tail chain while I put snibbles on the wheels. The weight of half a hutch of water was perhaps about as much as the pony could manage, but it was almost too much for us as we struggled to coup it. We heaved and strained at that hutch for a while, grunting and groaning, and seeking new handholds, before we felt it begin to go over. When it finally went, we watched the rush of water down the old road with some satisfaction, but determined that the next time we would not fill the hutch so full.

Andy went off to fetch the timber we needed, and I returned to the work place. The Contractor, the man whose gang had developed the road, also arrived, in a hell of a temper. 'Whit's this ah hear aboot this place bein a proper shite house,' he shouted, 'There wis bugger aw wrang wi the place whin ah saw it last!' 'An whin was that,' I asked him, 'The year yin?' He brushed past me, and went off to talk to Jim, who I was sure would soon clip his wings. 'Aye,' he admitted, 'There's been a bit o a squeeze doon the road an ye'll hae tae dae some repair work.' Jim nodded. 'If ye git oot the road we'll git on wi it,' he said. 'Hoo many beels (hutches) o watter is that ye hae fult?' the Contractor asked, and Jim told him just the one. 'Hell, man,' he said, 'Ah put mair watter in ma whiskey!' I couldn't resist it, and replied 'Aye, an if ye had a tube fae that gob o yours intae that watter, an if ye could sook as weel as ye blaw, there would be nae bluidy watter there!' He was furious. He was a Contractor, and was being spoken to like that by a mere lad. He raised his voice and his fist, but Andy was there beside me, and it was clear we were not going to back down, so he did. He went off muttering about seeing us on the surface, leaving us to stack the timber.

Jim had erected a crown across the roof of the road. He stood back as we approached him. 'Aye,' he said, 'That's a bit warmer noo. It'll be safer like that. Whit was aw the argument aboot?' Andy told him, and he laughed. 'Aye, he wis the same wi me. Aa telt him to bugger off an let us git oan wi the work.' We began to bail the water out of the place into the hutch, and it took several more hutch fulls before the water level was low enough to allow us to get down to work. Finally we were able to start turning back the wet gum and filling the hutch with coal, instead of water.

Water was still dripping steadily from the roof, and we were soaked to the skins. We had no water-proofs, of course, and wore only our moleskin trousers and a singlet as we lay on our sides in that muck and sludge, turning back the cut coal. It was cold, wet, and thoroughly miserable.

At piece time, Jim and I decided to go over into Jock Taylor's road, thinking it might be a bit warmer there. It was a relief to pick up our jackets from where they were lying in just about the only dry place, and put them on over our soaking singlets. We hurried over to Jock's road, and found them just coming out from their roadhead. We told each other that our places were "a midden, a shite house", but I was interested just then in my piece. As always, I was hungry, and the luke-warm tea from the tin flask, wrapped in brown paper and cocooned in an old sock, was veritable nectar.

Ernie and I talked about the pictures we had seen recently, and then, of course, got on to our favourite topic, football. We could hear Jim and Jock still discussing the work places. 'Had ye a visit frae

Stewart, the Contractor?' Jim asked. 'Aye, he wis in, bit he didnae say much. He jist looked round an said it wis nae sae bad in here,' Jock replied. Jim chuckled a bit at that. 'Nae wonder. He had his wings clipped by Andy and the young un. He was a bit sarcastic wi them aboot hoo they wis gettin rid of aw that watter, bit the twa o them were not takin ony o his snash, an he went awa wi his tail atween his legs.' And so the talk went on, but we were getting cold, and it was time to get back to work.

There was another couple of hutches full of water to bail out, and Andy and I got on with that while Jim replaced a broken tree at the roadside. Andy found a couple of corrugated iron sheets, or berges, and we were glad to have them. We erected them over the place so that a lot of the water ran away to the low side. At least it was not pouring down on us now as we worked, but still we would have to bail it all out, and there was a lot of it.

That shift seemed endless, and it was a great relief when lousing time came. The men commented on our drookit state as we went to the pit bottom, and gladly let us through to be first up the shaft, and into the warmth of the showers, and dry clothes. It had been the worst shift I had ever worked, and Jim felt the same. We were also agreed that if it did not change, we would be off, and seeking pastures new.

There were plenty of pits around, and no shortage of jobs. But we knew that Ferniegair was one of the best for wages and conditions. Also, I realised as I stood under the blessed warmth of the shower, this was one of the few pits with baths and drying rooms. For most men, it was still a case of going home dirty, and wet, often enough, and washing as best they could at home, while wife or mother had the job of drying the pit clothes and cleaning up after the bath. The nearest pit with baths was the Priory, and that was about ten miles away.

We faced the next shift with little heart. We knew it would be miserable, but we also knew there was little chance of earning a reasonable wage till conditions improved in the place. I faced a good deal of banter from the men as we changed into our now dry clothes, but I was in no mood for that, and my answers were short and surly.

Jim told me that there was no need to go for the pins that morning. We had only sent two hutches up the previous day, and, as I reminded him, would probably not even get paid for them, since they were filled mostly with wet gum and slurry. Altogether, it was a miserable start to the day, and by the time we met Jock and Ernie, my mind was made up. Ernie asked if I was all ready for a swim. He had heard that the water was up again. 'If it is,' I told him, 'ah'll no be splodgin aboot in it.'

The fireman called to us as we checked with him on the way in, and handed us a set of oilskins each. 'It's a present for ye. Ye'll need them this mornin.' 'Aye' an hoo aboot a diver's helmet tae gae wi them,' I snapped, and I felt snappish, because if they were giving us oilskins, then the place must really be hellish wet. Besides, we all knew that you really couldn't work in oilskins for long. We hurried on, and caught up with the others. 'Oilskins are alricht,' said Jock, 'Bit whit we need is nae oilskins bit a wee pump to tae git rid o that watter, an keep the place dry'. We agreed, for he was right.

We got to our roadhead and squeezed past the empty hutch waiting for us. It was worse than the previous day. We couldn't even see the seam we were meant to be working, and more water was pouring down from the roof. I laughed, the first time that day, and began singing *My cup is full and running over*, but this was no joke. We were facing something more like a millpond than a work place. 'Ah wonder if there's ony fish in there,' I said to Jim. 'We'll no catch ony fish in that, only oor death o cauld,' he replied, grimly.

And it *was* a grim sight, dismal and miserable. The only sound was the steady drip of water onto the berges and the sound of an occasional stone falling from the roof. We were both angry and frustrated. I sat down on the oilskins and lit a cigarette, and threw a stone into the water. It disappeared. The water was two feet deep or more, and we were supposed to bail it out and then cut coal. It was a daunting thought.

I told Jim I had a good mind to go up the pit, and he thought about that for a moment. Just then Andy arrived, and looked round, and voiced his disgust. He asked what we were going to do. Jim instructed us to get rid of the hutch that stood half filled with water, and see if we could find any more berges. Darkie was hooked up to the hutch, and I went off with them, ready to give a putt (shove) when we came to the steep bit of the road. I put my shoulder to the back of the hutch and pushed hard as Darkie slowed. There was a jink in the rails, and a flood of filthy water poured out of the hutch and all over me. I was soaked, and I had not even started the shift properly. We emptied the hutch into the old road, and then went on to where Andy thought there were some berges. Somebody had been there before us, though, and there was only one left, a short piece, rotten and holed. We took it, anyway, and when we got back to the roadhead, found Jock and Ernie in conversation with Jim. They had come round to see what our place was like. Their's was bad enough, they said, but this was a bloody sight worse.

They went off, and Jim and I stood and looked around. It wasn't only the water, although that was bad enough. The roof was bad, with several large stones about ready to fall. It was both wet and dangerous.

'Jim,' I said, 'There's plenty mair holes in the grun. Let's gang up the pit.' He looked round again and said 'Richt. Get yer graith.'

So we left that miserable, dangerous place, and made our way out. We were lucky. A rake of hutches was ready to leave along the main haulage way to the pit bottom. We piled the tools on top of a hutch, and crouched beside the driver on his bogie and took a free ride. We had to drop off, though, when we saw lights. It might have been an official, and it was illegal to ride on a rake. Still we had ridden most of the way.

At the pit bottom we had to wait until that rake of hutches was hoisted, and then rode the cage to the surface. I felt no regrets at leaving that pit for the last time. I was sure we had made the right decision in leaving those truly atrocious conditions and seeking pastures new.

The onsetter greeted us as we stepped out of the cage. 'Was that your toasters (tools, or graith) that come up?' he asked, 'It's oor there in the corner. Are ye leavin? Ye're no the first and ye'll no be the last!' We left our graith, and started to make our way to the baths, but met the Manager on the way.

He told us to go to his Office, but Jim said that we would get washed up first, and see him later, and that is what we did. The Manager was fair enough when we met him after bathing. He said that the place we were working was only temporary, and that when the development was finished, the Pyotshaw would be the main section. He asked us to reconsider, and talked of better ton rates and deficiency payments, but eventually realised that our minds were made up. We were leaving Ferniegair, and that was that. Just the same, he said he was sorry to lose us, and that if ever we needed a job, we should come to see him.

As we waited for the bus, Jimmy, Jock, Andy and Ernie joined us. They too had decided to quit. We stood and talked. Andy and I decided to try for work near Bothwell. We had heard that the wages were pretty good there. I was young and confident in my skills, and knew that I could hold my own in any pit. I had been taught my craft well, chiefly by my own father, and was ready to try it out in a new place. I had taken my first step in the dark, and was ready to go on.

BOTHWELL CASTLE

The Second Step

In a way I was sorry to leave Ferniegair, because I had many friends there, but the atrocious conditions under which we had been expected to work made the move inevitable. The very next day Andy Strain and I travelled to Bothwell, and met the Manager. He outlined the conditions in the pit, and made them seem quite reasonable. It would be very different from Ferniegair, though. For one thing, this was a gassy pit, with a lot of methane, highly explosive and dangerous. That meant we had to use electric lamps and safety lamps, not the old carbide lamps I had been used to. It also meant that there must be no smoking or other naked lights down the pit, so it was "Goodbye" to the comfort of a cigarette at piece time. On the other hand, the seam of coal was no less than seven feet thick, as opposed to less than two feet at Ferniegair. It would be possible to work that standing up, a great relief after spending shift after shift lying on our sides in mud and muck. However, as facemen we would have to both fill and draw our own hutches out to the roadway. The Manager looked at us both, and said that as fit young men that should prove no hardship, because the road was pretty level.

We didn't really need to think it over, and signed on there and then, delighted to have found a job so easily, and ready to face a new challenge and a new experience.

Andy was to start on the dayshift next morning, and I was to start on the backshift, from two in the afternoon till ten in the evening. I was not best pleased at this, but was assured it would be only a temporary arrangement, and that Andy and I would soon have our own place, and work as partners.

Like many another glowing verbal description, the reality was rather different, as we soon found out. The excellent conditions existed only in the words, and perhaps the mind, of the Manager.

When I started work the following afternoon, the first job was to lift a token, a sort of brass identity disc, which always had to be carried when underground. The implications of this were clear, and a bit disturbing. I was heavily laden with all my graith, picks, shovel, saw and mash hammer, but the men waiting at the pit were friendly, and gave me a hand. I knew some of them, and was subjected to the usual sort of banter, although there was a serious note to it. 'Whit the hell are ye daein here?' shouted Bobby Cleghorn, 'Surely ye've mair sense than tae gang doon this bluddy hole!' I knew Bobby well, and had played with his son when we went to school together. He was always cheerful, and I was glad to see him and talk about the pit. He told me about the conditions, and I began to have grave doubts about the wisdom of starting my new job. However, I was stuck with it, and anxious to get down and see for myself.

To my surprise, the onsetter at Bothwell Castle that day was a woman. She was a tough customer, and more than able to give as good as she got in the way of backchat. More than that, the cage was a double, with two hutches coming up at once, and she was able to handle them both at least as well as any man could, and she could curse and swear as well as any man.

I was fitted with my battery lamp, a heavy burden weighing seven pounds. The battery was carried on our waists, and the lamp was clipped to the cap. In addition, I had to carry a Glennie lamp, an oil safety lamp. The purpose of this was to act as a warning and indicator of the amount of methane gas in the atmosphere. The flame behind the thick lamp glass reacted to the presence of gas in the atmosphere in the same way as the flame of the little carbide lamps we had used in Ferniegair. This was different gas, though, and highly explosive, so the flame of that Glennie was protected by a fine wire mesh, which prevented the gas from exploding, or even burning. This was exactly the same principle as that discovered so long ago by Sir Humphrey Davy with his original safety lamp.

The men warned me about a jink or bend in the shaft, and that it was necessary to hang on to the safety bar in the cage. They were right. The cage seemed to drop at a tremendous speed, and when it passed the jink, there was a heart-stopping jolt. My cap lamp fell off, and I wished to hell we were down. It seemed a long way, and indeed was much deeper than Ferniegair. I was glad when we reached the brightly lit pit bottom and could step out of the cage.

One of the men enquired whether I was the new starter, and offered to show me the road. He led the way past the men standing waiting at the end of their shift, and there was the usual banter between them all, the sort of thing that always happened, and that never ceased to amuse me, even if I was not taking part in it myself. After walking about fifty yards inbye, we had to climb a twenty-foot steel ladder onto another roadway and another level, and then walk along to the fireman's hut. When we got there, we were all searched for contraband such as cigarettes, pipes or matches, for this was a gassy pit, and a naked flame could have led to a devastating explosion. We all knew that, of course, and did not resent the daily search. I was standing talking to Jock Gault, the man who had shown me the way, when I heard someone calling: 'You there. Aye, you there, Ah'm speakin tae ye. Come here.' The voice was gruff and unfriendly. I turned slowly, somewhat confused by that manner of speaking. 'Me?' 'Aye, fuckin you. Come here.' That I was not going to take, and told him so. 'Wae the hell dae ye think ye're talkin tae? Ah'm no yer little collie dug! Don't talk tae me in that tone of voice!'

It was the fireman, of course, a big, burly, red-faced man. He was called Tam, and I got his pedigree later from the other men. They called him a big ba-heid, a big gruff and a big idiot, as well as a lot of other uncomplimentary things, some of which were true.

'Hear, you,' I told him, 'Get this straight from the outset. Don't ever talk tae me like that again.' He snapped back: 'Here's a richt yin! Ye'll dae as yur telt, young fella, ur ye'll no be here.'

By that time I wasn't at all sure I wanted to be there anyway, but I was not going to back down. 'Hear you. Ah'm here tae work, no tae be shouted at be you or onybody else. Your job is tae tell me whaur tae go, and if my place is safe fur workin. Dae that, an we'll hae nae bother.'

'Aye,' Tam said, 'Ye're a perky young bugger. Gies yer lamp.' He checked my headlamp. 'Glennie,' he demanded. I told him I had already checked it, but he insisted on checking it again, so I took it off my belt and handed it over. Tam blew into it, and all around the glass, and said it was fine. 'Ye'll be gaun wi Auld Bob. Here he is now.' An elderly and frail-looking man stepped forward. This was Bob Boyd, who was to be my neighbour(★). He was work-worn, perhaps not as old as he looked, but certainly showing the effects of a lifetime spent in the pits. His face was pasty white and his shoulders hunched, and his feet shuffled along the roadways. Of course he should have been retired, to enjoy whatever time he had left, but the existing system forced him to struggle on, scratching out a miserable existence, unable to earn a reasonable wage under the system.

★ *Neighbours:* The men you worked with.

We had a long winding road to walk into the section, and even the haulage roads were low. There were cross-cuts between the haulage roads, and we had to travel these, bent double under the low roofs. Dust lay thick, and as we walked single file, those at the back were choked with the thick clouds stirred up by the men in front. It was extremely hot, and sweat poured down our bodies. Our eyes stung, and our mouths were dry and parched. I realised the wisdom of those men who had stripped off at the pit bottom and left most of their clothes there, to be picked up at the end of the shift. Altogether, it was a miserable start to a new job, and I was glad when we got to the lye, and it was possible to stand upright and straighten my back. I was very grateful to the men who had helped me carry in my graith: to carry that lot by myself would have been almost impossible. We put all the graith into an empty hutch, and parted company, with each team going to its own road, and auld Bob and I into ours. I pushed the hutch along till we reached the face.

This was a strange experience for me. The road from the lye into our face was level, and the coal seam itself six or seven feet high. Every six feet the roof was supported by a carrier, a tree about ten feet long, or a wooden strap the same length, with two props on each end to support them. There were several screens of heavy, fire-proofed jute cloth, which we called Brattis cloth, used to divert air into the roads. Later, as our road advanced, a small fan was installed outbye, with long pipes leading the air along to the faces. Those pipes were suspended from the props. Our face was four yards wide. All this was a tremendous difference from the conditions in Ferniegair, where the seam was only about fourteen or sixteen inches thick. The roadways driven off from our level divided the coal into stoops, each about eighty yards square.

When we reached the face, I saw that it was a curious seam. Although so thick, a rib of stone ran right through it about the middle of the seam. In effect, it was like two seams, separated by that strange stone rib. We picked along the top of that stone, stelling up the headcoal as we worked underneath it, then bored and fired the headcoal. We filled that away in hutches, which we had to put out to the haulage road ourselves, and then bored and blasted the bottom coal. We then picked the stones out of that, and loaded the coal away. The stones we built up into supporting walls at the sides of the road. We had to test very carefully for gas at the beginning of each shift, and before firing our shots.

The work itself was easy enough, and the conditions not bad, although the atmosphere was hellish hot. On my first shift old Bob and I filled fourteen hutches, and the old man was delighted. It was the most that had been filled in that place for a long time. I was glad enough when lousin time came, and we walked back along the low roadways. Other men joined us, and asked what I thought of the conditions in the pit. I told them it was a big difference from what I had been used to, with coal seven feet thick, but I thought that hand-drawing hutches was cuddie's work. Even though I was so lightly clad, I had sweated so much that the sweat had even come through my moleskin trousers, and I was shiny black with the combination of so much sweat and the coal dust. The only white parts were the whites of my eyes and my teeth. I would be happy when I got home, washed in the big tub, and changed into other clothes.

I was glad to be teamed with old Bob. He was a steady worker, although not so able as he had once been, but he was a trier and an honest and skilled workman. I learned a lot from him, and became a better craftsman as a result. We worked together for quite a long time, and it was while I was still with him that we had a very frightening experience.

A number of us were grouped in the lye, waiting for a rake of empty hutches, and laughing and joking about the usual things. Then suddenly we all fell silent and there was a strange hush. We could hear nothing unusual, but an instinct told us that something was wrong. There was a low rumble in the distance, and that was strange. It couldn't be the rake coming, because it had not been signalled. The sound grew louder, and then the roof supports began to crack. The roof itself shuddered and shook, and there was a rumble like a train running over a viaduct. The whole place was shaking madly. There was a big squeeze on, and we were in the middle of it. There was no place to run, no place of safety, no way to escape. The props and trees and supports splintered and shattered under the inexorable forces of the squeeze. Would our roof hold? There was nothing we could do; there was no time to put up extra supports, even if we could have moved, and in fact we could not move. We all stood as though petrified.

I glanced round at the others. At least I was not alone in being scared and dumbfounded. Bob was beside me with his mouth open. His lips moved but he said nothing as the whole place shuddered and shook and the roof creaked and groaned. It seemed to last for hours, but in fact it could only have been a minute or so — long enough for the thoughts of being buried alive to cross all our minds.

Gradually the quake passed away overhead, and gradually it faded away into the distance. Eventually there was silence. None of us had ever experienced anything like that before. 'Whit the hell!' shouted Big Rab, 'That scared the shite oot o me!' 'It wis like a bluddy earthquake,' someone said, and indeed I think that was just what it was.

Two firemen came running up into the lye. 'Is onybody hurt? Ur ye men alricht?' they gasped. We told them that we were unhurt. 'Thank Christ fur that. Ah thocht the hale place was gonna cave in, and you all below it. Thur's a big fall in the main road so ye'll git nae mair hutches the day. Ye'll have to travel the aircourse, then oot tae the bottom.' We went off to examine our places, and, as Bob said, you would have thought a bomb had struck them. Trees and props had splintered and broken under the pressure. The roof had sagged, and coal had been squeezed out and lay in piles across the roadway. We would need hutches to fill that away and clear the rails. But there were no hutches, and we would have to carry in the props ourselves.

The fireman, Tam, began to curse and bawl out orders for us to get back in and start repairing the road. 'Here, Tam,' I said, 'Haud on. This is deficient wark noo. Hoo ur we gettin paid?' 'It's your bluddy road; ye'll hae tae repair it yersels. Noo git in there and git bluddy started!' Tam shouted back.

He was furious, but I was not too pleased, either. 'Tam', I told him angered by his domineering attitude, 'If we ur no gittin paid fur that work we ur no gaein in and the bluddy place kin close. We ur gaein up the pit an ye kin git repairers in.'

Tam was a bit subdued. 'Alricht, ah'll see ye alricht,' he said, 'Jist git the wark done.' That had to be enough, so we started the job of clearing up and making the place safe, and that repair work took up the rest of the shift. We expected a reasonable payment for it, but the following pay day, when we checked our slips, we found there was no payment for that shift. We found Tam, who told us that allowances had been put in, and if they had not been paid, we should see the oversman.(★) Elk and I were selected to act as spokesmen for the squad, and we went off to see the oversman. He was a a man from Fife, arrogant and bullying, and we did not expect an easy time with him. We did not have an easy time, either. We stated our case, and our calculation of the work done and what we should be entitled to, and we did it quietly and calmly. However, he rejected the argument, and a heated altercation developed when he declared that he was paying nothing for the work. It was Elkie who lost his temper,

---

★ *Oversman:* A senior fireman or deputy in charge of a section.

not me, for once. He had the oversman by the throat, shaking him like a dog shaking an old rag. 'Ye Fife bastard,' he roared, 'Ah'll fuckin kill yer, ye snivel-eyed bastard reprobate!' He might have done that, too, if I had not jumped in to pull him clear and calm him down. When some sort of order was restored, we decided to go off and see the Manager, but I warned Elkie that he had to keep his head this time.

We rapped on the Manager's office door, and a voice called us to come in. 'What the hell do you two want?' This from the Manager, sitting behind his big desk. 'Justice!' I replied, and told him we had come about the deficiency payment we were entitled to. 'I know all about your claim, and I'm not paying it. It's your work. Now get out of here.'

Elkie was still simmering from his encounter with the oversman. 'Ur ye gaein to pit us oot? Don't try that stuff wi me!' I told him to cool it, to "keep the heid", and told the Manager that we were not going out of the office till we were paid what we were entitled to.

The Manager was not so easily calmed down. He told me I was a little agitator, but that sort of accusation did not worry me. 'Na, na,' I said, 'we jist want the money we hiv worked for, so jist sit back an we kin discuss it.' Elkie, though, was still fuming angry. 'Pey up,' he snapped, 'Ur yer pit's idle.' The Manager snapped back 'Is that a threat? I'll not be intimidated!'

Elkie stopped him short. 'It's nae threat, it's a fact.' I told Elkie again to sit down and let us get on with the discussion. I sat down, but Elkie remained standing by the desk. The Manager glared at us, but I began to relate the facts about the work we had done and how our efforts had saved part, or maybe the whole, of that section. We told how the squeeze or tremor had crushed the roads, causing coal to spew out over the rails, and of the large number of props we had to replace to save a complete closure of the slope road. There was a heated argument about the rights and wrongs of the crush and of the work we had done, but eventually, after much argument, we reached a settlement. The Manager made a proviso that this would be the last such claim, but we rejected that, pointing out that he had established a precedent, paying us a half shift for the work we had done. We told him that if there was a similar situation in the future, he would have to pay the same.

'We'll bluidy see about that,' the Manager said, and stated that he would put the money in for the next week. This was not acceptable, either, and we demanded payment immediately. He grumbled about it, but wrote out a chit for the sum agreed. We went off then, and told our mates of the result. They were delighted. 'Ye baith did weel, better than ah thocht,' said big Rab, 'That's an arrogant, miserable bastard. He would steal money frae his Granny, that yin!' We went off to the pay office to collect what was due to us.

We had many confrontations with that Manager and his oversman. Bob Lawson, the under-manager, and I got on well enough together, and I usually took any grievances to him, although there were a few occasions when I had to go to the Manager to settle up when I had been paid short.

The Castle, as the pit was known locally, had a history of low roadways and poor ventilation, and a bad record for accidents. The heavy work involved in the hand drawing of the hutches caused many strained backs, while runaway hutches, rakes breaking away and roof falls were frequent. They often caused serious or fatal accidents. Conditions were always hot and dusty, and there was always the danger of the lethal, unseen methane gas, with the attendant danger of a gas explosion. It was for that reason we always carried a Glennie, an oil safety lamp, which we used to test for gas.

There was one occasion when chance saved us from what might have been a bad explosion. I was working with a partner called Eddy, and we had been going very well. We had filled a number of hutches and had bored up our place, ready for firing another round of coal. We had tested for gas, and although gas was certainly there, it was a low percentage. The shotfirer (★) came along, and we helped him in stemming up the holes, but then he was called away to an accident. He was a First Aid man, and could be away for quite a time, so Eddy and I finished the job, inserting the explosive charges, priming them, and doing the rest of the stemming. We could not do the firing, because that was the job and the responsibility of the fireman, and we had to wait about an hour before he came back to us. We were impatient, having already lost time, and urged him to hurry, but he insisted on checking for gas. When he had finished, he looked worried, and said he could not fire the shots because the gas concentration was too high.

Eddy and I could hardly believe him, because we had tested ourselves not so long before, but when we tested again our Glennies

---

★ *Shotfirer:* At one time all colliers bored the shot holes in coal or stone, stemmed them up with explosives (Gelly — gelignite) and fired their own shots. Later, it became illegal for the men to fire their own shots, and shotfirers, qualified in the use of explosives, came into being. They held deputy's or fireman's certificates.

showed gas concentrations of over three per cent, well above danger level, and certainly those shots must not be fired. If they had been fired earlier, we might well have set off a gas pocket, and had a major explosion. There was nothing to do but leave the place for twenty four hours, as the regulations laid down, and hope that the gas would be cleared by then. But there were the explosives and detonators already in place. They could not be fired, and so must be left, but had to be left behind a barrier and a "No Road" sign. So we erected the signs and the barriers, and left the pit, losing another day's wage.

You couldn't always be as lucky as that. Some time later I was working in another section with my old friend Jock Gault. It was good coal, five or six feet high, and we knew that we were working up to meet another road, and that we would soon join up. We would hear the men boring away on their side, but Jock and I had some coal to fill before we started boring, so we got on with that. We had filled five hutches when the fireman came in to us. He was called Hutchinson, a canny, likeable chap, who knew my family well.

He enquired how we were getting on, and we told him we had filled five, and were working on our sixth. He warned us that Hume Smith, the man on the other side of our place, and whom we had heard boring his shot holes a little while earlier, was about ready to fire, but would come and tell us when they were actually going to fire. We still had a couple of hutches to fill, and could hear the boring still going on, so there was no great hurry about things. We thought that Hume's shots might break through into our place, and if they did not, then surely our shots would break through the barrier. We took a couple of full hutches out, and brought empties in, filled them, and Jock went off first with his. I stooped down to take the snibble out of the wheels, when there was an ear-shattering bang and a flash of flame. I was thrown forward off my feet and banged into the hutch. Stone and coal slivers ripped into my back and arms, and there was a blinding flash in my brain as my head struck the hutch. I screamed with the agony and shock of it all.

When I stood up I felt as if my back was in tatters. There was blood pouring from cuts and I felt as though I was on fire. But I knew what had happened. The shots had been fired and we had not been warned. There was a blow-through from the next road.

I was in very great pain, and hardly knew what I was doing, but I grabbed an axe and started off down the road, cursing and swearing, and promising that I would cut the fucking head off Hume Smith. There was a sharp blow on my face, and my shoulders were held tightly, and then my face struck again. It was Jock, trying to calm me down, and also needing to examine my injuries. There was another light, and that was the fireman, a First Aid man. By this time I was shaking, but quiet enough in Jock's grip. They laid me down, and Jock went off for some water while the fireman examined the state of my back and shoulders. He told me it was a mass of small cuts, but altogether not too bad. I was lucky, he said. If I had been any nearer the explosion, I would certainly have been killed. He picked away at the slivers of coal embedded in my flesh, and again told me I was lucky. I was not feeling very lucky, since this was the second time I had been caught by shot firing in that way, but at least I was calmer now, even if my whole body felt lacerated and sore.

More men appeared, together with the other shotfirer and Hume Smith, but by this time I was really too sore to be very interested. It seems that men had been sent round to us to give warning of the shots being fired, but had been held up on the way, and had not reached us in time. It really had been an accident, a misunderstanding, a lack of communication, and I suppose nobody was really to blame. But that still left me with a hellish sore back, and even more blue scars on a body that already had its fair share. I lost a shift the next day, since I was simply too stiff and sore to work, but the following day was back in the pit, and happy to be there.

Somehow it always seemed more difficult to go down the pit on those glorious days of summer when the sun gilded the whole world, and the countryside seemed to breathe and relax in the heat. Down below it was black, and hellish hot, not hot with the clean heat of the sun, but hot with the stinking, Mephitic breath of the mine. On top a man could stretch, and reach towards the sky, but down below you had to stoop and guard your head. It always took longer for your eyes to adjust to the darkness after a bright sunny morning — gettin yur pit een, as we called it.

There was one such glorious day when we cursed our luck as we went down. It was grand weather, and to leave it behind at the top of the shaft was galling. But it was back to the old grind. Jock and I were doing well that day, and by the time we had worked half a shift, at about 6 o'clock, were ready for our pieces.

But we were not to get our pieces that day. The message was passed along that there was a louse oot. There had been a big fall, and the roof had collapsed in the main haulage road. There would be no more hutches that day. We cursed at losing work, and wages, though for me that was softened by the thought of getting up the pit and into the open for the rest of the evening and its glorious weather.

We had to take the haulage road for a time, but then had to take a cross cut. The route to the pit bottom was closed off by the fall, and we had to climb up and over the fall itself. Big Tam the fireman was at the fall, directing operations. I was the first to go over, and he warned me to keep to the left where there was a hole I could squeeze through. I had to be careful not to touch any of the stones. It was a bigger fall than I had expected, and very carefully I wound my way up it to the top. When I got there I stopped and looked around. Above my head was a huge hole in the roof. Big, dangerous stones were hanging precariously, ready to fall. It was a bad place, not a place to linger in, and I was very glad to see a small gap on my left. I slipped through that, and felt a cool current of air. That was very welcome, because I was sweating heavily. I had to crawl along slowly and very carefully, not touching any of the loose stones, because the slightest movement could have caused another fall. It was a great relief when I reached the top, and could slither down to the far side of the fall to safety. There was a group of men there ready to ensure that everybody got through safely, and I turned and yelled as loudly as I could for the next man, Jock, to follow me.

Jock's voice answered my call. He was to be the next man over, and after a few minutes I saw his lamp at the top of the fall. He seemed to hesitate there, and I shouted to urge him on. He shouted back that he was just getting his breath back, and then began the descent, and he was puffing and blowing when he joined me and the others at the foot of the fall. 'Christ,' he said, 'Yon wis some bluddy sclim. It's a guid job we dinnae hae tae that ivery day!' He was right enough, but it was not just the fall that was difficult. It was the acute sense of danger and risk and the loneliness of being under that very unsafe place, with big stones ready to fall at any moment.

We watched and waited for the other men to come over, then went off to the pit bottom. The repairers would get on with their job of clearing the fall and making the roof safe, but it was a big job, and clearly it would be several days before we could work that section again. The money would be a loss, of course, but I remembered the fine summer day I had left on the surface, and promised myself that I would get home, wash up, and then have an outing with my friends. Working the backshift meant that there was little time for anything in life but work and sleep, and I felt that I was ready for a break. There was the usual banter amongst the men as we gathered at the pit bottom, waiting for the cage. Some had money, and would head for the nearest pub; others, especially the married men with families kept more quiet. They had to face a very small wage packet.

At the pit bottom we ranted at the pit bottomer to get us up quickly, so that we could enjoy what was left of the day, but he ignored us. He was a rather surly, dour-faced man, and he just got on with his job, duggin on full hutches into the cage, and drawing empty ones off. At last he turned, with at least the imitation of a smile, and told us to go up. I was on the second tow, and we whooped with delight as we left the pit bottom and speeded up the shank. The cage lurched its way round the infamous bend in the shaft, but we were used to that, and ignored it.

But the terrors of the day were not yet over. It was one thing to face a fall, and have to clamber over it with the danger of new falls crushing us, but it was something else to have trouble with the cage, and we were not prepared for it.

We realised that we were travelling faster than usual, and somebody shouted 'Whit the hell's gaein oan. Ah hope this bugger kens whin tae stop.' There was a lurch, and we swept up right past the pithead, still travelling fast. 'Haud tight!' someone yelled, and I grabbed the safety rail and shut my eyes. We sped up towards the hoarels, the winding wheels above the shaft. If the cage hit those, there could be a major disaster, and we would be the major part of it.

There was a sudden jerk, and we stopped, just below the winding gear, and swayed ominously back and forth, with the empty mouth of the shaft gaping below us. My nerves were jangling, and I was shaking. This was different from climbing over the fall: there we had something to do, and could rely on ourselves, whereas now we were hanging helpless above the corrugated iron roofs of the pithead.

There was still a joke, though. Tassie Tamson looked down at the mouth of the shaft and said 'Hell, it's a guid job that rope is haudin. It's a gae lang drap frae here!' There were figures running into the pityard, and voices shouting up at us. 'Are ye alricht up there?' 'Hoo the hell can we be alricht! Git us doon oot o this,' Jock roared back.

'Enjoy the view!' someone shouted up from down below. 'Daft bastard,' roared Wullie, 'That git should be up here!' The cage had stopped swaying now, and was just gently rocking with our movements. We saw the winding engine man come to the door of the engine house, look up, and wave his arms. Obviously there had been an overwind or else someone had blundered. I determined that I would find out about it. Someone shouted up 'Haud on, fellas, we'll shin git yer doon!' 'We hiv nae ither alternative but haud on, an keep hopin that rope disnae break,' Tassie said, and was promptly told for Christ's sake to shut his blabbering mouth.

At least the view from up there was fine, as I discovered when I looked around as a change from watching the panic down below. I was surprised to see so many big houses, and remember wondering who lived in them. There was a bus on the road, going to Hamilton, and I wished I was on it instead of being stuck up there, in that gently swaying cage with the shaft mouth open so far below. There were two cars going towards Glasgow, and a horse cart dandering along. I couldn't see Bothwell Castle; it was hidden by trees, but some people were taking a walk by the bridge over the Clyde and up towards Blantyre. That was a bad thought to have, for it reminded me that Scotland's worst pit disaster had occurred there. Better think of something else.

Wullie was looking round with me, and said it was a braw sight, and indeed it was. The evening was lovely, with white clouds like islands in a blue sea, and the sun sinking orange-red towards the horizon.

Suddenly we heard bells ringing below, and the cage jerked. We were going down. 'Ah hope the bugger kens whin tae stop this time!' someone said, and we dropped a little further, then stopped again with a jolt.

I tightened my grip on the safety bar, and we dropped again, slowly this time, and stopping frequently. Everyone was silent now. Slowly the roofs came up to meet us, and we went on down, to stop finally about two feet above the original stop mark. The onsetter was there, looking anxious, as he signalled full stop. 'Richt,' he said, 'Jump!', and we jumped. There were other men around, ready to assist us if necessary, but we all jumped well clear of the shaft mouth.

It was nearly the end of a perfect day, but on the bus home, Wullie had to cap everything by talking about winding disasters when there had been an overwind, and the cage had hurtled up to wreck the winding gear, and of others when the rope had broken, and the cage had hurtled down the shaft, taking men to their deaths. I shuddered at the thought, and wished he would shut up.

The days passed, not all of them, fortunately, as traumatic as that day when we had the roof fall and then the cage overwind. I always looked forward to the time we spent every day waiting at the pit bottom to go up the shaft. It was then that the men talked amongst themselves, and it was not always pit talk or football talk. Not that I ever tired of hearing the older men talk about their pit experiences, of where they had worked, and of the conditions under which they had worked. They talked also of the men they had worked with, and it was surprising to learn about just who had been in the pits. For one, there was Harry Lauder, later Sir Harry, the great music hall entertainer. There had been champion boxers and international football players. Several men had become Members of Parliament, and there was at least one Provost. The range of talents was astonishing, but even more astonishing was how those talents had finally broken through and been allowed to flower. It was not easy to break out of the constant round of work and sleep that made up the pitman's life, but some had done it.

There were others still working in the pit who had talents that should have been flowering in a more fertile soil. One lad, of Lithuanian extraction, although born in Scotland, had the most beautiful tenor voice, and often sang us a song or two as we waited for the cage. It was eerie, and very touching, to hear that voice soaring in song in such a place. Another lad was a conjuror and comedian of genius. He often had us roaring with laughter, and would then puzzle us with his latest bit of trickery. It was not always song and laughter, though. Many of the men were extremely well-read, and would talk about books and the wider world above us, and we listened and learned from them.

Big Jock was a footballer, and a good one. He worked on the Pickrose, a small motor-driven winch used for hauling hutches to and from the lye. Jock had newly transferred from his local junior club to Albion Rovers, and clearly had a great future ahead of him. One day we were waiting in the lye for our empty hutches when an oncost laddie (★) came rushing along, breathless, and gasped that there had been an accident. A rake had run away and was off the road, with Big Jock under it. We rushed off along the low, narrow road to help, and found that one hutch was off the road, and had jammed Jock's leg against the Pickrose. The way was almost blocked, and only the smallest of us, like me, could squeeze through. We found the roadsman beside the agonised Jock, and other men rushing up from the other side. Between us we managed to lift the hutch and stell it up, and pull Jock clear. The Fireman arrived, and organised a stretcher party to take him up the pit, where it was found that his leg was badly broken. That should have been the end of Jock's football

---

★ *Oncost:* There were many different jobs in the pits. Colliers, or facemen, or strippers were the actual coal getters. Brushers made roadways, for example taking stone from the roof to make headroom. Stone drivers or mine drivers tunnelled in stone, making roadways, or even mines. Oncost men worked on haulage, and supplied material for the facemen. Often they were younger men, waiting for a chance to become facemen, or were older men, or injured men no longer able to do their stint at the face. Their wages were lower than those of facemen. Others were beltmen, who attended to the belt conveyors and repairers, who did odd jobs such as repairing roadways. In addition, there were tradesmen such as electricians and engineers.

career, but he was a determined chap. As soon as he could he started again, at first for a non-league club, and then he went on, finally to play for Scotland, and become the Manager of Celtic, and of Scotland.

They were rough and tough men, like all miners, and it was only after you got to know them that you realised how much talent, even genius, there was in the pit. One man, with whom I became very friendly, was a naturalist, with a very profound knowledge of plants, birds and animals. More than that, he was an artist, and his drawings and paintings of wildlife were superb. He was also a woodcarver, and his carvings of birds and animals, painted realistically, were wonderful.

There were other very talented men in Bothwell Castle, and indeed in every pit I ever worked in. I often thought that if they had only had the opportunity of developing their skills, if only they had not gone down the pits at thirteen or fourteen years of age, then Scotland would have seen a prodigious flowering of talent. They were hard men, working in hard conditions, but with a rough tenderness only too often displayed when men were killed or injured. That they were brave was self-evident — you needed bravery to face the conditions of the pit. But they were also kind and modest and self-effacing. Truly, it was a pleasure and an education to work amongst them.

There were some days, though, when there was no congenial gathering at the pit bottom. Those were the days when there had been an accident and a man had been killed. When that happened, the pit closed for the day, as a mark of respect. That was an old custom, but a little later it was changed, and only the section where the man had worked went idle. The rest of the pit continued working, and part of that day's earnings was donated to the widow or other dependents.

There was one night while we were waiting for an empty rake. Our full rake was ready to leave, and we stood around in the lye, some of us chatting, others eating their piece and slushing it down with a drink of water. The first indication we had of trouble was a "whoosh" of air, then there was a distant booming noise. Dust filled the roadway, blinding us for a moment, and we all stood silent. We knew it was trouble, and when there was trouble in the mine, there was always danger, and the possibility of injury or death, if not for us, then for our mates. What we had heard and felt seemed like an explosion, and the question was: where had it happened? Someone thought it sounded far away, perhaps at the pit bottom. Big Jimmy was a dependable man, and a vastly experienced miner. He told us to stay where we were and "keep the heid". I, for one was ready to do what he said. Jimmy said he would go out and discover what had happened.

He went off, but was not away long, and soon returned, breathless. 'Richt, men,' he told us, 'Git yer claithes. It's a louse oot. There's been an explosion in the Wee Ell. There's some men hurt and wan deid. Ah don't know if there's ony mair. We'd better git oot an see if we kin help.'

It took only a moment for us to get our gear and gather again in the lye. Then we hurried off to the pit bottom to give whatever help we could. The bottom was full of men who had all hurried there from all the other sections. We found that one of the injured men was already up the pit, and another was being loaded in to the cage. He was badly injured, screaming in agony, and I shuddered. Not that I was squeamish, but it was horrible to hear that man's torment. Carefully, but with some difficulty, the stretcher was loaded into the cage, and it went off up the shaft, with the man's screams gradually dying away as the cage rose towards the pithead. A dead man lay on a stretcher, wrapped in a blanket. He could not be helped, and he would not mind waiting till his injured comrades had been lifted up to the surface, where their injuries could be attended to.

When the injured men had been lifted, then it was the turn of the dead man, and he went up on his stretcher, wrapped in his blanket, with some of his mates riding with him, ready to be handed over to his family, who would take his body, wash it and mourne over it, and then bury it. Then they would have to face the struggle to live without the strength of their breadwinner. It was a hard world, and that family would find that they would not always receive the same consideration from others as they did from the miners, who handled that dead man with compassion and respect.

I rode up the shaft with a group of men who had known the dead and the injured, and we rode in silence. At the pit head, men stood around in small groups, speaking quietly, and waiting to see if there was any need of their services. There was not, and so I dropped in my token, to prove that I was out of the pit, and went off, across the railway siding to catch a bus and go home. On the bus, an old miner who had been working near where the explosion occurred told what had happened. He believed that the men had been very close to the centre of the gas explosion, perhaps right in the fireball, and that they would have breathed in the burning gases, causing severe internal burning, awful agonies, and a frightful death.

I had worked in that pit for six months, and I had had enough of it. By now, though, in the middle of a desperate war, it was not so easy to change jobs. There were many restrictions, and the Essential Work Order required that we stay working where we were. However, I determined to begin the process of moving away from Bothwell Casle, even if it took a long time to do. The roads were getting longer as we worked the seams, and we had much further to draw our hutches. I hated that part of the job, regarding it as cuddie's work. The roads were long, and some of them were steep. There was no wonder that so many men were suffering from strained backs, broken legs and so on. It was brutally hard work.

There were quite a few Lithuanians and Poles working in that pit. They had arrived in the 1920's, big, strong men who settled in very well around Bellshill and Bothwell. Even when I knew them, some of them could still speak very little English. Often, their names were difficult for us to pronounce, and they often took the name of the Gaffer or Contractor who employed them. Many of those greedy Contractors ruthlessly exploited the men, paying them well below the average. It was strange to have as your neighbour a man who spoke hardly any English, and yet was known as Jones or Brown. We even had a Rab McGregor!

I made friends with one of those Poles, a huge man called Tony Anskitus. At piece time he would sometimes hand me the Polish newspaper in which his piece was wrapped and teach me how to pronounce the words, although the sense of them was beyond me. If I pronounced them well, Tony would slip me a small reward, a Polish home-made cake or something of the sort, saying 'You boy wee! Tack this, make you big like me'. Then he would flex his arms, showing off his big biceps.

There was one time when I was the only Scotsman in the section, my mates all being off ill or injured. I couldn't understand a word they were saying to each other, and I could not say a word to them. Many of them did not wear boots and socks, but simply wound lengths of cloth round their feet. The food, too, was strange to us, being mostly Polish bread and sausages, with chunks of fat on their meat. We did not fancy it much, although they offered to share. We joked that it must be horse meat or even cuddy!

I did not work alone with the Poles and Lithuanians for long, and was glad when my own mates returned. I was still working with Old Bob, and Jock had the next place, working with Big Rab. Our road out to the ley was steep enough, but theirs was even steeper. It was as much as we could do to push the loaded hutches up the incline. Indeed, the task was really too much for Old Bob to manage, so I claimed the right to have a "Putter" a young lad whose task it was to help push the loaded hutches. Even so, we cursed and strained and sweated heaving those hutches inch by inch up the road.

Big Rab would laugh at us as we struggled. 'Ha,' he would say, 'You not strong like Rab. You should eat Polish food, make you strong. Rab push that hutch out myself!'

We joked and bantered about it, in broad Scots and fractured English, but he insisted that he could do it, so we determined to try it out. I was sure he could not do it, because it was taking Old Bob, the putter and myself all our effort to get those hutches up the slope. So when the next hutch was ready, we gave Rab a shout.

I had filled the hutch myself, and had built up a good heading past the top, rimming it with big lumps of coal and filling the centre with small coal. It was perfectly dressed, and heavy. If we had been going to put it out ourselves, certainly I would not have packed so much into it, but this was a test for Rab.

He came into our place when we shouted, swaggering and chest out, but I was sure it would be impossible for one man to shift that hutch up the steep road. He looked at it contemptuously. 'Ha,' he said, 'You try to trick me!' Perhaps I had, in a way, but I had also been fair in greasing all the wheels. He rubbed his hands on his chest and spat on them and flexed his shoulders. He really was a big man, with a splendid physique, and I felt small and puny beside him. Rab dug his feet into the pavement and took some deep breaths. He gave a loud gasp and a grunt and heaved at the hutch. His shoulder muscles bulged and the veins in his neck stuck out. Every fibre in his body was straining, and the hutch began to move.

His face was red and distorted under the strain. His foot slipped, and he scrambled to get a new foothold. Inch by inch that hutch moved up the slope, with Rab growling like a wild animal and with sweat pouring down his body. He got the hutch to the top of the slope and we snibbled it there. Rab grinned at us and winked. 'Am ah no the strongest man in this section!' We could not argue about that, and Old Bob stood quiet, disbelieving what he had just seen. Rab grinned again, and swaggered back to his road. He would tell others about his feat, and so would we. It was a remarkable demonstration of human strength and determination.

I worked with several different neighbours for the next few months. Apart from Old Bob, there was Eddie, Wee Dickie Johnnie, Yad, and then Jock Gault again. The particular heading I was working for a time was different in that in was above the level of the ley. Therefore we just had to push the empty hutches up, and take the full ones down the incline. That was a lot easier, of course, but it could be very dangerous. Those full hutches were heavy, and we had to keep them under control going down what was in fact quite a steep slope. We had various ways of slowing them down. Sometimes we spread screen cloth on parts of the road, and then used double snibbles or snags on the wheels, with sand on the rails to give the locked wheels a better grip. We had to hang on to the handles at the back of the hutch, and dig our heels into the roadway between the sleepers, trying to control it. Even so, with everything we could do, there were occasions when a hutch ran away with us, and then we would race along behind it, shouting as loud as we could 'Runaway! Runaway!', and race along, hoping that it would not jump the rails as the hutch sped down the track at a tremendous speed. If it did jump the rails, there was a wreck, and at the very least we had to labour hard to get it back, and at the worst it could hit someone, or else knock out props and cause a fall.

There was one night when Jock and I were working at the face when a call came that there had been a bad accident. We dropped our tools, and raced out to the lye to see what we could do. A man was lying on the pavement, screaming in agony. The fireman was already there with Jimmy Graham, a First Aid man. The injured lad was an oncost worker of about my age, who had not long started in the pit. He had been dragged along by the rake, his foot caught in the haulage rope. His screams had alerted the oncost men who immediately stopped the rake and ran for assistance. The lad was in a terrible state, with his pulped face a mass of blood, his hands and arms torn and lacerated and his right foot lying at a grotesque angle.

This was an emergency alright, but there was only very limited First Aid equipment available. Jimmy took command, and barked out his orders. 'We'll hae to compromise here an mack a make-shift stretcher. Let's hae some jackets an shirts an some screen cloth. Fetch some stemmers.' These were the wooden poles we used for pushing explosive charges into the bored holes. Quickly the stemmers were pushed down the sleeves of jackets, screen cloth tied on with wire and the whole contraption lashed up as quickly and securely as we could. Carefully we lifted the lad onto the makeshift stretcher, and Jimmy detailed the stretcher bearers, and who would relieve them. We set off with our burden to the pit bottom, and it was a slow and terrible journey. We had to travel bent low under the roof, churning up dust and sweating in the heat of that poorly ventilated place. The injured lad was moaning, and occasionally lapsing into a coma. Fortunately, when we came to the outbye lye an empty rake was waiting there. We uncoupled a hutch and padded it as well as we could with shirts and jackets, then laid the man in it. I was the shortest of the squad, so Jimmy detailed me to ride with him, crouching down and cushioning his head and shoulders as much as I could from the jerks and bumps of the roadway. Then we went off, with men pushing the hutch, and hurrying as much as they could. In places the roof was only a couple of inches above the hutch, and I had to lie down with the injured man, holding him as steady as I could, and comforting him. I could only see one eye in his bandaged head, and my singlet was soaked with his blood. He began to scream, and I felt terrified in my helplessness. He was shaking and twitching, and I sent up a prayer 'Oh God, don't let him die!'

In fact, he didn't die, although it was a close thing. We finally got him up the shaft into the ambulance room and then off to hospital. He paid a terrible price for that accident. He lost an eye and a foot and had a permanently crippled arm. One more lad who would never work again.

Somehow it seemed that the coal we took out of the Bothwell Castle demanded a constant sacrifice of blood. I added some of my own.

The entrance to our road was only hutch-high, and the crossing had several broken crowns or roof supports. To make things worse, the curved rails (turns) were not fitting properly. They were natched, as we said. This made handling the full hutches difficult, and in fact it was a two-man job. One man had to be in front of the hutch and slew it round the bad joint while his neighbour pushed. You had to be alert and quick on your feet to jump clear when the hutch had cleared the bend.

I had been caught once there already, and had a three inch scar on my arm to show for it. This particular day I was in front again, tense, and ready to jerk the hutch round when we came to the curve. Suddenly I glimpsed a light coming into the roadway and shouted a warning as I prepared to heave the hutch round. That momentary lapse in concentration was enough. There was a sickening crunch, and a sharp pain up my arm. It was wedged tight between a broken crown and the full hutch, and I had the full weight of that hutch on the jammed arm. I screamed with the shock and pain, and Jock, who was at the back of the hutch, did his best to pull it back and clear, but despite his tremendous effort could only ease it slightly, not enough for me to get free. The light I had noticed was suddenly alongside, and to my enormous relief it was big Rab, the very man who had confounded us all by his single-handed pushing of a very full hutch up a steep slope. There was no-one I would rather have seen at that moment. He put his big shoulder to the hutch and called 'Heave!' Jock heaved and Rab pushed, and the hutch moved. I was free, and dropped to the pavement while the others snibbled the hutch wheels and came to my assistance. They carefully examined my arm, and found that I could move all my fingers although I winced with the effort. They bandaged my elbow, and asked what I intended to do. As it happened, this was Hogmanay, and I was looking forward to a bit of Hogmanay fun, so I was reluctant to quit work. We decided that I should carry on working, and that if I could finish the shift, then certainly I would be able to lift a pint or two that night, even if I had to do it corrie-handed, because it was my right arm that was damaged.

I tried filling an empty hutch while Rab and Jock took out the full one, but it was not much use. I could not use the injured arm, and swinging a shovel full of coal with one arm was beyond me. It was a pity, because there was enough coal cut to fill two hutches, and we could have done with the money. But I could do nothing, and so when Jock came back I decided I would quit and go home.

We wished each other a Guid New Year, and I went off. It was a long and lonely walk, and I felt distinctly queasy from the pain in my arm. There was no chatter of men and no companionship, and I was far from happy as I went along, bent double and kicking up clouds of dust. What a way to earn a living! Burrowing and scratching around far underground, with heat and dust and gas and danger as constant companions. It was unnatural, unfit for man or beast. And what was there at the end of the day? A wage packet with a few pounds in it, just enough to let you carry on for another week. And what was there at the end of your life? A body wracked and bent by years of toil, a body, like that of Old Bob, beginning to give way under the strains, and then finally perhaps, if you escaped all the ever-present dangers of death and mutilation, a few last years to hirple around before the final curtain.

'Hell,' I suddenly thought, 'I must be in a state of shock.' I was not normally given to such gloomy thoughts. Suddenly I could hear the rattle of a rake, and could see lights in the distance. I went out on to a haulage road and there was a welcome blast of cold air, which make me shiver, but was refreshing, and my gloomy thoughts evaporated.

But the problems of the day were not over. The pit bottomers were busy, uncoupling hutches ready to push them on to the cage. The head bottomer looked at me when I approached. He was far from being a popular man, and in fact was notorious for being difficult. We had nicknamed him Bela Lugosi, after the actor who always played a monster in the films we saw. He had a gaunt white face and small eyes and he always seemed to snarl when he spoke.

He was his usual cheerful and helpful self that day. 'Ye're not gittin up the pit. We're too busy,' he said before I had the chance to speak. He pushed a full hutch on to the cage while his mate pulled off the empty and belled the cage away. I told him I would get the next tow because I had injured my arm. 'Like hell you will. You bastards come oot here and demand to be put up the pit at all times. You're not getting up till lousin time.'

I felt the old familiar red rage begin to descend on me. I roared at him: 'You can't keep an injured man or a sick man waitin. Ah demand tae git up the pit. Ah need tae see a Doctor, and that's ma richt.'

He wasn't going to give way, though. 'You're not going to tell me what to do. Git oot the way!', and he made to push me. I grabbed his hand and twisted it behind his back and slapped my bandaged arm across his throat. 'Noo, ye white-livered, white-faced git, am ah gittin up the fuckin pit or not?' I jerked his arm further up behind his back, and he moaned 'Aye, alricht, ah'll put ye up the pit.' It was really a very silly thing I had done, because fighting down the pit was a serious offence, and we could both have been instantly dismissed for it.

The next two cages would take up the rest of that rake, and then I would ride. I released him, and he threatened to report me. He knew as well as I knew that he would do no such thing. An injured man had to be taken up as quickly as possible, and I was injured. If there was any reporting to be done, I was the one who would do it.

The last of the rake went up, and then I entered the cage, along with the other bottomer. Bela signalled "Men riding", and I grasped the safety rail as we sped upwards. 'Haud on,' the bottomer shouted, 'This bastard still thinks he's winding up coal!' We racketed round the jink in the shaft, and slowed as the surface approached. Geordie held my shoulder in case we jerked to a stop, and then we were at the pit head, with all the lights and activity. As we left the cage, I asked Geordie how he got on with Bela, and said that I thought he was like Death warmed up with a dreep on his nose, just like a zombie. Geordie thought he was not as bad as the other Head Bottomer, "a sleekit git, a Manager's clipe" (tale-bearer). Well, I did not have too much to do with either of them, and at least I had won my point about getting up the pit.

We laughed and joked for a moment with the on setter, saying that there would be no air raid alerts that night, because Jerry would be taking the night off to have a few drinks at Hogmanay. I was still feeling rather shaken from the accident to my arm and was anxious to get into the Ambulance Room for it to be attended to, so called for Geordie to hurry up. We went into the blackout and across to the Ambulance Room and opened the door. The light spilled out across the yard, and someone inside shouted: 'Shut the fuckin door! Dae ye no ken there's a war on!' That was the common cry in those days, an excuse for everything from a shortage of pit props to shops having no cigarettes and pubs no whisky.

'Ye daft git,' Geordie said. 'Hoo the hell can we get in if we dinna open the door?' But he closed it quickly behind him, for we were by this time well trained in never showing any light that might, just might, help an enemy bomber to find a target. The ambulance man on duty was Tam, who worked in the lamp cabin, and he gently unwound the rough bandages from my arm and examined it. He cleaned out the wound and put a fresh bandage on, joking that there would be no First Footing for me that night. It was going to take more than an injured arm to stop me doing that, though, and I told him so. He smiled and gave me a cup of tea, and I was glad of that, because I was feeling a bit sick with the pain from his ministrations, gentle though he was. His fingers moved down over the wrist, probing and pressing. He concluded that there was nothing broken, but that tendons were damaged, and that the best thing was a tight bandage. So that was what he did, and gave me some fresh bandages to put on after I had washed. Geordie offered to see me out to my bus. On the bus the conductor sympathised with me for being injured at Hogmanay and said that I could hardly lift a pint with that arm. He was right, and I told him so, but also assured him that I could, and would, lift a hauf or twa with the corrie arm. And I did.

When I got home through the blackout, my mother fussed over me, and tried to insist that I stayed at home that night and nursed my injured arm. But it was Hogmanay, and I was determined to go out and celebrate. We argued, quietly, for a while and she told me that I was as stubborn as my father. Of course I replied that there was no better man to be compared with, and she had to smile in agreement. Mother had sent for my brother Jim, a qualified First Aid man, who was always ready and more than willing to dress and attend to any injuries, and Jim carefully examined my arm. He put a new dressing on the cut, but was uneasy about the injured wrist. He did not think anything was broken, but believed it needed the attention of a doctor. That did not suit me at all. A doctor might well tell me to stay at home, and his instructions could not be ignored as I intended to ignore Jim's advice.

As we sat over our tea, Jim finally told me to go and see a local man called McCormack, a skilled bonesetter who had played for the Lesmahagow football team, and was now their trainer. In those days, there was hardly a pit village without its bonesetter. They were just ordinary working men, without any formal training, who had a profound knowledge of bones and muscles. Often their knowledge had been handed down from father to son for many generations, and they were highly skilled in treating all kinds of injuries and dislocations. They were the precursors of the osteopaths and physiotherapists of today, but they had no professional standing, although their skills were legendary.

I was quite willing to see McCormack, but told Jim that I would wait a couple of days because he would not want any disturbance on Ne'er day. Jim agreed, but warned me not to wait too long. So that was settled, and we sat round the fire, enjoying the warmth and comfort and the crack. My father joined us as he always did at Hogmanay, just after the pub closed. On that one night of the year he never missed going out for a quiet drink, and to bring back the necessary bottles for the celebration.

Finally, the bells rang out to mark the New Year, and we wished each other the customary things, and had a drink together. Then I picked up my bottle of whisky and a few bottles of beer and went off into the night. I was not alone. The streets were busy with people out First Footing, greeting each other with 'A Guid New Year tae ye, an mony of them!' in the ancient tradition. I was going to Peter's house, an old friend from school, and had a very warm welcome there. Drinks were exchanged, and good wishes and firm handshakes, although I had to shake with my left hand. I had to lift my glass with my left hand also, but fortunately it was my voice, and not my arm, that was exercised that night, as we sang all the grand old songs and a lot of new ones. We sang and ate and drank and laughed together, and the pit seemed a long way off. So did the war and all its horrors, but we did not altogether forget those who were absent on other business, nor those who would not see another Hogmanay. We drank a toast to them, and silently sent them our wishes.

I was wakened quite early the next morning by my father. It seemed early, anyway, because in fact I had not long been in bed. Hogmanay did not finish until the last person went home, and that was usually not until the drink ran out. But I was never a drinker, really, and although I had certainly had my share of New Year cheer, I had returned home well under control. I think perhaps my Mother's frequent tirades against drinking had some effect, although she had no reason to lecture any member of our family on that score. Anyway, my father asked me if I would go and feed his pony while he went off on some business connected with the small holding he had recently acquired, although he was still working in the pit.

I was quite happy to do that, although I found that my arm was very stiff and sore, and I had trouble in getting dressed and eating breakfast. When I finally went out the whole world was still asleep. It was a fine, bright, frosty morning, but there was not a soul in the streets, and hardly a chimney smoking. Folks were still in their beds after their Hogmanay. Mother had given us a lecture again as we sat over breakfast, and the idea of the Demon Drink was fresh in my mind that day. Indeed, perhaps I had a bit of a hangover, because certainly my thoughts were gloomy enough after the revelry of the night. Folks were still stinking in their beds, many of them had been blind drunk and had spewed and then drank again. 'Ah had a great nicht! Ah wis unconscious! Ah dinna mind gittin hame! Oh, ah hiv a big heid this mornin!' I had heard all the expressions and seen the reality. It was not that I detested drink: in fact I like a drink, but I did hate the effects it had on some men when they fell into its grip.

It was a few days later, and my wrist was no better, although the cut on my arm was healing well. I was still unable to get back to work. Jim came round to see me. He had not been well himself, otherwise I am sure he would have been chasing me about my injury. He looked at it carefully, and prodded around the wrist. His fingers found some very painful places. He then told me I really had to go to see Mr. McCormack, since the injury was not healing. In my usual way, I had been putting this off, hoping that time and rest would do all that was necessary. But that was obviously not working, and it did not take much persuading from Jim to make me agree to visit McCormack that very day after he finished his work (he was a painter) in Lesmahagow.

I found Mr McCormack to be a chubby, cheery, middle-aged man, who chatted away to me about football as he washed his hands. He remembered my brother well, and thought it was a pity that he had not followed a career in football, as he could well have done.

McCormack's reputation was well deserved. He was very gentle as he examined my arm, and then his hands moved rapidly backwards and forwards, up and down. I watched in amazement as my fingers moved in response to his touches on various tendons. It was as though I was playing a piano, but without any conscious movement on my part. My fingers responded to McCormack's touch, and for the first time in days were moving easily and naturally. It was a strange sensation. I had no control of my hand, just a slight touch of pain now and again, and yet the fingers were moving rapidly.

His treatment took only a few minutes, and then he told me that I should take it easy for a day or two, but that the injury was healed. He asked me to grip his hand, and I did, and felt no pain. It was amazing, and I thanked him for the trouble he had taken, and praised his skill and gifts. When I offered to pay him, he wanted to refuse, saying that since I was off work, money must be short, but finally consented to accept a couple of bob — ten pence — only after ensuring that I had money for my bus fare home.

Wherever Mr. McCormack had got his skills from, they were certainly effective. My wrist and hand felt almost normal, and I could move all my fingers. It was a great relief, that now I could get back to work, because so long as I was not working, there were no wages.

Altogether, that Hogmanay and Ne'er was memorable in more ways than one. I was injured in the pit; I had a good Hogmanay with good friends; I had a skilled man cure my injury; I went to the dancing with friends; and I met the girl who was to be my wife. Not many many weeks in anyone's life can have been so filled with incident.

It was at the dancing that I met the girl. It was usually there that couples met, but this was special, and it just happened by chance. I asked her to dance and she agreed. We found that we danced well together and enjoyed being with each other. I can't say what she found in me, but I found enchantment in her, and we went through all the rituals of courtship with joy. We have gone through our married lives with joy, too.

I went back to work with my arm almost healed, although I wore a leather strap on my wrist for extra support. I had a new neighbour, Wee Dickie Stewart, a hard worker for six days a week and a dead loss every Sunday. The trouble was that he was a drinker, on Saturday nights at least. We worked dayshift on Sundays, and the booze was still reeking in Wee Dickie's noddle when the shift started. It was always about piece time before he was any use at all, and I ranted and raved at him week after week, but to no effect. He wanted his Saturday night booze-up, and he had it. In the throes of his hangover he would moan 'Oh, ma heid! Niver agin! That's the last time!', but it never was the last time. Still, he worked hard, and was a good neighbour for the other six days, so we were making a reasonable wage.

The heading we were working was a long way from the lye, and the road led quite steeply up to it. This was a lot better than having the road slope the other way. We were pushing the empty hutches up the slope, and getting the full ones down as best we could. Only too often a full hutch ran away with us, usually when one of the wooden snibbles broke. There was little we could do to control it then, so we had to race along with it, screaming like a Banshee to warn everyone to keep clear. It was not too bad so long as the loaded hutch stayed on the rails, but if it jumped them, then the load would be scattered. That held up the work for ourselves and everybody else until the hutch was back on the rails and reloaded. The man who brought down a runaway was never popular.

The further our roadways advanced, the worse the ventilation became. The air was hot, and there was little movement to it. We sweated heavily from the moment we got in there until we ended our shift. Even our moleskin trousers were soaked through. The air was musty, and heavy with the reek of gelignite fumes, which made our eyes sting and water. Often, just for a moment's relief, we would stick our heads into the end of the airbags which carried fresher air from the fans into our workplace. Periodically we had to check the air with our Glennie lamps to be sure that there was no methane present.

But gas was not the only hazard in that ghastly place. The roof was bad and constantly working, so that there was the ever-present danger of a fall which could either crush us or trap us. Fortunately, that only happened once, when we were trapped in our place for about an hour, and had to dig our way out, while others dug in to us from the other side. No-one was hurt in that fall, but it showed us how unstable the roof was.

It all reached a climax one day when Jock Gault came rushing into our road shouting a warning that the junction was on the move, an expression that meant the roadway was in danger of collapsing. We hurried outbye and found the roof creaking ominously. Props were already beginning to splinter and bend under the enormous weight that was going on to them. Our neighbours were working furiously sawing props to replace the breaking ones, but these in their turn were giving way.

Big Rab was anxious, sawing away at a prop, and saying that we would never hold it. I looked around, and realised he was probably right. All our graith was still in the workplace, so Dickie and I raced back to get it out, being called stupid bastards as we did so. We picked up all our tools and jackets, and got back to the collapsing roadway to find the roof still working and the props still giving way.

We were called all kinds of idiots and told we were fucking mad for having gone back, but at least now if the roof did collapse, we had our graith with us on the far side. To replace all our tools would have been very expensive, and without them we could not work.

We all got stuck into the job of trying to prop up the roof, but it was getting lower and lower, and all the new props we erected were snapping and splintering. Finally, Big Rab realised that we were losing the battle, and shouted for us to get out. So we did, and raced back to a safe place and then turned to see the whole roof settle down and close tight with a mighty roar.

'Christ,' someone said, 'It's closed tight as a daisy. Aye, well, we tried as hard as we could to save the bloody place. Come on, we're loused out. We can dae nae mair here.'

We were enveloped in a pall of dust as we set off along the roadway to pit bottom. We met the fireman, Big Tam, who was not pleased to see us going. He demanded that we wait while he inspected the fall. That did not take him long, and he had to agree there was nothing else we could do or should have done. So we loused out and went home.

Wives and mothers were always alarmed when men got home early from the pit. There might have been an accident, and other members of the family were probably still at work. So the first task was to reassure my mother, who immediately began heating the big pots of water for me to wash. I stripped off my pit clothes, laying them carefully on newspapers spread ready on the floor and got cleaned up while mother made me a meal. I planned to get out of the house in time to go to the pictures, and that was what I did, and thoroughly enjoyed seeing *The Walking Dead*.

But that was an uneasy pit, and the earth movements had by no means finished. After our road had been closed by the fall, we started on a companion road to the one that had been abandoned. We were going along pretty well, because the road was much shorter, although it was still steep, and we could foresee that as we drove in the work of getting the hutches out would be as bad as it had been before. But for the moment, at least, the work was a little easier and we could make our "dark" quite comfortably. "Dark" was our expression for the number of hutches we had to fill and draw to make our wages.

One day we sensed that something was radically wrong. We were waiting in the lye for an empty rake, and there had been a strange rush of air along the roadway. The rake was long in coming, so long that Rab went off to see what the problem was, while we sat down and blethered for a few minutes. He was back very quickly, and his expression told us that there was trouble.

There had been a fall in the main road, and it was a bad one. We had to get out as quickly as we could, but when we reached the fall could not see how we were going to do it. Some repairers were already at work shoring up the roof, and they showed us a small opening high up on top of the rubble. That was the way through, but they warned us that it was very unstable. 'Ye kin git oot if ye kin climb up through yon wee hole, then keep tae the left and mind an keep the heid doon an no disturb onything, ur ye'll be here all nicht and mebbe for keeps.' We did not laugh at his joke, but one at a time began climbing to the top of the fall.

I was following Dickie. As he clambered through the small hole he struck a stone and it fell down. My heart leaped. 'Hell's fire, Dickie,' I shouted, 'gae fuckin easy. We all want tae git oot.' We had to worm our way along a small tunnel, with every movement slow and cautious lest we disturbed more rocks. It was a slow progress, agonisingly slow, and every moment we spent in that tunnel was a moment of great danger. We had to crawl on our bellies and twist and bend round the stones.

I heard Big Rab up ahead shout that he was through. If he could make it, then so could I, because he was a much bigger man than me. There was a sudden and welcome movement of fresh air, and I was at the top of the fall, and slithered down to final safety — if indeed there was such a thing as safety anywhere in the pit. That was the second bad fall I had had to climb over, and I felt it was enough. My luck surely could not last for ever.

There were no injuries or deaths caused by that fall, but only a very short time afterwards the mine took its toll. Two men were killed in successive weeks while working the dayshift, one by a roof fall and the other by a runaway hutch. But that was not sufficient sacrifice, and another man died on the surface, crushed between two wagons while shunting.

There were also quite a lot of serious injuries about that time, and the Bothwell Castle pit began to get known as The Slaughter House. In fact, a number of men decided to get out of that pit, and did so, although their places were soon filled again. There was not only the pit to contend with, but there was the war and all that it meant.

For one thing, of course, it meant relatives and friends off in the Services. At home, it meant shortages and rationing and blackout, and a constant dread of what devastation there might be on the surface amongst our homes while we were in the pit. If there was an air raid alert when we came up the shaft we had to douse our lights and get across the blackness of the pit yard as best we could. We all noticed, though, that however intense the blackness on the surface, it was never as intense as the blackness down the pit when your light failed. On the surface there was always a glimmer from somewhere: in the pit there was nothing.

The vicious air raids on Glasgow and the towns down the Clyde were certainly the worst we experienced. We were not directly affected, but for night after night there was the unending hammering of the guns and the distant thunder of falling bombs. We could see the glow as the towns and homes burned and could watch the slim searchlight beams as they groped their uncertain way across the sky in search of the enemy. The pit was closed at the height of the raids, for fear that some stray bomb might destroy the pithead gear and trap a whole shift of men. There was no other way out than up the shaft, although in fact an escape road was being driven. It was done too late, of course. While the pit was idle, we wanted to get into Glasgow or Clydebank to do what we could in the way of rescue or demolition work, for which our experience and skills were suitable, but we found that the city had been closed off to all but members of the rescue services, and that there was nothing we could do. We thought this was rather stupid. We were skilled at tunnelling and supporting falling walls and roofs, much more so than the folk in the rescue services. But we were prevented from getting in to the city, and so our skills went for nothing in that crisis.

I had determined to leave Bothwell Castle, and started the process of getting the requisite Green Card. This was in fact a permission to change jobs. At that time, during the war, mining was held to be an Essential Occupation, and you could not leave it. To change pits you first had to have the offer of a job in another pit, and then appear before a Tribunal which decided whether or not you could make the move. I had put the machinery for this in operation, but it was always a slow process, and I had to continue working as usual.

One thing happened while I was waiting that taught me a good lesson. I had the pleasure of watching an experienced Union official handle a grievance, and reach a settlement with a recalcitrant Manager. I learned a lot of useful lessons from that, lessons that I was able to apply in the future.

It happened this way. When we got to the Fireman's Cabin at the start of the shift one day, we were told there was gas in our heading, and it would have to be cleared before we could work. We were told to erect screens up the roadway to divert a current of air up there, and two repairers were detailed to help in this. When we tested, we found there was quite a lot of gas in our heading, perhaps as much as three percent, which was dangerously high, certainly far too high for working in or for shotfiring. A large part of the shift was spent in erecting screens and getting some fresher air up there, and as a result we had little coal to show at the end of the day. We expected to be paid for the work we had done in putting up the screens, but when pay day came there was nothing on our slips, and our money was short.

Of course we protested to the oversman, but he would not listen, and the argument grew heated. Eventually we went off to see the Manager, but he, as always, was obdurate and refused our case. Again the argument grew heated, with bangings on the table and strong words and threats. It happened that the Union Representative came into the office at the height of the argument, and he took over the presentation of our case.

First of all he got us all calmed down, and then it was a delight to listen to him as he marshalled the facts quietly. Soon he had the Manager nodding in agreement as the argument was presented. He even got the Manager's signature on a slip that allowed us to draw the money we were entitled to that day, instead of having to wait for the next pay day. And he did it all in quiet tones, without the table banging and shouting and threats that had seemed to be essential every other time I had argued a case with the Manager. Yad, that Union Representative, was an expert, and if he had not been a coal miner and a Union man would surely have had some high-flying career in politics or diplomacy.

Permission finally came through for me to leave Bothwell Castle, and I had the offer of a job at Loanhead. So it was goodbye to that pit, and I was not sorry. My body carried a lot of blue scars from the time I had worked there, but equally I had learned a lot. I was ready for wider pastures. Whether or not they would be greener I did not know.

We had a good night together in the local pub before I left. All my friends were there, and the drink flowed freely. So did the songs and the stories. That was one of the happiest nights of my life, and I was touched that so many men had come along to see me go off.

Of course, it was not just a matter of leaving that pit: I was also leaving home, and for the first time. My mother was a bit tearful about it, and worried lest I fall into bad company. I promised to write every week, and to visit in about a month's time. Then I went to bed, for my last night in the family home. Inevitably my thoughts turned to the friends I was leaving, Dickie and Jock Gault, Big Rab and Auld Bob, and to the men I knew who had died. I thought, too, of

Adam 'Yad' Russell, the Union Representative, with whom I had talked often after I had listened to him presenting our case to the Manager. But I was not sorry to leave that pit with its gas and low roads and hand drawing of heavy hutches. It had been my second step in the dark, and now I was ready for the third.

BURGHLEA, LOANHEAD

The Third Step

I was well loaded with all my graith and a case full of clothes when I went off on the bus. I was bound for Loanhead, a village on the outskirts of Edinburgh, where I had found a job in the Burghlea Colliery.

It was a Saturday, and a glorious summer's day. I enjoyed the bus journey, and was filled with anticipation at this new venture on life's road. The end of the trip was an anti-climax, though. I was directed to the Hostel where I was to stay, and found it was a locally notorious place called The Train. Indeed, it was a train: two rows of old carriages on a siding in the colliery yard, converted to living accomodation. One row was sleeping quarters, and the other the dining hall, games room and kitchen. A path of old sleepers was laid between the carriages as a footpath. There was washing slung between the carriages, ragged shirts, underpants and singlets, still grimy with pit dirt. There were roars of laughter coming out from what I learned was the games room. I was greeted by a barefooted man dressed only in trousers, his body covered in thick matted hair. He took me along to where another man was sitting on a stool peeling potatoes and throwing them into a bucket. It seemed that going half-naked was the accepted thing to do, because this second man was also dressed only in trousers. I was shown into one of the coaches, and allocated a bunk and a locker. It all seemed a long way from the warmth and homely comforts of the family I had left behind.

At least the place was clean, and it was all a new experience. Shortly afterwards Terry Rafferty came in and introduced himself. He had the bunk below mine, and I was glad to find he was a cheerful lad, always ready with a laugh and a joke. Together we went off to have a meal in the canteen, and I found the food strange and dubious. But at least it was eatable, and I actually enjoyed it. Of course, I was hungry, and anything would have tasted good — it always did in those days.

We talked about the pit and the conditions, and I began to feel more at ease in those strange surroundings. I was told about the various characters living in the hostel, who was a drinker and who was a gambler and who was a steady worker. This was a strange community to me, and far removed from the ordered life I had left behind. There was a constant game of cards in the games room (there was nothing else but cards, dominoes and darts), and some of the men were inveterate gamblers there. If they won, they were generous with their winnings, but if they lost then it was a long wait to pay day and another chance. There was dancing in the village, and it seemed that anyone going to the dancing borrowed whatever clothes they needed from anybody else who was staying behind. Shirts, shoes, ties and suits circulated amongst them all, because it was a point of honour to go out looking well-dressed, however rough and tink-like the conditions under which they lived.

There was a fine comradeship in The Train, and the lads tended to stick together in their pleasures as well as at work. On my first night, there was a big fight in the dance hall between some of the boys and some soldiers. It started in the usual way, over some girl or other, and ended in a general free-for-all with police and Military Police involved. One of our lads received a bad beating, but by the time the rest of us received the news and got there, the fight was over, and we all went off to the back room of a local pub, and had a good evening of beer and singing. I learned more about the hostel and the pit. There was plenty to eat, even if it never looked particularly appetising. There was always porridge and soup, as much as you wanted, and generally the rations were much more generous than those we had at home. There were all sorts of men in the hostel, a mixture of miners, facemen, brushers, oncost lads and even some Bevin Boys. These were youngsters who had been conscripted to work in the pits, and I had never met them before.

The working conditions were very different, too. I had always previously worked stoops, that is, short sections of a seam, separated from other work places, but in the Burghlea we worked Long Wall, where a whole length of seam was exposed, and we all worked at it together. This, of course, had the advantage that there could be a lot of mechanisation, because the machines could work along the full length of the wall. There was a conveyor, too, and that meant no more hutches to be filled. The conveyor ran the full length of the wall, and all we had to do was shovel the coal on to it. A big difference from filling hutches and then hand-putting them up the slopes to the ley. The seam stood about five feet high, so there would be plenty of head room.

As a newcomer to the pit I was classified as a Spare Faceman. This did not please me particularly, because I was an experienced and qualified faceman. However, that was the rule of the pit, and I would have to wait my turn to be a full time faceman. It was not too bad, though, because I was guaranteed three or four shifts at the face each week, and there was plenty of overtime if you wanted it. Besides, by this time the Union had won a guaranteed wage for all miners, so at least I would get my money.

The next morning I was awakened by Terry pushing me from his bunk below mine. It was time for work. There was breakfast first, though, a good helping of porridge, followed by a fry-up, served by a cheerful young girl. Not a bad beginning to my first day, I thought.

The Burghlea was a strange mine, or at least I thought so. There were three different ways to get to the pit bottom. One was by the normal shaft and cage. There was another entry down an airway, served by a little carriage which just fitted neatly into the steeply sloping passage way. I was told that it was called the Yo-Yo, and it got its name because it always went up the road in a series of jerks, three feet up and two feet back. Instead of using the cage, we entered the pit by the main roadway, which was a tunnel leading into the ground, and then sloping sharply dowwards. We travelled inbye seated in a train of little carriages hauled by a rope as thick as my wrist. I was shown the engine room, where there was an enormous pulley wheel over which the rope ran, and which was driven by a very big engine. So we were to ride into work! It seemed like a very gentlemanly thing to do.

However, I was hardly prepared for the stomach-churning reality of it. We took our seats in the little carriages, and were belled away. The rake of carriages moved off, and suddenly we were in the darkness of the pit mouth. Then we started going down, and all the seats swung backwards to stay level on the steep slope. And it *was* steep, and we seemed to be travelling at a hell of a speed. It was strange to me, and I thought I would rather have been going down in the cages I was used to. Some minutes later there was a gentle tug, and we slowed down and stopped at the pit bottom. I sighed with relief, but no-one else seemed in the least perturbed, and I reckoned that if they could get used to it, then so could I.

From the pit bottom there was another steep incline to walk down before we reached the fireman's cabin. There, after explaining what experience I had at face work, I was detailed to go in the stint next to Terry, who would show me the ropes. I was anxious to get started work, and get the first shift over, because I knew from old experience that the first shift was always the worst after you had been off even for a couple of days. Your body always complained about having to get used again to all the strains and efforts of the job, and you could expect a bit of stiffness and soreness. So the sooner you started, the sooner that would pass.

We got to the stint, and I looked around. It was all very strange. I was used to steel props, but had never seen as many as there were there. A huge pile of gum (small coal) lay waiting for us. This was from the machine, which had undercut the full length of the face. It seemed like a lot of coal to be shovelled on to the conveyor, and that was before the facecoal itself had been dropped.

Terry showed me my stint. It was about fifteen feet long, marked off from the others by broad chalk marks on the roof. The machine had undercut to a depth of five feet, and the seam itself stood about six feet in height. It was a hell of a lot of coal, and it all had to be shovelled by me on to the conveyor. While I shovelled the gum, the shotfirer and the holeborer (★) would bore my place for firing, and fire the shots. Then they would come back and give me a hand if necessary, at least until I was broken in to the work. Terry reckoned that the stint would be between 20 and 23 tons of coal, all of which I had to get on to the conveyor. He advised me to put as many big lumps as possible on by hand, and to keep the lumps as big as possible: that would mean less shovelling.

So I got down to the job, and was soon sweating heavily. Fortunately, the ventilation was good and the air fresh enough, because it was hard, gruelling and rather monotonous work. As I looked down the long wall of the coal face I could see lights bobbing up and down as the men went about their work. That was strange to me, because I had always worked in places where you could see nobody but your neighbour. There were all sorts of jobs going on simultaneously at that coal face. Apart from those of us who were shovelling coal on to the conveyor, the shotfirer and holeborers were busy. Other men were building pillars of stone and rubble in the waste—that is, the area behind us where the coal had already been won. By building those pillars, the roof was supported over our work place, and the pressure taken off the coal we were working. That system was later changed, and the waste allowed to close up totally.

★*Holeborer:* Another sign of how specialisation was creeping into the pits. Previously facemen did their own boring and shotfiring, but now those jobs were increasingly being done by men who specialised in them.

I was glad when it was piece time, and even more glad when the end of the shift approached. I had cleared up my stint, but as I looked along the face I could see that others still had a good bit to do. So I knew that I had held my end up well enough. The fireman came down the face line and spoke to me. 'You wull be lyin on,' he said, rather snappily, I thought. That meant I was to be working overtime. 'Not bluddy likely,' I told him. It was not so much the idea of working overtime that upset me, although I felt I had done enough for one day, but rather his attitude that I found objectionable.

I told him I had stripped my stint, and was finished for the day. 'You'll be lyin on,' he repeated. 'Ah'm the oversman, an what ah says goes.' Here I was, my first shift in a new job, and already getting into an argument. It was not a good start, but I was not going to back down.

'Ye micht be the oversman or a fireman or whitever, but git this straight. Naebody tells me whit tae dae or no dae. Ah'll say it agin: ah'm no lyin on. Gie the overtime tae a married man.' It seemed like a stalemate, but fortunately the Pool Leader of the section, a chap called Donald, appeared on the scene. He seemed to know what the problem was, and told me that I did not need to lie on. He said I had done well for my first shift, but explained that in future I might have to do overtime. Actually, I did not mind working overtime, and the extra money would be welcome, but I was damned if I was going to be *told* to do it, rather than be asked. I thought I might have made an enemy already in McLean, the oversman/fireman, but in fact he and I got on well enough together after that little incident.

I was glad to know that the pool leader was a reasonable man, and reliable. They were our team leaders, elected by the men themselves to do the job of allocating the men to their particular stints. They also assessed faceline problems, and agreed payments with the firemen. It was their job to keep the rota of men "lying on", that is, working overtime, and ensuring that all the men had their fair share.

I was pleased with myself as we walked off to the pit bottom. I had proved that I could work as a stripper and could work alongside anybody. I knew that at first I would only get three or four shifts a week at that job, but there was plenty of other work for an experienced miner, and there would be plenty of overtime if I wanted it.

It seemed that there was a constant stream of minor conflicts with management in that pit. There was no strong tradition of Trades Unionism there, and no particular spokesman for the men had appeared. In addition, there were quite a number of Bevin Boys, young lads conscripted to work in the pits, and most of them were from areas and even parts of society that knew nothing of mining and its struggles and of the solidarity of the mining community. Of course, I was not always directly concerned in each conflict with the management, but certainly I had my share of them.

On one occasion, I recall, a conveyor had broken down and a gang of us was repairing it. The job was not quite finished when the shift ended, and the fireman told us to work overtime and get it finished. I refused, and my neighbours were aghast. So was the fireman: indeed, he was furiously angry when he stormed along and asked me what the fucking hell I was doing. I explained that there was no point in my just working overtime for one hour. I would miss my special bus back to the Hostel, and would have to take an ordinary service bus, and that would cost me more than I would get as wages for the hour's overtime. Furthermore, I would miss my meal at the Hostel, and would either go to bed hungry or else try to find, and pay for, a meal in town. He was obdurate, though, and insisted that I do the job.

I was obdurate, too, and after a few wordy exchanges of the nature of: 'Ah didn't come up the Clyde on a banana skin,' and 'Dae ye think ma heid buttons up the back?' I went off to the pit bottom. To my surprise, the rest of the gang followed me out, and told me that the fireman was threatening to sack the lot of us if we did not do the overtime. That was pouring petrol on the flames, and we were more than ready for him when the Manager stepped out into the pit bottom. Obviously he had been told of the trouble.

He was always a fair enough wee man, though, and prepared to listen, once he had had his first barking session. So he barked at us, with a couple of threats, and then he listened as I explained the problem. He told us to go back to work, finish the job and then pick a spokesman to see him in his office after the job was done. That was not good enough, and we told him so. It was not just this particular job we objected to, but we felt we had a legitimate complaint about the general attitude of that fireman.

He listened, and, as was his habit, wrote everything down in a little notebook. Then he told us to select two, not one, spokesmen, and he would see us, together with the fireman, in his office after the job had been done.

That seemed about as far as we could get without actually going up the pit there and then, and making the pit idle. So we went back and finished the job, and then I was chosen as one of the spokesmen and went to the office. I think the outcome was really very satisfactory. It was agreed that if we were told to do overtime, then our payment would include an allowance for bus fare and for food. In addition, I believe that the fireman must have been roasted by the Manager, because certainly his attitude after that was less of the bully.

The Train, where we had been living, was closed down, and most of us were transferred to a hostel. Some of the lads decided that they would find their own digs instead, and we were all, I think, sorry to see the end of The Train. It had been a happy community, in which we lived a care-free life, looking after ourselves and making up our own rules of behaviour. The hostel was a complete contrast. It was a group of Nissen huts, each holding eighteen men. We had a large locker each, and a low camp bed. The Ablutions block was large and clean, and there was a Dining Hall and a Tea Bar which was open till ten o'clock every night. There was a laundry, and a First Aid Clinic with a full time nurse. There was also a full time manager, a wee man who wanted to be known as Major Helliwell. I suppose he had once been in the army, and certainly that is where he imagined he still was.

The Major tried to run the Hostel as his memory told him an army camp was once run. That might have worked with the Bevin Boys, who were all youngsters and new to the life of the mines. There was no way it could work with the rest of us, particularly when we had just come from the self-governing, anarchic community of The Train.

We set up a Residents' Committee to meet once a week and discuss the running of the Hostel. All complaints had to be aired there, and the committee saw some grand battles. Of course, there had to be some rules of conduct, and we accepted that, and honoured the rules. But there was no way we were going to accept petty restrictions and arbitrary decisions imposed by the Major. And certainly we were not going to have him addressing us simply by our surnames, for example, while he insisted on being addressed as Major, or at least as Mister or Sir.

As the weeks passed, we gradually got a reasonable sort of organisation and understanding, but it was hard going, and certainly we were never as free and easy in that Hostel as we had been in The Train. We did have all kinds of entertainment, though, from darts and dominoes tournaments to classical music concerts given by professional groups. We also had a weekly dance to which most of the local girls came, and thoroughly enjoyed. After a disagreement with the local band which had been playing for the dances, we found that there was a great deal of talent amongst our own lads, and they set up a dance band, which was not only a lot better than the one we had been hiring, but was good enough to have engagements all around the countryside.

Altogether, it was a very interesting group of young men living in that Hostel, and our leisure time was by no means all taken up with beer and dancing. There was Bob Currie who was studying for the ministry and who was a keen actor. He loved to dress and make up and then do his version of Hamlet or Macbeth. Johnnie Gilmore was an ex-Navy boxing champion, and he was happy to demonstrate his skill in the ring we put up. Donald McKenzie was from Skye, and he had a wealth of knowledge about the history and folklore and song of his island. Mick McGahey was in our hut, and spent most of his time reading and studying. We were good friends, and he introduced me to many books, and was prepared to spend endless hours discussing what we had read. We organised a discussion group, and the arguments raged loud and long into the nights. This was during the war, of course, when along with our Allies, the Soviet Union and the United States, we were fighting for our national lives against a truly evil empire. It was the period when Britain was united as never before or since in a determination to change society in such a way that most of its evils and sorrows would be eradicated for ever. We were young and strong, and *knew* that we could change the world, and we never tired of discussing just how we would do it, and the precise shape of the new world we would build.

There was one Irish chap in our dormitory, inevitably called Paddy, who was quiet and a bit morose. He kept very much to himself, but one night he and I happened to be the only ones in the hut. I was reading, and he came over and offered me a bottle of beer. Drink was supposed to be banned from the Hostel, but no-one took notice of such a stupid regulation. Paddy asked me about the book I was reading, and we talked about it for a while, and he asked to borrow it when I had finished. He then began to talk about his life, and it had been a hard one. With his long black hair and darkly-stubbled chin, Paddy looked a tough customer, and indeed he had lived a rough life at times.

His family had been small farmers, and as the only child Paddy had been expected to work hard even as a youngster. I knew something of how hard farming could be, but I had done it only intermittently, whereas Paddy did it constantly. He spoke of the haymaking, the mucking out of the three cows and the six or seven pigs, of the potato harvest, the singling of the turnips, and, worst of all, the shawing of turnips on a frosty morning. I, too, remembered those ice-cold fingers and soaking legs, and knew it for a miserable job.

Paddy's parents both died when he was still a young man, and the farm had come to him. It seemed like a rosy future, especially when he met a bonny lass, and they agreed to wed. It was not to be, though. The bonny lass called off the wedding just a few days before it was due to happen.

Paddy began to hit the drink, and hit it hard. It did not take him long to drink his way through the farm and everything else he could sell. He was an alcoholic bankrupt, and he took to the roads of Ireland, doing what jobs he could find to earn enough for his drink, and living rough in barns and hedgerows. Eventually, and not surprisingly, he became seriously ill, and was taken off to a hospital. He recovered, and determined that he was going to change his life before it was too late. So he came to Scotland, and began work in the pits, and there he found a friendship and comradeship that he had never known before. He was a hard worker, and a quiet man who would take a drink, but was never drunk. I knew him for a long time, and I am convinced that without the support of his fellow miners he would have perished as a miserable rag of a drunkard.

There was one thing special about working with miners: your education was never finished. There was always someone around who had read deeply in whatever subject you might find interesting. And it was not just book learning. The boxers, for instance, were delighted to share their skills. They thought I was promising in that game, and took me on and taught me a lot. Then there were the others who had read widely in history and politics.

One of these was Geordie, an engineer with whom I worked for a while. We had the job of dismantling a conveyor that had lain for some time in an old section. The roof there was bad, and I had to repair it before we could work safely. It was a long way from the airway, and ventilation was poor, and there was methane gas about, so I had to carry a safety lamp to test the air periodically. We were left very much alone on the job, and only saw the fireman twice a day when he came on his inspection.

Geordie, the engineer, was a tall, thin, middle-aged chap, a good craftsman, and a happily married man. He often invited me home with him, and we spent hours by his fireside talking, after enjoying our tea. His real love was history, especially the history of the miners.

He told me of the Truck Acts, and of how they ensured that, not so long ago, the miners were held in a condition of total servitude to the mine owners. He spoke of the old regulations and conditions in the very communities in which we now lived. I found it all almost unbelievable, and wondered what kind of people they were who would accept such conditions. Had they no guts, no fight in them? Of course, they had, and they did fight hard and endlessly, but it was a terrible struggle.

Geordie explained that the company owned you body and soul. You lived in their house, drank in their pub, bought from their shop, worked in their pit, and was even buried in their graveyard, after buying a coffin from the company store. If you lost your job, you were out in the street that same day, and you could not quit, because somehow you were always in debt to the company shop. And all that was not so long ago there in Newtongrange, where we sat by Geordie's fireside. 'Things are changing, lad, and changing for the better. You young ones can do it if you learn from our mistakes. Fight for better conditions, better wages and a better future. A strong Union is what we need, and that's coming now that you lads work here.' That was the theme of many of his lectures, and I have never forgotten what he said.

It was while working with Geordie on that same conveyor job that I had one of the strangest experiences of my life.

We had been taken off that job for a few days, and I was quite glad when Geordie called me as I arrived at the pit bottom one day, and said we were to go back and finish up. Nobody had been up those old roads since we had left them, and they were even lower and hotter than before. Cobwebs hung in great sheets from the roof, and it was unpleasant brushing past them. The old road was hot and stoorie, and the stoor rose in clouds as we walked along. There was one place where we had to crawl, throwing our graith along in front of us in stages. This created even more dust, which caught us by the throat. When we reached the section where the conveyor was, the place looked even more evil and forbidding than before, and we were both happy to realise that the job would take only a few days to finish, and we could get back to somewhat better conditions.

We had some tea from our bottles, and Geordie asked what I was doing for the weekend. I told him I was going home. I had done a good deal of overtime, and was taking the weekend off. I had not seen my girl, May, or my family for some weeks, and I was looking forward to the rest. Geordie told me that I should bring May over to stay for a while, and said that she could stay in their house. That was a kind thought, and I determined to try to organise it.

I went to hang up my jacket, and disturbed a large rat. The stone I flung missed by a yard. Geordie threw a spanner at its mate, and also missed. I told Geordie I hated those bastarding things, and indeed I did. More than that, I was quite nervous about them. Geordie assured me that they were harmless enough, and would never touch you unless they were cornered. He said they were really very intelligent animals, but I told him that was not possible, otherwise they wouldn't choose to live in the mine. Geordie laughed, and reminded me that we were here of our own choosing.

We got on with the job, and made good progress, with Geordie carefully laying out all the parts of the conveyor as he dismantled it. It was going to be a hell of a job for the transport men to shift that lot to pit bottom through old roadways. It would all have to be manhandled most of the way, and I was glad I would not be doing it.

The shift ended, and we went off, back the way we had come, and I was particularly glad that day to get up the pit and into fresh air. I wanted a good wash, and to get the dust out of my nose and throat and the sticky cobwebs and old grease off my body.

That day happened to be Friday, "The Day the Bear Dances", and I had a few pints in the company of my mates. Wee Wullie, one of the lads in the hut, had recently got married, and was going off to work at Blantyre, near his home. We gave him a good send off, but the result was that I was not happy the next morning when the nightwatchman woke me for the early shift.

Still, it had to be done, and a quick sluicing with icecold water made the world seem a somewhat better place. I could not face the porridge that morning, but the soya-link sausage-substitute slipped down easily enough. I slapped the fried egg on a slice of grey wartime bread, and ran for the bus, eating as I went.

Geordie was waiting for me, and looked rather unsympathetic when I told him I had a big heid on me. 'Drink and work don't mix,' he said, and patted me on the back. The dust and the heat and the cobwebs and the ventilation seemed even worse that day, and I was sullen and short tempered. Geordie tried to cheer me up. 'We don't have to rush,' he said, 'We can finish the job tomorrow.' We rested for a moment when we reached the conveyor, and then got up to start. I told him nature was calling me, and that I would be back in a minute with his tools. I went off down an old road, and found that I was not the first there for that purpose. There was plenty of newspaper lying about, and I settled down. Nature was indeed calling, but it was calling more than my bowels. There was something strange about that place, a strange feeling of foreboding, even danger. The hair tightened at the back of my neck.

I could detect nothing really wrong about the place. It was an old working, but the roof was no worse than usual and the ventilation normal. But there was something far from right. Suddenly there was a loud crack, and an old rotten prop collapsed some distance away. There was a squealing and a squeaking and a rush of something moving.

My lamp showed me a dozen or more huge rats dashing about. As I turned my head, my lamp was reflected in the eyes of many more rats crouching in the side walls. They leaped down onto the pavement, and I leaped to my feet, struggling with my trousers. I screeched with sheer terror, and raced out of that place. I wanted human company, and when I got back to Geordie I was sweating heavily and panting. 'If you want your fucking toolbag, you'll have to get it yourself,' I told him. He looked at me in amazement. 'Rats,' I told him, 'Dozens of them!'

I don't think he believed me, but we armed ourselves with wooden sticks and went back the way I had come. I was braver now, with Geordie at my side. That old road was seething with rats of all ages and sizes.

They ran, leaped and squealed. That weird assembly seemed to be forming into some semblance of ranks with the big rats pushing the smaller ones into place. The army grew even as we watched, and certainly we were not prepared to face it. We had to get Geordie's tools, though, and crept very slowly and quietly along until we reached the toolbag, and then we got the hell out of that. My graith was further down that passage, but there was no way I was going to go for it.

We had had enough, and seen enough. We got out of that place, crawling through the tunnel more quickly than I would ever have thought possible. We met the fireman and made our report. 'Aye,' he said, 'I heard there was plenty o rats, but no that they're on the move.' He wanted us to go back with him so that he could see for himself, but that we refused to do. Wisely, he decided he would not go through on his own, and instructed us to put up "NO ROAD" signs, and leave it.

That night the old roads where we had been working closed up completely. Everything in them was buried for ever, including my graith and jacket and flask, and of course the conveyor we had been working on.

I told my story in the Hostel that night, and to my surprise found that others had had similar experiences. None of them had known it happen in the pit, but certainly it was not an unknown thing for rats to move *en masse* out of a building or an area before a disaster of some sort. The old saying about rats leaving a sinking ship must have had its origin in that sort of migration. Donald, with his profound knowledge of the legends of Skye, took the opportunity to tell us about ghost lights and other things not of this world. His stories were creepy, right enough, and Donald was deadly serious about them.

My story about the rats was creepy enough for me, especially as I had always had a strong fear and dislike of them. To see them in such numbers, and acting in such a fashion was something I never wanted to experience again.

Gradually, conditions in the pit were improving, mostly due to the efforts of the Union. More and more men were joining, as they saw for themselves how the Union was struggling on their behalf, and as more men joined, so did its strength increase, and as its strength increased, so did its ability to improve conditions. This seemed so self-evident to me (it still does) that I could not understand those who stood out against the Union.

Although I had no official Union position at that time, I was often called on to help in settling some dispute or putting some case forward to management. As always happens when someone is becoming prominent and proficient in such matters, the management tried to get me on their own side. More than once the Manager himself tried to persuade me to study for my papers, so that I could look for promotion to deputy and fireman. He told me that he had been watching my work, and that although I was an awkward wee bugger, I was the sort of man he was looking for to move into management. He offered to help me with studies, and said he would provide a house for me and my wife if we got married and settled there.

I suppose it was good of him, and I feel sure he meant it well, but that was not the pattern I had chosen for myself. I had no desire to join the management. My place was working as a miner, and I was proud of my skills and strength. I had done a good deal of studying already, and had a sound theoretical knowledge of the mining industry — much more than many of the management had or ever would have. But I was a miner, and I was going to stay a miner, with my mates and comrades.

I was beginning to feel that there was not much more I could learn at Burghead, and thought that another move would be in order. My brother Jim was working in a mine in Sanquhar, in Dumfries-shire, and he told me that the pay was good, and conditions reasonable. I decided to join him there, but we in the pits were still subject to wartime rules and regulations. We could not just pack up our jobs and go as we wished. We had to get approval of the new job, and it had to be in the pits. We could not decide we had had enough of mining, and find a job outside the industry. So I started the long-winded process of getting permission to move.

While I was waiting, I had several more conversations with the Manager. He still hoped to persuade me to stay at Burghead, and to study for my certificates. It was very strange for me to meet a Manager as a friend, rather than as an official. I had found them always dictatorial, brash, and arrogant. They cut your rates of pay and your ton rates: they squabbled over deficiency payments you were entitled to. In return, I was just as arrogant, always at loggerheads with them. Now I found myself sitting and talking in friendship with a manager, and learning a lot from it. In fact, his attitude was not much different from mine. We shared much in our views of life, and our differences in the pit were forced on us by circumstances which put us on opposite sides of the fence. He was very persuasive in his arguments about becoming an official, and several times I almost succumbed. But basically I could never change. I was a collier, a man amongst men, and that was going to be my life.

The war in Europe ended, and we marked the occasion by a grand booze up. We were told the news as we came up the pit one day, and, as though by magic, supplies of whisky and beer appeared in every room of the Hostel. It seems that most of us had been saving up supplies for that occasion. Every time a man appeared in the door of the room and asked what was going on, he was told 'Shut up by drinking up', and a whisky and a bottle of beer was thrust into his hand. In no time there was a good sing-song going, with all the songs that were so popular in those days, including the appropriate *Roll Out The Barrel.* By some feat of organisation, someone arranged buses to take us all home, and we filled the time until the buses arrived by more drinking and singing. It was a grand party, and those lads who would not be coming back were not forgotten. Everyone drank a toast to them, which, if it would do them no good, at least ensured that they were remembered on that day.

When the buses arrived to take us home, those who were long-sighted (or experienced) made sure that they carried an empty bottle or two on to the bus. This was to be a non-stop trip. It was a non-stop singing trip, too, and a non-stop drinking trip, so long as the supplies lasted.

Back in the village arrangements were made to meet later and carry on the celebrations. But not by me. I had a lass to see, and maybe there would be some dancing to go to. That would be the best of celebrations for me. Besides, I was never a great drinker, and had already had a lot more than usual.

So I went straight to May's house, and was met at the door by Mary, her mother. The welcome was warm, and May was blushing with delight. The kettle went on to the fire, and food put on to the table. Mary was a good cook, almost as good as my own mother, and there was always something worth eating in that house. It was Irish stew that day, I remember, cooked as Mary had made it when she had been a cook in a big house in her younger days. It was good, and I was ready for it. That was Mary's way: she could always rustle up something tasty just while you coughed. May and I made our plans for the evening, and then I left to go home and see my parents.

The atmosphere in the village was just like Hogmanay, with everybody in festive mood. And it was not all just because of having a drink or two. There was a great deal to be festive about. The Allies had defeated an evil wickedness whose like had never been seen in the world before. The sacrifices had been great, but there was no-one who did not consider them worthwhile. Not so long before that day we had learned of the untold horrors of the German death camps. As the Allied troops had swept on to final victory, they had over-run those places of terror and agony. Our newspapers and cinemas had shown us pictures. We did not know the full extent of the horrors, but certainly knew enough to be doubly glad at the defeat and death of those responsible. So there was real joy in the festivities that day, and real relief that it was all over — at least in Europe.

My mother and father greeted me warmly, as always, and I had to sit down again at the table, for it was tea time. I protested that I had just eaten, but was told to sit down and eat up. My mother told me that I could always eat more, because I was always eating, and Pop thought I must be putting it all into a bad skin because I was not very fat. This was a regular piece of family badinage, and I believe we both spent time thinking up new comments on that subject. Pop bent over to knock out his pipe in the fireplace, and I told him that I might be a bad skin (which was how he always referred to animals which did not "do" well), but that I was the fittest in the family. But he had his answer ready, as he always had, and told me that I might be the fittest, but I was certainly the cockiest. We laughed, and watched my mother produce a large, newly-baked Soda Scone with roasted cheese. This was a favourite, and we wasted no more time in joking.

May and I went to the dancing, and as always I felt very proud and about ten feet tall to be the partner of that beautiful lass. She turned heads whenever we walked down the street, with her smiling face and the most lovely hair I have ever seen. 'It's a bonny lassie ye've got,' I was told repeatedly, and I always replied 'Yes, an it's me that knows it!'

After a couple of days at home, it was back to the pit and the old grind. I was impatient for a reply to my application for a transfer, but eventually it did come, and I was told I could move. I gave in my notice at the office, and then had another meeting with the Manager, who again tried to persuade me to stay on at that colliery and take my exams. for management. He was good enough to say that there would always be a job for me there if I found that I did not get on in Dumfries-shire.

THE TOWER MINE

THE FOURTH STEP

So I started at the Tower Mine in Sanquhar. I had hoped that I would have been working with my brother Jim, driving a new mine, but that job did not transpire. Instead I was engaged as a Spare Stripper. If a faceman was off work, I would take his place. This did not happen very often. Indeed, the joke was that you would get a regular faceman's job only if one of them died, or you shot him. So my wages were more often than not just the basic fall-back rate, rather than the Strippers' rate, and I was dissatisfied. There were several arguments about overtime, and I found the rules in that pit very different from what I had been used to, and I thought little of them. So I set about trying to change them.

I attended all the Branch Union meetings, and spoke up for a different set of rules. I was called a lot of rude names at that time, but gradually found that others were beginning to support me. My main argument was for a rota system for the Spare Facemen, which seemed only fair and elementary to me. I had not reckoned on how close-knit that little community was, and how many and varied were the numerous cliques. I learned a lot about this aspect of life in the village from a good friend, who happened to be the only Catholic employed in the pit. We walked a lot over the hills, and both enjoyed a pint after it, and he told me a great deal about who was who, and who mattered where. Altogether it was a long battle before my ideas for a more fair system began to take effect.

There was not a lot of entertainment in that small village, but occasionally there was a dance. That was my line of country, and I looked forward very much to the first one of the season. Two of us from the Hostel where we were staying got ourselves dressed up to the nines for that occasion. We polished and brushed and cleaned, and then had a couple of pints before going off to the hall. I could hardly believe it when we had paid our money to a very fat woman at the door, and elbowed our way through the crowd. This was no dance hall, it was a barn! It was whitewashed halfway up the walls, and the rafters were exposed in the ceiling. It really did look like a barn, and perhaps it had been not so long before. Not only that, but the dancing was strange to me. I prided myself on my dancing. I had visited pretty well every dance hall in Glasgow, and could hold my own in any of them, and at that time the dancing in Glasgow was the best in the country, and we danced to the best bands and in the best halls. Here we were in a barn, and the dances were not mine. There was a Dashing White Sergeant, and then a Reel, and the air was filled with wild cries and "Hooches!" as the dancers swung and leaped, and the accordion and drums (the only music) banged away. I could not handle that, but fortunately the M.C. announced an Old Time Waltz.

That was my country, and I confidently approached a girl I recognised. Her name was Linda, and she was a friend of my brother's wife. 'Hello, Linda. Care tae shuggle yer bains wi me?' That was a standard sort of approach in the sophisticated dance halls I knew, so I did not see why it should not work in that little village hall. It did work, and Linda and I moved on to the floor. She was a good dancer, and we made a good pair.

We finished the waltz, and stayed together for a Quick Step. 'Do you come often to the dancing?' she asked, and I burst out laughing, to her considerable surprise. I had to explain that her question was the regular question every young man in the Glasgow dance halls asked when he first took a new girl on to the floor.

The next dance was a tango, and that was a special one for me. Linda was nervous, and said she was not good at it, but I was confident. There were only four other couples on the floor as we swept off into the rhythm, and I whispered each move into Linda's ear. I did not notice, but two other couples dropped out, leaving the whole floor to just six of us. It was almost like an exhibition, and I enjoyed it, and so did Linda, as soon as she relaxed.

There was a round of applause as soon as the music finished. My mates from the Hostel were registering their approval of Linda and me. I told Linda she was great, and kissed her as I left her with her friends, and went back to my own. Doc. told me that we had danced well, and I said that Linda was a marvellous dancer. Doc. punched me gently on the shoulder, and said he was going to find out that night.

He did find out, and purely by the chance of my choosing Linda for the first dance in that village hall, I had become a sort of Cupid, for Linda and Doc. got on well together, so well that in a short time they were engaged, and soon married.

I was really not enjoying either the work or the life at Sanquhar. There seemed to be no prospect of getting a permanent job as a stripper in the pit, and as a spare hand I often had to work much overtime to get a decent wage. And although Sanquhar was a couthy wee place, it did not offer the range of entertainments and pleasures that I had been used to. I was still a very young man, and felt that I had to visit dance halls and cinemas as an essential part of life.

Besides all that, there was May. We wanted to get married, and there was no chance of getting a house in Sanquhar. So, for many reasons, I began to look round yet again for another job.

Not that my life in Sanquhar was altogether without its pleasures. There was the dancing occasionally, although I never did really get to grips with the country dancing that was so popular there. The cinema seemed to show nothing but old films that I had seen already, but I was glad enough to see some of them again. I learned to play quoits, and enjoyed it. And of course there was always the odd pint or two with my friends. Another advantage of Sanquhar was that May could occasionally pay me a visit, travelling by train. That was fine, but it served only to sharpen my desire to get away and find a place where we could have a house, and be married.

V.J. Day, the final end of the war, came while I was in Sanquhar. We learned of it in the early evening, and I was in my bed. I had had a particularly hard shift, and then had worked overtime for an hour or two. I wanted a bit of sleep before going to bed! There was to be no sleep that night. I was awakened by the banging of doors, shouts, whistles, hammering of dustbin lids and all sorts of row. It was the end of the war, and we celebrated. Drink came out from all kinds of unexpected hiding places, and was pressed into every empty hand. There were impromptu dances and sing songs and parties everywhere. Every house was open and welcoming, and there was hospitality in every one. The boys from the Hostel, together with the women and girls from the staff, gathered in the square, and then marched off to the pub and hammered on the door, demanding that it be opened up, or we would break it down. It was opened, and we settled down to a rare night, one I shall never forget.

The next day, quite early, a number of us decided to organise a bus to take us home for the day. We got it all arranged, and had a good day back in the village with our folks. Somehow it seemed right that we should celebrate with our own families rather than amongst strangers. It was a good day, and our own village was bursting with impromptu parties and celebrations. When the time came to get the bus back to Sanquhar, naturally some of the men were missing, but they were soon found, in the nearest pub, and we set off back to where we were staying, to the pit, and to work.

I was even more unsettled than before, having spent a day with May. She had not much cared for Sanquhar when she had visited, and, I reminded myself, that had been in the summer, when the village was at its best. The long months of winter were a different thing. Even if by some chance I got a house, May would not be happy. That was a consideration that weighed heavy with me.

For some of the time in the pit I was employed oncost, which I did not like, because the wages were poor, and, besides, I did not feel it right that a skilled faceman like myself should be employed on casual work of that kind. There was one day I was carrying supplies, girders for the brushers in the Main Road and then props for the facemen. We did the latter job by using the jigger, a conveyor that shook backwards and forwards, so that the coal — or the props — slid down to where they were needed.

There were four of us in the team, and things were going well. We were on the last load before our piece time. My job was putting the props on to the conveyor as Mick threw them at me. The roof was low at that point, and I was kneeling down. I was loading a prop on to the jigger when Mick shouted at me. He had thrown one of the props and had misjudged it. I turned sharply away from the flying prop, but I was too late. It caught me on the hand, and crushed my fingers against the jigger. There was a stab of pain, but not too bad, and I looked at my left hand. Two of the fingers were badly mangled, and the palm lacerated. Fortunately, it was still numb, and I was able to call for Mick, and able also to curse him for his carelessness. He was very concerned and sympathetic, of course, and together we did what we could to staunch the blood. It was flowing fast, so I tied a piece of string tight round my arm above the elbow, washed the hand with water from my bottle, and took a good swig at the same time, because the pain was coming now, and I was feeling it. We bandaged the hand as best we could, and in a moment blood was seeping through the clean dressing.

Obviously I had to get skilled attention, so I set off down the face, prepared to go up the pit. The fireman met me, breathless with his exertions as he hurried up the face. He had heard about the accident, and insisted that he must dress the hand properly. I protested that we had just put the bandage on, but he insisted on taking it off and dressing the wounds himself. By that time I was in no condition to argue, so let him unwind the bandage, which was already well soaked with blood. He told me to turn my head away, and listlessly I did so. Why not? He was the fireman, and a First Aider! Then I thought that he must have pushed my arm into a fire for some reason. Agonising pains shot up from the injured hand and racked my body and exploded in my head. The stupid bastard had poured iodine all over the wounds. He got a right cursing and I think I would probably have floored him if only I could have stood up. But I couldn't, and he wound another clean bandage round my hand. He told me that I had a bad wound there (as though I didn't know that for myself) and encouragingly said that I might lose at least one finger. I could have done without that sort of encouragement, and rather despondently I set off up the road to go out of the pit.

My confidence that I could get up the mine unaided was really a bit of bravado, and I was feeling very weak and shaky as I went my way up the incline. I was going out of a drift entrance, not up a shaft, so I had to walk all the way. Halfway along the Main Road, the haulage rope began to move, and I heard the distant rattle of a rake of hutches. I realised that no-one had told the surface that I was on my way out of the pit, and that I had to find a manhole, and find it quickly, to escape from the rake. Fortunately there was a manhole not too far away, and I crouched in it while the rake of empty hutches thundered past a few inches away, and then stayed crouched while the full hutches followed a few minutes later. I spent the time cursing the fireman, who had not informed the surface that I was on my way out, but then I realised that I should have shown a bit of initiative myself, and informed the surface of my movements. I waited there till the haulage rope was still, and then twice signalled the surface with the signal wires. Only then did I resume what seemed to be an endless climb up a steep hill to where, finally, I could see the little disc of daylight that indicated the surface.

I must have been losing quite a lot of blood still, because certainly I was growing weaker by the minute, and I was more than happy when two of the surfacemen came hurrying down to meet me and help me along for the few final yards. They had just been warned to expect me, and were very angry about the lack of communication and the confusion that had allowed an injured man to be walking alone up the main haulage road when rakes were running. At the surface, they sat me down and gave me a mug of sweet tea, the best they could offer. There was no transport available, no First Aid Room, no skilled attention of any sort.

The fireman's iodine had certainly not stopped the bleeding. The new bandage was soaked with blood, and dripping with it. Clearly I had to have proper treatment, and, what is more, the fireman's pessimistic statement that I would probably lose at least one finger was in my mind. It had to be a doctor. One of the surfacemen helped me out to the pit gate, and I leaned up against a gate-post, holding my injured arm up against the opposite shoulder, with blood dripping from the elbow of my jacket. I had been sick and weak earlier, but I was a lot sicker and weaker by this time. And there was no bus, although one was due shortly. I tried thumbing a lift, but no-one would stop for that man, filthy from the pit, and with his arm dripping blood from a blood-soaked bandage.

Eventually, a lorry driver did stop for me, a man who could not have been kinder or more helpful. He assisted me up into the cab, and then went well out of his way to find a doctor in his surgery. The waiting room was full, and I had to stand by the door, still with blood dripping to the floor, and feeling both weak and sorry for myself. Patients went through the door into the doctor's consulting room, but it seemed that my turn would never come. At last, one old lady, who had been watching me closely, insisted that I take her turn, and I was glad to do it.

The doctor, a gentle, gray-haired man, stripped off the soiled bandages and carefully cleaned the wounds before dressing them again in wrappings that made my hand look like a boxing glove. Not only that, but he made a sling out of a large triangular bandage, and put my arm into it. He expressed concern at the wounds, and said that I would certainly not be working for a while. I could not argue about that! He gave me some pills to take, and told me to return the next day to have the dressing changed. I was feeling much better by that time, and indeed was quite jaunty as I went off through the village to see Mary, the wife of my eldest brother. She was sure to have the tea ready, and I was ready for it. Besides, Sanquhar was a small village, and if I did not get there first and reassure her, she was sure to be told by someone else that I had been injured. Mary was almost like a mother to me, and treated me always like a grown son. Her welcome that day was warm and concerned, and, as always, the kettle went on immediately for tea. I refused to eat any of the food she pressed upon me — rationing was about at its worst then — and instead ate my pit piece. No point in wasting it, and I was certainly ready for something to eat by then. But I was always ready for something to eat!

I told Mary that I would be heading for home as soon as I had washed and changed at the Hostel. Already I was thinking of how I would enjoy a few days at home, days with May and my family. Perhaps I could even get our future sorted out. So I went off for the bus, and back to the Hostel in a cheerful frame of mind.

I was greeted by big Doc., who was not working that day. I explained what had happened, and what I was planning to do: first a shower, then some food in the canteen, and then a bus for home. It didn't work out quite like that, though. I stripped and got under the shower, and it felt wonderful, so wonderful that I decided I would have a bath. I filled the bath and slipped in, and that felt even more wonderful. Should I stay in the Hostel until the morning, or should I go home straight away? My thoughts wandered, and I must have dozed off. Big Doc. had not forgotten I was in the bath, though, and he came crashing through the door. 'Hell,' he shouted, 'Are you bathing in red dye?' I looked down. The steaming water was indeed dyed red. The warmth of the water had started the bleeding all over again, and I had lost a second lot of blood. It had been warm and comfortable in the bath, and I was dozing, as my blood trickled out. I suppose it is quite possible that I could have died there in that bath if Doc. had not been concerned about me.

He helped me out of the bath, and then went off to find the nurse while I groggily dried and dressed myself. I wanted bandages from the nurse to replace the soaked ones that the doctor had put on. Doc. was soon back, with the Hostel Watchman. The nurse was not in, but the watchman was himself a qualified First Aider, and he gently took off the old bandages. Then he looked with dismay at the wounds. He thought I should go to the hospital as quickly as possible, because I might well lose a finger. That was what the fireman thought, too, and I was uneasy.

I was more than a little dismayed by his view of the injury. That was two people who had told me I might lose a finger, first the fireman, and now the watchman, both First Aiders. I had to put a brave face on it, but inwardly I was very worried. 'Cum oan, man, tie the bloody bandage! Git oan wi it!' I told him, and he did just that, but reiterated his view that I should go off to the hospital.

Instead I went to the canteen, where Doc. was waiting for me with Ann, one of the helpers there. She had kept a meal ready for me, and she served it herself, on a tray — real V.I.P treatment, that was, and I was properly appreciative. We talked about what I intended to do, and I said that I was set on going home. They could not dissuade me, and so finally it was arranged that I would have a couple of hours sleep, and then go off. Doc. said that he would waken me in good time, so I finished my meal, and went off to bed.

It seemed only a moment later that I was awakened by all sorts of noise, Doc. shaking me, and shouting 'Wake Up! Wake Up!' When I opened my eyes, people were standing round my bed like visitors in a hospital, all looking concerned and worried. 'Whit the hell's wrang wi ye all?' I asked, and sat up. They looked relieved, and some laughed. 'Whit's aal the fuss?' I demanded. I was soon told. Big Nell had come into the dormitory to make the beds up and saw me lying there, with a pure white face. She couldn't see me breathing, and had ran out of the room shouting that I was dead.

I told them that I was far from dead, but that obviously there was no more sleep for me that day, and so I got up. I thought my hand was feeling better, and so I firmly decided that I would not go to the hospital, but instead would do what I wanted to do in the first place, and that was go home, where, of course, May would give me her usual welcome.

It was dinner time in the canteen, so I had yet another meal, and then went off with Doc. and Nick to visit my brother, who would have heard about my injury, and surely would be worried. We had the usual warm welcome from Mary, and chatted happily for an hour or two until Mick began looking at the clock rather too casually and often. We all knew what they meant. It was time for some beer. Jim would not join us, but the rest of us went off to the pub. It was there that we would meet all our mates, talk and laugh and perhaps sing, and converse seriously or lightly about the things that interested us — mostly the pit and conditions there.

It was an old-fashioned pub even for those days, with sawdust on the floor, and a high bar at one end of the long room. There were a few tables, and we took one of those to have a game of dominoes. I was really feeling very much better by that time, and greatly enjoyed the few pints of beer, the games and the crack. At closing time we went off quite happily to walk the two miles back to the Hostel and our beds.

I asked the night watchman to give me an early morning call, so that I could catch the first bus home, and packed my case. The watchman, an old miner himself, had every sympathy with me as I struggled one-handed. He helped, and like so many others, told me I should get out of the pits. He had been badly injured, and had decided that was enough. Although my injury was not really all that bad, he urged me to use it as an excuse to quit the industry. I listened, but I had heard that song many times, and really it had little effect on me.

Doc. and the others were still in their beds when I left the Hostel the following morning. I rather think they were nursing their heids, but I was feeling bright enough as I had breakfast and then went off for the bus and the three hour journey home.

My mother met me at the top of the stairs, and her worried look told all. She enquired anxiously about my arm, and jokingly I told her that I had been biting my nails again. She was not to be put off by jokes, though. She was the wife and the mother of pitmen, and was accustomed to dealing with their injuries, although she could never be hardened to them. So I told her, seriously, that I had two burst fingers, that they had been properly dressed, and that I would probably be home for a day or two. That took care of her worries about my injury, but there was something else troubling her. There was a visitor wanting to see me, some sort of official from Edinburgh. He was there, a tall, vaguely military-looking man, waiting in the kitchen. 'Are you Bob Smith?' he asked me. I dropped my case on the floor, already feeling irritated at this intrusion into my mother's home. 'Ye ken bluddy fine that's ma name, an whit aboot it?' I replied. The battle lines were being drawn immediately, and we had not been together for ten seconds.

'It's about your absenteeism,' he said, as he pulled a sheaf of papers out of his bag. Absenteeism was not being at work without having some reasonable excuse for being absent. During the war years, and especially in a Reserved Occupation like mining, absenteeism was more than just a dirty word: it was a criminal offence. 'You worked at Burghlea and lived at the Hostel?' I answered "yes" to both questions, and he went on to say that his papers related to a large number of days when I was off work with no reasonable excuse. His tone was sharp, and I was fast getting irritated. I demanded to know what he was basing his accusation on, an accusation I knew must be false, because my record of work was almost perfect. He read out a series of dates when he said I was absent. I began to smile, and then laughed at him, which did not please. Clearly, he was not used to having anyone challenge him. Like so many others with a little brief authority he enjoyed exercising it, and hated to see it treated with contempt. But he was going to get nothing but contempt from me. As it happened, I could show beyond a shadow of doubt that I had worked on the dates he was quoting. Indeed, I could do it right there and then, and did so, by producing my pay slips. I had the habit of keeping them, and they were all there at home, in a drawer of the bedroom.

That was the end of his arrogance, of course, and after he had checked the payslips against his list of alleged absenteeism, he acknowledged that mistakes had been made somewhere. I could not resist having a final little dig at him, of course, and warned him that he had better be very careful if he was going to go around accusing miners of absenteeism. There was very little of it in the pits, and if he falsely accused a miner who had a less calm and equitable temperament than me, he might be in trouble! Anyway, my mother offered him a cup of tea, and we sat down together over tea and a scone, and I found him to be actually quite a decent and interesting man who had a rather difficult and unpleasant job.

He left shortly afterwards, and my Mother said that she had been very annoyed when that man turned up on her doorstep. At first she thought that something had happened to one of her men, and had been very concerned. I told her to stop worrying and gave her a cuddle, rejoicing that I would be home for a day or two. I said that I had just burst a couple of fingers, and so had to run home to ma Maw. We laughed about it, and were still joking away when Pop came home. He, too, was concerned when he saw me, but I told him that I had just put my hand where it should not have been, and this was the result. I told my parents I was needing a holiday anyway, and this was all very convenient.

However, all my family, and May, insisted that I must go to the hospital in Glasgow the next day, and there was no way I could refuse. May offered to go with me, so that was some sort of recompense. My mother arranged that Arthur, my brother-in-law should also go along in case I needed a strong arm. I objected, but it was no use: when my Mother finally made up her mind there was no moving her, and she had made up her mind about that. Actually, I did not mind too much, because Arthur had just been demobilised from the Army, and we had a lot of news to exchange.

Besides that, he had not yet met May, my lass, and I never tired of showing her off to my family and friends. She was waiting at the bus stance as Arthur and I approached, and I pointed her out. Arthur whistled softly in appreciation, and told me, what I already knew, that I could pick them, and that May was a smasher. He thought she was very young, though, and that I should have waited till the mark of the school bag was off her back. I laughed, and told him that May was eighteen, and that we were going to be married. 'Well,' he said, 'She looks like a bonny lass still in school.' And so she did, and I was proud to be with her.

I introduced Arthur to May, and we chatted away happily on the bus into Glasgow. Now that I had Arthur with me, May decided that instead of going to the hospital with me, she would visit friends, and we would meet later in the day. I was really glad about that, because I did not want May to be around when my hand was being treated.

The out-patients waiting room was full, and it was almost two hours before my name was called. That was a miserable two hours, and I felt something of a cheat when I looked around and saw all the lame and injured waiting their turns. There were broken arms and legs, damaged skulls, ribs strapped up, and more than one foot was missing. And I was going to take up the time of the doctors and nurses with a simple little damaged hand. Still, two first aid men had strongly advised me to come to the hospital, and had warned me that there was a danger of losing a finger, so perhaps my visit was justified.

The nurse who finally attended to me seemed to think so. She was gentle and kindly as she unwound the bandages, and cleaned off the hand in warm water. The doctor came across and examined it, and then spoke quietly to the nurse. She looked at me for a moment, I thought with sympathy, and then told me to turn my head because I would not want to see what she was doing. In fact I knew what she was going to do, and I was ready for it, so I told her to go ahead. 'Don't go under the table, then,' she said, and tweaked the blackened nail off the forefinger with a pair of tweezers. I did not go under the table, but I wouldn't have minded doing so if that would have eased the pain that shot through my arm and jolted up my head. The lassie wiped off the nail-bed with cotton wool and looked at me again. 'Are you ready for some more?' she asked. I nodded, because I could not trust myself to speak, and deftly she took the nail off the next finger.

The first time was bad: the second was hellish. I am sure that young nurse knew how painful it was, and she was quick with the sympathy and encouragement. There were no other nails to be taken off, and she assured me that the wounds should heal cleanly and be less painful now that the pressure under the damaged nails had been released. Quickly and efficiently she dressed the hand and told me that I must go to my own doctor for fresh dressings. I thanked her, and she said that she wished all her patients were as co-operative as I had been. She had seen many a man slip under the table when his nails had been removed, but I had watched quietly. It certainly was not any particular sort of courage on my part, but a kind of bravado, a determination that I would face up to whatever happened. I realise now that it was exactly the same sort of behaviour that dominated all my activities in the pit, both working and dealing with management.

My arm was throbbing with pain when I met Arthur in the waiting room, and my stomach queasy. However, that was not enough to prevent us from going off immediately and having a meal together. At that time, both of us were always ready to eat. As we sat in the cafe, I asked Arthur about his time in the Army. This was really the first opportunity we had had to talk since he had been demobilised, but he was reluctant to speak about those years, and kept deflecting the conversation to what May and I were hoping to do. I explained that we hoped to get married, but that first we must save some money, and find a place that did not look out on to pit bings. Sanquhar was alright in its way, but could be dreary in the winter time. It was not where I wanted to start my married life.

That injured hand kept me home for a week or two, and it was not fully healed when I went back to Sanquhar ready to start work. I had enjoyed the weeks at home, especially the time May and I had spent together, but I had to get back to work and earn some money.

When I arrived in Sanquhar on a Sunday evening after a long bus journey, I went straight off to visit Jim and Mary. They were delighted to see me, and the tea was on the table immediately. Jim told me that the Hostel was to close, but that I could certainly stay with them. That was a kind thought, but really it only re-inforced what I had determined to do. And that was to leave that pit and seek a job somewhere else, probably nearer home.

I found the Hostel half empty, with several of my friends already moved away, and that, too, strengthened my resolve to seek another job. The war-time regulations were still in effect, though, and I had to go through the usual rigmarole of interviews and bits of signed paper. To get one particular signature I had to go to Dumfries and be interviewed by some official there. This was a woman, and she was very awkward and off-hand. At one point she actually threatened to have me prosecuted for not being at work, in spite of the fact that the doctor had not yet signed me off as being fit. Altogether, that was a frustrating few weeks before eventually my permission for transfer came through, and I began looking for work in the Shotts district.

I already knew one pit manager there, and went to see him, but unfortunately he was just in the process of moving to a pit in England. He asked me to go with him, and promised a good job, particularly if I would agree to study for my qualifications, and for a little while I was tempted by that offer, and talked it over with my family. They were not happy at the prospect of me going off again, and neither was May, so eventually I decided that really it was not for me, and looked for a job at Shotts.

I had heard that facemen were wanted at two pits in the Shotts district, so went over to look at the prospects. It was a sixteen mile road journey from the village to Shotts, and when I left the bus and started walking up the pit road it seemed that I was right out in the moors, the countryside was so bleak. There were two pits close by each other, and at the first I found that the Manager was underground, so I sauntered over to the other and talked to some of the men there. They told me that there was a lot of trouble with water in that pit at present, and the men were being paid only sixpence or a shilling per day wet money. That did not sound very promising to me, so I determined to get a start at the other pit if I could. There was no point in working in atrocious conditions if they could be avoided.

At the first pit I was in time to catch the Manager coming up for his breakfast. I asked for work, and he looked me up and down. He told me that I did not look like a miner, and enquired what I could do in a pit. I told him acidly enough that I was a stripper, and had stripped coal from eighteen inches to seven and a half feet. Moreover, I could turn my hand to any job in the pit. He laughed, and took me off to his office, where a blazing coal fire was a welcome sight on that cold day. In the office, the manager, Mr. Stewart, enquired closely about all my experience, and then said he could start me on the Monday as a faceman. That was alright, and that was his part of the interview. Then it was my turn, and I enquired closely about conditions and payments and ton rates. I was satisfied enough with the answers, and the manager told me that if I could strip coal as well as I could talk we would get on well.

I signed the necessary papers, and so was taken on at Shotts, to work the Millcoal seam. There were no baths at the pits and so I would have travel dirty in the special buses back to the village every day, and bath in the old tin tub in front of the fire. In a way, this new Step in the Dark was a step backward to my very first days in the pit.

SHOTTS
THE FIFTH STEP

It was my bad luck that on the day I was to start work the bus broke down and I was a late start. As it happened, there was nobody else off that bus working at the same pit as me, and when I got to the pithead, burdened with all my graith, I found the pit working and the cages busy with hutches. I told the onsetter that I was starting work, and he replied that they were winding coal, and I would have to wait. The Undermanager was due up shortly, and he would give instructions about getting me down. That was alright with me, and I strolled around for a few minutes, and then went back to the cage.

It was a bitterly cold day, and a brazier blazed near the shaft mouth in an effort, quite unavailing, to keep the cage and shaftmouth clear of ice. I told the onsetter I thought the cage looked like an ice cube, and he laughed and said he had seen it worse. He slapped his cold hands across his shoulders to try to get some warmth back into them after pulling a hutch out of the cage. He thought he had a good job in the summer time, but a bloody cold one at times like this. I had to agree about that.

Eventually the jangling of bells indicated "Man Riding", and then the Undermanager stepped out of the cage. He was a big chap, and he seemed a bit gruff and bad tempered as he demanded the count of hutches up the shaft that day from the onsetter. He looked down at me as I stepped up to him and explained that I was a new start. 'Aye, I heard you were starting,' he said, 'But you're too late. Your place is filled.'

This was not a good way to begin a new job, but he could not be allowed to get away with that. 'Steady on ' I told him, 'The bus broke down, and it is not my fault I'm late.' 'There's nae work for you this morning,' he snapped back at me.

I had not even started work, and here I was engaged in a dispute already! I hoped it would not continue that way. Still, it had to be done. 'Well,' I told him, 'If there's nae work for me, you'll pay me a shift, a Bevin shift.' I was referring to a war-time regulation introduced to the mines by Ernest Bevin when he was Minister of Labour. Bevin was a Labour Party stalwart and the leader of one of the biggest trades unions. Churchill took him into the war-time coalition government, where his undoubted skill at organisation proved a boon. Later, he became Foreign Secretary in the Labour Government of 1945, and made his mark in that position too, although not everyone, by any means, would agree that his mark there was to his credit, or the credit of his party and country. Anyway, he introduced various new regulations into British industry, and one of them was that a man must be paid for his shift if he turned up for work and no work was available. That was what we called a Bevin shift.

So that was what I was demanding from the Undermanager, and he was wrathful. I reiterated that I was claiming a Bevin, or else he could find me work at my full rate. 'Huh,' he snorted at me, 'You're a smart wee bugger. Alright, you can work the day advancing the tip of the bing,' and told me to find Big Tam in the yard, and he would set me on.

Big Tam was sitting on the bench by the onsetter, and it was easy to see how he had come by his name. He was a really big man, and I learned later had been badly injured in the pit, and had for some years now been employed on the surface. He greeted me kindly, and told me to sit down for a while until it grew light, because we could not work on the bing in the dark. Gradually the day dawned, a winter's day, and a cold one with a red sun in the east and all the rest of the world cold and black and white. Big Tam and I went off to the bing, carrying his tools, and climbed up to the top. It was not a very high bing, but it left me breathless, and when I got to the top, I was glad to sit for a while and admire the view. Tam pointed out various places, including the Forth Rail Bridge in the distance.

The sun had risen to a blaze of glory that I have never forgotten since that day. There was the most remarkable variety of colours in the sky, reds, yellows and blues combining to make lovely patterns. I constructed a great tropical scene of islands and blue seas out of that sky, with glorious beaches and surf breaking. I was running along that beach with May, which really was quite remarkable, for the nearest either of us had been to a tropical beach was in the shilling seats at the local cinema. One day, perhaps, I told myself — then turned to the job in hand.

Our job was to advance the rails on which the hutches ran to be tipped. I stooped to pick up the first rail, and gasped with surprise and pain as the frozen metal stuck to my hands. Gently I disengaged them — to have pulled away sharply would have torn the skin off my hands. Big Tam saw my predicament, and fished an old pair of woollen gloves out of his bag. I was dressed and equipped for working underground, not on that frozen Siberia of a pit bing. Still, we worked away, with me mostly man-handling the rails into place and Tam bolting them down. Soon enough, it was piece time, and we went off down to the bing to the pithead, where I was glad to see several more braziers clustered round the shaft.

I stood and thawed out at one of them, and was still there when the Gaffer (the Undermanager) came by. He laughed as he asked if I was getting thawed out, and this irked me, because it was obvious what I was doing, and why I was doing it. I simply did not have the clothes for working in such an exposed position. So I told him that I would not work again up there: this was my first and last shift. He said I would be at the face tomorrow, if my bus was on time, and laughed again. So I told him that if that did happen, and this was the only work for me, then it was Home Go.

There was a little gang of us sitting around one of the braziers, enjoying its warmth and having our piece and a smoke. Tam told me a good deal about the pit and its practices. There were two sections underground, the Main Coal and the Mill Coal. In the Mill Coal the flat rate for facemen was one pound and two pence, and twenty one shillings in the Main Coal. Hand drawers were paid seventeen shillings and sixpence, and eighteen shillings, but men on the face earned a bit more, being paid by the ton, and then they themselves paid the hand drawer his wage. I was surprised at this, and said that I thought it unfair. Hand drawing is a hard and heavy job, and should be paid equal to a facemen. I had done the work in the Bothwell Castle, where the facemen drew their own hutches, and knew it to be heavy graft.

Piece time finished, and we went back up the bing. The glory of the dawn had gone, and it was just a bitterly cold winter day, with nothing moving or growing, not an animal or bird in sight. It was a desolation, and I thought of the summer, when the moor would be alive and a blaze of colour. But that was not getting the job done. We continued laying rails, and soon enough it was finished. Tam looked at the job with satisfaction. ‘A guid job, weel done, an cheap at the price!’ he laughed, and went off to tell the Foreman that they could now start to tip the rubble that lay waiting in the hoppers. I spent the rest of the shift around the yard in various odd jobs, but I was glad when it was time to pack up and go home.

The next day was just as cold again, and braziers were still blazing round the shaft mouth. Men were waiting there for the cage, and I joined them, picking up my graith from where I had left it the previous day. The cage, when it came time for winding us down, was ice-bound, and I was glad to hand over some of my graith to my mates so that I was able to hold the safety bar tight. It was a small cage, and the shaft was not particularly deep, but the trip was far from reassuring, with lots of ice breaking off the shaft and falling down on top of us.

There were even icicles hanging from the roof of the cage, and the floor was several inches thick in ice. The usual noises of the shaft were hidden by the crunching of ice, and altogether I was not the only one to be glad to reach the pit bottom and walk along to the Fireman's Meeting point. I was met there by Tony, who was to be my neighbour, and the two of us, with Wullie and Sharp, our drawer, went off to our places. I was glad of their help in carrying my graith, for it was a long twenty minutes walk, and then a low roadway before reaching the face. I was sweating heavily from the trip, and found myself thinking that I would not have minded being back on the bing! But I was a faceman, and I looked with interest at the Mill Coal. I did not much care for what I saw.

The seam was about fifteen inches thick, with a rib of "tumfy" or soft stone on top of it, and then the real stone roof. I could just stand upright at the roadhead, and a taller man then me would have had to stoop. I examined the roof, and immediately saw a bad stone there. It looked dangerous, and I took my pick and levered it out. There was a loud crash as it hit the ground, and Tony hurried back in to the place from where he had been outbye stripping for his shift. He was worried until he saw what had happened, and then I think he was relieved to have had a practical demonstration that I knew what I was doing in the pit.

I stripped off too, leaving just a thin singlet. Already I was sweating heavily from the effort of getting in to the place, and the air was not very good. Soon it would be thick and heavy with reek from the shots we would have to fire to break up the coal. Tony, quite fairly, allocated me to the "leich" side, where I had to turn the coal uphill, and soon I was into the swing of the work. We had to secure the roof as the coal was stripped away, and also had to dispose of the tumfy. This varied in thickness from four to six inches, and had to be broken up and shovelled back into the cundy or waste. That was the space where the previous shift had cut their coal as we advanced the face. We were paid an allowance for that work with the tumfy, so much per inch thickness. This was what we called a "deficiency payment", and we had to negotiate and haggle about it with the fireman, who noted your rate in his report.

My first shift ended, and Tony looked at the results with satisfaction. He said that was the first time that side had been stripped properly, and that the brushers would not be pleased. They were the men who worked behind the strippers, making the roof safe and generally cleaning up. They had been having a good perk for themselves by loading any loose coal that the stripper had left. Well, it would be a gae strange thing if any brusher got paid for coal I had stripped! I left them nothing.

May and I decided that we would wait no longer, and we got married. We had both scrimped and saved as much as possible, and we had money to set us up in life. Together we had the sum of £39:00! It was a struggle then, and it continued to be a struggle for many a year afterwards.

At first we lived in a rented room in Whitshill, paying more for that room than the occupier of the house paid for the whole dwelling. We searched every day for a house of our own, and after several months of that, my mother stopped our work bus one day, and told me to go as quickly as possible to a factor in Cambuslang who had the letting of a vacant dwelling in the building beside our family house. I went off as soon as I had bathed, and got the flat.

We did not have a lot to put into it. We had bought a table and four chairs — wartime Utility Pattern — and our parents had given us a bed and two fireside chairs and a sideboard. There was a rag rug from my mother, and a small carpet from May's mother. My sister and brother had given us a hand wringer, pots and pans and dishes. Cutlery we had bought at a sale. Neighbours gave us all kinds of necessary small things — like Mrs. Simpson, an old lady I used to tease when I was a small boy, and who used to chase me. She gave us a clothes rope, a basket and two dozen clothes pegs.

So we set up our own home, and soon knew there was to be a third member of our family. We had not much wealth and few possessions, but we had a warmth and a deep contentment that made every day a delight.

I had been working only a few days in Shotts before I was given my own place. My drawer was a lad called Wattie Short, a strong young chap, and a good worker. He was a year or two younger than me, and we made a good team, helping each other whenever we could. We were partners for quite some time, and never lost a shift. Or, at least we never lost a shift except for the day when the bus caught fire.

I had a bus journey of about twenty miles each day. The buses were far from reliable, being the oldest and scruffiest on the road. One winter's day the bus did not even stop to let me aboard, but just slowed down, and then stuttered off up the road with me struggling through the door. The driver told me he had had trouble getting it started that morning and did not dare risk stopping again. I went to my usual seat at the back, but soon complained about a strong smell there. Tom, the driver, told me it would be paraffin from the heater that had been there all night, but it did not smell like paraffin to me. Gradually the bus filled up, and we went off up the lonely frost-bound road. Gradually the smell grew stronger. Eventually it was unmistakeable. It was smoke, and the bus was on fire.

It seemed like only an instant before smoke and thick reek filled the bus, and we were coughing and spluttering. Men jumped out of the door, and I struggled with the emergency door at the rear until finally it flew open and I jumped clear. Not everybody got out, though, and we had to go back inside and drag out some of the men who had been overcome by the smoke. We were all badly affected, and vomited and retched for quite some time after vacating the bus.

Then there was the question of what to do. Some men were for walking the miles in to work. Others wanted to wait for a replacement bus. I was decided, though. It was home go for me. I certainly did not feel in any condition to face a shift that day. As I waited for a bus going back towards home, a number of other men joined me, and we discussed what we could do about the time lost. It was the money we were worried about.

We felt that we were due payment for the lost shift, and for any time we might be off in the future as a result of the bus fire. However, we did not know who we should claim against. If it was the pit, then we could handle it ourselves, but if it was the bus company, then we needed help. Finally, it was decided that we should consult a lawyer about the problem, and that is what we did.

It was months later before we got a final settlement, but when we did it was reasonably satisfactory. On production of a doctor's certificate that we were unable to work because of effects from the bus fire, we were paid £5 each for each lost shift. From that amount, the lawyer deducted half a crown in the pound (twelve and a half percent) for his fee, a deduction which I felt exorbitant. Still, we came out of it not too badly, even if I would rather have been able to deal with the whole case in the usual way we dealt with pit problems.

And that was the only shift I lost in that pit.

Mind you, there was many a day when I wished I could find an excuse for not going down. There was no pleasure about the work, no exercise of skill and craftsmanship. It was just a long daily slog in atrocious conditions, and the only reason for doing it was the money at the end of the week. And the money was needed. Not only was there May, but now there was also Janet, our wean.

I was working an end road, and it was wet. It was so wet that the roadway was flooded at times, and water dripped and poured constantly from the roof. The coal gum left by the machine cutter was slodgy and difficult to move. The seam was only about fourteen inches high, and I was lying on my side shovelling away under that height for most of my shift. In those conditions of constant wetness your hands and body grew soft, and cut easily, so that you were constantly treating fresh wounds and injuries. It was winter again, and I had a long journey home in unheated buses. There were times when my moleskin trousers actually froze solid during that bus journey, and I could stand them upright by the fire when I got home. There were no baths at that pit, so I had to bath every day in an old wooden bine (tub) on the hearth rug. Even with the joy and comfort that May and Janet brought to the house, it was a miserable existence, and I had had enough.

Conditions in that place were so bad that I was being paid three shillings per day water money. Even so, that was hardly enough to make up for the misery and hardship in involved. One day all my frustrations exploded.

The fireman came along to assess the deficiency payments, and told me he was cutting my water money from three shillings to one shilling and sixpence. We argued back and forth for a few minutes, then he closed his book with an air of finality, and told me that was all he was paying, and I could stuff it up my arse. 'Well, if that's all you're paying, I'll share it with you,' I shouted, and showered him with shovelfuls of dirty water. 'You can stuff that up your arse! I wouldn't work for that in these conditions. Do it yourself. I'm for home go!'

Wattie, my drawer, agreed with me, and said he was going too. We would see the Manager. So we went up the pit, only to find that word of the fracas had gone ahead, and that the Manager wanted to see us.

We found him in his office, warm and comfortable, with a big fire blazing at his back. It was a far cry from the conditions we had just left, a fact I was not slow to point out. He listened quietly enough to our complaint, just now and again telling me to calm down. I told him about the conditions of work and the water, and of how I had a long journey home and my trousers had actually frozen during that journey. He was sympathetic, and after thinking about the problem for a moment, said that he would restore the three shillings per day water money, and that he would make up our money for the time lost that day. Furthermore, he suggested that I should bring some extra pit clothes with me, and change in his office each day, and dry my wet clothes before his fire. He was fair enough, and the only other thing I asked was that he get that fireman off my back. He laughed about that, and said that the fireman was in charge, and would remain in charge. However, we noticed that after that the fireman left us alone, and we always got the highest possible deficiency payments.

After some time, the water in my place dried up, and working was a lot more comfortable. However, since a pit is always a pit, and coal seams are always unpredictible, there was more trouble just ahead.

We ran into a hitch. That was what we called a geological fault where the seam almost disappeared. There was only two or three inches of coal visible above the floor, and the rest was buried. This made for miserable working, although we knew it was only temporary, because we could see the seam further along, and it was normal height. I was working in just a few inches of height, crawling along like a worm on my stomach, cutting props only about six inches high, and trying to shovel coal along. You had to handle the coal several times, because there was no room to swing a shovel, and you could just drag it along till it was level with you, then crawl ahead and repeat the process until finally you were at the roadhead and could fill your hutch.

My personal miseries at that time were compounded by an eye injury which meant I had to wear an eye-patch. Another man was put on to help us over that hitch, but even so there was no way we could make a decent wage, and we were on deficiency payments. This was particularly hard for me, because I always had the practice of paying my drawer the same wage as I drew myself. As facemen, we were responsible for paying the wages of the drawer, and most facemen paid them a good deal less than their own wages. I never considered that fair, because the drawer worked very hard, and he could make the faceman's work a lot easier if he chose to. He was doing a man's work in a team of two, and to my mind was worth as much as his partner. Anyway, I always paid my drawer the same as I paid myself, and always insisted that our arrangment be kept secret from the others. When I was on deficiency payment, then my drawer suffered also.

At that time, the Flat Rate was one pound and two pence in our section, and the drawers, most of them, were paid seventeen shillings and sixpence, or maybe eighteen shillings. It was certainly not a lot for more than eight hours a day of hard labour in bad conditions.

I particularly hated wet work because it always meant a lot more hard work for May. So when water started to come into the place again, I was very fed up. First the hitch, and then the water. Wet clothes again, a freezing journey, and then extra hard work for my wife. May had to wash all my pit clothes each day, and arrange for a spare dry set to be ready every morning.

It was late afternoon when I arrived home from the pit, and my first job was to wash in front of the fire, in water heated by May on the gas stove. Then she took all my dirty, frozen clothes downstairs to the outside wash house. If she was lucky, she could get them washed right away, but often enough the other women were not finished their washing, and May had to wait. She worked in that cold wet wash house by the light of my pit carbide lamp, and then carried the clean clothes back up the stair and spread them on boards in front of the fire, where they would steam away and dry ready for the day after the morning. I needed three sets of clothes: one dirty, one clean but wet, and one clean and dry. It was hard work for May, a slip of a girl still, even though she was the mother of our daughter. She was not used to such labours, but she never complained, and I was very proud of her.

Quite unwittingly, I was the cause of a strike at the pit. The men were gathered in a meeting when I got into the yard one day, and I was called up to the front, and told that I was the cause of the steg, as we called strikes. Someone had learned that I was paying my drawer the same wage as I drew myself, and the facemen were objecting. Naturally, the drawers were not objecting, and instead were seeking to have that arrangement written into the rules.

There was a lot of argument backward and forward, and references to the pit agreements. I stood on the ground that the agreements laid down minimum payments but did not stipulate that they could not be exceeded. Tempers rose, as they always did on such occasions, and there were accusations that I was taking the bread out of the mouths of the facemen. I retorted that on the contrary I was putting bread into the mouths of the drawers, and at that someone took a swing at me. Naturally I swung back, connecting with a large brass belt buckle, and doing my hand no good, but the chairman and half a dozen others separated us before any damage was done.

Finally, I moved that the meeting agree that drawers should receive the same as facemen, wanting to put my own informal arrangement on a proper basis. There were various amendments moved, but when it came to the vote, my motion was carried, because of the unanimous support of the drawers, and even of a few facemen, to my surprise. So that was a little victory, I felt, for justice, although it did my popularity no good, at least for a while.

Another little conflict we settled satisfactorily was over the use of contractors. These were men who contracted with management to do certain jobs, even coal cutting. Having settled a price, they then recruited a gang of men to work for them. Naturally, the lower the wage they paid, the higher the profit for themselves. It was a system I detested, as my father before me had detested it. He used to call contractors "bloodsuckers", and in my view he was right. I would never work for a contractor, but on one occasion I found that I was, without my knowledge.

I was sent to a new place, and found it was being worked by contract. The contractor and I were at each others throats, verbally, immediately, and I made it clear that I was not working for him, but for the pit. We left it at that, and got on with the job.

On payday, my drawer and I found we were paid a shift short, and questioned it with the Undermanager. He explained that for one shift we had been employed by the contractor, and must draw our wages from him. There was no bother about that, and the contractor paid over our envelopes immediately. When I opened mine, I found he had paid me twenty three shillings and ninepence for the shift, which was a good wage. I was puzzled about it, and then I realised that in fact he was trying a bit of gentle bribery. He had paid me over the odds, and I might think that working for a contractor really was not so bad, and I might stop shooting my mouth off about "bloodsuckers" and "leeches battening on the workers".

Well, he was wrong. I checked with the men on his team, and found he had paid them twenty one shillings. So I showed my pay slip around and did everything I could to fan their dis-satisfactions, explaining that if he could pay me that much, then he could pay the rest the same. If he was not doing so, then it just showed how much he was taking off the labour of each man. Eventually, the contractor could find no men to work for him, and that was virtually the end of contract work in that pit.

Conditions in our place were bad and getting worse. Ventilation was sluggish, and the air was often thick with the reek of shotfiring. The roadways were getting longer, and soon that place would have to be closed. Meanwhile, water had broken in again, and we were working wet, with all the misery that entailed for us, and of course for our families.

I lost a couple of shifts because the bus got stuck in snowdrifts and I could not get through. Certainly it was not my fault that the shifts were lost, and I confidently claimed Bevin Shifts, believing that I would be paid under that scheme which allowed payment when a man was prevented from working by no fault of his own. The claim was turned down, though, when I presented it to the Manager, so I called in our Delegate, a senior Union official, who was confident that we would win it. But he was also turned down, and so the last recourse was the Agent.

He was a full-time Union official, whose main job it was to argue disputes with Management. He came over to the pit, and was closeted with the Manager for quite some time. When he came out of the office, he told me the claim had again been turned down, and that was the end of the matter.

I could hardly believe what I was hearing. The claim was a perfectly sound one, and indeed I had myself argued and won similar claims in the past. Now I was being told by the Agent that it had been turned down. Of course, he was right, there was no further court of appeal. I had lost the shifts. I ranted and raved at the Agent, but he kept very cool. I told him I had previously heard nothing but good about him, and yet here he was, losing a perfectly simple case. He looked at me, and said that an Agent's reputation was only as good as his last case. Some he lost: most he won. This one was lost. And it was, finally.

Our place kept on varying, but was never better than bad. The height changed all the time, and the rib of soft stone, or tumfy, above the coal varied too. Most of the time it simply came down on top of you as you worked, and that was uncomfortable, but it did give a bit more height, and we certainly needed that, since the seam was never more than a foot to fourteen inches high. Some weeks we managed to get a decent pay packet out of it, but then there were spells of low wages, and even of no more than the Fall Back Rate, which was the guaranteed minimum. How anyone could live on that Fall Back Rate I never knew, and yet if you were unlucky or had disagreements with management, that was what you would take home each payday.

I got myself a bad scaring one day. The place was wet again, and as soon as I got home May went off to wash my wet and dirty clothes. Meanwhile, I was bathing in the scullery, using the big tub. Janet was playing in the living room. Suddenly my father opened the house door and walked in. He had been in the neighbourhood, and was paying a visit. We shouted greetings through the open door, and then I heard him say to Janet 'Give me that, wee lass.' He came through to the scullery, and he was an angry man. He had found Janet playing with a bundle of three sticks of gelignite, complete with detonator, and with the fuse wrapped round the bundle.

He tore into me, and I had no defence. Janet had found the explosive in the big pocket of my jacket, where I was in the habit of storing it when in the pit. Somehow that shot had been overlooked, and I had carried it all the way home and into my house without noticing that it was there. No harm had been done, as it happened, but only too easily my house and my family, and several others, too, could have been destroyed. It was an example of utter carelessness, and I was determined that such a thing should never happen again. It never did.

Shortly after that incident the section I was working was stopped, and for a time I worked in the Main Coal. It was a big name for a little seam. It was still very low, no more than twenty inches high, but at least it was safer to work because it did not have that rib of soft stone above it, and so the roof was harder and safer. The ventilation was particularly bad, and the air quite putrid with reek from the shotfiring. I began to suffer from headaches from the bad air, and I was not sorry to move to another section, although I was warned that where I was going was a notorious hell-hole. It had earned its reputation, and deserved it.

It was not a regular place, and was only worked when development was taking place elsewhere, and work was needed for the men. The roof was low, and the roadway both long and low. It was so low that the drawer constantly had trouble with his hutches scraping along the sides and roof. The conditions were such that there was no way we could earn a decent wage, and we were earning just a few pence above the fall-back rate. We did get excess water money, and that helped a bit, but it was a foul and dangerous place. The roof was bad and the coal thin. There was a lot of extra work in cutting props to support the roof, and then I had to lie on my side, in three or four inches of water, under an unstable roof, and shovel coal. It was altogether a hellish place, and I determined that I was going to get out. The Manager saw me one day, as I came out of the pit, ready for the long bus ride home, wet and dirty and dog-tired. He looked at me sympathetically, and again offered the use of his office to change and dry my clothes, and assured me that soon my own place would be ready, and I would find it very different. I could not accept his offer, even though it was kindly meant. There was no way I was going to accept favours that were not given to all the men equally.

The time had come to move on, though, and I began the process of getting permission to go to another pit. The wartime regulations still applied, and it took some time before permission was granted. In a way, I was quite sorry to leave Shotts, and the friends and workmates there, but I was quite ready for a change. As always, I was confident that a change would necessarily be for the better. The fact that they had not up to then did not weigh in my calculations.

However, Shotts was not going to give me up quite so easily. The departure had to be marked with blood. We had got our own place back at last, after working in some wet and dreary conditions. The roadway was level, which meant easier work for the drawer, and although the roof was unstable, we should be able to make better money.

For once, my bus was early that first morning, and as we met together on the surface, I was beaming, for there was the prospect of a flying start, and therefore of an early louse. Wullie, my drawer, was happy, because the road was short and level, with plenty of height and width. We should be able to make a decent wage at last. We were at the fireman's meeting point when I discovered that my saw had been left at the pit bottom. I needed it, and so turned back to get it, while Wullie went on, and started to fill the gum. By the time I got back, he had filled most of it, and I could start work right away breaking into the cut coal.

I hadn't been working at it long when the call came that there was to be Mine Firing. That was when a whole series of shots were fired at once, and it meant that the whole face had to be vacated and the men had to take shelter right back in the Main Road. We went back, and gathered there, resting and talking, and listening for the shots. Soon there was the first of the blasts, and then they came in rapid succession, vibrating and echoing down the roadway, shaking loose some stones that fell harmlessly away from where we crouched. Soon there was silence again, and the man next to me said that would be the last. We listened, and there was no sound, so I crawled off along the faceline to my section, and began erecting a prop where I thought the roof looked a bit unsteady. Then smoke began drifting down the face, and I did not like the look of it.

I turned and crawled back into the roadhead, only to be engulfed in a thick cloud of really heavy reek from the blasting. The whole roadway was filled with that white smoke, and it was sweeping along into every cranny, pulled by the ventilation fans. My eyes stung, and I began coughing. I had to get to hell out of that, and quick, so I dropped to my knees and began crawling as fast as I could along the faceline, heading for the roadhead, and what I hoped would be clean air. It seemed that the faceline was endless, and I began to despair of getting out. My eyes were streaming and my lungs felt as though I had been breathing fire, and I was just about at the end of my strength when I heard voices and came out into the roadhead. No-one had realised that I had gone back into the face, and I could well have smothered there without any help coming for me. I had done a very stupid thing, in fact. That was the first firing we had experienced on the new face, and I should have waited in the roadhead until I saw how the ventilation coped with the reek. Instead, I had assumed that the air flow would clear it away quickly. It didn't, and I might have been killed.

I was lucky enough that day, but one man was not. We had just resumed work after the reek had cleared when Wullie came in and told me there had been an accident. We went out immediately to the roadhead, and found several men there, awaiting instructions. An official told us that stretchers and a stretcher party were needed. Big Jim was dead. He had been firing the shots, and had just lit the last fuses when the first ones went off and caught him. They went off on top of him. He was still alive when they got to him, and all he said was to ask whether his neighbour was alright. Then he died, in the arms of his neighbour. Jim had sent him away when he was lighting the last of the fuses, and he was clear when the first round went off. He heard Jim calling, but there was nothing he could do. If he had gone back he would have been killed too.

A stretcher party took up the body of our friend, and went off to the pit bottom. The rest of us went back to the faceline to secure the roof and make everything safe for the rest of the day. The shift was over for us. We were going up the pit with Jim. We were paying him the miners' last mark of respect for a comrade.

We went back to work the next day, but my heart was not in it. I was dissatisfied with conditions in that pit, and with the conditions of my family.

I was young and prepared to work hard. Indeed, I revelled in the physical challenge that pit work represented. And I greatly enjoyed being part of the comradeship of skill and hardship that was the miners' life. But I had to think of May and my daughter. May was a young lass still, and a lovely one, and she had taken up the part of the miner's wife with skill and joy. We men worked hard in the pit, but the wives worked just as hard at home.

May was out of her bed at four o'clock in the morning to make breakfast for me and see me off to work. There was the washing of wet, dirty pit clothes every day. The scraping of mud from pit boots, and the anointing of them with dubbin were daily tasks. Then there was the house to attend to, and the children, and the meals to make. It was a hard life, and I was determined that I would do something to make it easier. That would mean moving from Shotts, and I set about getting the necessary permission.

ALLOA

THE SIXTH STEP

When I had first visited the Alloa area in September 1948, to look at the prospects for work there, I had only stayed two days. The wages and conditions seemed good, much better than we had in Shotts. The seams were higher, and that meant no more crawling about in wet low seams, a prospect which pleased me. What's more, the flat rate of wages was 26 shillings a shift, and that was an increase of five shillings on the rate paid at Shotts — a weekly increase of thirty shillings.

I stayed in the Hostel overnight, and gleaned as much information as I could from the men there. Altogether, it seemed as though the new step in the dark would be a worthwhile one, so I was quite happy as I gathered up my graith, collected the essential Green Card and travel voucher, and set off with high hopes.

Of course, I should have known better, and the high hopes soon evaporated as I travelled, needlessly, for weary hours on the route laid down by the travel voucher. Of course, I should have demanded that the voucher be changed to the direct route, but for once I accepted the stupidity of those in authority without protesting. Consequently, I was weary and angry when I arrived at last at that new Utopia where I was to work. Things were not eased when the receptionist at the Hostel told me there was no room available. I heaped abuse on her head, but of course it wasn't her fault, and soon I had calmed down enough to apologise to her, and get directions to the Coal Board office.

I reached the Board's office just about midday. There was a little window labelled "Receptionist" and "Enquiries". I rapped on it, and seconds later it opened, and a girl's voice asked if I could call back on Monday, because they were busy at the moment. I was already tired from the long, roundabout and unnecessary journey, and annoyed at finding that there was no place reserved for me in the Hostel. So the old temper flared up yet again, and in no uncertain terms I demanded to see the Industrial Relations Officer there and then. The lassie was taken right aback by my obvious anger, and hurried off through a door, returning a few minutes later to say that Mr. Kennedy would see me now.

I went through, and found Mr. Kennedy sitting behind a big desk drinking coffee. He wasn't exactly helpful at first, saying that there was nothing he could do just then, because the Office was closing in a few minutes, so he, too, got a blast. He was told that I hadn't come halfway across the country to be treated like this, and if he didn't get off his arse and do something, I was going straight back to Lanarkshire to report what had happened, and that surely someone's head — his — would fall. Obviously, he had not expected such a reaction, and obviously was not accustomed to it, and he was shaken. He thought about it for a moment, and then asked if I would like to go into private digs. That suited me, so he went off, and returned a few minutes later with an older man, John McEwan, who said he would try to find me digs. John was friendly and sympathetic, and listened to my complaints quietly. He asked me to go up to his house, where his wife would be glad to give me some food. We did that, and while I was eating, I could hear Mary and John whispering in the kitchen. Eventually Mary asked me if I would like to stay there with them. I liked the pair of them, and certainly Mary's cooking was fine, so there was no hesitation in my acceptance of their offer.

Later that evening I went out for the usual Saturday night drink with the pair of them, although, like me, they were certainly not drinkers. Still, a couple of pints on a Saturday, and a good blether with their friends was the routine, and I was glad to join them.

One of the men we met was a machineman in the pit where I would be working, and the other worked in the Glasshouse, which was a factory making bottles. Jimmy Todd, the miner, was able to give me a lot more information about the pit. He told me there had been a serious spate of accidents recently. One man had been killed by a runaway rake and another killed at a nearby pit by falling down the shaft. Several men had also been injured by another runaway rake. I wondered whether I had come to a slaughter house by mistake, but Jimmy assured me that it was not so, and that the area had a good safety record. I told him that was a relief, anyway, but privately determined to be extra careful. I had had more than enough accidents already.

On the following day, Sunday, I prepared for starting work the next day. I cleaned and overhauled my carbide lamp and sharpened my saw, and generally put all my graith into good order. Then I went out walking in the countryside. It was beautiful, but somehow I felt that I had moved back in time. There was plenty of work around for various trades, with the pits, engineering works, the Glasshouse and Breweries, and obviously the area was booming. But some of the housing was really deplorable, with rows of old-fashioned pit houses, still with their open ash-pits (outside toilets) and open drains. Still, I was told, it was all to be changed soon.

Monday morning was fine, but cold, and I was glad to walk briskly over to the pit. I knew I was to be on night shift, but there were things to be arranged. There were no baths at the Meta mine where I was to work, so I had to arrange for a locker at the Devon pit, where the baths were situated. Also, I had to see the Manager, and, amongst other things, make sure that I was on top rate. It seemed that there were two or three different rates paid at the mine for the same job, and that was a system I did not like. Certainly I wanted to be sure I was on top rate: I had no intention of working there for sweeties.

I walked off through the village, again noting that it was very dilapidated, with many blackened and broken windows, and broken chimneys belching smoke from the coal fires that burned night and day in the miners' houses. I was lucky: the house where I was staying was fairly new. It was a couple of miles up a tree-lined road to the pit yard, and when I got there I found it was not just the pit yard, but there was also a coal briquette factory.

The Manager was not immediately available. He was down the pit, but I was assured he would be up shortly for his breakfast, and sure enough, after a short time a tall man in a boiler suit passed me, wished me 'Good Morning', and went into the office. I was told, rather to my surprise, that he was the Manager. I was not used to Managers who looked as though they were doing a day's work, and wore a boiler suit.

I followed him into the office, and found him eating his breakfast, but just the same he was quite happy to talk as he ate. He asked about my experience, and I was able to tell him that I was an allround miner, with experience as stripper, faceman, brusher, mine driver and even machine work, although I stressed that I was really a faceman, and did not want to work machines. We had a long conversation, and then settled on a rate, which satisfied me, although I fancied that if I pressed a bit, a bit more might be forthcoming. That would be for the future. So I went off happily enough to the baths to arrange for a locker, and then strolled back to my lodgings.

I had a few hours sleep before night came, and my first shift. It was a fine night of heavy frost and a full moon, and I was pleased with the sight of the trees as I walked along the road to the pit yard. The fireman in charge was a tall, active man, who greeted me as I approached, and told me to go with two of the men, and wait for him at the mine mouth. We walked along together, and I felt I could get on well with the two of them. We waited for Eck, the fireman, in a shed at the mine mouth, grumbling, as normal, that the previous shift had almost let the brazier fire go out. It was quickly re-lit with a good dash of waste oil, and we each had a cup of tea and a piece of bread while waiting for Eck. When he appeared, we were told off to load a rake with props and straps, and some girders. That was fine, but when I went to lift one end of the steel girders, I felt the skin of my hands stick to the cold metal. The night was so cold that I feared I might lose the skin off my hands. Paddy tossed over an old bit of rag, and I used that to keep my bare hands off the freezing metal.

It really was a cold night, and we were not dressed for working outside. We were underground men, used to working in warmer places than that mine mouth, and we dressed accordingly. However, the work was hard, and we soon had a good sweat on. When the rake was loaded we had another short break and a smoke by the fire, and then set off underground. I had not realised we were going to ride the rake, and I was worried about it, especially since I had so recently been told about the accidents in the area. However, Paddy told me that the engineman knew we would be riding, and that he would be careful. It did not seem to me that he was particularly careful, since the rake hurtled down the slope at a hell of a speed. I was riding the last tub, and held on tight. The others were screaming like banshees, and that, with the noise of the rake rattling over the joints, made for an unnerving journey. 'Heid doon', screamed Paddy at one point, and I ducked, just as a torrent of cold water from the roof descended on us. I hoped the engineman really was in control, and was very glad indeed when the speed lessened and we gradually drew to a halt. Paddy, still exhilarated, asked me how I had enjoyed the ride, and I told him that it had scared the shite out of me. He said I would get used to it, and I told him you could get used to anything but hanging, but that you did not have to like it. He laughed, and we got on with unloading. As Paddy said, the sooner we got started, the sooner we got loused (finished). We all worked together to the end of the shift, on several different jobs, and I felt that this was a good team of skilful men.

It was a stiff climb up a steep slope to the mine mouth, and I was tired at the end of that first shift. I was not used to having to walk out at the end of a shift, and found it irksome. However, it was part of the job, and no doubt I would soon get used to it. At one point, where the water had soaked us as we rode down on the rake, there was the sound of rushing water. Davie went off to the side and brought back a mug of crystal clear water. 'Here, have a drink on me,' he said, handing it over. I took it, and drank it off. It was delicious, icy cold and pure. I refilled the mug and passed it back to him. 'Ye'll have a hauf yerself,' I said, and he laughed, and drank it off. This water rushed down the roadside in a channel made by the mine drivers, then flowed into an inset like an underground pond. It was deep, but the water was so clear that you could see the bottom. It then overflowed, and disappeared into the old mine workings.

Although this was a good team of men, and we worked well together, it was a strange thing that each Thursday night, when we received our pay slips, a different mood came over them. Each would slink off to a corner to study his slip, and no-one would give a direct answer when asked what the rate was. I was not accustomed to such secrecy, and found it strange. For myself, I was receiving a higher rate than when I was at Shotts, and was happy enough with my wages.

It all came out one Thursday. I had worked some overtime, and used a bit of chalk on a steel plate to work out the rate. I had been paid short, and loudly complained about it. Paddy came over and looked at the figures I had chalked. 'You don't get paid all that!' he exclaimed, and his face was a mask of fury. 'I've been here longer than you, and I don't get that much!'

'You get what you fucking deserve!' I snapped back at him. 'You're all that bloody sleekit you don't want your neighbours to know what you're making. Well, here's my wage slip, look at it, study it, then get up there and demand your entitlement. But I'll tell you, I'm going in first, because I'm short!'

We all went off to the office, and I was indeed first in. It did not take long to settle my query, and I was glad I had raised it, because there was an extra ten shillings that I had overlooked — a rare thing indeed for me. The others followed me in, and I hoped that they would stick together on the question of wages. I could hear a lot of shouting and cursing going on in the office, but when they trooped out, I could see by their faces that not everything had gone well. The Manager had given way on some points, but had stood firm on others. Although he was not prepared to pay them the full rate, which I was getting, they had gained quite a bit, and a promise that he would look into it. Another week went by, and the next wage slips showed that the promise to look into it had produced no results. Davie and I were elected to argue the case with the Manager, and the whole matter began to look like a dispute.

At the meeting, we put our case, and the Manager listened. We argued back and forth for some time, but he would not give way, so we stamped out of the office and reported back to the men. We decided to strike, and went back to tell the Manager that his shift was not going down. He was furious, and the argument got very heated, but we were rock-solid. Unless there were concessions, we were going home. Eventually there *were* concessions, and we went off to report to our neighbours. They accepted, and the shift started. There was an increase on the rate, and other minor improvements in conditions. We were satisfied.

Development of the mine was moving fast, and many more men were being started. The first face line was complete, and cutting began there. This was a dangerous period, for it was not unknown for a whole new section to close up, but we seemed to be lucky, and a week went by with no problems. It was too good to last.

The previous shift had reported that the section was on the move, and when we went down for the night shift, we knew that extra care was needed, because for some reason most closes take place around midnight. We were working in pairs now, and I was partnered by Shultz, an old machineman. Our job was mostly repair work, and strengthening the existing timber props. It was a job that was badly needed that night.

Each pair was allocated a stint, an area, to secure. Oncost men supplied us with the timber, and some of the paired men were packing up the roof with stone packs or pillars six or so feet long and four feet wide, with stones that had already fallen from the roof. Others were erecting pillars of special hard timber about three feet long. Others again, like Shultz and I, were putting in props in the dangerous area, trying to prevent the roof from closing. The roof creaked and groaned and gave out loud cracks. It was on the move, ready for its first break. As fast as we cut props and put them in place, they groaned and splintered under the inexorable weight coming on to them. We cut and placed props as fast as we could work, in a lather of sweat, lit only by the flickering carbide lamps. It was a wretched and a savage place, and a dangerous one. As props shattered, we pulled them out and hastily built them up into pillars and thrust new props into place, hardly having to wedge them, for the roof was working so fast under the crush.

There was a rumble nearby as part of the roof collapsed. Calls of 'Are ye alright?' echoed around, and we shouted back our answer. But it was not alright for two men. They had been caught by falling stone. One was cut badly about the head, but was rising shakily to his knees as we reached him. The other had a broken arm, and we helped the two of them out to the safety of the roadway, where Eck treated their wounds and sent them off to the surface.

Still the struggle continued, with props and even pillars giving way and the roof continuing to work. I felt that no-one who had not experienced such a place could possibly understand it. Here we were, far underground, giving of our utmost strength to stop that roof from closing. We could have gone off and left that raped earth to heal its own wounds, but instead we fought on. Far above our heads, men, women and children slept, lovers murmured into each others ears, babies tossed in their cots and young men vomited up the night's beer. In the almost total blackness we sawed and hammered and swore, and feared that we would be the next to get a stone on the head, or worse. In the cundie, the waste where the coal had already been worked out, there was an almost continual noise of falling roof, and where we worked, the squeeze continued.

'Ur ye feared?' Shultz asked me, his face screwed up with tension. 'No,' I replied, although in truth I was very afraid, and so was everyone else. 'Well, ah'me scared,' Shultz said. 'This is enough to scare the shite oot o ye!' And he was right.

Still, we won. The roof was held, although at a cost of blood and broken bodies, and production went on. Each night we had the same battle, and indeed it was a war that seemed to have no end and no victory. How could it? We were fighting against the very nature of the earth itself, and finally could never win.

There was the usual toll of blood to be paid for the coal that came out of that pit. One night it was Chick's turn. He was one of our neighbours, a middle-aged man, and totally bald. He always wore the old-fashioned cloth cap with a metal plate in front to hold his lamp, and he got struck by one of the new-fangled steel props that had just been introduced to the face line. It had sprung out without warning, and caught him right on the head. The roof fell where the prop had failed, and we dragged him clear, with blood streaming down his chest. We poured water from his bottle over the wound, and saw it was long and deep. I always carried some filters from face masks, and after washing out the wound as well as possible (joking as I did so that I baptised him "Chick"), I gently put one of those on the wound, then we helped him out to the roadway, where the fireman could dress it properly, and arrange for him to be taken out of the pit. Chick was not the only casualty, by any means, and in fact, they were all in vain, for, after struggling with that roof for two weeks, it finally closed completely. It was "as tight as a wulkie", as we described it, and we had to start all over again.

It was a dangerous job re-opening that section, but eventually it was done, and as work progressed, gradually the roof became sounder, and the work less dangerous, if not easier.

Now that we were under a better roof, more men were starting at the mine and the teams were re-organised. I was started on back-shift, a shift I did not like. I called it the Old Man's Shift, because there was no chance of a social life at all, although fortunately we could sometimes get an early louse — finish — if we completed our stint in good time.

I was made a team leader, along with Jimmy Gilchrist, who had been a fireman before joining our team, and we had a good run for a few months, with reasonable conditions and a good roof. One day, quite unexpectedly, we broke through into some old workings. These were not shown on any maps of the district, and management knew nothing of them. This was a dangerous thing to happen, because old workings could fill up with gas or water, and unexpectedly breaking into them could, and sometimes did, result in a disaster. But these ones were dry and clear of gas. They presented a challenge I could not ignore, and Jimmy and I set out to explore them when we had finished our stint.

These were workings of a different type, and I think much older, than the others I had been through when I was a laddie working with my father. The air seemed fresh enough, and I wondered if somewhere there was an entry to this old working. The low roof was arched to give a little more working height, and we could still see the marks of picks on the stone roof. That must have been hard and tedious work, and skilled, and one had to admire those old miners, ancestors of ours, who had worked in this pit.

It seemed that ventilation must have been poor in the days when the section was working, because a gauton or trench had been cut along the lower side of the roadway, and this was covered by boards of wood to direct air to the headings. Marks on the roadway seemed to have been made by sledges dragged along, for that was the way coal was moved in those days, with women usually doing the dragging, crawling along on hands and knees, with chains running from their waists to the sledges. Those were truly the bad old days, when men, women and children were bound, serf-like, to the pits and the coal-owners. As we went further along the old road, the air began to get heavy and stagnant. Cobwebs hung from the roof and stuck to our faces as we crawled along, and finally we decided that it would be dangerous to go any further, so we went back, still filled with awe and admiration of those miners of a past age, and reported what we had seen to the fireman. Another man and he then went through, and over the next few days most of the men in the section explored the old workings, always two at a time, for we all knew that it could be dangerous to go alone.

The work we were doing in that section was hard and rough. On each shift we had to build about ten packs in the waste to hold up the roof, and then move the pan conveyors forward into their new position for the next cutting shift. These conveyors moved the cut coal from the strippers at the face down to the main roadway, where it was filled into the hutches. The pans were ten feet long, made of heavy steel channels, bolted together, and resting on rollers. They shuggled backwards and forwards, driven by the pan engine, and the coal slid along, and eventually tipped off the end into the hutches. It was all a lot easier than the old method of hand filling and hauling the hutches, but there was still a great deal of rough and heavy work to be done each shift, moving them forward into their new position. Each one had to be man-handled, and they were awkward.

About this time my family joined me in a new house near Alloa, and that made a tremendous difference to me. I was more content, and even the work seemed to be easier.

The roof had become difficult and dangerous, and a lot of time and timber was used in trying to keep it safe. There was one night when we working rather desperately on the roof when we ran short of timber. It was the task of the on-cost men to keep us supplied, and they had run short. I went out to see what was happening. As I approached the haulage engine, which should have been running and bringing up our timber, but which was idle, I could hear someone talking softly. I thought the engine man must have gone off his head, because there was no-one else around, so I called out to him, before reaching his position. 'Cam on, Geordie, what's up wi the supplies?' He looked round quietly, and I could see him smiling. 'Ye've scared ma wee pal, Whiskers'. 'Whit the hell are ye talkin aboot? Cam on, we need mair wood!'

He smiled again, and called softly: 'Whiskers! Coom on!'. A large rat then appeared from under his seat, jumped up to Geordie's lap, and settled down to be stroked. I had never seen anything like that before, nor have I since, but Geordie and Whiskers were friends for a long time, although I made it quite plain to both of them that their friendship must never again interfere with the supply of the timber we needed.

Although it was routine enough, the work we were doing always had its dangers, and I must say that some of our practices in the pit added to that danger. We did things that enabled us to finish our work, and finish it properly, but which were not really permitted under the Coal

Mines Act. One of these was the firing of what we called coo-coo shots.

We worked in the waste, with just enough packing under the roof to keep it safe. Sometimes we needed more stones than we could find lying around to build a pillar for the roof, and when that happened we would fire a shot in the roof itself to bring down more stone. We were not supposed to do it, but the officials turned a blind eye to the practice, so long as we kept the section working. Those shots were what we called 'Coo-Coos', and I have no idea where the name came from.

One night as we were working in the waste the call went out 'Fire! Fire!', and we knew a shot was imminent. We took shelter behind a pillar, and the shot rang out, and soon the heavy drift of smoke and sulphurous fumes reached us, then was drawn swiftly along the airway by the fans. That was when we should have gone back to work, but this time there had been an accident, and a man was injured. The cry went up, and I leaped onto the conveyor and slid along as fast as I could to where the rocks and fallen stones lay in a vast heap. I was horrified. Were they under that? There were great stone slabs lying in the waste, brought down by the shot. If the men had been caught by that lot, they were dead for sure.

There was no-one under the stones, but Paddy had been caught by the leg, and was lying on a ledge, with a great slab holding him down, and the roof above quite unsupported and dangerous. It could collapse at any moment, and if it did, Paddy and the rescue team would be gone.

We got a lever under the slab, and raised it an inch, then chocked it and got a new purchase with the lever. Again we strained and groaned with the effort, but the slab moved, and Paddy was free. We pulled him loose, and carried him to safety up the roadway. The rest of us scrambled away over the pans, and we were just in time, because a few minutes later the roof closed down over where we had sweated and strained to get Paddy free.

The fireman, Jimmy, examined Paddy, and found his leg was broken and severely lacerated. He was bandaged up, both legs tied together, and carried off on a stretcher, severely shocked, but lucky to be alive. There had been two other similar accidents in the area lately, and each had been fatal. In each case, when the roof was coming in, the men had leaped towards the face for safety, but each had died. Paddy, for some reason, had leaped to the side, and lived.

We were working around an old disused shaft, that used to belong to the Meta Pit, and it created a lot of problems and difficulties for us. The roof was still unsafe and restless, even though we put in steel props set no more than a foot or two apart, but still there were ominous surges and intermittent falls. At the end of one shift the fireman asked for volunteers to lie on (work overtime), but I thought I had had my share of overtime, and so left it to others, and most of us went off to the baths. We were still washing when word came in that the whole section around the shaft had caved in, although fortunately without loss of life or even injury. One of the men who was there, Jimmy Russel, a pan shifter, told me later that the whole place just gave one extra surge, and then black sludge poured into the section, covering everything in it, conveyor, pan engine, everything. He said it was closed end to end, and he couldn't see how anything could be salvaged.

He was right enough, as I saw for myself the next day. An electrician and I were taking out some panel boxes near the old section, and I took the opportunity of examining it. I could hardly believe the destruction I saw. Untold tons of sludge had poured down the shaft, even bringing branches of trees with it. Everything in the section was buried, and the section was indeed closed end to end. That was the finish of it.

Fortunately, a new section was ready to start, and our men were transferred to it, and production was not halted. I was working with a chap called Russel, a hard worker, but very hashy, taking risks where they were unnecessary, and cutting corners on many jobs. This did not suit me at all, because I had always been taught to take safety first. That had been my father's constant cry, and it was a precept I followed always. Now, with Tam Russel I found I was constantly at him for being rash and hashing on, regardless of the risks. There was one night we were building a pillar and I was on my knees behind it, filling the centre of the pack with rubble. We had not reached the roof, so the pillar was giving no support, but just the same Tam began knocking out props. 'Whit the fuck di ye think ye're daein, Tam,' I roared. 'Leave that steel alone or the bloody roof will come in on me!'

Tam continued hammering at the support, and I yelled at him again, more strongly that time. He turned, and for some reason his face was a mask of hate. 'You bastard,' he snarled, 'Don't tell me what to do. Ah'll cut yer fuckin heid aff!' and he came towards me waving his axe. That was his favourite tool, and he was forever sharpening it. I certainly did not want that buried in my head, but I was on my knees in a low place, and there was not a lot I could do. Feeling around behind me as Tam waved his axe above my head, I felt my pick and gratefully dragged it around to the front. At least I was not quite helpless now. Tam still had that strange, almost mask-like look of hatred on his face, and I knew that somehow I had to talk him out of it. But I felt he would not respond to kind words. 'Look, Tam,' I told him, 'You bring that axe near me again and I will bury this pick in your fucking guts. Now put that axe down and keep your head.' He looked at me and there was indecision on his face. There could quite well have been murder done that day, because if he had come at me with his axe, I would certainly have attacked him with the pick, and someone would have died. But fortunately he backed off, his face became normal, and he threw the axe to the floor. I told him that if he had pulled the steel before the back of the pillar was tight, the roof would certainly have come down on me. He looked at the roof and at the pillar, studied the situation, and then said: 'You're right, old son, let's get it packed up.' And we simply got on with the job.

Tam occasionally had those dark moods, but usually we got on pretty well together. I only once saw him really give way to his violence, but fortunately was not on the receiving end. We had finished a job, and were going to send our graith along the conveyor to the next place. Tam slid off down the metal pans, and when he shouted, I began loading the tools on to the conveyor, where they would travel along until Tam picked them off. Suddenly I heard almost maniacal screaming, and realised it was Tam, so I jumped on to the conveyor and skidded along it as fast as I could. A few yards down, there was Tam, axe flashing and thudding as he hacked at something. I felt my heart turn over: had he really attacked someone? What the hell to do now? But it was not a 'someone', but a 'something'. Tam was methodically chopping up a rat, and screaming as he did so that he hated the bastards. I swallowed hard, slid on past him down the conveyor, and went to pick up our graith where it had tumbled off the end of the conveyor.

Tam and I got on famously for some days after that, although I still found myself watching him carefully. He was one of the first to reach me the night I got caught by a fall.

We had finished building one pack and had just started on another. Tam was building the foundation, and I needed a prop to stabilise the corner. There were none lying handy, but I noticed a wooden prop under the roof just on the waste side of a steel strap. That would do the job. I tapped at the roof to test whether it was safe to draw the prop, and it sounded solid, so I gave the prop a light tap with my heavy mash hammer. You had to be careful when withdrawing wooden props because they had a tendency to spring out. That tap was enough. There was a sharp crack and I felt a blow on the head and saw a blinding flash. I was thrown forward to the floor and, although numbed by the blow to the head, immediately realised that I could not move my legs. I was trapped by the steel strap, which had come down, and had let down a large stone. I was half under the pans, with blood trickling down my face, while the strap lay across the pans, holding up the big stone, which otherwise would certainly have crushed me. My leg was pinned beneath the strap.

I heard the shouts of men, and the scrabbling of boot nails on the steel pans as men rushed to help. 'Holy Christ! Is he under that? Is he dead?' I shouted back, feebly, 'No, I'm not dead! Get the bloody thing off me!' They were all good miners, experienced and skillful and strong. They heaved and strained at the strap, using it as a lever to ease up the stone, while others stood by to guide the stone away and drag me clear as soon as the weight came off. They pulled me clear and then below the pans to safety.

I was badly shaken, and glad of the water bottle that someone passed me. My head and shoulders were cut and my elbows bruised. My ankle, where I had been held by the strap, was badly bruised. They washed me off and put dressings on the wounds, but I refused to go out of the pit on a stretcher, as they wanted. I would walk out, but just the same was glad enough to have a helping shoulder to lean on as I went up the mine and into the baths. I was very glad of the pullover that someone gave me, because the shock had left me cold and shivering. The hot water of the showers was a blessing, and Tom Gavin, the bath attendant, a qualified First Aider, dressed the wounds, using a black ointment that he kept specially for such injuries as mine. He joked that he had seen the last of me for a while, but I assured him that I would be at work the next day. He carefully covered his ointment with bandages, and told me to leave them in place for a day or two, otherwise the ointment would stain my clothes, and my wife would have trouble getting them clean. I have no idea what the ointment was, but certainly it soothed the aches of the cuts and bruises.

I caught the bus home, and May received me with her usual love and sympathy. Of course this, my wife and home, was the reason why I had to be at work the next day. I could not afford to be ill. Money was already desperately short. There had been several short stoppages recently, and although we had no debts, certainly there was nothing to spare. It was essential to keep the wages coming in.

However, it was not to be. The next morning May brought my

breakfast to me in bed, a sign that she expected me to stay there. Because she had brought it, I ate it, and then asked her to help me to get up. I was determined to get to the pit, but realised as soon as I got to my feet that it was out of the question. There was no way I could work, or even get to the pit. However, I realised that if I took two days off, and went back on Friday, there was a good chance of weekend work, which would help to fill the financial gap. So that is what I did, and when I went back, my neighbours ensured that I was given an easy job for a few days — tightening up the bolts on the pan conveyor when it was moved — until I was fit enough to go back to full labour. That sort of kindness and consideration was quite normal in the pit: it was no place for selfishness or the attitude of dog eat dog that is so prevalent elsewhere today.

This deeply engrained attitude of co-operation and mutual aid certainly did not apply to Management. They never lost an opportunity of trying to cut wages or rates, or the number of men on a team. We had had several short strikes when rates were threatened, and had managed to keep our wages up to a reasonable level, although we did lose two men off our team, or pool, as we termed it.

There were several such pools working, some with as many as a dozen men in them. Ours worked very well together, with each man helping all the others to finish the job. If a man was off work for some reason, then we took a man from the stott, or spare list to come and work in our team. That system did not apply in some pools. There, if a man was off work, the others would do his job, and split his wage amongst them. I thought this was greatly unfair, because men on the stott only had their fall-back wage, which was very low, and a few days working in a pool made a great difference to them. There was a lot of argument and some ill-will about this question, but our pool continued to take on spare men whenever we could, as an example to the others, and gradually our system began to be accepted throughout the pit, to the delight of the spare men.

I could understand why the men watched their pennies so carefully, and even why they sometimes acted selfishly when the pay packet was involved, but I could never get used to the way Management used every trick they could find to hold back a shilling or two from wages. After all, we were supposed to be working for the NATIONAL Coal Board, but we found that we had to be just as watchful and even ruthless as in the past.

The coal mines had been nationalised in 1947. This was part of the Labour Government's plan to modernise and revitalise British industry, and it was a step that both the Labour Party and the Union had been fighting for for many years — even a Conservative Government Royal Commission back in 1922 had advocated nationalisation as the only remedy for all the ills of coalmining in Britain.

When Vesting Day (Nationalisation Day) came in 1947, all the pits passed into State hands. The proud new blue and gold signboards outside the pits read: *This pit is managed by the National Coal Board on behalf of the nation.* We had all been to meetings and listened to speakers telling us about the new Utopia of nationalisation. We were told there would be a rosy future, wages increased, holidays with pay, improved sickness and injury payments — it all sounded good as we discussed it between ourselves. The more cynical asserted there would be no change. It would be the old team in new jerseys, they said, and they were right.

Former coalowners were paid vast sums for obsolete pits and even for pits already closed. Steel works owned by ex-coalowners were sold coal at far below the cost of production. The National Coal Board became a haven for ex-coalowners and their hangers-on, and for venal Union officials, where high salaries and much power were available, and little work done.

This was not the nationalised industry we had hoped for and which our fathers had fought for. This was a distortion, a perversion of what could have been, and it is not surprising that disillusionment with the N.C.B. set in so soon.

I had not been fully fit after my accident, and still felt weak. I struggled out to work each day, but May lectured me about it, saying that I had started work far too early, and that I really needed a rest. Finally I went down with the flu, and had to lay off for three days, although I again managed to start on the Friday, in hopes of extra weekend work. I handed in a Doctor's Certificate to safeguard my bonus, because the bonus was only paid if you worked a full week, but the bonus was protected if you had a Doctor's Certificate of illness. The following payday my bonus had not been paid, so I went in to the Office to see about it.

I thought it had probably just been an oversight, and I would be paid when I pointed out that I had handed in the Certificate, but the Manager was adamant. He was not going to pay, and pointed out that the Certificate stated "This man informs me" that I had lost time, but went on to say that I had flu. He was not going to pay on a Certificate that did not state I was unfit for work. We argued back and forth, but it was useless. Finally I stormed out of the Office, shouting that he could stick the Certificate and the bonus up his arse, and that somehow or other I would see that he paid it ten times over. By chance, it was not long before he did.

A few weeks later the oversman approached me at work, carrying a small book and pencil. The Manager was leaving, and a collection was being made for a presentation. I asked what the men were donating, and he told me five shillings or even ten, although some were down for just half a crown. What should he put me down for? I told him: Nothing, and said it loud enough for the rest of the pool to hear. 'Whoa, boy,' I told him. 'I am not giving you anything for that git. I'm glad the sod is leaving us. He is going to a better job, with more money. You don't collect if a worker leaves, or is injured, or has to retire. I don't believe in a collection for a Manager, and especially not that sod. You can tell him from me that I gave fuck all to his collection, and that he can shove the bonus money he stole from me three weeks ago up his arse.'

Old Davy, the oversman, was surprised at all that, but did not argue. He was not surprised, though, when the rest of the pool, and a good few others, hearing the stramash, also refused to contribute. So, in a way, I got my own back, even though I did not get the bonus, and May was a few shillings short that week.

The new Manager was quite an improvement on the old one. He knew his job well, and while strict about the rules, he was fair, and you could discuss things with him. On the whole, things were going quite well at that time in 1954 and 55. Wages were reasonable, and although there were still difficulties with bad roofs, production was high. There were few disputes, not like a few years earlier when there was strike after strike as we fought for better conditions and wages, and when we had to scrimp every penny to make ends meet. They had been poor and miserable times, and it was good to see the end of them. It was not that we were able to live in luxury; far from it, but at least times were better, and the men and their families more contented and settled. In spite of all the dis-satisfactions with the National Coal Board, at least some things had improved for the miners, although most of the improvements came about simply because the miners themselves, through their Union, fought for them.

But we were miners, though, and there was always something happening, something to upset and disturb. There was one time when we suffered very heavy rain in the district, much worse than anything we had ever known before. Flooding was widespread, and many houses in the pit rows were under several feet of water. We were lucky because the water did no more than lap at the front door, but others had to be moved out and given temporary shelter. For twenty four hours a number of us waded up to our waists in water, carrying furniture out of flooded houses, and trying to divert the floods. Accommodation had to be arranged for those who had to leave their homes, and meetings held with the local council to get emergency help.

I had hardly given a thought to the mine while all this was going on, but the mine itself was flooded. The men had been at work when water came rushing down a heading, and Willie McDougall, the Union Delegate, had immediately given instructions for the men to be withdrawn, and get up to the surface. Neither Willie nor the Manager could determine where the water was coming from, but it was rushing like a river down the headings, and the whole mine looked doomed. Fortunately, the water found its way through old workings into the adjoining pit, where the huge pumps managed to control it, but it left our mine in a bad state, with sludge covering everything. Days were spent cleaning up before we could resume production, and even after that no-one could be sure where the inrush had come from, although it seemed likely that it had come down the old shaft.

I had recently been elected to the Union Committee, and so was involved in all the meetings that were held to try and determine the cause of that flooding, and I listened with interest to all the ideas put forward. My own view was that the old shaft was responsible. As it happened, it did not matter too much, for shortly afterwards that seam was abandoned. There was plenty of coal still there, but we were all transferred to another seam, the Forty Inch.

The Forty Inch worked well for a time, and wages were reasonable, but there was one period when I was out of the pool for a while. The team was reduced because the section was shorter as a result of the seam meeting a fault or hitch. This was not unusual, and normally the hitch did not last for long. Anyway, I was on the stott, or fall-back wage, and I did not like it. Of course May did not like it either, because those few shillings short in the pay packet made a great difference.

May was pregnant again, and having a rough time. As a result I had lost some work when I stayed home to take care of her. Obviously that had come to the notice of the Manager, Jimmy Gilbreath, and one day he sent for me. I was a bit nervous about this, for I was fairly sure what he wanted to talk about. However, he was a fair man, and I knew he would not victimise me for circumstances I could not control. He did better than that, though, for he gave me a P.G., a 'Permission Granted', which allowed me to leave the pit whenever my work was completed, without waiting for the end of the shift. I could leave without losing any bonus or time. That was really very good of him, but typical of the interest he took in the welfare of the men in his pit.

A little later I was back on day shift, and working at the face, two circumstances that made me a lot happier. There was more time for a bit of social life, and a bit more money to spend. Not that we could live the life of Riley on a collier's wage! It needed only a few days of idleness as a result of accident or illness, and real hardship resulted. We managed to keep out of debt always, but often enough it was a near thing. I had a few accidents (we all did), but was never off work for more than a day or two. As always in the pit, the conditions constantly varied, and we never knew from day to day what we would find at the beginning of each shift. The condition of the roof was the main thing to consider. Come what may, it had to be kept safe, but in doing that we had to run many risks and work many hours.

Often enough there were big holes in the roof, and somehow they had to be timbered to make them safe. That was a nerve-wracking job, where you had to be constantly alert to hear the warning creak or crack of timber, or the rumble of a falling stone. You had to be constantly ready to leap to one side, hoping that you were leaping away from the fall, and not into it. Not everybody was lucky, and there was a steady stream of accidents and injuries. This was colliers' work at its finest, with all the men working together, and relying totally and implicitly on each other for their safety, indeed, for their lives.

Even in the ordinary work of getting the coal, men relied on their neighbours, not only for their own safety, but for help when in difficulty. Each of us at the face had to clear a 'stint', usually marked off by counting the pans, or sections, of the conveyor. Normally, the stint was 2½ pans. We had two men who could never make their full stint. One was 'Two Pan Dan' and the other 'One Pan Dan'. They were always helped by other men who had finished their stint, or who perhaps had an easier stretch. The coal was still won in basically the same way as it was when I first started, although now, instead of undercutting the seam with a pick, as I had done, and as my father had done before me, the undercutting was done by machine.

The machine undercut about 4½ feet along the full length of the face. Our first job was to clear away the gum, or the small coal left by the machine. That was shovelled on to the conveyors, then we drilled shot holes in the coal, fired them, and then shovelled the fallen coal on to the conveyors. That left an unsupported roof, of course, and as quickly as possible you then had to erect supports. You were working unprotected at that time, and under a roof perhaps weakened by the shots. You could not be easy until you had some props in. This was essentially team work, and at our morning break each day we discussed what was to be done, and who would do it. As I say, the work was not so very different from when I had first started years before. There was a lot more noise now, from the machinery, and the pace was more hectic, as we strove to keep up with the machines, but the risks and the sweat were just the same.

I had been elected Chairman of the Union Branch, and was now deeply involved in Union activities. I had always been a strong supporter of the Union, but now I was having to play an increasing part in all its activities. As it happened, the first time I had to use my Chairman's casting vote proved to be an important matter for the Union.

A circular had come in from the Head Office regarding Rest Days. We were entitled at that time to three Rest Days a year, and it was proposed to make Christmas Day a Rest Day, and forego one of the others. When it came to a vote in the Branch, the results were equal, so it was up to me as Chairman to decide. I argued that in fact neither side was right. We should most certainly have Christmas Day *and* Hogmanay as Rest Days, and I for one would certainly be taking them. However, they should be in addition to the recognised three Rest Days, and not instead of. That idea was well received by the Branch, and was put forward to Headquarters. Eventually it became Union policy, and in not too long a time was accepted by Management, and we had won those two extra Rest Days.

We had been having a fairly long spell of incident free work. That was unusual in the pit, and we all wondered how long it would last. I was making reasonable wages, and getting an occasional extra shift, so that we could save a little bit of money. We always liked to keep something on one side for the times when money was short, but of course could never save enough to ensure that we could get over the bad times without some hardship. However, we managed a holiday in Dublin, and that was something we all enjoyed and savoured for many a day afterwards.

Of course, since the pit is always dangerous, and always unpredictable, it was not long before trouble struck.

We were having our break one morning, laughing and joking as usual, when a a young oncost lad came running in, breathless, and gasped that we were all to get as quick as we could. We told him to calm down and tell us what the trouble was. He said that the engineers had been using a gas cylinder for some job, and that it had blown up and there was a fire with a lot of smoke. I told him to get along up the face as fast as he could, and tell the men, while we would come along behind him and we would all go out by the top road. We could get out straight away because so far nobody had been hurt or needed help. Already I could see a thick and menacing cloud of smoke rolling up the roadway towards us. It filled the whole roadway, and I wondered for a moment why it was moving so slowly in the air current. The air should have been moving it more quickly than that, and I thought that perhaps the main fan was off. As quickly as possible we all scrambled up to the top road, making sure as we went along that no men were left behind. I thought our best plan would be to follow the air circuit out along the top road, but some men disagreed, and indeed the top road was already filling up with sluggishly moving smoke. Some men wanted to go back down the face line and get out by the bottom road, but I argued that the bottom road was already full of smoke, whereas the top road had just begun to fill up with the reek. Anyway, two or three of the men decided to go by the bottom, and the rest of us started along the top.

I warned everybody not to rush, but walk normally, and keep their heads as low as possible, and we set off, with me and the young oncost lad bringing up the rear. As we moved along, someone at the front called out that the reek was getting thicker, but we had to keep moving, with tears pouring from our red eyes, and lungs aching as they struggled to find air in that smoke-filled atmosphere. Our lamps were useless, and we were soon bent double, holding the bogey rails as a guide as we shuffled along, sweat pouring from us and heads throbbing. It was a fiendish place to be, and I was not surprised when I noticed that I could no longer hear the young lad who should have been behind me.

I called out to Jimmy Brown (or croaked out, rather) that the lad was missing, and we went back into the reek, which was even thicker behind us. The lad was there alright, stretched out in the roadway, vomiting and retching. We picked him up, and gave him some water. He was far gone, and very frightened. So were we. Half carrying him, and half dragging him, we went on again, silent except for the sound of our tortured breathing.

I shall never forget that first breath of fresher air when we got to the trap door into the main roadway. The air down a pit is never fresh, but that tasted and smelled like the very essence of spring days and cut grass. We were safe, but there was still a big question. Who was the stupid bastard who had stopped the air flow in the top road when he knew we would be coming that way?

We were the last out, and other men helped the oncost lad away and took him out of the mine. We sat down for a while to recover, still with eyes streaming and lungs aching, and then I set about finding out who was responsible for changing the air current. Whoever it was, he had almost caused our deaths. In fact, it was the oversman, Matt, and he readily admitted it. I thought he should have known that we would be taking the top road, following the air current. In fact he had sent a man in to tell us to take the bottom road, but we had already left. He had done what he thought best, and had not acted carelessly. Just the same, it had been a very dangerous incident, and could easily have had disastrous consequences.

We sat for a while, some of the men still coughing and vomiting, and let our jangled nerves settle. We were not given much time for that, though, because the fireman appeared and demanded that we get back to the face. We had been out long enough, he said. I told him to go and get stuffed and that some of the men would have to go up the pit. Indeed, they all said they were leaving, and the fireman went off, muttering that we would hear more about that, and that our time would be cut. When Matt returned we reported this to him, and told him we were all going up the mine. And that is what we did, still coughing and sometimes vomiting. It was a bad experience, but ended well enough, and only a few of the men had to take any time off, although the oncost lad lost a week's work.

One unpleasant and unpopular job I had to do at that time was help to decide whether Trainees could join the regular teams of miners. The Trainees were mostly young, single men who had joined us in the pit, and were learning the trade. Now they wanted to join the ranks of the faceworkers. The Trainees were all still Oncost, and their wages were lower. There could only be a limited number of faceworkers, though, and already we had some trained miners who were not in any regular team. If a team was short of a man on some shift, one of those trained men would join it, but only temporarily.

At the Union meeting to discuss the Trainees' claim, various arguments were put forward on both sides, but personally, though sympathetic to their claim, I felt it was not right that they should take over our jobs. We had struggled hard for years, even for generations, to get reasonable conditions. Now they were amongst the best in the area, and I felt strongly that those men who had taken part in the struggle should benefit. Although there was no prospect of further development in our own pit, there was plenty of work for the Trainees elsewhere, if they could get taken on as face workers. So I spoke out against them coming on to our lists. We had trained them, but had trained them to be miners, not to take over our jobs. If they were capable, let them go elsewhere. Most of them were young and unmarried, while we had our family responsibilities. My attitude was not popular at that meeting, but eventually, as always, a compromise was found, whereby we took a few of them on to our lists, and the rest, if they wished, could go elsewhere, but would receive first chance if they ever wanted to come back to us when work was available.

There was always something strange going on in the pit, which is really not surprising when you consider that a coal mine is a totally unnatural environment. Nature never lets you forget that. Sometimes you are reminded in a harsh way, as when our mine was flooded. At other times, nature intrudes itself very gently. There was one time when I was walking out of the mine and saw wee Geordie Burke scattering breadcrumbs on to the roadway, and whistling softly to himself. I asked him what the hell he was doing, encouraging rats in that way. He told me it was not rats he was encouraging but his wee birds. I looked at him as though he must be daft. Birds? Here, in almost total darkness, sixty or seventy yards from the mine mouth? Geordie laughed at my astonishment and disbelief, then showed me that indeed there was a nest, high up in the corner of a girder, and that the nest held four eggs and a totally unafraid swallow. It was only a few feet from the bogey rails, where rakes of hutches roared along every few minutes, making a tremendous din, and close by a place where water poured ceaselessly from the roof, and yet those eggs were hatched, and the youngsters reared in those conditions. We watched over them very carefully, but it was the parent birds who did all the work. This was such an unusual thing that word of it spread wide, and even our local newspaper heard, and sent a photographer along to record it. I bought one of his photographs, and still have it, as a permanent record of the courage and devotion shown by those birds in such strange conditions.

For part of this time I was working as a spare faceman, and was given all kinds of different jobs to do. I enjoyed that, not only for the variety of work, but also because I had the chance of working with different men. It was always interesting for me to see how different men tackled the same sort of problem, and at the same time I had the chance of learning more about my trade from a number of master craftsmen.

At one time I was sent to a new development section to take preliminary cuts off it before it went into production. That was interesting, to see a brand new face, newly prepared, seeming almost tidy and clean. It was almost a shame to dirty it up with our machines.

I quite enjoyed working on the machines, too. I was not a machineman, though, and the actual operation was not in my hands. My job was to set and reset props as the machine pulled itself along the face. I also had to set up the anchor rail. This was a heavy girder which was set up in holes I cut in the floor and roof. The machine's draw chain was attached to that anchor rail, and it then pulled itself along by the chain. When the machine had pulled itself up to the anchor, the anchor was moved on again to a new position, sometimes further along the face, or perhaps back the other way.

There was one occasion I remember when I was working with Wullie MacGregor, the machine operator. I had dragged the chain up into the far corner of the face, as far as I could go, and was trying to fix the anchor. However, both the roof and the pavement were soft, and every time strain went on the anchor, it pulled out. There was only about eighteen inches of height to work in, and I was getting very frustrated. Finally I called to Wullie to pass me the boring machine and a short drill. I would try something else. I bored into the coal at an angle, hooked the chain over the drill, and called to Wullie to start up. He looked over to see what I had done, grinned, and started the machine. The chain tightened, and there was a loud ping from the drill, but it held, and the machine began cutting. We had won again.

It was Wullie MacDougall who first aroused my deep interest in the miners' diseases of silicosis and pneumoconiosis. Of course I knew that miners had bad chests, and that many old miners could hardly breathe or walk. But they were 'Under the Doctor', and were getting Doctor's bottles for their chests, so they must be alright, I thought. Bad chests were just something you got in the pits, like blue scars all over your body. Wullie enlightened me.

Silicosis and pneumoconiosis were industrial diseases, caused by the dust we were inhaling all the time we were at work. There was no cure for them, and they were irreversible, but because they were an industrial disease, those who contracted them were elegible for compensation, and a pension if they were unable to work. In no way would this compensate for their misery and pain, but at least it was something. Most men were unaware of their entitlement, and never made a claim. Others knew about the entitlement, but had no idea of how go to go about making the claim. This was a deplorable situation, and we set about ending it. The Union set up what was virtually an advice bureau, pressing men to apply for compensation, and showing them how to go about it. Many men had been fobbed off by their Doctors with stories of 'weak chests' and 'a touch of bronchitis', and them we advised to demand an X Ray (which was their right) to determine whether or not they had an industrial disease. If they had, and most had, we showed them how to apply for pension and compensation. It was great to see how this initiative made an enormous difference to the lives of those men and their families, bringing perhaps a little comfort and safety into what was still a harsh and borderline existence.

Of course, like all miners, I had known that old men suffered from their chests. We expected to suffer in our turn. But I had not realised just how widespread and horrifying that suffering was. Only when I began going about amongst the retired miners did I come to appreciate the size and depth of the problem. I never got accustomed to seeing those men, old long before their time, gasping for air, their lungs (the bits that had not already been turned to stone) racking their bodies, their throats wheezing. It was a sad sight, the more so because I knew those men: they were my comrades, we had worked together and drank and laughed together We had depended on each other in the deep brotherhood of the mines. Now they were husks of men. It was one of the greatest delights of my life to be able to do something for them, however little, and however late it might be.

Of course, it was not enough for the Union to fight and win compensation for these men. We also had to fight to eliminate the conditions which led to those diseases. This we did too, always arguing and fighting for better ventilation and dust suppression. We also fought for, and got, mobile X Rays to come to the pit head, where all the men could have their chests examined at the first suspicion of trouble. This sort of everyday activity by the Unions is never publicised. We are always represented as being a bunch of rapacious hoodlums, out only for ourselves, and determined to wreck the industry. In reality, most of our Union work is taken up with such things as I have just described. And if it had not been for the Union, those men would never have had a penny in compensation, nor would all the better ventilation and dust suppression be in place today — where there are any pits left, that is.

It was about this time, in 1959, that the blow fell. Our mine was to close, and we were to be transferred to Bogside, eight miles away.

BOGSIDE

The Seventh Step.

I had worked a long time in that mine. My first two years there I had spent on nightshift, working at a variety of jobs, such as brushing, packing, steel drawing, laying pan conveyors and cutting coal for the dayshift strippers. Another ten years I spent on backshift doing much the same work, and than I went on dayshift stripping coal. Now we were to be moved to Bogside.

Management Relations Officers descended on us, and gave us briefings about what we could expect in the new pit. It was all modern, the very latest techniques and methods. There would be the very latest steel props which tightened automatically to the roof when you drove in a wedge. There would be a disc coal cutter, a shearer, that cut the coal from floor to roof, two feet wide at a time, and travelled along the scraper conveyor. No more undercutting, then, and dropping the coal by shot and hand.

Altogether, Bogside was made to sound like some kind of colliers' Utopia. There would be revolutionary new technology, a complete contrast to how we had worked in the past. Labour would be much less arduous, and wages better. That was what we were told, and that is perhaps what some of us believed. The more cynical knew it would never be like that, and the cynical were again proved to be right.

We found, when we got to the pit, that most of the men already there were Trainees. They were inexperienced miners, not long in the pits, who had worked in factories or shops before coming down the mine. They did not have our traditions of tough Union activity, and they had accepted conditions we found unacceptable.

We were on a basic wage, which was lower than that in the other pit, so the first thing was a battle for wage contracts. There was no formal severance arrangements or payment in the transfer from one pit to another, so there were many difficulties to be ironed out. A joint meeting was called between the new men and those already working there. It was a total chaos, one of the longest and hottest meetings I have ever attended. Our main complaint was that those inexperienced men were willing to work long hours to make a decent wage. Somebody said they worked longer hours than the mine pumps! That was not our idea at all. We wanted a decent wage for reasonable hours. There were some bitter arguments at the meeting, and it soon became clear that their officials, inexperienced as they were, had no idea how to conduct and control a meeting. When tempers flared, the Chairman lost control.

We called for him to resign, and then called for the resignation of the Delegate when he could not answer questions we put to him. At that, the Secretary also threw in his books. The Chairman thereupon called for nominations for Secretary, and our group put me forward, as I was the only one present with experience of Union office.

I really did not want any position in this Branch, but I had no alternative. I thought for a moment, then agreed to accept the nomination on condition that it was temporary, and that I would later resign in favour of Charlie Burke, who was the obvious man for the job. It was put to the vote, after two other nominees, both from the other Branch, had been named. I was elected and then conferred briefly with the Chairman. I told the men I had taken careful note of what had been said, and would confer with the Management at the first opportunity. The Chairman then closed the meeting, and thus the heat was taken out of a situation that had seemed very tricky.

About twenty of our men started work at Bogside the following Monday, but the rest of us had to work on a few weeks more till places were ready for us. We were keen to get started in that miners' Utopia, and delighted when word came down that we were to move on a Monday. At the end of that shift, our last there, we tied up our graith and left it at the mine mouth. It would be picked up and transported for us. In a way, in spite of looking forward to what we believed would be improved conditions at Bogside, we were quite sorry to be leaving that mine. Wages had been reasonable, relations with management good, and conditions no worse than elsewhere. The new was the unknown, but as always one hoped it would be an improvement.

On the morning we were due to start at Bogside, we were picked up by buses from our home villages and taken straight to the pit yard. It was all very different from what we had been led to expect. The pit head consisted of no more than a few wooden sheds, and they were the offices, workshops and stores. Another wooden shed was supposed to be the baths, and it was like nothing but an old barn, with half a dozen showers and two large sinks, and stinking of sweat and wet clothes. Altogether, it was far indeed from the glowing descriptions we had been given.

An oversman, a chap called Davie, with whom I had worked before, came over to us as we waited in the yard. He began to allocate places and men. There was only one faceline, and several development roads. He went through all the names, and told them that firemen would be waiting down the pit to show them to their work places. Most of our men were disgruntled at the allocation of jobs, because few of them were on facework.

As the Union representative, I raised this with Davie, but was surprised at his response, which was, briefly, that what he had said was final. They were the jobs, and those were the men. Furthermore, he said, I had fuck all to do with it.

That was enough. I called the men over, and explained the situation, reminding them that we had been promised there would be no down-grading. The lads were all for going home straight away, but I told them I would talk to the Manager first, and that going down the road immediately would solve nothing. So three of us went in to see the Manager. I told him I was the Union Secretary, and that he had a problem. I thought it could easily be sorted out, and that it was no more than teething problems with a new pit. He replied that the men should be down the pit and working by now, and I told him that the reason they were still on the surface was that they were dissatisfied with their job allocations. They wanted assurances that they would not suffer wage loss by doing that work, much of which was on-cost. The Manager replied that he was not paying face work rates to men doing on-cost work, but I told him that it had been agreed, and minuted, that those men, Grade One workers, would retain their basic wage. He repeated that he was not going to pay more than the on-cost rate for on-cost work.

There seemed no point in continuing the discussion, so I went back and reported to the men, telling the manager that his pit was idle. He called us back after a few minutes, but had no offer to make, so we still got nowhere. Eventually, he agreed to phone the area office, and they confirmed what we had told him: we were to be paid the rate for our grade, irrespective of the job we might happen to be doing. That was alright with us — it was what we had agreed in the first place. So we went down the pit, and started work.

It took a while before we really got settled in to that pit. Relations with those who had been working there before we arrived were not easy at first, and there was a strike one day when those lads objected that we were claiming all the best jobs and being paid higher rates than they were. They did not want to accept that the best jobs (that is, the highest paid) should be shared between us. The Pool Leader, Cuggie, took our lads up the pit, and had a meeting with Management, which merely confirmed the agreements we had already reached. It took a long time before that rift between the old and the new miners healed over. Those lads had us classed as agitators, while we adhered to the values we knew — sharing of jobs and overtime and a fair deal for all. We certainly could not accept that some men consistently had high wages, while others only had the Fall Back Rate.

The first few weeks there were hectic for those of us who were Union officials. Fridays were a nightmare, as numbers of men came up and reported shortages of wages. It was a constant battle with management, and took a lot of time. Conditions at the pit head continued to be atrocious. What they called the baths could not accommodate all the men, and many of us had to travel back home dirty. This was a real reversion to the bad old days. We got off the buses black and sweaty and wet, sometimes shivering with cold, still in our helmets, pit clothes and knee pads. Teeth gleamed in black faces, and our own children cried in fright when they saw us. Our wives resumed the drying and cleaning of pit clothes as though we had never fought and won the battle for pit head baths. But we *had* fought that battle, and were determined to press management to get the baths in to Bogside as quickly as possible.

Will MacDougall had been our Delegate at the last mine, but he had left his job at Bogside. Because of his disability, he had been put on light work, and placed in charge of the Explosives Magazine. Wullie took one look at the Magazine and declined to accept responsibility for it. There were no proper locks on the doors, and the shed itself was unsafe. It was a blow to us when Wullie left, because he was an experienced Delegate and a very skilful negotiator. One Union meeting sacked our then Delegate for incompetence (in fact, it was inexperience, rather) and a delegation was sent to ask Wullie MacDougall to come back. There were discussions with managers and with the Board's Agent, and Wullie was offered some other job. He accepted, and was immediately elected Union Delegate, and straightaway brought all his skills to bear, and very soon conditions and rates of pay were vastly improved.

As Secretary, one of the most worrying things I had to deal with was the spate of accidents. This was partly due to the inexperience of the young miners, and with our old timers, the new system of coal getting.

The new coal cutting machines were causing most accidents to the face workers. We were not accustomed to them, and felt that at times the workers were left very exposed to roof falls. The machine itself moved along on top of the scraper conveyor, and when the scraper had to be moved forward, the men had to cross over the conveyor to shovel up the gum and allow the scraper to move forward. They were under an unprotected roof while doing this, and accidents from roof falls were frequent. Also, there were frequent falls of coal from the face on to the men. The scraper itself was moved forward by operating hydraulic rams, pushing against steel posts set at an angle between the roof and the pavement. Steel posts and props were always a menace, being liable to spring out without any warning.

There was one fatal accident. He was one of us, an incomer, and we knew him well. He had been working up by the scraper gear head when a part broke loose and struck him on the chest and head. He died as his neighbours carried him from the face. There was an investigation, of course, and as a result new regulations were introduced that certain parts of machines, previously welded, must in future be bolted together. That was all very well, and it might have saved problems in the future, but it did nothing for poor Sailor or his family.

It was strange how management was so often short sighted and stupid. They seemed to think that by scimping on spending a few shillings they were being economic and efficient. In fact, the reverse was true. Only too often their 'economies' led to extra expense in labour and lost production. They would have led to more accidents, also, if we had not been constantly vigilant about it.

We had no set neighbours at this pit, and you never knew who you would be working with, nor where you would be working, from one shift to another. There was one occasion when three of us were sent off to a development road, and when I examined the face, I did not like it at all. The roadway itself was reasonable, apart from a few broken trees that could be replaced, but the air was foul, and the conveyor belt in a sad state of repair. I told the other lads about it, and we agreed that it was not a fit place to work, so we sent for the fireman. When he arrived we told him about the bad air and that the belt was torn in places, with holes in it, and in some places only about a foot wide. We pointed out that it would not carry coal, and that we would be spending most of our time shovelling up what the belt spilled. He was not a bit sympathetic, and simply told us there was nothing he could do, and we had to get on with the job.

So we told him that if there was nothing *he* could do, then there was something *we* could do. We were not going into that place until there was a fan installed and a new belt provided. If he could not do it, then we were for up the pit. He asked us to wait, and went off, and shortly afterwards the oversman arrived, bawling at us to get in there and work. We sat still, and looked at him.

'I'm telling you: Get to your bloody work!' he roared. Some people never learned, and he certainly had not. He was not dealing with youngsters just out of school or young men from shops and factories, but with seasoned miners who had spent years learning their trade and their rights. I replied, quite politely, that he was telling us fuck all, and he could not dictate to us. The air was bad and we were not working in it. If he got a fan along, we would install it, and also the place needed new belting. The stuff there was as thin as a ribbon, and would not held the coal. He pushed past and into the place. He looked around, took a deep breath and then said: 'Ye know, it's no good, but it's no bad'. We looked at him in wonderment. What the hell was that meant to mean? Eventually he admitted that we were probably right, and that we could go and pick up a fan from a certain place, and he would send an electrician along to fit it. Half a shift later, it was installed, and the air became fit to breathe, and at the same time a couple of oncost men dragged in a hutch laden with new belting. So we got our way, but only at the expense of threatened industrial action, and were able to start winning coal in an atmosphere that did not threaten our health and safety.

Altogether, Bogside was not being a happy mine, in spite of the fine promises which had encouraged us to move here. Where were the excellent prospects and good wages? In the light of what we had been told of those, we had not negotiated any severance payment, and now we found our wages several pounds a week less than before. Furthermore, there were other things, and especially the lack of pithead baths, which caused so much extra work for our wives, and also a certain amount of discomfort and even illness for us, when we had to travel so many miles wet through and dirty.

It was only a short time after the death of Sailor that we had another fatal accident. This time it was a fireman, Tam Smith, who had been killed when the gearhead of a faulty scraper conveyor fell on him. We never did find out what had caused the accident, in spite of serious investigation.

Another man, Davie Patterson, had a lucky escape. He missed

death by inches, and only because of the sheer physical strength of one of his mates. Davie had been working behind the shearer, a coal cutter, when his foot was caught by a stone and he was dragged under the scraper conveyor. His shouts attracted his mate, a big Polish chap called Bruno. Bruno grabbed at Davie and held him against the pull of the machine, until their shouts attracted the attention of the machineman, who switched off and came to their rescue. It took some time to release Davie, whose leg was jammed by the stone and severely lacerated. His foot was also crushed, and he was off work for a long time.

So bad was the spate of accidents that Bogside became known as The Slaughterhouse to the the staff of the local hospital. A great deal of my time as Secretary of the Union was spent in filling up accident report forms and visiting injured men at home or in hospital to get their story. So bad did the situation become that we set up a special committee to investigate the reasons for each accident, and try to ensure that they were not repeated. We reported to the Union, and took up with management everything that needed changing, and without doubt we managed to end a lot of dangers and dangerous practices in the the pit.

I had been elected Union Secretary permanently by this time. Our old Secretary had decided not to join us at Bogside, and the Branch chose me in his place, presumably thinking I had been doing a reasonable job as a temporary Union official.

As time passed, there was more harmony between the two groups of Bogside workers. The old squabbles and jealousies disappeared in the common labour and the common dangers of that labour. Instead of being two groups, we were one, the men of Bogside. A lot of effort was devoted to charitable concerns there. Not only did we organise collections — sometimes as much as thirty pounds — for injured men, but we also collected for retiring men. Another thing we did was adopt the nearby Dr. Barnado's Home, and give the children various treats, especially at Christmas time. This tradition continued until the mine was finally closed down.

In fact, the mine was almost closed not very long after it had opened, and while it was still being developed. Water broke in from somewhere and the pumps could not cope. The working face seemed safe enough, and production could continue, but all other men, such as the developers, were put on to diverting the water and getting pumps into place. Three of us were building a dam of sandbags and heavy clay, and were working over our ankles in water, with the stream rushing along like a burn in spate. We had not been working long when it became obvious that the water was rising. It was no longer ankle deep, but up to our knees. It was time to get out of there, and to get the men out. Wullie MacDougall came along just then, and he agreed, so he went off to warn the facemen and I went off to get all the developers out.

In places it was like walking through a waterfall, and where the pavement dipped the water was already dangerously deep. However, I got to all the places where men were working, and gave them the message to get out. Then I wondered whether Wullie had been able to reach all the facemen, and I turned back and worked my way along the face, but there was only one light there, a fireman who was checking that all the men were out. I confirmed that all the developers were out, so we decided to get out ourselves, if we could.

I was alone when I got to the pit bottom. The fireman had gone off down a side road just to be quite certain that no-one was down there. The pit bottom was like a lake, with water well over the top of the minecars standing there. Somehow I had to get across, and certainly I could not swim. There was nothing for it but to go hand over hand along the armoured cables that looped across the roof, and that is what I did, until I could jump on to the last minecar, itself deep in water, and then work my way along that to the roadway and the main incline. When I got to the surface Wullie MacDougall and Matt, the oversman were preparing to go down to find me, and of course they were delighted that was not necessary, and that I was safe. I was able to give them a report of the situation, and then we went off to report to the Manager. More pumps and pipes had to be sent underground, and men were detailed to go and fit them. Of course, I was soaked, and had no dry clothes, so a van was organised to take home those of us in that condition.

It took several days before the pumps were able to bring the water under control, and several more days before the muck and sludge were cleared away and we could get back to production and development. For a good while after that we encountered very wet conditions. They were so bad that sometimes when a hole was bored in the rock and the drill pulled out, there was a jet of water as though from a hose pipe. That was something I had never seen before.

Those wet conditions presented new problems and dangers to all of us. I was working on the face at the time, pulling out Dobson props and erecting them nearer to the faceline. The Dobson was a steel prop, which worked hydraulically. You put it into place, and then operated a lever to pump the top up and wedge it into position. To release it, you simply turned a key, which released the hydraulic pressure, and the top retracted. All very simple, except that often enough the prop would collapse on top of you when you released the pressure. That was bad enough when you were working dry and with good pavement. When we were working wet, and struggling in several inches of sludge, it was a recipe for trouble.

Because it was still so wet, we were working in oilskins and gumboots. The skins were provided for us, but the gumboots we had to buy ourselves. When we started work, outer clothing — jackets, shirts, trousers — came off, and we put on our oilskin trousers and jackets, with a square of oilskin under our caps, hanging over our necks. The only bare skin was face and hands, and we tied our wrists with string to keep the water out as well as possible. The water was cold, of course, icy cold, and it poured down steadily from the roof. They were bad conditions, and made worse by the several inches of sticky sludge on the pavement.

One day the Manager came down, and he was accompanied by the N.C.B. Agent, Jock Wallace. Jock looked at the atrocious conditions in which we were working, and he virtually exploded. He said that never in all his years as a mining engineer had he seen such hellish conditions. No men, he said could be expected to work out full shifts in conditions like that. He told the Manager that he wanted the men on half shifts, and he wanted it done that day, and he wanted it to continue until we were out of the wet. There was no argument from the Manager, who was himself appalled at the conditions, and not only did we work only half shifts, but also had an increase in the water money we were paid.

There was no doubt that we earned that extra money in terms of ill health and sickness. There were few of us who did not suffer from boils during that time when we were constantly wet and cold, and the incidence of rheumatic illnesses of various kinds also rose in later years. I myself got a poisoned hand. It happened simply enough. I picked up a loop of broken strands from a wire rope and threw it into the waste, where it should have been in the first place, instead of lying half submerged waiting to trip somebody up. It had been left by a rope splicer who had cut it out of a cable before doing his repairs. He should have disposed of it safely, but had just left it in the roadway. Anyway, I picked it up and slung it away, and in doing so got a prick from it through my gloves. I pulled off my gloves and sucked the spot of blood on my thumb, and then thought nothing more about it.

The next day my thumb was red and throbbing and swollen, and when I went into the pit, I reported the accident to Jimmy Gilchrist, the section oversman, who had actually seen what had happened. That was a Friday, and I had the weekend to do the necesary doctoring, with water and vinegar as hot as I could bear, and cold water compresses. This kept the swelling at bay, but when I got to the pit on Monday I asked Matt McEwan, the day shift oversman, for some pain killers, and for a fresh dressing. He took off the bandage and exclaimed 'Good God! You can't go down the pit with a hand like that!' I told him that I couldn't go down without it, and that all I wanted was a fresh dressing. We were going on holiday that weekend, and I would have time to attend to it then. I worked that day, and the following day, but then I had to go to see the doctor. He gave me a right tongue-lashing and told me that to be tough about things like that was just plain stupid. Did I not realise the danger I had caused myself? I realised that alright, but I wondered whether he realised what a few lost shifts meant to us. If it was possible to get to work, and do the job, then we went.

The doctor cleaned up my hand, and then gave me an injection of penicillin, the new wonder drug which acted like magic on all such cases of poisoning. He told me to see him again in two days, and that he would have me back to work in no time. When I went back two days later, I showed him a large swelling in my arm pit, but he told me not to worry about it, and that the penicillin would take care of that. I was worried, though, especially as we had arranged to go on holiday to Ayr on the Saturday of that week. When I told the doctor that, he gave me a note to take to the hospital in Ayr, where I would get the final dressing and treatment.

The swelling under my arm burst before the Saturday, though, and thick, foul-smelling pus poured out of it. May dressed it and bandaged it, and we were able to get off for our holiday. The hospital in Ayr, when I went there, were very complimentary about May's dressing and bandaging of my arm-pit, a place difficult to bandage, but one which she had done neatly and efficiently. The hospital gave me a clean bill of health, and we were all able to enjoy our week in Ayr.

That was the first time I had been treated with penicillin, and I realised what a wonderful thing it is. Poisoned hands and other wounds were common enough amongst all working men, and very often in the past they were very serious, not only causing a lot of pain and lost work, but even more serious results, like lost limbs and even lost lives. We all knew about poisoned wounds, and all dreaded them. All old miners had their favourite ways of treating them, most of which involved water as hot as it could be borne. There was little a doctor could do to help: his treatments were just the same as our home remedies. Now, suddenly, there was a new treatment that could be guaranteed to stop the poison dead, and without any of the pain and uncertainty of the old hot water treatments. There had rarely been any scientific advance which gave so much immediate benefit to so many people as did the discovery of penicillin.

When I got back to work, I found that the big clean up after the flooding was still going on, and that there was a remarkable degree of harmony between men and management. Both sides realised that the very future and existence of the mine was in the balance, and that if it could not get back into production quickly, it was likely to be closed permanently. Consequently, everybody was working hard and co-operatively, and as a result, production was soon restarted, and development work resumed.

It was a pity, in a way, that those harmonious relations did not continue. For some reason, management began a campaign of guerilla warfare against us. Officials would cut men's time or rate without even informing them, let alone consulting them. Contracts were broken and attempts made to impose worse terms. Men were consistently paid short in their wages. It was quite normal to have a queue of disgruntled men outside the manager's office every pay day, trying to get their wages right. All the Union officials were kept busy with these claims, and only too often tempers would flare on one side or both. There would be disputes, and men would walk out and off the job. In those circumstances it was not surprising that a new solidarity developed between the men. If one section was in dispute and on strike, there was no way that the other men in the mine would work. They were all on strike till the dispute was settled.

It was out of that period of managerial penny-pinching and incompetence that our Union became so strong and militant. It was an alliance and a comradeship justly renowned throughout the Union movement. Not only were our men ready to fight for better conditions for themselves, but they gave willing assistance to all others, wherever they were to be found, who were fighting in a just cause. That policy was to continue through the years, and we were properly proud of it.

It was sometimes difficult to combine being a Union official and a collier. There were so many calls upon the officials to settle matters with management that not only working hours were interfered with, but family life also. We were working three shifts at that time, changing shifts each week, so that your body really never got a chance to adapt and adjust to the different times of sleeping and working and eating. For me, night shift was the worst, for I slept little in the day. When I came home from the pit, the children would be up and waiting for me. There would be time for some games and stories before I went off to bed. Then would come the interuptions. Milkman, postman, insurance man — it seemed that half the village called at my house when I was trying to sleep. May had her housework to do, and would do it as quietly as possible, but it seemed that I was alert to every rattle and scratch. It would often be a relief when someone would knock at the door and enquire for me. May would explain that I was on nightshift, and sleeping, but often enough I would call through that I was getting up, and the caller should come in.

A quick wash, and then I could sit down with the caller, and usually with a cup of tea, and find out what his trouble was. It was great to be able to give advice and help, and solve problems, and I never begrudged the time and effort it all involved.

The new pit head baths had at last been opened, and they made an enormous difference to us all. There was no more travelling in cold buses, sometimes wet through, and always dirty and tired, and cleaning up in the kitchen at home, leaving a real mess for our wives to handle. Perhaps having the pithead baths was the greatest gain my generation of colliers had made over our fathers, more important than almost anything else.

I lost a good friend about this time. 'The two Js', Jerry and Jock were inseparable, and I was happy to be working in the same team with them. Jock was an outdoor man, and I enjoyed his tales of fishing and observations on the birds and beasts he knew so well. Jerry was the family man, and always spoke with great pride of his children and their various talents. He was a happy man, who had had a difficult childhood. He had grown up in Ireland during the Troubles there, until his father brought the family to Scotland in the hope of a better and quieter life. His stories of the Troubles told of strife and disorder such as we could scarcely comprehend. Jock was off work ill, and Jerry went to see him often. One day he asked me to call and see Jock, and when I did I was shattered at the sight. He was withering away, that man of the outdoors, into just a husk of humanity. I visited a few times more, until one day Jerry told me that Jock wanted no more visitors. Just a few days later he died, and Jerry, in tears, brought me the news. We attended his funeral, and were deeply moved at the death of that man we had liked so much as a workmate and as a friend.

Neither production nor development were going well in that pit. It seemed that wherever we went, we encountered solid rock, and that the seams were very faulty. I was working on driving a road, but after blasting through solid rock for a long time, hope of finding the seam again was given up, and I went back on the stot, that is, without any particular job, but doing odd jobs each day, and only getting the fall-back rate of pay. That meant a considerable drop in wages, and it went on for a long time.

I was sitting with my neighbours having my meal break one day (we were allowed fifteen minutes for our piece) when the Manager together with the Area Manager walked past the abandoned roadway where we sat. The Area Manager saw me, and sent the Manager to call me over. He wanted to talk to the Union Secretary, and that was me. He began by saying that the mine was in dire straits, which I knew better than he did, and that he wanted to call a meeting of selected men, perhaps a dozen or so experienced miners from different departments to discuss what could be done. I accepted the idea, pointing out that our jobs were on the line here, just as his was.

We met the next morning in the office. On our side there was Wullie MacDougall and the other Branch Officials. Jimmy Russell represented the conveyor men and George Grindley the Pool Leaders and Drivers. There were others, all experienced miners, and now all worried men. The Area Manager approved of our choice of men, and we settled down to a long discussion. All the maps and diagrams of the mine were produced, and we talked long and deeply over the problems.

At first it seemed that there could be no solution, but gradually, out of the accumulated experience and wisdom of that group, men and management and union officials, a way forward was found. Ways to get back to the coal seam were devised, and it seemed that production could be resumed, and at a healthy rate. It would all need hard work and a certain amount of sacrifice by both men and management, and a certain amount of forebearance by both sides, but we all knew that the very future of the mine, and of our jobs depended on making it all work, and we were determined to do it.

At the end of the long meeting, Management undertook that they would play their part as agreed, and the Union Officials arranged to call a meeting of the men immediately and put it to them. This we did, and the response was good. They agreed with all the suggestions made, and really got tore into that mine until we got it back into full production. The whole episode was one of the best examples I ever came across of real co-operation between men and management, and it convinced me all over again that what the National Coal Board needed was a change of top management. If only management had worked *with* the men, as surely they should have done in an industry owned by the nation, instead of continuing the antagonistic practices inherited from the old days, then the National Coal Board would have been a great and undoubted success. We were lucky in having an imaginative Area Manager and pit Manager, as well as Union officials of the calibre of Wullie MacDougall, who could sit down together and really pool their knowledge in the interests of the industry.

As Union Secretary I had to deal with a whole range of problems, and sometimes in so doing had to make myself quite unpopular with the men. There was one like that about rats. We had a circular from head office informing us of the danger of Weill's disease in the pits. This is a particularly horrible disease, crippling and sometimes fatal, which is spread in the urine of rats, and in no other way.

We always had rats down the pit, and usually they were everybody's enemy, but we never really did anything constructive to discourage them. Now we were told to embark on a safety campaign. Instead of carrying our sandwiches in paper, which we screwed up and threw into the waste, usually with a crust or two, we were instructed to use tin boxes. No waste food was to be left behind. Generally, every effort was to be made to discourage rats, and in the posters I made to tell the men about these new rules, I stressed that already several miners had died from Weill's Disease. There was a bit of opposition to the new rules, but gradually they took hold, and were fully accepted. We also went on to cover other safety aspects, such as not using glass bottles for our drink down the pit. These were often broken and thrown into the waste, where several men had suffered severe cuts. We stressed also the importance of using gloves and goggles and masks when necessary, and made sure that these were supplied. Our efforts in that direction gradually paid off, and there was a noticeable decline in the numbers of days lost through illness and accident.

Amongst the more pleasant tasks of the Union Officials was arranging for retirement presentations and retirement nights for men who had reached that age. We always had a collection, and a night out in the local. There was a presentation, and speeches, then a good sing song and entertainment. They were good nights, and I always enjoyed them, although for me they were invariably marred by the parsimony of the Coal Board. Their presentation was no more than a framed scroll, recording that So-and-so had worked for so many years in the pits, and had given long and invaluable service. The frame for this was edged in black, and I thought the thing in very bad taste. The miners' pension was a disgrace, hardly enough to pay the rent of a house, far less live in any sort of dignity, and I constantly strove to have this issue of pensions raised in all negotiations with the Board. Ironically, all Coal Board officials and even office girls had a pension scheme, while the miners themselves did not.

This was a time of rapid change in all mines. There were new methods of coal cutting, and new systems of conveyers. The output per man was rising rapidly, but our wages did not follow. In Bogside we had finally overcome the problems of faults in the seams, and there was a lot of development work being done, and two facelines were producing.

We all had to learn new methods of working, and adapt to new machines. Generally, the accident rate was low, but of course there was still a goodly crop of them, especially, we found, in the transport of materials. In an effort to reduce accidents, the Union and management jointly set up a Safety Committee to advise men on the proper procedures, and to check on machines, conveyors, haulages, and, above all, on ventilation.

As Union Secretary I received many circulars from Head Office on safety, and we tried to implement them all. Usually management was very ready to listen to us, and to help in all safety measures, but with our claims for compensation for miners stricken with pneumoconiosis it was a different story. They insisted on basing compensation on a medical evaluation of how much damage had been done to a man's lungs. To us then, and to me now, that was ridiculous. If twenty percent of a man's lungs had been turned to stone, should he have only a twenty percent disability pension? In that case, you would have to have no lungs left at all, and be dead, before you could get a full pension! I remember a speech by our General Secretary at the time, saying that for each day of the year a miner in South Wales died of pneumoconiosis. If three hundred and sixty five men had died in one day in a pit disaster, the nation would have responded magnificently. The same number died in a year, and died in pain and misery, and usually poverty, and it seemed that no-one, except other miners, cared. I watched one man die, a neighbour of mine from the

Meta mine. When I visited him in hospital he had been cheerful and optimistic, talking of the Pipe Band in which he played, and of his plans for the summer. He was discharged home to die, and when I saw him a few days later, death was already sitting on his shoulders. He was no more than a skeleton of a man, struggling for every breath, and knowing that each might be his last. And yet, according to the doctors, that man had only a low percentage of pneumoconiosis, hardly enough to receive any pension at all.

Wullie MacDougall was so intent on overcoming the problems of dust that he never missed an opportunity of speaking out about it. In fact, he was very proud of his nickname 'Stoury Wull' or 'Dusty'! He always insisted on good ventilation and the use of water sprays to suppress dust and on cleaning up the mine generally. He was respected by both men and management, and always listened to, and I know that he did a very great deal to improve safety in the pits.

Although things had improved considerably since we first started work in Bogside, our wages were still a lot less than we we had had before. There had been so many stoppages that the little we had saved was long gone. Our wages were just enough for the everyday needs, and there was very little to spare. Our social life consisted of an occasional trip over to Lanarkshire to visit our folks. Always the children came first, and any sacrifice was made cheerfully if they could benefit. Just occasionally I would go out on a Saturday evening and have a couple of pints with my friends.

There was one New Year time when we had saved enough to have a short holiday over in Lanarkshire. It was bitterly cold and there had been heavy snow followed by frost, so road conditions were bad. We enjoyed our visit, but when it came time to go home, we found that the transport services were greatly curtailed, because of the holiday. First we had a long wait for a bus into Glasgow, and in spite of being well wrapped up in all our clothes, we were miserable with the cold. At Buchanan Street station, we found that the train we had hoped to catch had left already, and there was another long wait for the next one. The shops and the buffet in the station were closed, so there was nothing else to do but huddle close and wait. Eventually a porter appeared who told us that our train would be leaving from the lower level, and that there was a waiting room there, and there might even be a fire.

There was a waiting room alright, but no fire, only the cold ashes of a fire long dead. There was nobody else around, only a solitary porter at the far end of the long platform, packing boxes onto a trolley.

The whole place was cold, and damp, with paint flaking off the wall, and inexpressibly dreary. It was better to walk up and down the platform than sit in the dankness of the waiting room, and that is what we did. A signal bell sounded, and we looked hopefully up the line. A loco came steaming out of the tunnel, and we were sure it was our train. But it wasn't. It was just a loco. We moved back into the waiting room. At least it was a change of scenery. Then there was the rattle of a trolley over the slabs and two porters appeared, pushing a trolley on which there was a coffin. One porter was tall and thin, the other short and fat. They were quite unaware that we were in the waiting room.

The tall one lifted his cap and scratched his completely bald pate. The short one rapped on the coffin and then addressed it. 'Hey, you in there! Ye'll be warmer in there than we are oot here. Ye ken it's bluidy cauld the nicht.' He chuckled wildly, and so did his lanky companion. Encouraged, the short man went on: 'Hey, we cannae wish ye a Happy New Year, fur ye'll no be here next year!' They shouted with laughter and the tall one said he was sure the wee man had had a good drop that night to be in such good form.

When they caught sight of me in the door of the waiting room they came over and wished me a Happy New Year, and shook my hand. I found their hands icy cold, and I shuddered. However, they assured me that our train would be along in a few minutes, and they were right. I left them still leaning over the coffin and exchanging their patter in the time-honoured Glasgow way.

That was a bad journey home. The train had been standing idle all day, and there was no heating. The journey took over three hours, and we were standing for over thirty minutes of that time in freezing fog. I wrapped the children in my overcoat, and used my scarf to wrap May's feet. We passed the time by drawing funny wee men on the steamed up windows, but it seemed to take for ever before we pulled into our station, only to find that the last of the buses had long gone, and we had to walk home. When we got there, I kindled the fire, while May made tea, lighting every one of the gas burners in an effort to get some instant heat into the house. Then hot water bottles were filled and every spare blanket piled on the beds. The holiday was over, and it was back to work the next day.

As always after Hogmanay, there were aches and pains and sore heads the next day, with fervent promises of "Never again!". But even while the promises were being made, those making them were wishing that they had the price of a drink, just enough to get them over the day. It was not that they were all boozers, by any means, but the traditional over-indulgence at Hogmanay takes its toll. Fortunately, that was a problem that never touched me.

Just a short time after that I was working day shift on development work when Wullie Ramage came and told me that there had been a serious accident at the face, and I was to go and inspect. I collected my jacket and the bag with my book and pens, and we went off. On the way we passed a phone that was ringing, so I took it off the hook, and just as I was about to speak I heard a conversation on the phone. Obviously there was a crossed line. 'Is there anything I can do at this accident site?' asked one voice. 'No,' came the reply, 'That bloody Union Secretary, the Workmen's Inspector, is on his way down, so you better stay out of the way.' 'Alright then,' the first voice said, 'I'll just come up the pit.' The phone went dead. I was unable to distinguish the voices with any certainty, although I had a suspicion about them. We went off down to the face, to find that the accident had been a fatality and that the men had, in the old tradition, all left the section. The dead man was a youngster, killed by the cutting disc of the machine. After overhearing that conversation, I was even more distrustful than ever, and checked and double checked all the measurements, but could find nothing wrong. I made my sketch, and put all the dimensions in, and then we went up the pit.

I was doing that job as Workmen's Inspector. I had done quite a lot of studying before being appointed by the Branch to that position, going to night school and various courses organised by the Union. It was an official position recognised by the Coal Mines Act, and was in addition to the permanent Workmen's Inspector from Union Headquarters, who inspected the mine each quarter, and whenever there was a serious accident. Together with all the usual work of a Branch Secretary, being the Workmen's Inspector meant a considerable amount of time spent on various sorts of union activity.

It was my job to make a full report of that particular accident, and all other accidents, both to Management and to the Union. Later, our own Workman's Inspector came from Edinburgh to make his own inspection, but neither of us could find anything wrong, and nothing to explain that strange telephone conversation I had overheard. So far as we could discover, nothing was being covered up.

That lad's funeral was a moving experience. Of course, I attended as Union Secretary. All officials attended all funerals, and none of us ever got hardened to that obligation to pay our last respects to our comrades. On this occasion, it seemed that the whole village of Coalsnaughton turned out and lined the road to the cemetery. Workmates walked with the coffin, and it was easy to see how well liked and respected the lad had been.

Things in the mine seemed to be going well. We had overcome the faults in the seams, and production was high. The contracts were satisfactory and the men seemingly contented enough. There were no more of the strikes which had bedevilled the place and eroded our standard of living in the earlier years. We were better off, not so much in the sense that our wages were high (they were never that in coal mining) but that they were steady. Some men left, and others joined. Almost twice as many men were now working in the pit as when we started. It all seemed secure and the future safe. We should have known better.

About this time, in the late '60s and early '70s, we began to see very clear signs of a change in the economic climate of Scotland. Works began to close down and workers laid off as machines were developed to take their places. It was a slow process at first, but obvious enough if you looked for it, and we in the Miners' Union tried to warn our fellow Trades Unionists about it, and to take some steps to prepare for a different future, and to protect the interests of our members. Our warnings, though, even in the local Trades Council, seemed to fall on deaf ears. They would agree that something would have to be done, then go away and do nothing.

In the meantime the Miners' Union remained in the forefront of every battle that had to be fought, and every campaign to improve the standards of working people, not only in our own country, but everywhere in the world. We campaigned for the Right to Work, for Equal Rights for Women, for Better Pensions, and we participated in many demonstrations and contributed to campaigns. No-one came to us for help and went away empty-handed.

Our own jobs were changing dramatically, too, as new machinery came into use. Coal getting now was totally mechanised. Instead of picks and shovels and saws and mash hammers, we had to learn how to use the very latest technology in cutters and conveyors.

Not all of it was good, and in fact some of it was downright dangerous, exposing the men to roof falls or bringing them far too close to cutter bars and discs. In safety meetings with the management we discussed all of these things, and tried to find ways of modifying them and making them safer. It seemed that all improvements in coal getting brought new problems. The new machines which cut and automatically loaded coal in a continuous cycle were extremely noisy and produced masses of dust. Ventilation was never good, and the air always hot and humid. In those conditions men sweated heavily, and the dust settled on them thick and black. Only their eyes and teeth stayed white. The air bags which were supposed to control the ventilation and bring fresh air in to us were often torn by debris or falling coal, and did not really do their job well.

We were supplied with masks but at first they were crude and inefficient. Later models were better, but without doubt they did hinder a man's breathing, and a lot of men found they could not wear the masks when doing heavy work. And, in spite of all the mechanisation, it was still, as always, very heavy work. Everything about a pit is heavy and built to last, and everything is constantly being moved from place to place. That is in the nature of the job, but it meant that miners still had to rely to a great extent on sheer strength and agility. Since we were all paid on contract, there was no time for resting and catching your breath. It was work from start to lousing time, with a few minutes for a break at piece time.

I was lucky, in a sense, because I was often called away off the job to investigate an accident or on other Union business. That gave me a break from work, but it also meant that I had to claim an allowance for the lost time.

One morning as we rode to work on the bus, Wullie MacDougall called me to his side. We would have to have an important meeting as soon as we got to the pit yard, he said, and asked me to get round the buses as they arrived and call the men up. He explained that the Devon pit was on strike, and that the men were holding a stay-down strike there in protest at pit closures. We had been closely linked with the Devon when we worked at our previous mine, the Meta. The Devon men were asking for our support. It was indeed our policy as a Union Banch to fight to safeguard jobs, and we had often talked about it at Union meetings, warning that pit closures would have a devastating effect right through the district, as unemployment would spread outward from the miners to all the other workers.

The men gathered round in the pit yard, and Wullie took the floor. There was no difficulty in persuading the men that we had to support the Devon strikers, and soon the buses were filled up with men turning round to go home. We were on strike again.

A little later there was a meeting of the officials to plan our campaign, which included arrangements to donate food and drink to the men staying down in the Devon. Various officials were detailed to go off to the various pits and put the case, and by the afternoon the whole of the Area was on strike. Various men and officials were also selected to go outside the Area, and I went off to Fife.

The reception by the Branch officials at the first pit we visited was not exactly warm, although the men we talked to while waiting for the officials to appear seemed sympathetic enough. At the meeting in the Branch office we argued strongly that the closure of the Devon was only the first step — it could be their turn tomorrow. I had worked in the Meta mine next to the Devon pit, and knew there was still plenty of coal there, but the mine had been closed, and we had been transferred, and only now were we back to the financial position we had been in when working the Meta, despite all the fine promises that had been made. We again asked them for their support, but they were very lukewarm. 'Well, that's about it,' said the Chairman, 'We'll discuss your problem.'

Jimmy McCaig, one of the men from the Devon pit, had had enough. 'Our problem?' he roared, 'Can't you see it'll be your problem tomorrow? This is everybody's problem, everybody's future is at stake. Do we get your support or not?

The Chairman replied that they had heard what we had to say, now we should leave it with them and they would call a Branch meeting for Sunday and put it to the men. 'Sunday!' shouted Guy Bolton, another Devon man, 'What's wrong with today? Let us speak to your men!' The Chairman refused to do that, but said he would put the case sympathetically on Sunday. We told him, strongly, that we needed support today, not on Sunday, but we could make no headway with him. We left, not on the best of terms.

The next pit we approached received us better, and we were allowed to address the men. When it was put to a vote, there was an overwhelming vote to strike, and that pit was idle. We had some food in their canteen and then went on to another pit in the Fife coalfield. There, too, we were succesful, and the pit was idle. I was not surprised at this success. Indeed, I would have been surprised if they had not come out in support of the Devon men. It was a long and honourable tradition that miners supported each other in their struggles.

Back in the strike centre, our own Area, we were told next to go off to Bathgate and seek their support. This was likely to be difficult, because the Bathgate men had long held the reputation of being moderates.

When we got to the pit we went to the baths and found some of the men changing into their work clothes. We explained what our mission was, and they all promptly changed back into their other clothes. However, one old chap warned us that it would be difficult to get the pit out, although he certainly agreed with us. He did say that if we got this pit out, then the whole coalfield would follow. We were still talking with him when someone, obviously someone in authority, asked what we were doing there. I told him that it was a fine night, and that we had been talking about the dogs: they had not run well for us that night. He was not fooled, though, and ordered us off the premises, saying that it was private property. I corrected him on that. It was property belonging to the people, but he as the pit manager, still had the right to order us off, and we went, after telling him he could expect his pit idle by that night.

We went outside the gate and as the men came up from the shift we gathered them around us and Jimmy McCaig spoke about the stay-down miners and how they were living underground. I spoke about how essential it was to save jobs now. I told them that we were only the temporary custodians of those jobs. We had inherited them from our fathers, and we had to be sure we could hand them on to our sons. It was their future we were fighting for. We must learn not to believe the promises made to us. In the Meta we had been promised a veritable heaven on earth, with a better future, easier work and higher wages if we moved to Bogside. The opposite was true in every case. There had been plenty of coal left in the Meta when it was closed, and we had had to battle for years to get back to the same wages and conditions that we had left in the Meta. Now the Devon men were faced with the same position. They were fighting for their future, and we must support them. When the meeting was opened to the floor, the old chap I had spoken to in the baths gave his very strong support, and when it came to a vote there was no question: they were on strike.

Our delegation (or Flying Picket, as we were proud to be known) arrived back at headquarters at two in the morning, and then we went off to rest for an hour or two. The next morning a big meeting was being held in the strike centre when we got there, with all the top Union officials present. There had been discussions with the Board, and the strike was called off. We were to go back to work on Monday. Devon was not to be closed immediately, so to that extent, the strike had achieved its aims, although it was closed later that year, and we had an influx of Devon men into our mine. They were experienced miners, and soon fitted into the more modern methods of coal getting, although like us with the Meta, they often regretted the closure of their own pit.

In those years I was very deeply involved in Union activity, not only as Branch Secretary, but also as Workmen's Inspector and Delegate to the Trades Council. There was little time for any social life, and there could be no doubt that our domestic life suffered. May, as always, was a gem. While I sat at the kitchen table for hour after hour, filling in forms and reports, she held the family together, and never lost patience with me or with the job. She would always produce a cup of tea for the men who came along with their problems, and listen to them with understanding. Certainly without her patience, gentleness and understanding, I could never have done the Union work I did.

Most of that Union work revolved around accident and damage claims. When it came to disputes, Wullie MacDougall was usually around to take the leading role, although there were occasions when I had to do that, and when it was necessary, I did not hesitate. It was always a great satisfaction to me when we won some claim for compensation for an injured man, and that was about all the rewards one got. Certainly there was no money in it. We did receive what was called 'Remuneration Money', but almost all of that went on stamps, and the little remaining, and a good bit more, on things like bus fares. Wullie always called Union work a labour of love, and he was quite right. And we never gave up on a case.

I was at a meeting of Delegates and Secretaries once, and, chatting after the meeting, I was amazed at the attitude of some of the Secretaries to some accident claims. 'I just told him he had no claim' was a standard remark. I was astounded and angered at this, and hotly denounced them. I told them I would never refuse to fight a case, and that we were not qualified to be judge and jury. Each case had to be submitted on its merits and argued to its conclusion in the best way we could. That was our duty, and that was what the men trusted us to do. Anything less was a betrayal.

I also pointed out that in many Damage Claims men were being offered £50 or £60, and because of debt or bad advice, were taking it, while others, fighting the case, were getting awards of £700 or £800. This was wrong and ridiculous, and the Union should be seeking ways to improve the system, first by looking at the actions of their own legal advisors who were supposed to advise members on the merits of the case. The N.U.M. Compensation Department was good, very good, but they were advised by outside lawyers and I felt that they were the ones not doing their job properly, and that it was up to us, Union Officials, to give advice from the point of view of the men and the workers, not from a narrowly legalistic attitude.

Now that there were two sections producing coal, a lot more men were employed, and it was my job to keep the lists of men and their places of work. Inevitably some men were dissatisfied at their placing on those lists, but the Union rules had to be followed, and they were, since that was much the fairest way of allocating the jobs. I myself was on the spare list for a while, and that meant one had to take any job that was going on any particular day. That I always welcomed, as it meant a variety of work and a variety of work mates, and I always felt that learning about other jobs and other techniques was worthwhile.

When I went back on to the Faceline, I had an accident that laid me off work for a few weeks. I was working with a young trainee, shifting the conveyor. As the machine cut a slice from the coal face, all the equipment of coal cutter, conveyor and everything else had to be moved forward by the width the machine had cut from the coal. The empty space where the coal had been removed was the waste, and generally it was allowed to collapse, but of course we had to support the roof where we were still working, close up to the cutter and conveyor. That roof was supported by pillars built up from stout wood, and these are knocked down and advanced each time the conveyor is moved forward. That was the job I was doing. Meanwhile the young lad was moving the conveyor.

That was done by a steel joist being inserted into the roof and an arm worked by hydraulic pressure pushing against that and moving the conveyor section into its new position. On this day I was getting ready to move a pillar, and was a bit anxious about the roof, which was unstable. It looked as though it would collapse when the pillar was removed, so I erected a prop to protect myself, and prepared to knock out the pins jamming the pillar against the roof. Meanwhile the trainee lad was busy with the conveyor.

I slid into position to hit the pin and just as I raised my hammer I found myself pinned to the pillar by the hydraulically operated steel rod which should have pushed the conveyor. It had not gripped the roof as it was intended to do. I screamed for the lad to reverse the action, and he immediately did so, and I rolled clear. Just then, though, in his excitement and distress, the lad hit the valve again, and again the rod shot out and this time pinned me by the chest. It was only for a moment, and then Johnnie got it right, and I was free, coughing and in much pain. Johnnie was with me in an instant, greatly concerned and trying to help. When I could, I told him to stop worrying and blaming himself, that it was an accident that could have happened to anyone. Workmates were soon on the scene, and offered to get me up the mine, but I told them I would manage on my own. There was no doubt I had to get out: certainly I could not work. Breathing was difficult, and a deep breath agony. I had to move carefully so as not to jar my body. It had to be kept in a certain position, and I had to take short breaths. Not the easiest way to walk out of a mine. The road was low, and you always had to walk bent double, and I groaned with the pain as I stumbled along.

And then the haulage rope began travelling, and I knew a rake of hutches was coming. Manholes, I thought, where are the bloody manholes? Normally I knew exactly where they were, and where I could find shelter in safety and let the rake pass. Now I could not think where they were, and could not move quickly to find them. So I lay down on the pavement between the legs of a roof support and hoped that I would be clear of the rake and its load. Lying down did not ease the pains in my chest, just the reverse, and it was still difficult to breathe, but at that moment I could not think of any thing else to do but lie there. Fortunately the rake did not have a wide load, and it all just cleared me.

I lay still in a sort of stupor of pain and sweat until I heard the hiss of the haulage rope over the pulleys die away. The rake was at the other end of the track, and it was time to go. I managed to roll over and get to my knees, with knives and red hot pokers and hack saws going in and out of my chest. Then I pulled myself to my feet and went on, doubled over under the low roof and almost blind with the sweat I could not wipe from my eyes.

It was a great relief when the height of the roadway increased and I was able to work my way to an upright position. It all seemed a lot easier then, and I got to the mine mouth without any further problems, although the pain was not less. I reported the accident there, and went off to bath and change, while arrangements were made for a van to take me to the hospital. There, an Indian doctor, who seemed no more than a young lassie, examined me and arranged for X rays, which showed three broken ribs and two badly bruised. As she strapped me up from my neck down to my waist, she said that she saw a lot of accidents from Bogside, and did I find it a very dangerous place? I told her that it was no more dangerous than any other mine, but that all mines were dangerous, and that accidents could always be expected. And that is true: no amount of new machinery, no amount of new training, no amount of skill and care will ever make mining a safe occupation or one in which accidents are not a regular and expected feature of every miner's life.

It wasn't easy climbing back into the van, which had waited to take me home, since every breath was like a knife. Nor was it easy climbing down again at home, where May came running out, greatly concerned when I had been late off shift, and more concerned now. I was able to reassure her that there was nothing seriously wrong, but just the same was glad of her help into the house, and into my chair by the fire. I tried smoking a cigarette, and that was a mistake. Every drag on it was a new knife into my ribs, so it went into the fire. May tried to make me more comfortable, and brought me tea, and my wee daughter appeared, woken by the noise, and tried to comfort me. It was a relief to be home, but I was beginning to want my bed.

Eventually I managed to get into bed and into a reasonably comfortable position, and then the pills I had from the doctor took effect, and I went off into a deep sleep, much deeper than I usually managed in the day time. The next thing I knew was May bringing me a meal. She had to help me up into a sitting position and then back again to lie down after the meal. That was the order of things for the next few days, with May having to help me along. I was lucky to have a wife loving and caring as she was. It certainly helped when things were rough and painful, as they were at that time. Rough, because money immediately became very short as soon as I was off work. The compensation benefit did not go very far, and our little savings soon vanished. The doctor had given me another sick note for a further three weeks off work, but two days later I started work, and then went and told him, and asked for a signing-off certificate. He warned me that I would have to be very careful, but I knew that anyway. Certainly if it had not been the pressing need for the money, I would never have started work so soon.

To return to work after any spell of idleness means being stiff and sore with aching muscles, tired arms and legs for several days until you regain your physical fitness. It was worse for me this time, because as well as the expected stiffness and aches, I still had the pains from the broken ribs. Fortunately, I was listed to go on development work with two good neighbours, who took some of the weight off me. We were a good team, although sometimes they were a little resentful when I was called away to settle a dispute or investigate an accident.

That happened not long after I had restarted work. There was a phone call for me: I had to go immediately to a neighbouring mine, Castlehill, where there had been a serious accident. I met our Manager when I got to the surface, and he was grim-faced. An accident, even if not in our our pit, affected every one of us. He told me that a van would take me straight over to Castlehill, and that he would see me when I got back. At Castlehill the officials I met were stony-faced, and they told me what had happened, and that a man had been killed. Our inspector, George Montgomery, had already been sent for, and I went into the office to wait for him. When he arrived, we went underground to the scene of the accident, where the man had been killed by a mine car. We examined the car and the whole area, took measurements and checked the warning bell system. The Government Inspector arrived with the Manager, and did his own examination. We then compared notes and ideas on what had caused the accident. It did not seem that any regulations or rules had been broken, and yet a man was dead, with all that that meant for his family. We had to check and double check, to ensure that the accident was never repeated. It was easier, in a way, if there had been carelessness or broken rules, but there was nothing of that sort here. Consequently we had to examine every rule to see if it needed changing. It all had to be done, and we all co-operated in doing it.

When we had finished our reports, George drove me back to Bogside, and I took him home for breakfast. We had always got on well together, and I learned a lot from him. He was concerned then at the increasing amount of noise in the pits, caused by the introduction of more powerful machinery. For some time we had been advising men to use cotton wool in their ears. He told me that he was actually writing an article on the subject, and said he would send me a copy when it was ready, and would value my opinions on it. When he did, I found it very valuable, and used it to raise several points on noise abatement at the Safety Committee meetings. Between George with his emphasis on noise abatement, and Wullie MacDougall with his committment to dust suppression, I always had something to raise at the Safety Committee, and I know well that as a result of our efforts conditions were greatly improved and safety increased.

I was still working with Matt and Bob on driving a roadway. We had reached the coal and driven on through it. Now we were backbrushing the roadway, that is, cleaning it up, and erecting circle arch supports. We had been joined by an extra man, Alex McEwan, a big and powerful chap and an excellent worker. We worked together for some time, and worked well as a team, and it was then that I got perhaps the biggest fright of my life.

We had moved the conveyor, and I was putting in a Dobson prop. This was a steel prop with a moveable head actuated by a hydraulic pump built into the prop itself. As I was pumping it up my key slipped and I lost my balance with the weight of the Dobson on me. I stepped back and my foot went into the scraper pan. No problems about that, except that at that very instant the chain running the pan and operating the scrapers reversed and caught my foot firmly between one of the scrapers and the barrel end of the conveyor. I was horrified, and called for help. Jimmy leaped to the signal wire, but it was not working, so he shouted to men further down the face to stop the scraper. He and Alex came back to where I was lying, sweating with fear. If that chain reversed any further, my leg was off. 'For fuck's sake hurry up, Jimmy,' I pleaded, knowing well that he and everybody else was hurrying as much as was possible for men to hurry. Jimmy got a strap under the top plate and heaved, hoping the plate would ease enough for me to be dragged clear. The strap snapped. They could not see a pinch bar that I knew was lying somewhere. Alex raced up with a steel strap. Sweat was pouring down my face and I shook with fear as they put a chock under the plate and manoevered the strap under it. 'When we lift, pull your foot out,' Alex ordered, and put his enormous strength under the strap. I watched the strain show on his face and neck, and feared that the strap would bend, and that my foot would go into the machine. 'Pull out now' he hissed, and Jimmy heaved on my leg. I was free, and at that moment the chain reversed again. That was when my leg would have been off.

I pulled the lace of my boot loose, and dragged my foot out of it. The sock stayed in the boot, and my foot came out startlingly white. After a moment, as the blood rushed back, it went red, and I was able to move it. No bones broken, then, and no bad crushing. When I looked at my boot, I saw deep gouges in the leather, the heel almost torn off, and the steel toecap squashed almost flat. That stout boot had certainly done its job of protecting my foot, but I still shuddered at the thought of what would have happened had my neighbours not succeeded in getting me free. I took my girder key and hammer, and beat out the toecap to almost its original shape, and worked my foot back into the boot. Again I thanked the lads for their help, and we went back to work.

The first job was to examine the signal wire and find out why it had failed. That done, and having repaired it, we got on with the job.

The drivage we were working on was a long one, first into the coal, and then back to rip the roof. That was what we called back-brushing. It paid reasonable wages, and although we ran into some small faults, we were always hopeful that things would improve and we would have a long spell of earning really good wages. That never happened.

It was while we were driving that level that I received a message one day to go at once to a particular drivage off a heading. The fireman wanted to see me. It was some distance away, and when I got there I found the fireman standing waiting for me. He had a concerned look on his face. He was an older man, a good miner, and not one to panic. 'I thought you should know about this,' he said, 'You being the Union Secretary and Workmen's Inspector. I want you to take a look at this road. But don't mention I sent for you.' I assured him I wouldn't, and went into the road. He had reason to be distressed with the conditions there. Even out at the gearing there was a lot of spillage, and I told him he should get that cleared up. He promised to get someone on to that straight away, and went off.

I scrambled over coal that had spilled from the scraper, and made walking difficult. This was shoddy workmanship, and I was already getting angry. It should all have been cleared up, and all the broken props replaced to make for safe walking. I reached the slusher, the small moveable haulage engine which dragged buckets of coal from the face to the beginning of the conveyor, ducking under air bags, and as I moved further into the road, I was shocked to see how they were working. One man was at the slusher and another at a turn in the roadway. He signalled to the man at the slusher by waving his lamp. Another man was up at the coal face. I was astounded to say the least, and called for an immediate halt. 'What the bloody hell is going on here? Are you all mad?' 'We're only doing our job,' said one. 'We're on contract!' said another.

'Contract?,' I replied, 'Contract my arse! Being on contract doen't mean to say you take risks and perhaps kill yourselves. This road is stopped till its safe. I want this road cleaned up and proper signals installed. Nae mair waving yer lamp. I want all broken and missing props replaced. I want this road made safe and secure. I don't want any of you men hurt. Now start and get that done, and I'll come back later to see if it has been done to comply with the Coal Mines Act. Now get mobile.' I was called a smart bastard, and other things, but I was sure that the job would be done, so I went off into the heading, where I met the old fireman. I told him I had stopped the road till the various requirements had been carried out. He agreed that was the right thing to do, and said he would get an electrician in to put up the signal wires. I went back to my place and had a long drink of water, then started writing up a note of the inspection. Then I saw a light hurrying up the road towards me. It was carried by an angry oversman. He had only recently been started but already had the reputation of being an arrogant bastard, and was known as The Whiz Kid.

He roared that I had no fucking right to stop any road in the pit. I had no authority. He was in charge, not me. He was going to make an example of me. He would put me all the way. The Manager would get the report. I told him to calm down, to keep the heid, that I had the authority to enter any workplace, operate any machine, make any inspection. I produced the certificates and authorisation papers from my box, and further told him that as a Union Official and Workmen's Inspector, I would stop any place I considered dangerous until it was made secure.

He glared at me, and I really hoped he was going to strike out. But all he said was: 'I've started that road up again just after you left.' I told him alright, but it was on his head. If any of those men was hurt, he would be responsible and answerable as being in breach of regulations. He made no reply, but hurried off up the roadway.

I had hardly started work again, after explaining to Bob and Matt what the trouble was, when a young oncost lad came running up and told me there had been a bad accident, and that I had to get there quick. It was the place I had stopped and the Whiz Kid had restarted. Bob and Matt came with me as I raced up the roadway, ready to give what assistance they could. As it happened, their help was not necessary. The two injured men were already up the pit. I went on to inspect where the accident had happened, and met Matt MacEwan, the oversman. We always got on well together. He was strict, but fair and knew his job and his men. Together we inspected the site of the accident. There were two girders lying on the pavement, as well as some props. Obviously they had been dragged out by the slusher bucket. There was nothing more to see, but as we came away, I pointed out to Matt the broken props and the lack of a signalling system. He made a note of all that, and we went up to the surface.

Wullie MacDougall met me there, and reported that the two men were not seriously injured. One had a suspected broken leg and bad bruising, the other had body bruises, and could expect to be back at work shortly. Wullie asked me exactly what had happened, and I told him that I had inspected the place, found it unsafe and stopped the road till it had been rendered safe. It had been restarted by the official, and I argued that my decision to stop the job had been vindicated by the accident happening immediately work had restarted. I was angry, and wanted an example made of that character. Wullie listened carefully, and then told me to go and get washed and we would go and see the Manager.

The meeting was brief. I made my statement, carefully referring to the notes I had made, and the outcome was a decision to stop the road, and our own permanent Union Inspector would be called in.

Our inspector, Lance, was due to arrive the following morning. I was told to wait on the surface for him, and sent a message to Matt and

Bob that I would be delayed because of an inspection, and that they had better get another man. I waited in the canteen for Lance, who soon rolled up in his usual bright and breezy manner. 'Hello, lad,' he shouted when he saw me, 'You've set the heather on fire this time. You've set the cat among the pigeons! MacDougall was on the phone last night, but let's hear your side of the business. Can we get some tea or coffee in the canteen?'

'You back again!' shouted the woman in charge. 'And I haven't cleaned up the night shift mess yet.' I laughed, and told her to belt up, that she was always the same, moaning. In fact, she was a cheery and very obliging woman. 'Two coffees, please,' I asked, 'Please!'

She smiled, and said I was always the same with the patter, thinking I was God's gift to women, but God wisnae good to women when I had come round. I told her that wasn't fair, and that I always gave women the respect they deserved. She agreed, and said that was why she would make some coffee, even though the canteen was closed. What's more, she would even bring it over for us.

Lance and I settled down to business and I told him exactly what had happened the previous day and the attitude of the newcomer official, the Whiz Kid. I reported that he had started the road up again after I had stopped it to allow the men to get it cleaned up and renew the broken legs. It was definitely unsafe, I told him, and in breach of the Coal Mines Act. I would not allow men to work in those conditions even though that character pressurises them into doing so. Lance made notes as he listened.

Then the door burst open, and in came Davie Allen, an old friend. He was always bright and breezy, and always had a joke. Today was no different. Had we heard the one about the young lad who took his lassie out on his motor bike? They went up a country lane and stopped and did a bit of smooching. Then the lad asked her if she believed in the hereafter. 'The hereafter?' she exclaimed. 'Aye,' he said, 'The hereafter. Because if you're not here for what I'm here after, you'll be here after I've gone!' We all laughed at his joke, and wondered where he found them every day.

We finished our coffee, and Lance went off to see the Manager, and I waited for him in the canteen. He was only away for a few minutes, and then came back in his overalls, with lamp on his head and safety lamp at his side. We went underground and along to the drivage where the accident had happened. I began to point out the things I believed to be dangerous and in breach of the Act. We stopped under the last girder that had been erected, about fourteen or sixteen feet from the face. Lance noticed it was bent, and I pointed out that several were in that condition. There had been a steel strike, and steel was in short supply. Those girders had been withdrawn from old roads and erected in there. Lance said I did not miss much, and must have eyes like a hawk. 'No, Lance,' I told him. 'Like a cat: we're down a pit now.' He laughed, and we went on with the inspection.

Lance was obviously determined to discover everything he could about that place, and made a thorough inspection of it, even testing for gas. He asked me what I would do if gas was found, and I replied that I would close the section. He asked if I had any experience with gas, and I was able to assure him that I had quite a bit in Bothwell and the Lothians and in Ferniegair. He seemed satisfied, and we went out. That was not the end of his inspection, though. We went along to the faceline. The road in was long and low, and several times Lance stopped and measured the height. Eventually he said that it would never do, it did not comply with regulations. I had to agree with him, but pointed out that they intended to start backbrushing that road, and that in any case it was the tailgate, only a supply road. He thought that was all the more reason for it to be the specified height, and made another entry in his note book.

We travelled along the faceline, stopping several times to inspect Gullick props or the rams of the conveyor. When we reached the shearer coal cutting machine Lance called to the operator to stop the machine, and asked him several questions about the dust suppression system, then asked him to turn on the water sprays. Some of the sprays were not working, so he instructed that the machine should not run until all sprays were working effectively, and told the operator to send for the engineer. The machine man was open-mouthed as I scrambled over the machine. 'Smart bastard, that!' he said to me. 'Yes,' I agreed, 'He is smart. That's the Union Inspector, and you had better do as he asked.'

'Alright,' Tam said, 'But it's not my bloody fault the sprays are not working.' I turned on him. 'Listen, Tam, you are the operator in charge of that shearer. If the sprays don't work, stop and have them fixed. Don't give me that old guff about it not being your fault. It might not be your fault, but it is your responsibility.' Tam looked at me open-mouthed, and then turned away and shouted into the Tannoy. He told the engineer to get his rag out and drag his arse over there. I smiled as I crawled along the faceline, where the air was still heavy with the dust from the cutting. Lance had been quite right to stop the shearer. When we reached the main gate Lance made a few more notes in his book, and then we made our way out. On the way Lance talked about the problem of dust, and said that cutting without water or with faulty sprays was dangerous, and that I should stop any machine I saw like that. We commented that only one man had been wearing a mask, and he said that we should really be impressing the men with the importance of wearing the masks. I told him that a lot of men said that they had difficulty in breathing with the mask, but Lance said that if they did not wear them, they might soon not be breathing at all. Of course, he was right enough about that, and he knew that Wullie MacDougall in particular, our own "Stoury Wull" was constantly on about the same thing.

We rode up on the man riders, and it was good to be out in the open air again. Lance went off to see the Manager and I went off to the baths, and we arranged to meet later. I was waylaid by a number of men wanting help with filling in accident or compensation forms, and some wanting help with putting a grievance. I was sure I could help them by a meeting with the Manager, but Lance had been waiting some time before I was through with the routine business.

I told him my bus was away already, but he said I was not to worry about that: he would give me a lift home. He still had a number of questions he wanted to ask me, about the names of the various roads and sections we had visited. He had to be very precise in writing his report, but it was a job he was good at, and it was soon completed. He and I always got on well together, but I was a bit upset when he asked me to show him the road to a new mine at Solsgirth. At that time of night! I had been away from home since six o'clock in the morning, and I knew that even when I got home there would be more forms to fill in, more reports to prepare. I had had enough for the day, and when I told Lance that, and said there would surely be more Union work waiting at home, he asked about my spare time. Did I play golf? He was a golfer, and had his clubs in the car. I did not play golf. I hardly had time to play a game with my children. 'Dedication, that's what I call it,' said Lance, and asked what I got out of it. I told him bugger all except the satisfaction of helping my fellow men. There was a remuneration of (and I started to laugh) £10 a year from the Branch. Wullie MacDougall had the same, and I explained that we did not believe in using the Branch funds for remuneration, but only for vital issues, like expenses for delegations. Lance, who was paid by the Union, listened with interest, and repeated that he thought we should have a better remuneration from the Branch for all the work we did. I disagreed, though, and we were still discussing it when he dropped me at the corner of my street, and I pointed out the way he should take to the golf course.

A couple of chaps were waiting for me when I got home. They had been waiting quite a while, and May offered to make some tea for us all. The lads wanted help with some forms that had to be completed. Well, that was no problem, but I wanted my tea first.

'Here,' said the elder of the two when I sat down, 'That's a braw dug you've got.' 'Ay, that's Jamie,' I told him. 'He's a rough collie. I bought him for my son.'

'Ay, he's a braw dug alright,' the man repeated, 'But ah wouldna like tae dae anything wrong when he's there. The lad can do anything with him, an so can yer wife, but we've had tae sit here on this couch and not move. He kept his eyes on us and sat there between us and your wife all the time.' I laughed at that, for it was Jamie all over. I called to him, and he raced over and put his lovely head on my knees for me to rub and caress. But as soon as May whispered his name, he was off to her with his paws up on her knees and nuzzling up under her chin. 'Jamie's a good dog,' she whispered to him. 'Who's worth his weight in gold then?' Jamie squirmed with delight. I told the lads the story of how Jamie had saved us from being burgled one night.

May and I had just gone to bed and were half asleep when she thought she heard the back gate latch being opened. She told me to wake up, but I told her to lie down and let Jamie attend to it. I was still half asleep, but I did hear Jamie give a soft "woof", which meant that he was awake. I told May, in joke, that I was not going through there. I might get a tanking, and then there would be no work in the morning. Just then I definitely heard someone at the back window, so I was up like a flash. In my hurry to get out of the back door, I had forgotten that the door was locked, and by the time I had found the key, the intruders had vanished. Which was just as well for them, because when I got the door open, Jamie went out like a thunderbolt and I am certain would have pinned any one he found.

There was no-one in the garden, but it seemed plain that they had slipped through the hedge into the next garden, and would be making off down the street. I raced round with Jamie, and ran down the road, but there was no sign of any intruders, so we went back. When we got back into the house, May was up, looking a bit anxious, but when she saw us she burst into peals of laughter. It was a hot and humid night, and I had gone to bed dressed only in my swimming trunks. That was all I was wearing when I raced down the street. 'Good job there was nobody about to see you!' May laughed, but I was not particularly amused. I inflated my chest and posed with biceps straining, as I had seen in advertisements for Charles

Atlas body building. 'There,' I told her, 'If they saw a splendid figure of a man like that it would be a treat for the women, a real eyeful.' She smiled, and agreed.

And that was how Jamie, with a bit of help from me, saved us from being burgled.

There was one fatal accident while I was working in that mine, and as the Workmen's Inspector I had to investigate it and make my report. Our Union Inspector and the Board Inspector were also involved, of course. Chick, the lad who was killed, was well known and liked, and his death was a shock even to us, who were somewhat hardened by our constant exposure to danger and injury. He had been a prisoner-of-war, taken at Singapore, and had survived the Railway of Death. It was sad indeed that he should somehow have been crushed by a rake near a manhole in that mine.

There was no doubt that Wullie MacDougall and I made up a good team. A lot of our Union work was dealing with shortages in men's wages, and those Wullie usually handled. I was kept busy dealing with accident and sickness cases. There were spells when I did not have a great deal to do, and then Wullie and I shared whatever work he had. At other times I would be exceptionally busy, and Wullie would help me, usually grumbling about it, but always willing, and always saying that I should have an assistant. I told him I had one, and that he was the assistant. Generally speaking, he did the talking and I did the writing, and we got the work done that way, and never grudged the time spent doing it.

If any of our members was in hospital or sick at home, we always tried to visit them. Here, again, Wullie came into his own. He had a real bedside manner, a gift that few people possess, and could chat away and keep the sick man entertained for as long as we stayed. I could not do that: I would talk for a few minutes, and then was stuck for something to say. Actually, I don't think it mattered very much what we talked about, it was the fact that we visited that was important to the men.

We had the practice that, when a man had been off work for, say twelve weeks, we would have a collection for him. These were generous, and only too often a Godsend to the man and his family. They would have been living on Sickness Benefit or Compensation for a long time, and that was damned little. There was one collection, though, taken up for a man who was considered to be a sponger, and who rarely contributed when the bag went round. The collection for him amounted to Two Pounds Fourteen Shillings and Two Pence. Some jokers had put in a few steel washers, indicating that the man was not liked. It was not much of a collection, even when Wullie and I dipped into our own pockets and made it up to a round Three Pounds. It was my job to deliver it, and I was not looking forward to it. However, old Sandy, one of the Committee Members, offered to do it for me, and I was glad, for I could not think how I could explain that small sum, so uncharacteristic of the men of Bogside. Besides, it meant that I could get home at a reasonable time on a Friday.

I saw Sandy on Monday, and asked how it had gone. 'Fine,' Sandy said. 'Ah just telt the bugger I wisnae here tae be hoofed, poofed or laughed at, and here's yer money. He just gawked when he saw all it wis. "The miserable bastards. Is that aal ah git?" he asked me. Ah telt him that was mair than ye deserve. Ah ken you, you niver put into a collection in yer life. Alwis remember it's better tae be the giver nor the receiver. Ye were niver the giver, and ah left him cursing at his door.'

Old Sandy was a character and I always enjoyed his company at meetings and demonstrations. He was a real old timer, a jovial man with a tremendous sense of humour. He loved to tell of the old times. There was once when he had been off work ill, and his wife began to think he was shamming, and told him so till Sandy had had enough. So he took her out for a bit walk, up through the cemetery. He stopped at several headstones. 'Aye, auld Tam. Ah kent him weel. A hard grafter. Here's auld Rab, he was a guid brusher, a real hard worker. An here's auld Jimmy, a guid man. Ye kent him weel, he wis niver oot o the pit. A grand worker he wis.' And so it went on till they went out through the cemetery gates again, when Sandy turned to his wife and said: 'Aye, hen, an whit dae ye think noo. Would ye no hae Sandy here beside ye, or lyin up there amang the guid men?' We never did learn what Sandy's wife replied, because he always began laughing at his own wit.

It was Sandy who called me to the scene of another fatal accident. This time it was a lad working on the surface. I knew his father well. He was Polish and had come over to fight during the war. At the end of the war, he had married a Scottish woman, and settled down here. The lad had been late in getting home from work, but his folks thought he had probably gone to visit some friends. It was much later that they grew concerned and contacted the pit. It was found that his clean clothes were still in his locker, so a search was instituted, and his body was found under a conveyor.

He had been cleaning up under there, and his clothes were caught up in the moving belt and he had been drawn up to the rollers and strangled. It was a horrible death, and he was just a young lad. Wullie and I went to visit his family to bring what comfort we could, and to help them in the distressing business of filling in all the necessary forms.

Wullie and I were both members of the Safety Committee and also of the Consultative Committee. The latter did good work in ensuring better co-operation between workers and Management. It was important work, because in the past our record for strikes was dismal — although I should add that the majority of those strikes was caused by the arrogance and incompetence of Management. This, happily, was changing, and there was much more harmony and co-operation, a situation which was good for both men and Management.

The Safety Committee sat and discussed accidents. A list of accidents was produced at every meeting, and we discussed them, and how they might have been avoided. Steps were then taken to ensure that whatever was wrong, whatever had caused the accident, was put right. The accident rate gradually dropped, but we could never be satisfied. Continually, we had to instruct the men in working safely within the Coal Mines Act.

As a Workmen's Inspector I was sometimes none too popular when, on making an inspection, I found men taking terrible risks, and came down heavily on them. I found that some officials turned a blind eye to some of the dangers and hazards in which they allowed men to work. When I found that, I would stop the job till the place had been made safe and secure. This greatly annoyed some of the officials, but gradually most of them came round, and eventually would tell us of any working that they considered dangerous, and discuss ways of making it safer. That sort of co-operation and harmony, of course, resulted in both better production and safer conditions, and was good for all concerned.

Some accidents were caused by sheer stupidity, like the day the Whiz Kid flooded the mine. He was the oversman I have mentioned before. Our team of Bob and Matt and myself were still on development work, and after some rough patches, had began to make good progress, and of course rather better money. I had been called out to some incident, and on my way back saw water running down our road. I shouted to Bob and Matt, and heard Bob call back that I was to come quickly. I ran through a cross cut, and saw a heavy flow of water, which was getting heavier by the second.

'Get tae hell out of here!', I shouted, and Matt and Bob charged off into the water. It was almost up to their waists. I followed them, and, being so much shorter, the water was already well above my waist. I shouted that they should walk on the bogey rails, and hold the monorail for support. This was an overhead rail on which pulleys ran to bring us supplies. As we struggled along, the water got deeper and the current stronger.

I was wearing gum boots, and of course they had filled up with water, but I was unable to get them off. As the water got deeper I got more and more worried, and finally was pulling myself along the overhead rail. I heard a voice shouting that they were sending a pulley down, and that I was to catch it and hold on. I could see three lights up ahead, and heard the pulley coming along the monorail towards me. It arrived, and I clutched it thankfully. The men began hauling it back, and I felt myself floating along through the water. 'Hell, we should have let the wee bugger drown!' I heard someone say, but by that time my feet were touching bottom, and I let go of the pulley and walked up the rest of the incline.

'Well, thanks, you shower of bastards,' I told them, and pulled off my gum boots to empty them and wring out my socks. I noticed that one of the men was Jimmy Dick, a rather dour oversman with whom I had had some disagreements. This time I had to thank him, though, for it was his quick thinking that had sent the pulley down to me. If that had not been done, I doubt that I could have got through the flood and the current. One of the lads said that a valve had burst at the dam up the slope.

However, somebody else reported that the Whiz Kid had opened the valve for some reason, apparently to see how much water was in the dam. That seemed likely, for the inrush had eased, as though a valve had been closed, and the water was pining away off. It did not surprise me that the 'baw-heided bastard' had done something else daft. The only surprise was in how he had got the job in the first place.

Jimmy Dick asked if the three of us in our team would salvage some electric panels that were just above the water, and we agreed, although it was uncomfortable and cold working in our sodden clothes. Other panels could not be salvaged, at least not yet. They were further down the road, which was still flooded almost up to the roof.

We had just finished moving the panels when we heard a voice we knew well shouting abuse at some oncost lads, and saw a light coming our way. It was the Whiz Kid himself. He pushed past us, and went off to make his own inspection. Quickly he was back. 'Now this is what you will do. You will all have to lie on. I want you all.....' He began, but I stopped him dead. 'Get this straight,' I told him. 'We are not lying on. We are in no condition to lie on. We are soaked to the skin and we are going up the pit at lousing time.'

'You are not!' he screamed. 'We are, you know,' I responded. 'I'll sack you!' he shouted.

'Look,' I told him, 'If anyone is going to be sacked over this lot, it's you. It's lousing time now, and we are going up to get these wet clothes off.' I turned and picked up my jacket and bag. The squad followed me. The Whiz Kid raced up and told us that we could not go, and when I said we were on our way, he repeated that we were sacked. That was a threat that had no content, coming from him, so we ignored him, and moved away.

We met Wullie MacDougall on our way out. He looked at us in amazement and enquired what the hell had happened. We told him that the whole of the south level was flooded, with hundreds of pounds worth of damage and that there was a team of men in there now salvaging what they could. I added, as an afterthought, that we were sacked. I would be seeing the Manager as soon as I got up the pit. Wullie sent us on our way, handing me his anorak which he said he would not be needing for the rest of the shift, and told us to get changed as quick as possible, or we would all be down with a chill. He went off to see the place for himself, and we went on up.

We met the Manager at the pithead, and while the others went straight off to the baths, I told him what had happened. He listened, and then said he had heard we did a good job in salvaging the panels. I told him that we had been sacked, and all he said was that he would deal with that, and I should get off to the baths.

Later, when we were sitting in the canteen waiting for our bus, the flooding was the centre of interest. Some of the men had heard of our squabble with the Whiz Kid and wanted to know what the Manager intended to do. I think they would have walked off the job there and then, and taken the rest of the pit with them, if I had not been able to reassure them that Wullie, the Manager, had not taken much notice of what the Whiz Kid had said.

One of the lads said he had heard that big Jimmy Dick had pulled me out through the flood. I told them it was a good job he was there and had the idea of sending the pulley along the monorail. Without it, I might have drowned. My gum boots were full of water, and I could hardly move. It was Bob and Matt who pulled me through the flood, but the idea came from big Jim, and all credit to him. But that could not make big Jim any more popular. One of the lads said that just last week he cut some men's time, and that one of them caught up with him later. 'You rotten big cunt,' he said. 'If you were lying needing the kiss of life nae bugger wid gae ye it. Ye're rotten baith inside and outside!' Well, maybe so, but I had something to thank him for that day.

I don't know what happened privately between the Whiz Kid and the Manager, but certainly not another word was said about us being sacked.

As a result of the flooding, the South Level was closed for some time, while various teams sought to salvage what they could. Our team was split up and we were on the spare list, which meant a different job each day. Bob and I worked together quite a bit, fireproofing a road up to the hopper. One day the fireman came along and asked us to clear away all the steel material that had been picked up from the conveyor belt by the magnets. There was all kinds of things, bolts and nut and picks from the cutting heads, and a mass of other steel. We put to one side all the stuff that could be used again, and then dealt with a big pile of wire that had been used to bind wooden straps in their bundles. This was a tangled mass, and we pressed it down into the hutch we were filling. I was just picking up some keys probably dropped by a tradesman when suddenly I felt a searing pain in my eye, and saw a bright flash. I cursed and swore and asked Bob what the bloody hell he thought he was doing. He could not understand what was wrong at first, and then we realised that a long length of wire he was handling had somehow sprung out of the hutch, right over to where I was standing, come over my shoulder, and struck me in the eye. It was the sort of thing that no-one could have foreseen.

Of course, Bob was blaming himself, and I was not in a condition to contradict him, although I kept assuring him that it was an accident. The pain in my eye was excruciating, and I was blinded with tears. I got to my jacket, and reached for one of the bandages I always carried. It was a burn bandage, a big cotton swab, and I used that to dry off my eye and my face. The pain was no better, and obviously I had to go up for attention. I told Bob to tell the fireman what had happened, and that I had gone up the pit to get attention and a proper dressing.

On the surface I went to the First Aid Room, where my old friend Tommy Gavin was on duty. 'Oh, aye,' he joked,' a sore eye for the puir wee man. Well, there's some say ye see too much, anyway!' I told him I was in no mood for joking, and would he get on and dress my eye. He sat me down and gently used a swab, then took out his magic eye, as he called it, a big magnifying glass, and took a close look at my eye. He whistled, and said it was a bad one. I would have to see my doctor. He would put in some drops to ease the pain, but I should get off straight away to the doctor. I yelped with pain when he put the drops in, and Tammy told me to take it easy. I would live, but would have a damned sore eye. He said I should go and get washed, while he made out his report, and then I should come back and get some more drops before going off to the doctor's surgery.

I was only off work for two days with that injured eye, and went back very much against the advice of the doctor. However, it was the old story — compensation and sick payment just did not go far enough to keep the family. It was work or go hungry. Well, I could have gone hungry, but there was no way I would watch May and the children doing so. There were plenty of jests when I got back, with a patch covering the injured eye. I was called the One-Eyed Bandit and Long John Silver, and a number of other things, but it was all in good fun. The oversman helped by giving me work in places where the dust was not so heavy, so that there was more chance of keeping it out of my injured eye. I had to wear the eye patch for quite some time before the eye was back to right and I could work normally.

It was not long after I had returned to work after that injury that I was elected to go to London as a member of a delegation to lobby our Executive during some negotiations they were conducting with the Coal Board. That was the 1969 negotiations on wages. There was a special train from Scotland, and we arrived in London in the early morning. We made our way towards the Board's headquarters, and hoped to find somewhere nearby where we could get something to eat. It was a wet morning, I remember, and we were hungry.

As we marched along, and turned a corner, we suddenly heard singing. It was part of the Welsh contingent, giving *Land of my Fathers* with great gusto. That was a fine uplift for us, tired and hungry as we were, because we had left home immediately after work, and had no sleep on the train. We all joined in the singing as best we could, and the Londoners passing on their way to work must have thought us mad, marching along and singing in the rain. A passing policeman obviously thought so. He looked at us in amazement, and we explained what we were and where we were going. Did he know of a good place to eat?

Yes, he did, it was a good place, and cheap, just a couple of streets away, and if we went along with him, he would show us where it was. So we did, and he was right. There were already quite a lot of other miners there, mostly Welshmen, and, like the lads with us, they were singing too. The policeman declined our invitation to have breakfast with us, and went on his way, while we got stuck into bacon rolls.

There was still plenty of time before the meeting between our Executive and the Board, so we went off for a stroll around London, although it was still drizzling with rain. We did not mind: our spirits were high, and we had every hope that we would be able to influence the members of our Executive who were considered to be weak in their stand against the Board's plans.

When the time came and we arrived at the Board's headquarters many other delegations had also turned up. We mingled with them, and the Welsh lads again began their singing, in which we all joined when we could. Singing in the rain, perhaps, and singing to keep our spirits up, but it all added to the atmosphere of the occasion. Most of the people who passed by in their cars and buses just glared, but some did give us a wave, and we waved back and smiled at them.

A few policemen appeared, and took up their positions. They seemed friendly enough. One near me claimed to be a Scot. Anyway, his parents were, although he himself had been born in Carlisle. His father had been a miner, but had received a serious injury and had to leave the pits. He himself would never go down the mines, but he had every sympathy with miners.

A little later our good opinion of the police was changed rather when three busloads of them appeared and shoved us into line. We were in two groups, with a clear entry into the building. The lad I had been talking to was still there in front of us, and we continued to talk and exchange remarks. There was a good deal of pressure now from behind, as men tried to get through to the front so that they could more easily say what they wanted to say, and make their points to the Executive members as they entered the building.

The Executive members began to arrive in ones and twos, and we chanted our slogans and shouted what we expected of them. There were some we knew would fight for us, and they were whole-heartedly cheered. It was only a half-hearted cheer for Lawrence Daly, our General Secretary, mixed with a few boos. There was a surge forward as he slipped into the building. Mick McGahey followed, from Scotland, and there was no doubt where he stood, or what he would do. He smiled and waved as there was a loud cheer for him, and he took the time to stop and shake hands with some of the older chaps he knew. Now we waited for our President, Joe Gormley.

When he arrived, there were cries of 'Traitor!' and 'Don't sell us out again, you bastard!' Joe's face was sullen and strained as he scowled at the crowd, and made his way through. It was a tense atmosphere for a moment and the police had to force a way through for him. Later it was alleged that both Joe Gormley and Lawrence Daly had been struck, but I was right there at the front of the crowd, and I saw no blows. Certainly there had been shouts of abuse and some pushing, but nothing more, and nothing like the scenes of riot that the grossly exaggerated reports in the evening newspapers described.

We spent the morning walking around London, and when the rain began coming down again, we dropped into a pub. There we met some of the Welsh lads, and had another song or two from them. When the time came, we made our way back to the Board's headquarters, and were met with the news that we had again been sold out. 'That Gormley, the gutless bastard' had done it again.

It was quite shattering, because for once we had had high hopes. Now they were gone, and we were angry. Back at the same cafe we found a lot of other men already there, all angry and disillusioned. It was Joe Gormley, 'the gittering sod' who was the subject of our talk. A Welshman said he was in the pocket of the Coal Board. Another said that we should have been represented by Mick McGahey, and we agreed with him, not just because Mick was a Scot, but because he was a man who would never surrender to expediency or bribery. 'We'll always be at the bottom of the league despite all Gormley's fine talk — that is, if anyone can make him out, the muttering bugger.' So it went on. 'You'll see, he'll get a slap on the back and be told he's a fine chappie, and then when the time comes he'll get some honour, all for selling us short.' That was the opinion of an old Ayrshire miner, and of course he was quite right.

There was a laugh when Tommy Coulter came in with the evening papers. He told me I was a thug, a bloody wee menace, fighting with the polis. There was a picture of me, with the caption "Miners in Brawl with Police", and there was Frank, the policeman I had been talking to, with his helmet falling off his head, and me with one arm in the air as though I was going to strike him. I remembered the incident. There had been a surge from behind and I was pushed forward into Frank's sturdy back. We had laughed about it at the time, and no harm was done to anybody. However, an alert photographer had caught it, and it looked as though the wee Scots miner, five feet seven and weighing ten stone, was attacking the poor polisman, well over six feet and fourteen stone. We passed the paper around, and then I stuck it in my pocket to give May as a keepsake of her aggressive, polis-bashing husband.

We had called a Union meeting for the Sunday after this delegation, and there was a good turnout. Wullie MacDougall gave a full report of our experiences and his opinions. I followed him, and confirmed that we were dissatisfied with the outcome of the meeting between the Executive and the Coal Board. This was not only our belief, but that of many other Delegations we had talked to. I expressed the opinion that trouble was coming to the coalfields. The future showed that I was right.

It was back to the old grind on the Monday, and I found that I had been allocated a driveage. It went well for a while, and we made reasonable wages for a week or two. Then we hit a fault. There was stone the full height. The management decided that we should drive straight through, in the belief (which was correct) that we would pick up the seam on the other side of the fault. We worked it like a stone mine. The noise when we bored that stone for blasting was incredible. We had to use Blast Borers, worked by compressed air, because the electric borers could not handle it. The Blast Borers were very noisy, and we had to stick cotton wool plugs in our ears. Even so, at the end of each shift it took quite a while before we could hear properly again. It took about a month to get through that hitch, and then we were back in coal again.

Shortly after that, at a meeting of the Consultative Committee, I was able to give vent to a personal grievance. Those meetings between Union and Management gave us a chance to discuss all the workings and problems of the pit. It was an example of the sort of co-operation we sought, and in which we believed. Everything was discussed openly, and as a Workmen's Inspector, I was very interested in the discussions on safety and the accident reports. On this occasion, the Manager, who was Chairman, opened the proceedings by reading the correspondence, which consisted of a letter from the Coal Board, from Head Office, from the Top Brass. Congratulations and thanks to the Management, officials and men. We had broken two records, one for coal output and the other for a fast driveage. Would we keep up this excellent work, and so on. The Manager was flushed with pleasure and pride. He said that a member of the Committee, myself, was one of the Team Leaders of this driveage. Did I have anything to say?

I laughed at that, because I always had something to say. I told the Committee that I well remembered that driveage, not because we broke a record, in fact my pay slip made no mention of a record. But it took me three weeks of argument and meetings to get the money I was due for the period when that record was broken. 'That's true, isn't it,' I challenged Big Willy, the manager. He was upset at having his moment of triumph spoiled. Wullie MacDougall jumped in to relieve the tension. He rebuked me for bringing up a question of wages, when the rules of the Committee forbade that. I addressed the Chairman again, and told him that I was not speaking about wages, but was merely stating a fact. I was not impressed by letters of that sort, and why didn't we get on with the business of the meeting? So we did, and had a full discussion of several things, including some accidents, of which I was able to give full and detailed reports. I had talked to witnesses and had visited the men in hospital, and so was able to talk with knowledge about what had happened, and make recommendations to ensure that type of accident did not happen again.

After the meeting I was walking away with Wullie MacDougall, and he asked me what had caused my outburst against Big Willy, the Manager. 'Hell, Wullie,' I told him, 'That sort of thing makes me bloody sick. All this backslapping. It's a load of shite. That letter thanking and congratulating the Manager. What the hell did he do? And the Officials. If it was left to them we would get nothing done. All they are good for is to cut men's time. Useless prats some of them! Sure, I remember it well. Hell, I had a shock when I saw the pay advice. I went in to see Big Willy. "I am no paying that, so I am no"was all he could say.'

'Wullie,' I went on, 'The pit has been on strike for less than that! We were pounds short in our pay, and my neighbours wanted to strike. I had a hell of a job to convince them that they would get paid, and it took me three weeks to recover the money. Letter of congratulations and thanks to the Manager! My arse!' Wullie listened, and laughed, and the talk turned to some injured men in hospital. Wullie said he would visit them, and I was glad, for he was much better at that than I was. He was, I told him, the patter merchant of the team.

When I got home that day there were two men and a woman waiting for me. May had given them tea, as usual, and they were all chatting away. Old Larry had recently retired, and he had shown them the watch he had been given. May said she had seen it already, because she was the one who chose it. That delighted Larry, who was even more pleased to tell us that as a result of having his picture in the local paper when he retired, a long-lost brother in South Africa had written to him, and so had a cousin in America. They had thought he was dead until they saw the picture.

All three of them wanted help with forms to be filled in, and I was glad to do it. We had a joint grumble about those forms. Why could they not be written in such a way that people could understand them? It wasn't everybody who was at ease with writing, and even the simplest forms sometimes gave a lot of trouble to some people.

While we chatted, I wrote away at the table, and soon had the job done. Meanwhile, Jamie, our dog lay watching everybody, and keeping, as always, between May and the visitors. They laughed when I pointed it out, and were impressed when Jamie bounded up to me when I did no more than whisper his name, and then went off to May when I asked him where Mum was.

When they left, I had an hour's sleep in the chair, for it had been a long day, and then we went off for a walk, with Jamie, of course. We were joined by our son, who was always ready for a walk and a wee look for birds' nests.

It was a lovely evening, with a spectacular sunset. The wee boy thought it looked like a volcano, and since none of us had ever seen a volcano, we could agree with him. I never tired of watching the beauties of nature, whether they were tranquil and quiet like that sunset, or great storms and gales. Perhaps it was a reaction to having to spend so much of my life down the pit. Anyway, we went into the woods, and sure enough found a few nests, which delighted the laddie, and pleased me. The old skill was still there. I showed the boy how to cover up our tracks so that no-one coud know we had been there.

For some reason I remember that day well. As we strolled along, May and I and our son talked about nature and all its delights and terrors; about how birds and animals lived and loved and killed; about how man was destroying so many things of beauty. I was reminded of my own boyhood days when my wee companion Cha Downey and I had wandered through the woods and learned the ways of the wild creatures.

When we got home that evening, our daughter and a friend had already prepared the tea, complete with a dish they had baked at school, and very good it was, too. My daughter then told us, with delight, that she was first in her class at school. Altogether, it was a good evening, that, and one I have remembered.

I remember it particularly, perhaps, because it happened just before we went on strike. This was the first nation-wide strike of miners for some time, and we had to re-learn a lot of lessons. Not the least of the lessons was how to scrimp and save and manage on very little. Our small savings soon dwindled away, and all the little luxuries we had grown accustomed to had to be sacrificed. I was away from home many hours each day, and sometimes for days on end, and only saw my children when they were asleep in their beds. Fortunately for me, May, as always gave her full support and help. Our parents, too, having themselves known the hardships that strikes cause, and also being convinced of the necessity of fighting for better conditions, gave us all the help they could. It was not a long strike, and we were soon enough back at work, although it would take some time to reach a reasonable standard of living again.

Fortunately we were working on a good driveage, and making good money, so we were able to make up our losses fairly quickly. Those men unfortunate enough to be working bad places had to struggle for months before they were back to financial stability.

There was one day we were working away at our driveage when an oncost lad came running up and told us that the Flipper wanted to see us. We asked him who the hell the Flipper was and he told us it was the Whiz Kid himself. 'Aa the oncost lads caa him that, after that dolphin show on the telly. He's always splashin through water, nae oilskins or onything, he just wades in or dives in, cleans oot sumps and such like, an comes oot like a drooket craw. The bugger is always rushin aboot daein this. That's why we caa him Flipper. The cunt is daft, jist plain daft, an he expects us tae be the same!'

I told him he should not be speaking of any man like that, but I had to stifle a smile at the name they had found for him. The lad told me he was in the sump, which was an abandoned driveway which we now used as a catchment for water.

There was no sign of anybody when I entered the sump, but when I called, a light appeared some distance away. 'Come here,' shouted Flipper the Whiz Kid, 'I want a hand to fix this pump.' I could see he was waist deep in murky, oily water which stank. There was little air in the place, and altogether it was highly unpleasant. He walked towards me, and he was a sorry-looking sight, soaking wet, with no oilskins. He had just plunged into that greasy stinking water in an attempt to start the pump, which had clogged up. He asked if we would get the pump going, and I said we would, but told him that we would have to be paid for the time we spent fixing it. He agreed, and I left him standing there waving his arms about in an attempt to shake off the oily water in which he was soaked.

My neighbours came back with me. We were properly prepared with our keys and oilskins, and it took us about an hour to get the pump clear and running Matt was the expert on pumps, and we left him to it, while Bob and I cleared the sludge that was clogging up the hoses. Flipper worked alongside, and was delighted when Matt called out that he was ready to try the pump. He switched on, and after a stutter and a splutter and a sharp "woof" it began chattering away quite happily. The Flipper said he was going up the pit, and would see us when we loused. He disappeared off up the Sump road, and we returned to our normal work.

The shot firer had just finished firing for us, and the air was clearing. He had already been back in, and said it had been a good round, although there was a bad bit of roof on the right hand side, which would have to be watched. A couple of legs had been blown out, but he had replaced them, so all we had to do was start shovelling. 'Bell on when you're ready,' he told us, 'And I'll tell the switchman you are ready to start up.'

We told him that was fine, and that we would get that round redd up and bore another round which we might get fired in time for the backshift. He told us he would not be far away, picked up his battery and cables and walked out to the switchman.

We were soon hard at work, shovelling coal onto the conveyor, with sweat dripping from our faces. We worked fast to make up for lost time. The roof had collapsed in one place, so we had to repair it with temporary supports till we had cleared enough coal to put in proper supports. When that had been done safely, and most of the coal filled away, Matt and I started to bore the next set of shot holes, while Bob shovelled away the last of the coal before coming to help us with the boring. When we had finished, we hauled the electric borer out to the road where it would not be damaged by the shots, and coiled up the cable.

We signalled to the switchman to call the shotfirer, while we measured the amount of explosive we were going to use for each hole. Rab, the shotfirer, was soon with us, and he selected the number of detonators we would be needing. We agreed the last shot had been a good one, and hoped this would be as good. We always liked to leave a good supply of coal for the backshift, to give them a start. When all the shots were primed and the holes stemmed, we withdrew to a safe area and Rab coupled up the cables to his battery and turned the key. There was a series of muffled bangs, and then silence. All the shots had fired, so we waited in silence for a few minutes to give the fans a chance to clear the reek before we went back to ensure that the roof was safe to be left for our partners on the next shift. Everything looked fine, so we erected a few poles and straps to hold the roof, and left for the surface.

My neighbours went off into the baths, but I went looking for the Whiz Kid. I wanted to settle the price we were to be paid for the job on the pump. He and I went into a small office, and he did a bit of figuring on a piece of paper, then tossed it across to me. I looked at it, and nodded in agreement. That price would suit us. He reached out for the paper, but I folded it and put it into my pocket. 'What's that for?' he asked. I told him I was keeping it for reference. 'Don't you trust me?' he asked. 'Frankly, no,' I told him, but I was satisfied with the price he had given. I advised him to make sure that his pump was not clogged again, and he asked if we would take a look at it from time to time. This I said we would do, and that I was sure we could come to some arrangement about it. All in all, I was quite pleased with our work for the day.

Altogether, we worked about six months in that driveage before it was stopped when we hit another fault. Other developments were planned, but our team had to split up, and for a time we were on the spare, taking any job that cropped up. Of course, this meant a drop in wages, since we were on the Fall Back Rate some days.

A gang of us was busy one day assembling a gearhead and a new conveyor when one of the young lads, an engineer, said he had a bone to pick with me. I was a bit surprised, because although I knew him well enough, our paths rarely crossed. 'Yes,' he said, 'I saw you coming out of the station the other day with your daughter and you ignored me. I'll tell you, she's a lovely girl, a smashing bit of stuff, and I would have liked an introduction.'

I looked at him and thought back. 'A few days ago, at the station? Well, I'll tell you something: that was not my daughter, that was my wife!'

He was astonished at that. 'Your wife! Well, she looks a lot younger than you! Tell me, how did you get as braw a woman as that?'

'Aye, well, that's a mystery to me, too. It wasn't my money, for I have none. It definitely was not my looks, so it must have been my charm. But I'll tell you this: I don't know whether what you say is an insult to me or a compliment to my wife. When I tell her what you said, she will be delighted.' And, of course, she was. That was not the first time I had been told such things about May, and I was never surprised, because she looked so young.

There was quite a spate of accidents around that time, and I was kept busy making investigations of them and writing reports. In addition, I had to make inspections to ensure that all the regulations were being followed. This sometimes led to a certain amount of friction, particularly when I stopped a job or a machine in the interests of safety, even though it meant that the men would be losing money.

However, I had the full weight of the Union behind me in the job, and there was no way I would scamp it. Both the Safety Commmittee and the Consultative Committee backed me up in those inspections of machinery, and everything else in the pit.

I became really angry one day when I was carrying out an inspection. I found material of all kinds, girders, props, wooden straps, all thrown down carelessly at the end of the bogie road. It should have been stacked properly, so that the men had a clear road for walking in and out. The way it was represented a hazard, and I immediately instructed the oncost material squad to make the area safe by stacking the material properly by the roadside. There was some grumbling about the amount of work involved, but I told them I did not give a damn about that. I insisted on having a clear passage for the men, and told them to bring no more material in until that had been done. The lads did a bit of glaring at me, but started on the tangled mass of material they had allowed to accumulate. I told them I would be back, and moved off into the faceline. I heard one lad say: 'He's a proper bastard, that.' Another replied: 'Maybe, but he's right. It's his job to see you nits do your work properly, and he's a guid Union man!' I smiled to myself as I went off.

At the roadhead I gave a hand for a few minutes to a brusher who was erecting Dobson props. We looked at the roof, and it seemed heavy to us, needing more Dobsons. The brusher told me it had been bad all week, so we put the Dobsons into place before I went on up the faceline, crouching along between the gullicks supporting the roof.

George, the fireman who was to accompany me, was waiting. 'Hello,' he said, 'I thought you had got lost.' I told him there was no chance of that, and I knew the section well. I told him also that I thought the roof was bad further back, and he agreed. He was worried in case they were working into another hitch, a geological fault in the coal.

We went on, and soon could hear the roar of the cutter as it ate its way into the seam. When we came alongside, the roar was deafening. I crawled past it for a few yards, and was astonished by what I saw. Clouds of dust, thick and menacing, were rising from the cutting head. I was surprised by the amount of stour, and horrified also. Men were working in that. Did they never listen to all the times they had been told about the dangers of pneumoconiosis? Did they never see all the old miners, struggling to catch a breath? Here they were, working in a positive dust storm.

I bellowed for the machine to be stopped, but no-one heard me, so I pulled the signal cable, and the roaring machine came to a halt. The machine man, surprised, came to see what the problem was. He got an earful of problem. I asked him, in forceful terms, why he was cutting without dust suppressors and without a drop of water from the sprays going on to the disc. That machine was not to move one inch until the sprays were working properly. Tammy, the machineman, said mournfully that he was just cutting to the roadhead before he had it fixed. There was no way that was going to happen. The machine was to be stationary until the sprays were working, otherwise Tammy would be off the job. He was shaken by my outburst, but I was really very angry about what I had seen. It was a complete denial of everything we had struggled for so long to get. Generally speaking, all the safety regulations had been introduced only as a result of constant pressure by the Union, against opposition from Management, especially the old mine owners, and here we had the men themselves ignoring all the most basic safety requirements. Tammy called on the Tannoy for the engineer, whose job it was to fix the sprays.

Another light came along the face, accompanied by a loud voice calling out, enquiring what was wrong, and why was the cutter stopped. It was the Manager himself, demanding to know who had stopped the machine.

I was ready for battle, and explained that I had ordered it stopped because it was cutting without water and you could have cut the stour with a knife. There was no way I would have the men breathe that. I expected trouble, but Big Willie agreed with me. He warned the machineman never again to cut without water, otherwise there would be trouble down on him like a ton of bricks. All dust suppression systems must be working at all times. I gave a silent cheer for Big Will. At least one Manager had learned some lessons.

The engineer soon appeared, and got to work on the sprays, and I went off towards the Tail Gate road. With the machines silent, the whole section was quiet. I could plainly hear the roof making, a sure sign that the waste was going to close up. We were safe enough under the Gullick supports, but very soon there was a loud crash and the roof in the waste collapsed in a great cloud of blinding dust. Well, there was nobody under it, so it didn't matter, and I went on to the Tail Gate stall, where some men were sitting about waiting for the machine to start up.

They asked what was wrong, and I told them I had stopped the shearer, and why. One of the facemen said he thought the sprays must have been off, because the stour had been very heavy, and that they should not be working in dust like that. I agreed with him, and said there was no reason why most of them should not be working behind the machine.

However, I asked them, why were they not wearing masks? There was only one man wearing his. 'What's wrong with you chaps?

You are supplied free of charge with masks to protect you against dust and you are so pig-headed you won't wear them.'

I heard the usual excuses. Ah canna wear them. Ah canna breathe. They're nae fuckin use. I told them it was all a load of balls. They had to persevere with wearing them. They would get used to it. Were they so little concerned about their health that they were prepared to finish up coughing their lungs and guts out? I wore a mask in development, and that was harder work than they were doing. They just had to persevere.

Somebody wailed that I was always getting on about something, and I rounded on him. Too bloody true I was always getting on at them. It was for their own good. That's what I was there for, to look after their interests, their safety and their health. But I did expect them to behave like responsible adults and experienced colliers, not like spoiled brats. 'Wear your masks,' I told them, 'otherwise I just have to waste my time going to your funerals and helping your widows to sort out your bit pension.'

There was not much else to do on that inspection, just checking the panels and the roof, the sump, the pumps and the belt conveyor. It took a whole shift, and writing up the report took hours more, but that had to be done later, in my own time, at home.

At least I had a good home to go to. Not everybody was so lucky, and in spite of the vaunted welfare state that was supposed to take care of us from the cradle to the grave, some people managed to slip through the cracks, and had to survive in the depths of degradation and poverty. I did not see a lot of that, but it was brought forcibly to my attention one day.

I was greeted one morning at the pit head by Tammy Gavin, who asked me if I had any good in my heart. It was early morning, and just at the start of the shift, and I was not feeling like indulging in cross talk, so I asked him what the hell he wanted now. 'Well,' he said, 'It's auld Jock, him that worked around the yard and in the baths. He's been been off work sick for a long time now, and there is a pile of letters and forms to be dealt with. Will you come down with me to his house as soon as possible?'

I told him I would go that very night, and we should meet at pit head at lousing time. He was waiting for me when I came up the mine, and we went off in the bus, and then had a walk of about a mile to Jock's house. Tammy knew the way, and led me up to a dilapidated, broken-down place with broken windows and with ashes and rubbish strewn around. In the short and stinking close that led to the door, Tammy observed my look of disgust, and laughed. 'That's nothing,' he said, 'Wait till you see what it's like inside. You'll need a strong stomach.' He opened the door, and went in. I hesitated on the threshold. The stench was overpowering and nauseating, and what I could see of the interior much worse than the outside. Tammy called for me to go in, and, swallowing hard, I did.

It was utter chaos. The table was littered with dirty plates and half empty cups of tea. The floor was unswept and covered in ashes and filthy clothes lay around. Tammy called me from the bedroom to say that the auld yin was in bed, and I went through. That was even worse. I had never seen anybody in such a disgusting and degraded state. The old man was obviously very ill. His face was grey and he stared at the ceiling, unaware of our presence. Tammy took him by the shoulder. 'Come on, Jock,' he said, 'you have visitors.' Jock moaned, and rolled around in that filthy bed with its torn blankets and grey sheets. He heard my voice, and tried to say he was glad to see me, but when he tried to sit up he slumped back into the horror of his blankets. When he moved, a vile smell came from the bed. 'The poor old bugger has done a shite in the bed, maybe several. We'll need to get him cleaned up. Give me a hand to move him over.' When I grasped the old man's shoulder it was just like gripping a skeleton through the shirt he was wearing. He groaned, and I asked if I was too coarse with him. 'No, no,' he said, 'I am just done.'

'Hell tae the fear o that,' I told him. 'Ye've a lot o damage tae dae yet. Tammy is going to clean ye up an put clean blankets on the bed.' Tammy came back with blankets and a sheet he had found in the drawers and said he would manage now. He was used to this sort of job, he said, and, truth to tell, I was glad to leave him to it. I had little stomach for that job, and already I was struggling hard to keep from throwing up.

I went back into the other room and boiled the kettle and washed up the dishes, and cleaned up as well as I could. Then I boiled the kettle again and made some tea and took two cups through. Tammy had finished cleaning up the old man, and they were both ready for a cup of tea. 'Where's yours?' Tammy asked. I told him I did not want any just then, that I did not want to spoil my dinner. He smiled, knowing well what the trouble was. He handed me a pile of letters and asked me if I would deal with them. He had already arranged for two of the women from the canteen to come over and clean the place up, and I was glad that he was to have some help with an unenviable task. For myself, I was glad to be out of it. Tammy came to the door with me. 'Now you see what conditions some folk still live in. What a state this poor old bugger's in! I knew you would get a shock here. You are not used to this sort of thing.'

'No, Tam, indeed I'm not. I can scarcely believe that people exist in these, they (*I was fumbling for words*) conditions, circumstances. This is hellish. I would not have believed it if I had not seen it for myself.'

'There was a women living with him,' Tammy told me, 'But she buggered off when things got bad and the money stopped coming in.'

'Well,' I said, 'He needs someone to look after him properly. I am going up into town to see what can be done and I will get an appointment for a doctor to call here.' I hurried away up the close, feeling a bit gutless under those distressing circumstances, but determined to do what I could for the old man.

Even out in the open, and through the cigarette I immediately lit, I could still smell the stink of that place, and the disinfectant Tammy had used so abundantly. The contrast when I got home to the bright and shining place that May had made for us was so startling that I could hardly settle down. I told May where I had been, and how fortunate I felt. I told her of how Tammy was caring for old Jock, and how I could not have done it.

The next day Tammy called me over to his room in the baths. 'Well,' he said, 'Now you know how some folk live. You'll be happy to hear that the two women came over from the canteen and cleaned that place up a treat; it's shining like a new shilling. And the Doctor's been, and he's trying to get Jock away to some place where they will get him on his feet again, the poor old bugger.' I was glad to hear all that, and passed over the pile of forms and letters that I had dealt with overnight. I showed Tammy where they needed Jock's signature, and he said he would attend to that.

Later, I learned that Jock had been found a place in a home, and that he was much better, and on his feet again. But the shock of seeing one of our own men living in such conditions of squalor and poverty distressed me very much, and made me more than ever determined to continue fighting for improvements which would make such poverty a thing of the past.

The opportunity for a bit of fighting to improve conditions came soon enough. This was the first of the big strikes. That was in 1972, and we struck for improved wages. As a Union official I was involved day and night. May and the children saw little of me during that time. It was a matter of a few hours sleep, and then out again, travelling all over the area. Of course, like everybody else, we suffered from the shortage of money. My cigarettes were the first thing to go, and then began the time of scrimping and saving and economising. Even when we won (and I never doubted that we would), it would take a long time for us to get back on our feet again. And yet we heard and saw ourselves being attacked for calling a 'frivolous' strike. There is nothing frivolous about a strike. When men see their children sitting down to a dinner of a slice of bread and dripping, and their wife has not had a cup of tea all day, and they themselves have not had a cigarette for a week, there is nothing frivolous about it. But we went on with the struggle.

I came near to being arrested. Not that I had done anything wrong, but you did not have to do anything wrong to be arrested if you were a picket. Sam Dalziel and I as officials, and about a dozen pickets stood at the road leading to Longannet power station. A panda car and a police van were parked at the roadside. Somebody joked that there was a polis man for every one of us, but I warned them to be careful. I did not want any trouble, and so told them again of what was allowed to us as legal pickets. It was a cold night, and we huddled round a brazier, with Sam and I taking turns at the gate with a token picket force to stop and speak to all lorry drivers, and ask them to support us.

There was no harrassment and things were going smoothly. I was standing at the gate with three pickets and two policmen, chatting away when a car approached and stopped at our signal. I moved forward to speak to the driver when he suddenly accelerated away and I had to leap to one side to avoid being hit. I landed on my elbow on the road and I caught a glimpse of a picket being struck by the bonnet and thrown to the other side. There were angry howls from the pickets. 'Stop that bastard! He tried to run us down!' The car was away by this time, and there was no way we could stop it. I rose shaken from the road, and was astounded to see three policemen dragging the lad who had been thrown by the car off to the police van. He was being arrested. Not that he was going easy, indeed he was struggling hard, but just the same they got him into the van.

The lads on the gate wanted to go over to the van, but I told them to cool it. We did not want trouble. I would see what was happening. I went over to the van, followed by Sam. The policemen were making notes when we approached them. 'Hello,' I said, trying to remain calm, although I was already seething inside, 'What's happening? What's this lad being booked for?'

'Fuck off,' snarled one of the policemen, 'Or you're next.' 'Listen,' I told them, 'I'm a Union official.......' That was as far as I got. 'We know who and what you are, and you're next.'

I was beginning to lose my control — which would have been exactly what they wanted. 'Listen, you lot,' I told them, ' I want to know why that lad, who was knocked down by a car the driver of which ought to be arrested, is himself being arrested. I demand.......' Again that was as far as I got.

'Look, you, you fuck off!' snarled another policeman, and gave me a hefty shove. I staggered and almost fell, but still managed to keep cool enough to protest about the arrest of our picket and their failure to do anything about the car that tried to run us down. Sam saw that I was getting perhaps uncontrollably angry, and he pushed between me and the group of policemen. He took me by the shoulders and told me to leave it be. 'They want you to go for them, and if you do we will all be in the nick. Leave it!' He led me away, reluctantly.

I was angry and frustrated and when we rejoined the rest of the pickets was hardly able to report what had happened. Sam told them quietly that one of the lads had been arrested, and how it happened. 'Come on, boys,' they said, 'Let's go and see about this.' They moved off across the road. Sam moved smartly to the front of them, holding out his arms to stop them. He told them again that violence was just what the police wanted, and they would have liked nothing better than for us to attack them. We would only make things worse for the lad already arrested, and for ourselves. If we had a go at them, it would give them the excuse to have a go at us. I joined Sam at the front of the group, and added my arguments to his, and eventually the flaring tempers receded, although there were a couple who still wanted to have a go.

Thankfully, and largely due to Sam, it ended peacefully, although the lad who had been knocked down and then arrested was eventually brought to court and fined heavily. Of course, we made a report to the Action Committee, and found that similar things had happened to other pickets. It seemed possible that the driver of the car had himself been a policeman, provoking trouble.

The strike dragged on, and as Branch Officials we had to bear the brunt of the work and the struggle. We saw little of our families and little of our beds during the seven weeks that strike lasted. It was a tremendous struggle, and when it ended, we had won only a partial victory. *But we had not been defeated.*

Some time later the gutter press carried a report that Mick McGahey had spoken about £100 per week miners. It was a totally untrue report, but it was carried widely, and people believed it. The fact was that miners had barely half that amount.

There was one Friday night I was walking home after work, tired after a strenuous day, and loaded down with all the reports, Branch business and accident claims I had to deal with over the weekend. There were three of us in the group, Frank, who had been a faceman but had lost an eye in an accident and was now working oncost, and Wull, who was a surface foreman. As we passed the Club, some men staggered out, clearly a bit worse for their drink, although they were quite cheery. When they saw us they shouted: 'Hey, there go they cunts, the hundred pound a week miners!'

Someone added: 'Aye, and they dae fuck aa for it!' I was for just walking on, although angry enough, but Frank, who knew the men, stopped and told them they should get their facts right. Wull, too, was furious, and pulled out his payslip. 'I'm an official,' he told them, 'A foreman. Here you are, a full week's work, with overtime, sixty two pounds.' Frank produced his slip. Forty eight Pounds. I produced mine. As a faceman on the highest rate, it showed sixty five Pounds.

They could hardly believe it. 'No,' I told them, 'But you will believe the shite you read in the papers. Here is the proof. Here are the facts!' They couldn't dispute it. They were bucketmen, they said, and they got more selling scrap than we got in wages.

One of the papers I had to deal with that weekend was a report on old Jock Carberry, a friend of mine who had died of pneumoconiosis. His own doctor, two doctors in Stirling Infirmary, and two others in Mearnskirk who specialised in diseases of the chest agreed that he had the disease. There was a postmortem which seemed to show that the disease was not present, so the Union arranged to have a second examination, which proved positively that pneumoconiosis was the cause of death. This was important for us, because Jock had left a widow who would be entitled to a pension if we proved our case.

His widow had lodged the claim, and the Union was to represent her. That was my job. I spent the weekend diligently studying the documents and reports, translating the medical terms into layman's language with the help of the Oxford Universal Dictionary. I made many notes, and was finally confident about the case. I had recently been a member of a team that had won the title of Scottish Champion in a national Safety Quiz, so felt that I could put a good case.

The hearing was held locally. The Union representative and I discussed the case, and then I was given permission to speak on behalf of the widow. I put the case as well as I could, gaining confidence as I went along. When I had finished, the Union representative and I retired into the waiting room while the Tribunal discussed the case. As we sat down, the Union man told me the case was lost. I was dumbfounded, and asked what he meant. He opened his document and pointed out that the Medical Advisor to the Tribunal was the same man who had done the first post mortem. There was no way he was going to admit to a mistake, especially if it was pointed out and argued by laymen like us. He was right. The decision was against us. I was fuming mad. The whole thing had been a farce. There should have been a neutral man in there, not someone who perhaps felt his reputation was at stake. I told the Union representative I was going to write to Edinburgh and demand an appeal against the decision, which was grossly unfair. I felt worse about it because Jack had been a friend of mine, and I had watched him die, and had comforted his widow. I felt that somehow I had let both of them down. So a strongly worded protest was sent off to our Head Office, who replied that the points I made had been noted, and that every effort would be made to help the widow, and they would be in touch with her in due course. After a lot more paperwork and argument and of course delay, a pension was eventually granted to that widow, which she should have had in the first place, and without all the obstruction and procrastination.

For some time about then Jock and I were employed on Special Duties. That was doing any work that required extra special skills and experience. It was dangerous at times, but we enjoyed the variety and the challenge of it. We were well satisfied to see a job well done and safe. On one occasion we were involved in securing a roadway high above a gearing. It was a simple job for us, and had gone well. Jock drew my attention to a heavy flow of sludge underneath the gearing. A build up of that sludge could cause a hazard, if it interfered with the smooth operation of the gearing on the belt conveyor, so we decided to clear it away.

We climbed down from the platform and stuck our shovels into the sludge. It was sticky, and it stank: so badly did it stink that we had to gulp at times. The sludge continued to flow as we shovelled, and we were not making much headway. The belt was beginning to stick and jam up, then free itself with a jerk. It was running heavy with coal and some big stones from the brushing road. Shovelling that sludge was hard work. It stuck to our shovels like.....well, we had a vivid description of how it stuck......and we had to stop frequently and clean them off. Then we had to throw the stuff high and away to make sure it did not flow back.

There was suddenly a bright idea. A barrow! That would make the job easier, so we decided that at piece time, which would be shortly, one of us would go and get a barrow, and in the meantime we would just have to keep shovelling.

I had picked up a big shovelful of the stuff, and it was resting on the belt while I prepared to throw it up and away. Suddenly a big stone on the belt struck my shovel, knocked it from my grasp and jerked it straight up into my face. It was a painful blow, and I shouted out in pain and anger, cursing and wiping the sticky mess from my face. That was enough, the bloody belt could jam if it wanted to: I was shovelling no more of the stuff until we had a barrow. Jock came over and looked at me in astonishment, then began laughing.

'I didn't know you had two mouths,' he said, 'One up and one across, like a bloody crossword puzzle. But from the way you're shouting maybe you need two!' I did not know what the hell he was talking about, but then he looked more closely at my face and gently wiped the muck off. 'Christ,' he said, 'Your nose is split from top to bottom. It's deep, and the nose could be broken.' He used water and a pad to wipe off more dirt, while blood flowed freely and dripped around my feet. He told me that I must get up the pit and have it seen to, and I was in no condition to argue, so off I went, holding fresh pads to my nose from time to time as they became blood soaked. When I reached the surface I headed for the baths and the First Aid Room.

The attendant cleaned and dressed the wound as well as he could, and put a plaster on it, and told me I had better come back at the end of the shift when the nurse would be in attendance, and she would dress it properly. So I worked the rest of the shift, and then Nurse Rose did a proper job of cleaning and dressing it. She did not think it was broken, and nor did I, but certainly it was a deep wound, and took some healing. Of course, I had to withstand a good deal of ribbing about it, on the lines of: 'Did your wife hit you with a frying pan?' and 'Whit like is the ither fella?' That did not worry me at all, but the incident left me with yet another blue scar, this time very visible on my face, to let the whole world know that I was a coal miner, and proud of it.

Although we had our share, and perhaps more than our share, of accidents, we rarely had a fatality, so that when they did happen, they seemed all the more shocking.

There was one bright sunny day when I was walking down the road with an old friend. He had called unexpectedly, and after a good crack and a cup of tea, we decided to go for a pint — just one — before dinner. As we were walking along deep in conversation a car squealed to a halt alongside. Wullie MacDougall was in it, and he shouted to me that I was the man he was looking for. I told him he was out of luck that day, and I was going for a pint, but something about Wullie's expression told me there was something wrong. Indeed, there was. There had been an accident, a right nasty fatal one, and I was to get over to the pit straight away.

I told him I would be over immediately, but first I had to go back home and tell May where I was going, otherwise she would worry if I did not return for my dinner. Wullie ran me back home in the car, and then we went off to the pit, and on the way Wullie told me the little he knew of the fatality. A man had been crushed by a machine. He was dead. And that really was all we knew.

The Manager and a few men were at the pit head. The men were the neighbours of the dead man, and had witnessed the accident. They would be able to give us their statements on what had happened. I could interview them in the next room, while we waited for Jim Pollock, the surveyor, who would go underground with me and take measurements. We did that, and then I changed into overalls ready to go underground. Wullie, unfortunately, was not fit enough by that time to go into the pit. When Jim arrived, he was accompanied by Abe, the other Workmen's Inspector, and after a brief discussion, we set off into the mine, accompanied by a deputy. There was no transport, no manriding cars operating that day, so we had a long walk to face, first down the steep incline and then along the level. It was a sad and quiet little group. Although none of us knew the dead man well, we did all know him, and even if we had not known him, a fatality always hits any mining community very hard. It was that lad today: who would it be tomorrow?

The driveage we were walking was familiar to me because it was one I had worked on. It was strange to be walking along it when there was no sound but our boots and the occasional click as one or other adjusted his lamp. There was no machinery running, no men working, and everything was silent. It was a weird atmosphere.

When we reached the site of the accident we sat down for a moment to catch our breath, because we had been moving fast, and wiped the sweat from our faces. Jim asked Abe to help him with his measurements and hold the tape, and I made my own sketches and comments. The man had been crushed to death by a machine they were moving. They were moving it by switching the current quickly on and off, so that it inched slowly along, under control all the time. It was a skilful team, and they were accustomed to using that method, and they knew its dangers. On this occasion, someone had been in error and the machine moved forward too far, and crushed the man against a roadside prop support. He was killed instantly.

There was one place that Abe, who was a burly man, could not reach to hold the tape. Jim asked if I would do it. I emptied everything out of my pockets and crawled through a small gap, and eventually, after much squeezing and wriggling was able to get the end of the tape on the point Jim wanted. Only then did I realise that I was lying in the exact position that the dead man had lain in just a short time before. I was very glad indeed when Jim called that he had got the measurement and I could come out of that.

We finished the job, and walked back, still silent. Fortunately a fireman had appeared, and had started the manriding belts, so we did not have to face the long walk back up the incline to the surface. Abe and I washed and then filled in a report of our findings. Wullie MacDougall was waiting for us and we briefed him. He had already been in contact with our Head Office, and told us that Lance Johnson, the Union Inspector, would be down the next day. Then we left for home, in the car again. Wullie and Abe dropped off for a pint on the way, but I was eager for my dinner, so went straight home, where May was waiting, and so was my meal.

When I arrived at the pit the next day, I was questioned by the men about the fatality, but I told them little at that stage. Whatever I had said would have been passed along from mouth to mouth, and would certainly have been distorted. It was better to say little, and wait for the reports. The pit was working, of course, which was different from the old days, when the whole pit would close for a day after a fatal accident, a mark of respect and mourning that I for one missed. I waited in the canteen for Lance, and when he arrived gave him a report on my findings and ordered breakfast for him – the bacon rolls and tea he so much enjoyed. The Manager joined us for a time, and was able to give Lance all the formal details of the dead man, his full name, age, address and where he had come from. Lance and I changed into overalls and went off underground.

It was very different from the previous day. The mine was in full production, and the machinery all working. No longer was there the eerie silence which had enveloped us on the previous day.

Lance always kept his eyes wide open every time he was down a pit, and often stopped to examine things. He was very thorough, and would always comment on what he saw, so that I learned a great deal from him.

At the scene of the accident, Lance probed around, making notes and sketches in his book, and asking me to hold the tape for him. We scrambled about over the machine, and Lance plied me with questions on how we normally went about flitting (moving) machines of that sort. Finally, satisfied that we had covered everything, we went out and into the Manager's office. There we had a discussion on what we had learned, and of how the fatality had happened, and of how we could avoid it ever happening again. We signed the various reports and books, and then went over to the canteen. It was Lance's turn to buy, and I was not slow in pointing that out, and ordering up yet more tea and bacon rolls. He grinned at me, but then looked upset when I lit a cigarette. 'You know you should give that up,' he said. 'You would have more cash to spend, and would feel better.' This was an old argument, and I was ready for him.

'See that big car of yours,' I told him, 'That's where you spend your extra cash! Your car does a lot more damage to health that me having a smoke. It pollutes the environment, kills wild life and can well kill your family and friends. It spews noxious fumes every time you even start the engine, and its a hazard to all forms of life. Think of that, Lance, and if you will give up your car, I will stop smoking!' He laughed, but made no answer.

Back at the Union office, Wullie was sitting at the desk writing letters and filling in forms. 'Just thought I would give you a hand,' he said, and I was glad to see him. I still had a lot of paper work to do before I could get home, and I had already been at the pit since six that morning. I was tired, and ready for a bit of sleep. Not that I regretted the time spent with Lance. I had, as always, learned things from him, and would be able to do my job better as a result. He had been a pit Manager before becoming an Inspector for the Union, and there was nothing he did not know about mining, and nothing ever escaped him.

I was lucky in having several friends and colleagues from whom I learned a great deal. Chief amongst them, of course, was Wullie MacDougall. He was a great man, one of the unsung and unrecognised heroes of Trades Unionism in Scotland. He was our Branch Delegate while I was Secretary, and we made a good team. He always quipped: 'I'll do the talking while you do the writing!', and indeed that was how we worked most of the time. He was a dedicated Union man, a fighter for human rights, and never once did he turn his back on anyone who required his help or assistance, despite the fact that he suffered from a lingering illnesss that at times laid him off work, and confined him to bed, for long periods. Even when he was ill in bed he would help anyone who turned to him. I had visited him several times when he was in bed, to seek his advice, and he never failed. He had been known more than once to rise from his sick bed, come over to the pit to solve some problem, then be rushed back to his bed again. Truly a friend and colleague to be admired and respected. Nor was Wullie the only one. The Trades Union movement was replete with men who sacrificed their lives for the welfare of the Union and their comrades.

It became clear that another strike was approaching. That was in 1974, and again the issue was wages, but this time there was also the very serious issue of a national plan for coal, which we, rightly, saw as determining the very future of our industry, as well as our own personal futures. And we were determined to protect them. Obviously it was going to be a bitter struggle, and we prepared for it. Strike committees were set up in local areas where we could contact them in the event of any emergencies or for arranging picket lines. We had two focal points in our district, the two power stations. We placed a caravan at each of those sites as shelter and headquarters for the pickets. It was my job to keep those caravans supplied and provisioned. There were also many meetings to attend, and much correspondence to deal with. A lot of that correspondence was concerned with keeping the picket lines quiet and peaceful and lawful, and I stressed the importance of that at meeting after meeting. Peaceful picketing is never easy, and tempers can flare quickly at times, but that is what we stressed at every opportunity.

On one occasion we had a picket at Kincardine Power Station. There were several of our men and two policemen, one of them a sergeant, and we chatted and joked to pass the time. Several lorries had driven up, and we had talked to the drivers and they had all turned round and gone away, refusing to cross our picket line. We cheered each driver as he drove away. Another lorry came up and we spoke to the driver. He also agreed to go back, and we gave him a cheer as he went. However, a couple of minutes later he came roaring back up the road and crashed straight though our picket line, scattering pickets and policemen as we all leaped to safety. Two pickets and a policeman were slightly injured, and the lorry went on to smash into a car containing some reporters, and wrecked it, before hurtling on into the power station. Some of the lads, screaming abuse and threats, raced after it as far as the closed gates. Others assisted the reporters from their wrecked car. They were only bruised and shaken, so we took them and the policemen back to our caravan for tea and food. We dressed the wounds and stopped the bleeding, and gave them all sympathy.

There were fearful threats uttered about what would happen to that driver when he came back. Wullie MacDougall, who was there also, and who had leaped into the hedge together with the police sergeant, had his work cut out to calm everyone down. He had this gift of taking the heat out of a difficult situation, and he did it again. We discussed the situation with the police. We were obeying all the rules and laws of picketing, onerous and unfair as they were, and in no way could we condone the action of that driver. He had been reckless and dangerous. He had wrecked a car and injured its passengers. We would have liked to have got our hands on him, and I suspect the police would have, too. However, justice, if that is the name for it, took its course. The man appeared in court, and was duly admonished. *Admonished! For what he did!* Some of our lads went to jail for even being on a public road leading to a picket line!

The strike went on, and our situation grew worse. There was no money coming into the house, except a pitiful DHSS allowance for my wife and younger child. It was a real struggle to keep afloat. My cigarettes were the first thing to disappear and I forgot the taste of a pint. As Branch Officials we were continually on the move, with picket duty, soup kitchens and meetings to keep the men informed. Wherever we went, we encountered the same closeness and comradeship and determination.

It was one of my jobs to keep our two caravans supplied with provisions, and I was amazed at the amount of tea consumed. I commented on this and one of the lads asked if I had heard of the saying that when the people had no bread, they should eat cake. Well, we had no beer, so we drank tea!

There was one morning when I arrived at Kincardine Power Station about four o'clock. I expected the lads to be drowsy and half asleep. Far from that; they were all there, all puzzled and alert. Mick Fox greeted me. 'Did you ever see the likes of this? Kincardine is full of police. The police are everywhere.' I told him not to worry, and together we walked down through the village. He was right. The police were indeed everywhere. There were panda cars and uniformed men standing in groups. They eyed us up and down as we walked along. It seemed like the British Army in blue uniforms. All the phone boxes were out of order, having been 'spiked', obviously to prevent us from contacting the other strike centres. We went back to the caravan and I arranged to get transport immediately over to Fallin, the other power station, to report the situation and get advice. I reassured our men on the picket, and told them they had to stay cool.

Arriving at Fallin I found Terry McMeel there. He was the leader of that section, and he laughed when I told him of the situation at Kincardine. He said it was all a hoax. Some bloody hoax, I told him, and reported how the village was full of policemen and of how the phone boxes had been put out of order. He explained that the previous night someone had rung up George Bolton, and asked about the situation at Kincardine. George said, jokingly, that a mass picket would be there, and that the power station would be stopped.

Anyway, there was no trouble at Kincardine that day, although there was a good deal of provocation, and I had to work hard keeping our lads cool.

The hours were long, and it seemed that I had not spent time with my family for weeks. Whenever there was a break from picket duty, there was a meeting to attend or correspondence to deal with. May was her usual kind and understanding self, and fully supported the strike, and was prepared to suffer along with the rest of us. The difficulty was the children. Not that they went short of anything essential, but everything had to be rationed carefully, and the one thing I wanted to give them above all else, my time, I had to give elsewhere.

So far as I was concerned, trouble first came when I was on picket duty at Longannet. When we arrived to relieve the nightshift, we found the police were already there in force. We were planning a bigger turnout ourselves that morning, so already the potentiality for trouble was present. More police arrived, and marched down the centre of the road, with our men lining both sides, and whistling Colonel Bogey as the police marched along. It was all good natured, and the police seemed to be laughing as much as we were.

The police then lined the road leading to the power station gates, and our lads were behind them. There was a bit of pushing, but it was all perfectly good humoured, and jokes and patter flew. Following the established procedure, each car and lorry was approached by two pickets, who attempted to persuade the driver to turn back. Sometimes they succeeded, and sometimes they failed. Each success was greeted with cheers, and each failure with boos. One lorry driver charged straight through the line, causing one picket and one policeman to leap for safety. There was a howl of anger from the pickets and they strained forward against the line of police. If the road could be closed completely, it would not be necessary to argue with each driver separately, and run the risk of being run down by some stupid person.

There were shouts of 'Heave! Heave!', and the police line wavered, swayed, and was broken. The men poured into the road and blocked it. There was a bit of pushing and shoving as the police tried to get the road clear again, but it was mainly quite good natured and joking. Eventually the lads did return to their lines, and again there was peace, and we got on with our legitimate picketing. Then a heavy lorry escorted by a police car thundered straight through the line, despite all the efforts of the pickets to stop it. Again there came the call to 'Heave! Heave!' and again the police line was broken, and pickets streamed across the road. Tempers were beginning to flare by now, with the police irritated by their inability to hold their line. There were some scuffles, and some kicking and punching by the police as they fought to get the pickets back off the road.

Our lads objected to this, and very quickly the atmosphere changed from one of reasonable good humour to bad temper and conflict. It was ugly, as pickets met police head on and battled with them.

Several arrests were made, and the Union Officials did their best to restore order, appealing to the men to stay cool and return to their ranks. Reluctantly, they did, but the arrests continued and this inflamed the situation, especially as those arrested were being beaten up in full view of their fellow miners. Graham Steel, a member of the Executive, appealed through a megaphone for restraint, and for a time there was restraint, on our side. But again the arrests went on, and the public beatings. Still, our lads were disciplined enough to recognise provocation, and refused to respond. The road was again cleared, and the lines restored, and the pickets on duty again began stopping vehicles. I was one of them, and enjoyed arguing with the drivers, especially when they told us of their sympathy with our struggle, as many did.

As I was relieved of duty and was heading back for the caravan for the tea I felt I deserved, there was a heave from the pickets, and a group of men, perhaps half a dozen, spilled out into the roadway, probably in fact pushed from behind. They were just by me, and suddenly we found ourselves surrounded by a group, a gang of police, who punched and kicked at us. That was no place to be, so I slipped between two policemen, and headed back for the lines, stopping a few punches as I went, but very carefully not retaliating. I got free of the struggling bunch, and then suddenly my arms were twisted up behind my back, very painfully, and a voice grated: 'We've got one of the bastards!'

'Hold it,' I called, 'I'm only heading back for our own line.' 'That's what you think!' replied the burly young policeman who was busy giving my twisted arms another heave further up my back. I was frogmarched away, despite my protests. 'We are having you, you little bastard,' the policeman snarled. 'We've had enough of your fucking kind!' I was held helpless, and beaten about the arms and legs, and then pushed over towards the policevan.

Some of the pickets saw what was happening, and they roared with rage. They heaved forward, the police line broke and our lads raced forward to where I was being half pushed, half beaten into the van. The two policemen holding me saw what was happening, and realised what was likely to happen to them in a moment. They gave one last jerk to my arms, then pushed me forward into the road and had one last kick at me. I felt a searing pain in my ribs as I staggered to my feet and stretched out a hand for assistance from someone. A big miner pushed his way through our now thin ranks and put his arm around my shoulder. He led me off and sat me down on a rock. Then a hand grasped me and pulled me up and round. It was a police inspector, and he was angry.

He was actually snarling, and his lips were really twisted with hate. 'You,' he told me, 'You get up that fucking road and if I see your fucking face down here again you will be in the clink.' I said nothing, and did nothing. He jerked at my arm. 'I know you,' he said, 'I know who you are and what you are. Now get to hell up that road or I'll have you in the van along with your fucking mates!' I still made no reply, but gently disengaged my arm and walked into our lines. He glared, and then walked off into the police cordon.

Back in the caravan we talked over the situation, and I was given tea, the usual remedy for all ills. It was difficult for me to breathe, and clearly I could do little more on the picket. Anyway, I had been there since early morning, and it was now late. Time to be away, so a car was organised for me and a few others who had been hurt. I was quiet on the way, and the others, who knew that I had been beaten up, told me that it was time I had a rest. I looked white and weary, and needed to take some time off. I had to agree that I was weary, and agreed that I would hand over for a while to others, and get some rest. At our strike headquarters I reported what had happened, and then told them I was off for a while. Everybody agreed, so I went home, to the care and love of May.

She dressed my wounds and bruises, a job she was well used to doing, fed me, and saw me to my bed. It was welcome, and I slept the whole night through, and only awoke the next morning when the smell of breakfast cooking drifted through from the kitchen.

The struggle dragged on, and to their eternal credit most of the miners stood firm. There were hazards and real hardship, but there was a determination to go on until we had won, and until the future of our industry was safe. That was what we were fighting for — the future of the coal industry in Britain. A great deal depended on local Branch officials who had the task of keeping up the morale of the men, and in ensuring that the aims were always kept in sight. Wullie MacDougall was superb at that, and every meeting he and I attended induced a feeling of confidence, a feeling that the struggle would be won. He made everyone feel that the destitution, hardships and suffering of today were necessary for winning a secure future for all.

Generally, we had lots of support from the public and other unions, although of course there were some people who detested our action. They failed to realise what our struggle was about, and were completely misled by the misrepresentations and downright lies in the press. There were vile insinuations made about Union officials, and threats of violence. Some officials had to have an escort whenever they went out.

There was one night I met some friends who were not miners, and they insisted I join them for a pint. They knew well that I could not stand a round, but that made no difference. We chatted for a while, and I headed for the toilet. I overheard one of a group of strangers say to Hugh McDonald, a striking miner, that all miners were nothing but McGahey's communist bastards. I laughed, and remarked to Hugh that if that was the subject of conversation, he should forget it. I went on towards the toilet door, and then something, I know not what, made me duck down, just as a pint mug hurtled past my ear and smashed against the door. It shattered, leaving a deep indentation. I spun round just in time to see one of the strangers hit the floor with a crash. Hughie had decked him. Two of the regulars grabbed

Hughie and held his arms as he attempted to have a go at the other two strangers. Seeing that he was held helpless, one of them leaped forward and balanced for a blow. I was there before he could strike, though, and grabbed his arm, spun him round, and slammed him against the wall. I was leaping at him again when I was caught from behind and a voice said 'Leave this one for me.' It was the Boss, Alex Brady, the publican. He took the stranger by the shoulders, shook him like the rat he was, and told him to pick up his mate and get the hell out of the pub, and never come back. He had seen it all, and knew just what had happened, and he was not to be trifled with. The strangers, rather the worse for wear, went off into the night. Alex set us up a whisky, and we talked over the event. It seems that the three strangers had been there for some time, and had boasted of their membership of the National Front.

A few days later Wullie MacDougall told me that he had also been set upon in a hotel, and when I described the three, he thought they could well be the same ones. He told me that other officials in different places reported the same thing happening to them, and it seemed as though there were hit squads out after Union officials. We agreed that we would have to be careful in the future, although we did not feel it necessary to have bodyguards, as some officials in other places had to do.

Wullie and I, and of course other union officials and stalwarts, spent what seemed endless hours on the picket lines, in meetings and in discussions. We met one day at a meeting, and realised that we would both have to walk home, and it was miles, because we were both stony broke. I told him that I had been away from home so much even the dog thought I was a stranger. Wullie laughed, and said that Sadie, his wife, thought he was the insurance man. We could still joke, but it was tough.

As we walked home that night with a group of other men, the talk was all of the strike. We had been out a long time, and would not go back until we got a real settlement, said one youngster. An older man said he had seen it all before. We would only get a bit of what we asked for. Some of our leaders are shite-the-beds. They would sell us down the river and then they would get a knighthood or a peerage for stabbing the workers in the back. The young lad said that would not happen this time.

I told them that I was not too sure. They might think I was sceptical, but I agreed with the older chap. Negotiations used to be a sort of Chinese Bargaining. You fought for a fifteen bob rise, and they accepted two bob, and called it a great victory. That was bullshit. I knew Lawrence Daly, and thought he was a good man, a fighter, but I had my doubts about Joe Gormley. I did not have any faith in him. He might have been a good man once, I said, but now he struck me as being two-faced, the sort who would sell us down the river for his knighthood. I told them that my father used to say "Once they reach the high life, they forget the roots. I never reached for the high life, so don't have far to fall!" Like all the old miners my father had seen plenty of betrayals by leaders, and was cynical about all of them. I had not seen as much, I commented that night, but I shared the old man's cynicism.

Eventually the strike ended. It seemed that we had won. The Coal Board and the Government had agreed on plans for the future of the industry. The Union accepted them as offering us the security we had demanded. Lawrence Daly was the hero of the hour, and was acclaimed all over the country. To us, the settlement looked good, and we were jubilant. Even the cynical amongst us, and I was one of them, had to agree that it was a reasonable settlement.

So it was back to porridge and pit claes, as I told the lads at the meeting when we announced the return to work. It was not back to normal immediately, though. It would take a long time to get back to normal. Not only had the pit been idle for a long time, but so had our bodies. It took a while to get them working again. Then there was the question of debts so many had to face. These had been incurred during the strike, and now had to be paid off. We had had no strike pay, as so many people thought. A small Social Security payment was made to wives and children, but the married men themselves got nothing. Worst hit of all were the single men. They had no income and had to rely on the generosity of their families and friends. Far from being actuated by greed and mercenary motives, as the press claimed, the striking miners knew well that it would be a long time before they even managed to get back to the relative financial security they had before the strike. It was not financial greed that had caused the strike, but a determination to protect the future of their industry. Now, they rejoiced at the belief that they had achieved what they had fought for.

Apart from regular work at the pit, there was a great deal of Union work to catch up with, work that had been postponed during the hectic days of the strike. It mostly involved report writing and form filling, and it got to the stage when May, normally so understanding and patient, said that the only sight she ever got of me was the back of my head stooping over papers at the kitchen table. I remember one day an old chap came up to me at the pit and handed over a form which was long overdue. He apologised for its lateness, and I assured him that it did not matter. It was an Accident Witness Report form, and I opened it out to check it over. I had to laugh at the answer to one question: *What was the injured man doing at the time of the accident?* The reply was plain and correct enough. "The poor bugger was lying on his back and screaming in pain."

That was the same day that the Under Manager told us the story about his new wrought-iron gates. They had just been fitted to his garden, and the Manager happened to come by. He admired them, especially the bonny way in which the initials "A.G.", for Albert Gibson, had been worked into the design. He thought he would have some made for his own front gate, until Albert reminded him that his initials would be "W.C." for Willie Chalmers.

One of the jobs I had to do as Workmen's Inspector was inspect any small privately owned mines where the men were members of our Union. There was one a few miles away, and not long after we had returned to work after the strike it became time to inspect it. They sent a car over to pick me up, and I went over in style. The Manager met me, and we went down the mine together. I was already a bit concerned about the state of the road into the mine, which was situated in wooded country. The entrance road was badly pitted, and indeed impassable for ordinary vehicles. It was used only by his own coal lorries, the Manager said. That was alright if he wanted to ruin the springs of his own wagons, but I had to consider how an ambulance could get in there if necessary. He agreed that he would have some work done on it.

We made our way into the mine by the return airway, the upcast driveage, which was low and slippery, with surface water dripping from the roof. Further down, we passed into old workings where dust rose in clouds as we walked. A little further on and we were into an old road, where the roof had fallen in several places. We had to clamber over the falls, and that made something else to go into my book. I told the Manager that he really would have to get that roof repaired. It was his return airway, and if it closed, he would be in serious trouble. He agreed, and said he would see that it was done. At a cross cut the Manager left me in the care of a fireman, and we crawled along for a while through a very low old working, where the air was stale and sluggish. Charlie, the fireman told me that this was just a short cut to the face, and not the return airway. We reached the first work place, which was idle. Charlie told me the reason was absenteeism, and asked, jokingly, if I would like to work a stint. He seemed to think I had never been in a mine like that before, but in fact it was exactly the sort of place I had worked in for so many years. It was like stepping back in time. There was no roaring of machinery here, no rattle of conveyors, no screech of cutters. I felt quite at home crawling along the faceline, but not enough to take Charlie up on his offer of a shift.

I asked him what rates they paid for the likes of that seam, and he explained that it varied very much. Everybody did all kinds of work, cutting, stripping, brushing, anything at all, and were more or less on a shift rate, with bonuses. He said the pay was good, and there was no hassle that way.

We went on crawling up the faceline, and moving over the coal gum or small coal left from the cutting. This had not been redd up, or cleared away to make an easier passage. I thought to myself that they did not know much about stripping coal. The first job you do after securing your roadhead is to redd up the gum. This is much better for the ventilation and makes for easier working all round. We reached a place where a man was working, stripped to his singlet and trousers, the way we used to be years before. He asked what I thought of this kind of work, and said I would never have seen the like of it before. Evidently he was confused by my overalls, safety helmet, gloves and dangling safety lamp into thinking I was some kind of visitor or official. He ranted on for a while about people like us not knowing what real pit work was like, and I let him rant, and laughed when he finished.

'Look, mate,' I told him, 'I was stripping coal when you were still at school. I would have had this place stripped by piece time. Why have you not got your gum redd away? It's beginning to block your airway. You are needing a set of wood up there, the roof looks heavy.' I took his pick and tapped the roof. It sounded bad. 'Get some wood up there before you go any further. You should know you are over your distance according to regulations.' I took a strap and a tree — a pit prop — and picked a needle hole for the strap to rest in at the top of the coal, measured the prop, took his saw and cut the prop to length, and hammered it home under the strap. That supported his roof.

I gave him a bit of my father's advice: 'The first thing you do in stripping coal is mind your head.' Then I split out a lump of the cut coal, and began to shovel out to the roadhead. 'There you are, son,'I told him, smugly, 'That's how its done! Now, don't let me ever see you working without supports again, or you will be for the high jump!' Putting on my most authoritative tone, I told him I would let him off this time, but he had better be careful in the future. He was a bit shaken, and called me "Sir" as he said he would be more careful. Charlie, meanwhile, in the background, was having trouble refraining from laughing out loud. When we went on, Charlie said he was glad I had put that bugger in his place. He was headstrong and careless, and needed to be taken down a bit.

A bit further down the road we came to the hand drawer, who was crouching there, cursing steadily to himself. His hutch was off the road, and well off, with the buffers resting on the rails.

He had some choice things to say, and amongst them was the fact that this was the second time that day he had been off the road at the same place, and that the bloody rail had sprung again. I asked him if he did not think it would have been sensible to take time out and fix the rail, but that in the meantime I would give him a hand to get back on the rails. As I strained and lifted at the front end, Charlie and he packed the wheels, and we swung it round. Then we did the same at the rear, and the hutch was back on the rails, which Charlie had knocked back into place with a heavy hammer.

The drawer went off with his hutch, and Charlie and I examined the rails. The sleeper was rotten, and needed replacing, so Charlie went to find one. He was soon back, and we prised up the rail, withdrew the rotten sleeper and slipped the new one into place. I measured the gauge in the old way with my elbow against one rail and my fingers against the other, and Charlie knocked the nails into place. 'Perfect,' we said, both of us having enjoyed using skills from the past, and proving to ourselves that we had not forgotten those elementary parts of the old colliers craft.

We worked our way back to where the incline led up to the surface, and I made several notes of things that needed to be done urgently if work was to be done safely there. At the foot of the incline we waited in a manhole till a rake of hutches had passed. Charlie phoned the surface to tell them we were coming up, and we set off up the steep slope. I noticed, and pointed out to Charlie that several of the manholes were in bad condition, and needed immediate attention. He agreed, and said he would see to it straight away. I noted also that the haulage rope had been sawing through some sleepers because pulley rollers were missing. There was also an absence of fire equipment and sand buckets.

At the surface, I told Charlie that I had finished underground, but that there was a lot to be done. I was far from satisfied with the safety precautions, and quite a lot needed immediate attention. I went off to the office, squelching my way through deep mud. I thought how miserable it would be to work in those conditions, especially on wet winter days, and with no baths at the mine.

I had a cup of tea with the Manager, and enjoyed some of his wife's dumpling, and then went off to inspect the explosives magazine. Rather to my surprise I found it in good order. A little later, sitting with the Manager in his office, again drinking tea and eating dumpling, I went over my report, stressing the things that needed immediate attention. He promised to have them seen to immediately, and I told him I would be back the following week to ensure that everything had been done to make working conditions safe, and in accordance with the various regulations.

The Manager commented that from some of my remarks it seemed that I had had experience of working low seams by hand. I told him that was the sort of mining I knew when I first started down the pits so many years ago. We exchanged reminiscences of the old days, and I told him that the strangest thing for me was the quietness in the old-fashioned mines like his. It was for me like going back in time. He himself had never seen the sort of machinery we were using, and listened with great interest as I described the shearers and conveyors. He said he would like to see this for himself, and I assured him that he would be very welcome to come over any time and be shown round. He was very interested also to learn about my own job of Workmen's Inspector. He thought I was doing that full-time, and was very surprised to learn that a lot of the work had to be done in my own time, that I was not paid for it, and that I was also Union Branch Secretary, with all that meant in terms of extra, unpaid work. We parted on good and friendly terms, and I told him I would be back in a week's time to ensure that everything I had reported to him had been put right. He assured me that it would, and asked if I did not trust him. I told him it was not a matter of trust, but that it was my duty to ensure that the men working in that mine had safe conditions, and I would carry out that duty. And that really was the situation. I was not being untrusting or officious, but was determined that so far as possible, all injuries, illnesses and accidents would be eliminated.

It rained over the next week, and when I returned to that little mine, I found a coal lorry well and truly stuck in the deep mud of the yard. It looked as though a tractor would be needed to get it out. The Manager was not at all the same cheery person that day, but by the time I had finished my inspection had recovered some of his good humour. The lorry had been dug out, and men were busy filling in the worst of the potholes. I found that most of the safety hazards I had reported had been attended to, and that generally conditions were reasonable. Back in the office, over tea and dumpling again, I told the Manager I was satisfied with the mine, but that he must keep up the standards. We both signed my report, and he offered me a lift down to the road in his Landrover. I was glad of that. It saved me a long hike through deep and sticky mud. On the way, he very seriously offered me a job at his mine, with good pay. I didn't even think about it before refusing. I had my job and my responsibilities where I was, and I was not going to give them up.

A van was waiting for me in the road. The Manager had phoned up and arranged for it. 'All part of the service,' as he said. I knew the driver, who had taken me around to various places in the past, and we talked as he drove me back to my own mine.

He thought that place was the back of beyond, and I agreed with him, saying it was a wee mine fifty years behind the times. Willie did not know that little mines of that sort still existed, and I explained to him that there were quite a few of them, privately owned, and licensed by the Coal Board. 'It took me back quite a bit, being down there, reminding me of how I used to work, with hand picking of the coal and hand drawing of the hutches. People complained it was cruelty to the ponies, so they got rid of them, and used men and lads instead. It was brutal work.'

Willie agreed, but said that at least men could refuse while the poor ponies couldn't. 'That's true,' I told him, 'But in fact it was not a job fit for man or beast. Still, it was done. That's all in the past for me, and I would never go back to it. All mining was hellish hard work in those days.'

I was on one of my favourite hobbyhorses by then. 'The good old days: my arse,' I told Willie. 'The Dukes, the Lairds, the Landlords, the Coal Owners, they got their fortunes and their big houses from the sweat and blood of the colliers. Poor buggers, they landed in the grubber, the poor house, when they were no longer able to work. They were treated like scum. Things have changed a bit since those days, although we still have a long way to go to reach a decent standard, a safe future and security when we retire.'

Willie had listened, nodding his head as he drove. 'My father was a miner. He's dead now, but he spoke the same way you do. He had a rough time of it before he died. He couldn't get out of his chair, knackered with working, no air, wet places and sheer bloody hard graft, that's what killed him.' There was bitterness in his voice. 'Aye,' I told him, 'There's lots of men like that. I've worked with them. It's an inhuman world, unjust. The rich get richer from our labours, the poor stay poor. Maybe some day we will have a more equal society, or maybe that's just a dream, but we must fight for that better and safer and more secure future for ourselves and for our children.' Willie's memories of his father had touched a chord with me. I did not know the old man, but I knew a hundred like him, and was filled with respect and admiration for them. They had fought a tremendous battle, not only against all the forces of nature in the pits, but also against the unscrupulous bosses and politicians of their day. We had other struggles. 'It will be a long drawn-out fight,' I told Willie. 'If only we had good strong Union leaders. One or two are good, but the majority are crawlers, lap dugs o the bosses. Here in Scotland the Union is strong only because we have a good leader in Mick McGahey. He is a dedicated man, a fighter for the benefit of the people. You wouldn't believe that from the abuse the media give him. That's their policy, they are the mouthpiece of the upper classes. Certainly some Union leaders are only there for what they can get out of it, and to take other highly paid jobs, and to hell with the workers who pay them. They sell the workers short. They are scum, and believe me, there are plenty of them, even at Branch level.'

We were pulling into the pit yard, where I would get bathed and changed. 'I can believe what you say,' said Willie, 'My father spoke the same way. Anyway, see you again,' and he swept away out of the yard, with a cheerful toot on the horn.

There was one thing about being so deeply involved in Union work and inspections. It meant that life was never dull. Even when a Union official was ill in bed, as I was on a couple of occasions, calls still came for assistance and work still had to be done. Very much against May's angry remonstrances I had to get out of bed, where I had been for a fortnight with a right dose of flu, and attend to the post mortem forms for Frank Logan. It was a waste of time, though, because before anything could be done, Mrs Logan was dead herself, and she had been so motherly to me when I visited her, telling me to get back to my bed, and take a hot toddy.

Sometimes the jobs were heartbreaking and dramatic, and sometimes they were childish and funny. It was dramatic when the call came to attend a fatal accident at the foot of the mine, where a rake of hutches had run away and smashed into the bottom of the slope, killing one man and injuring another. The damage done was awful, and took a long time to clear up.

It was funny when I was met one day in the pit yard by a group of men angry because the milk in the canteen was sour. When I looked at it, I realised that not only was it sour, but it had been watered. My experience as a boy working on farms told me that. The canteen lady had stacked the offending crates to one side, and as soon as the Manager appeared, I told him what had happened, and asked that he get the milk analysed. He agreed to do that, and when I came up the mine after my shift, he called me into the office to say it had been done, that the milk certainly had been watered, and that the contract with the supplier was cancelled. A new supplier had been appointed, and was taking over immediately. That was the end of the story, but it serves to point out the great variety of matters that had to be dealt with by a Branch official.

Of course being a Union Official did not save me from the usual rough and tumble of life in the pits. There was one occasion when it got very rough indeed. That was in the baths one morning, when I was changing ready to go down. Some sort of argument broke out between a couple of the men, and it began to look and sound nasty. I felt that being an Official I really should do something about it, so I called to them to cool it and get away to the job. 'Aye, Alright,' said Danny, a pool leader, and turned away to his locker. Under his breath he added: 'That big bastard is off his head. He's fucking daft.' The "big bastard" was big indeed, about sixteen stone, and powerful. He heard the whisper from Danny, and charged at him, pinning him against the lockers. He had Danny by the throat, and was squeezing.

I leaped forward, because Danny was obviously helpless, and tried to pry his fingers loose. That didn't work, so I thumped him on the wrist. Big John was still squeezing, and he was livid, with a wild glare in his eyes. I could not shift him, so I jumped on his back and shoved two fingers up his nose. He grabbed me with a free hand, and tossed me against the lockers on the other side. I came back, head down, and butted him in the ribs. He swept me to one side, and I fell under the seats. Clearly, Danny was weakening fast, and I appealed to the men standing round and gaping. None of them had come forward to help me. 'Give me a fucking hand,' I screamed at them, 'Or he'll kill Danny!' I grabbed John again by the head from behind, and tugged.

'Leave him, son, you haven't a chance,' said a voice behind me. It was Big Chris, a powerfully built German. 'I'll sort him out for you.

Chris grabbed John by the neck, using some sort of judo hold, and quietly led him away from Danny, who collapsed onto the seat, rubbing his throat. He soon revived, and when I looked round for Chris and John, they were standing a little way off, talking quietly. John looked over at me, and there was a pained look on his face. He told me he was sorry that he had hurt me. So was I, but I was not badly hurt. It seemed that Chris had in fact learned his unarmed combat in the German Army, and for once I was glad of it. I was more than a bit upset that our own lads had stood by and watched what was happening and not tried to intervene. In fact, I was a bit more than upset: I was frankly disgusted.

At the end of the shift I was approached by Brian, the Safety Officer. He wanted to speak to me. He had heard there had been a fracas in the baths, and that I had been involved. I put on a puzzled expression, and looked straight into his face, and denied that there had been any sort of trouble. 'Brian,' I told him, 'I saw nothing, heard nothing about any fight or squabble this morning. Your informants have got it all wrong.' He could not shift me from that story, and finally had to go off. If the matter of the fight had been been brought up at a Safety Meeting, it could have meant the immediate dismissal of both Danny and Big John, and I would be no party to that. Those standing around listening to the exchange between us grinned happily. They knew well what was happening.

A little later Wullie MacDouugall thrashed it all out in the Union office, and it all ended well by Danny and Big John shaking hands and agreeing to forget it. Wullie thought I had done the right thing in refusing to shop the two of them to Brian, although he said he would have had no hesitation about it if the fight had taken place down the pit. He thought I was a bit mad to have tackled Big John, and said he would have thought twice about that. If I had thought twice I probably would not have done it at all.

There had been some changes in Union office holders, although I was still Branch Secretary and Workmen's Inspector. Wullie MacDougall was now Chairman of the Branch, and was also an Executive Committee Member. George Bolton, an up-and-coming Union leader, was now Delegate. Wullie and I always worked well together, and George fitted in very well with us both. George had been opposed in his election, greatly to our surprise, by a man who seemed to have no qualification for the job, except the desire to use the position for his own ends. We had never expected that it would be a close election, and none of us could understand how it could ever have happened, because there just was no comparison between the two men.

There was really close co-operation between Management and Union in many things. We sat together in several committees to consider such things as safety, health, welfare and even absenteeism. One of the best things that came out of the Consultative Committee was the agreement to have more frequent visits from the Coal Board mobile X ray unit. I warmly welcomed this, and we had posters printed giving details of the times and dates of the visits, and arranged that officials should seek to persuade all the men to attend. It would take only a few minutes and would safeguard their future. They would be told of the results, and would be given proper advice and help if it was necessary. It was a chest X Ray , of course, and we were particularly interested in tracing the first signs of pneumoconiosis and silicosis. In the event, there was a very good turn out, although not as good as I had hoped for. When the results came through, some of the men had traces of dust in their lungs. Some had a disablement assessment, and a few had a very high percentage of dust. Most men had imagined they were free of dust, so this was a bad shock for them. We gave advice on claiming disablement benefit where necessary, and in consulation with the Manager found work for them in a comparatively dustfree atmosphere. This meant down-grading for them, and less wages, but there were other benefits to which they were entitled, and we did our best to ensure that they were not left worse off.

Absenteeism was always a problem, and a committee was set up to deal with it. The committee was chaired by the Relations Officer, and there were representatives of the various unions, a secretary and a safety officer. I usually represented the miners. Men with a bad record appeared before this committee and their record was discussed, and we tried to find the reasons for it. Sometimes the men had difficulty in adjusting to different shifts, and we tried, in those cases, to find some suitable arrangement.

Other men always found Monday mornings difficult. There was no real reason for that, so warnings were issued in those cases. Mostly the warnings were heeded, and the men did not appear again. Some cases angered me. Men who were physically fit were taking days off whenever they pleased. The first time they were given a severe warning, and told of the penalties if they persisted. Often we found a physical reason, some disability, which caused absenteeism, and we tried to solve that by offering different work. There was one big healthy lad for whom day shift was a killer. He just could not get up in the mornings, although he was fine on other shifts. His record was deplorable, and he kept bringing out different excuses. Finally I told him, 'Right, man, you have trotted out every excuse in the book except for being pregnant.' He looked at me, and gasped, then said: 'Ah'm not pregnant, but the wife is.' We had to laugh, and then the chairman asked him to leave the room while we discussed his case. The chairman said he should be sacked, and others agreed, but I argued that he should be put on a trial period of three months, and downgraded to oncost work. If there was no improvement after that, he should go. Finally, this was accepted, and the lad was called back and given a talking to by the chairman, who said that his job had been saved by his representative, and that he had better get himself sorted out. The lad hung his head a bit, and then cheered up, and thanked the committee and promised to do his best.

As it happened, his was the last case that day, so I gathered my papers and went out. He was waiting for me. 'See you,' he growled, 'I'll never speak to you again, you black bastard.' I was a bit surprised, after seeing him so contrite and thankful just a few minutes early, so I just told him he was lucky to have a job at all, even if it was oncost. Again he called me a black bastard, and walked away.

Each time I saw him after that he called me a black bastard, and I came to look forward to it, and always reminded him that he said he would never speak to me again. In fact, it became a bit of a joke, and when one day he was allocated to work with me on the same team, he refused to address me all day other than as the black bastard. Actually he worked very well, and had become a good timekeeper, so I had a word with the Manager, reported the change in the lad, and he was offered the first face work that came up. He gave the Absenteeism Committee no further trouble.

We were driving a cross cut in a development area, and making good progress. There was only about an hour to go on our shift one day, when we heard an unusual noise, a loud rumble, in the distance. 'What the bloody hell was that?' called Wullie, his head cocked to one side. 'That's strange, I've never heard that before.'

Nor had I, and I didn't like the sound of it, but there was nothing to do at the moment, so I called for help in getting the heavy borer out of the way. If we were going to have to get out of there in a hurry I did not want anybody falling over that. Suddenly one of the oncost lads who was supplying us with material shouted out. 'What the fuck's that?' and pointed out outbye. We looked, and it was an awesome sight. There was a huge, dense, reddish-brown cloud of smoke drifting towards us, completely filling the roadway, and about to envelop us. It was menacing and ugly. I shouted to everybody to get their Self Rescuers on, and snapped open the steel case to get mine out. These were respirators which we all carried at all times. This was a recent safety regulation, and although we recognised that the respirators could be life-savers, we often cursed them for being heavy and awkward. This was an occasion when we blessed them, not cursed them!

I checked that everybody had his Self Rescuer in place and adjusted properly, and then we began to walk out, not rushing or panicking. I had been through a similar experience before, and knew that at all costs we had to get to fresh air, and that we must head for the main roadway. We could see nothing in that dense cloud, and our eyes were stinging and watering. Our lungs were aching with the effort of breathing through the respirators, and we were sweating heavily. I was in the lead, groping along, and when my hand felt part of the gearing of the conveyor I knew we were nearly out of that road and into the main road. If it was filled with smoke too, then we would really be in trouble. I clambered over some supplies and across the conveyor, and suddenly there was brightness and a current of air. I whooped with delight as I pulled the Self Rescuer off my face, and thankfully drew in a deep draft of fresh air. A few minutes later we were all sitting around in the main road, drying off, and recovering. Certainly if it had not been for those Self Rescuers which we had cursed so often for being a nuisance and a handicap, we would have perished in that cloud of noxious smoke.

'Right, lads,' I said, 'It's lousing time for us. We can't get back in there today.' Our bags and jackets would have to be brought out by the next shift. We should get cracking now, and get up to the baths before we cooled down too much.

It was fine walking to the mine bottom, but when we caught the man-riding cars up the long slope to the surface, the icy air struck hard, and we were shivering. The warmth of the baths was welcome. But then, the baths were always welcome. I think the baths were the innovation that meant more to miners than any other, more than all the new machinery and all the new methods of work. It was my generation that saw the installation of baths, and mine was the last generation to have bathed every day in front of the kitchen fire or in a freezing wash house, and seen the pit clothes spread out to dry on the hearth, and the women cleaning and putting dubbin on the the pit boots. Now we had hot showers every day, lockers for our clothes and a drying room for the wet pit clothes. We travelled to work clean, and we returned clean. All the filth and wet was left behind at the pit, where it belonged, not in the houses our wives kept so trim and neat.

That day, just as I was about to enter the showers, with my towel tied modestly round my waist, I was accosted by Brian, the Safety Officer. He was upset. 'Who gave you permission to use the Self Rescuers? They will have to go off now to be tested. It's a reportable incident!' I looked at him angrily. 'Are you bloody daft? I gave permission, or would you rather have five dead men who had waited for a fireman to tell us to put them on like a lot of kids. Christ, man, you're daft! A man had to use his own initiative or his instincts in a situation like that!'

Brian bleated on for a few minutes about having to write reports, so I told him I would write his reports if he waited until I had bathed, and went off to the showers.

I made my report to Brian, and to the Safety Committee, which happened to be meeting the next day. They listened carefully, and plied me with questions, although none of the questions concerned itself with our use of the respirators. The fireman of the section also gave a report, which confirmed what I said. We discussed and drew up new rules to ensure that such an occurence did not happen again. In fact, what had happened was a peculiar thing, the like of which I had never heard before or heard of since. A valve had been opened on a big stretch of old piping used to carry compressed air to the blast borers, and those pipes must have been filled with fine rust and muck which blew out under great pressure, making that big cloud of what we had assumed to be smoke.

Some weeks later I was called into the office. Albert, the Undermanager was there, along with Brian and Matt McEwan, the oversman. Albert said he had a job for me. He was holding my last inspection report, in which I had pointed out that some roadways did not comply with regulations. He said he was giving our team the job of putting them right. We were to make sure that they did comply. I thought about it for a moment, then told him we would need a bigger team. Albert said that we should be able to manage, that we should take our time, plan it out and make a good job of it, 'but, by Christ, make sure it complies with Regulations.' I gathered that my report must have irritated him.

I told him that we would do it, but that there would be a problem about supplies. Matt said he would see that we got all the material we needed. Albert intervened again, with a new thought. He would give us another man, the only member of the Ghost Squad you ever saw.

The Ghost Squad was so named by Albert himself. It was made up of Wullie MacDougall, who was away most of the time on Union business, and Bobby McMeechan, who was partly disabled and lost a lot of time. The other member of the Squad was Adam Gollecky, and he was the one who was to work with us. He was a Pole, a strong man, and a good worker, and we were glad to have him with us. So we had a new team that was to last for some time. Matt McEwan gave us our detailed orders and we planned how to have the material transported to us, because we would be working well away from the main stream. We spent two days collecting wood, straps, battens, chockwood and many sets of circle arch girders.

Some of the work we knew would be dangerous, because we would be working alongside a fault, but we were a team of four experienced and competent miners, and were not deterred. In a week we had made good progress, and split into two pairs, each doing different work. I was working with Adam, and chose to work close by the fault where there had been a huge fall of rock.

The plan was to work over the fall, erecting circle arch girders as we went. We had to set the girders on straps, and then on blocks under the fault, and everything had to be firm and secure. We erected forepoles in front of where we were working, and they gave us a certain amount of security in that place. We made faster progress at the top, where the fault levelled out, although it was much harder work for the supply men, who had to drag materials up the slope to us. They were helped by our partners who were having an easier time with their work outbye. Soon we came to the point where the fault ended, and the enormous rock fall dipped down again towards the flat road ahead of us. This slope suited us, because we could couple up our girders and slide them down the slope, then just ease them upright into position.

We were short of straps to be used as distance pieces between the girders, as required by the Regulations, so we put out some battens ahead of the work, to keep us safe, and erected another set of girders, temporarily chaining it until the straps came up and we could secure it properly. We did that, and then we put out more battens, and I went on to make solid the place where the next girder, or perhaps the next two girders, would go. Adam had gone back to see if he could hurry up the straps, but I felt quite safe under the battens.

There was a shout from up the slope, and I knew Adam was back. He shouted that he had brought some straps, and I told him to get on with fixing them while I finished the job I was doing. I was standing in a hole and fixing a block into place when a warning shout echoed down the slope. I froze, and looked up. A girder was falling towards me. I threw myself sideways, but to my horror my foot was jammed in the hole. I remember closing my eyes as the girder hurtled towards me, and then it struck. Fortunately, I had got well to the side, and the girder only struck my battery case, knocking me further over, and causing some bruising and abrasions.

It could have been a lot worse, but I could not have found worse language than that I used on poor Adam. He was white with shock, and I was shaking with fright when he reached me. He got a mouthful or two, even before he bent to the girder and lifted it to free me. That was a tremendous feat, but I was not in any mood to appreciate it. Finally, I learned that he had taken off the chains securing the girder before he had put the straps in place. He had a bit more tongue lashing, more to ease my own fears than for any other reason, and then we dragged the girder back up the slope and fitted it into place.

I was not injured, just a bit bruised and shaken, but the incident — it was nothing more — made me think about how often I had been hurt and injured in the pits. It certainly was not that I was careless. Far from that. If anything I was ultra-careful, because in my job as Workmen's Inspector I so often saw the results of careless working. Pit work, by its very nature, was dangerous, and I had spent my working life in the pits. I had not had a really bad accident, but that had been a matter of chance, not skills. How long could the chances go my way?

Entering the Union office one day, after my shift and after bathing, I found Wullie there with a man I recognised, but could not quite place. Wullie introduced us. It was Dick Douglas, our Member of Parliament. He shook hands vigorously, and listened as Wullie went on about me being the busiest man in the pit. Dick said he was delighted to meet me, and gazed straight into my face. He went on to say that Wullie had been talking about how active the Union branch was, and of course he had heard about us beforehand, and about the good work we were doing in the pit and locally.

'Yes,' I thought, but did not say, 'And you are a proper pee-hee, all talk and no action.' So I excused myself and got on with some correspondence. There was one letter that needed Wullie's signature as well as my own, an application for a man to go to our Union Convalescent Home. I passed it over, and Wullie read it and signed. Another matter needed his opinion and he said it would be raised at the Branch meeting on Sunday. We checked that the notices for the meeting had been printed and distributed, and generally got on with the routine work of the Union Branch. Dick, meantime, sat and watched and listened, and we chatted away when we could.

Wullie was called away to see the Manager, and then there came a knock on the door and a head poked through. It was Bob Kane, an old friend of mine, from my youth, when we both worked in Shotts. I was a faceman, and Bob was my drawer. We had been good friends, but now Bob was leaving the pits. He was but a frail shadow of his former self. He was gasping for breath, and it was clear he had the dreaded miners' disease of pneumoconiosis. I sat him down, and enquired how he was, although that really was clear enough. He was dying. 'Oh,' he said, 'I'm buggered. I can hardly draw a breath. I'm knackered. I've got to leave the pit.'

He handed me over a packet of papers and asked me to fill them in for him. I did so, and Bob left, puffing and gasping. Dick had watched all this in silence. 'What's wrong with him?' he asked in a shocked voice. 'What's wrong with him?' I repeated, sarcastically, for I was upset at Bob's condition. 'That man suffers from pneumoconiosis, one of the hazards of our work. Now he is being tossed out of the industry like a load of garbage. Do you know what that man's entitlements are? He will get £800 and a pittance of a miner's pension and some piddling little sickness benefit. That is if they are granted. We have to battle even for them because it's not easy to convince a Medical Board however self-evident the claim seems.'

Dick asked if I had known the chap long, and I explained that we had worked together at Shotts. I was at the coal face, stripping the coal in a fourteen or fifteen inch high seam, sometimes with inches of water on the pavement, and always with water dripping from the roof. Bob had been my hand drawer. He filled the coal I stripped from the seam and loaded it into a hutch or tub. Then he pushed that loaded hutch out into the main road, along tracks that often undulated, making it heavy and strenuous work for the drawer. I had done that work, and it was hard. Wrenched backs and legs were common. I went on for a while about bad conditions and how things were a bit different now, but equally dangerous, and how all improvements had had to be fought for by the Union.

Dick listened to me ranting away — and I could do a bit of ranting on that subject, about which I felt so deeply. He put in a few remarks, but it seemed to me that he was a bit condescending. I told him that in my view he represented what was really wrong with the system. They went round all smiles before the elections, they listened, but they never heard; they saw, but they never understood. They were not interested in the conditions people lived in, or pensions or low wages. They were all gas and gaiters, all talk. It was time they came down amongst the people and learned something about them, about how they had to work and live, and do something to right the wrongs that bedevilled them.

Justifiably, Dick was a bit bewildered by my outburst, and said that they did what they could. I told him that was damned little, and that it was surprising to me that folks gave some of them a vote. Dick laughed, and said he could be sure of my vote. Yes, he could, I told him, but only because there was no way I could see myself voting Tory or S.N.P. But he had better be careful, I warned him, the S.N.P. was going to run him close. The candidate was a local man, and well liked. I heard the talk down the pit, and Dick had better not be complacent about his vote, or he would lose the seat.

Dick looked at his watch and said he would have to be leaving, and that it had been a pleasure meeting me, a sentiment which I rather doubted. However, we shook hands, and off he went, almost colliding with a faceman who was coming into the office. 'Who stole his scone?' the man asked, 'He didn't look too pleased.' I explained that he was the Labour candidate for the forthcoming elections, and that I had slagged him a bit, telling him they were grossly overpaid, and even so some of them had other jobs as Directors and so on. If they paid attention to doing what they promised to do in their election addresses, they would have no time for other work. Some M.Ps, like some Trades Unions Officials, are concerned only about themselves. They grab what they can, and even end up in the House of Lords for services rendered to the bosses. There are some dedicated to the cause, but they were the ones who got the big stick from the media.

Tommy asked me who I was going to vote for anyway, since it seemed I had booted the arse of the Labour candidate. 'Well, I'm going to vote for him, of course,' I replied. 'He's the least of the three evils.' I could never vote for the others, but I can't pretend that I voted with enthusiasm for Dick.

There was plenty of correspondence to keep me busy that evening, but I got through the homework, as it was still called, in good time, and went out for a pint, a game of pool and a blether with the boys. The local pub was bustling. There was a darts match with a team from Tullibody, and a good turn out from both pubs. Frank asked me what I would have, and went off to get the pint of heavy for me. Hughie told me a story of what had happened just before I came in.

He asked me if I remembered the chap from Tullibody who lost his leg in an accident a year or so earlier. I told him that, yes, I remembered him well. It seems that two of our lads, Jimmy McGillivray and wee Wullie Davidson were standing at the bar when that chap came up to order. 'Hello, pal, join our club,' Jimmy said. The chap gaped a bit, and said he was already in the Tullibody club. Jimmy laughed, and hammered his own tin leg with a pint glass, and then did the same to Wullie's tin leg. There were those three men standing at the bar, and they only had three legs between them. It was funny alright, in its way, but it also meant that the pits had taken three of the legs off those three men.

There was no escaping Union business even when I had come out for a quiet pint. The one-legged lad from Tullibody came over and asked to speak to me. He was concerned about the delay in getting his claim for compensation settled. I was able to explain that everything was going well, but that these things always took time. He should be hearing soon, and I was sure there were no problems with the claim. His mind was eased a bit, and he wanted to buy me a drink, but I told him I already had one, and was in company. So he went off.

When I got back to the others, we had been joined by Davy Pearson. He was great company, with a lively wit. He also played the tin whistle and sang songs of many kinds. There was never a dull moment when he was around, and an evening in his company was always good fun.

'Ah, here's ma wee pal,' he said. 'Come and sit doon and I'll tell you this. I've written a wee song about you.' And so he had. He played the tune on his tin whistle, a merry, Irish Jig kind of a tune, and thumped out the rhythm with his feet. Then he began singing. It was a grand wee song, all about the work I did for the Union, and soon there was a crowd gathered round listening and stamping to the rhythm. I was more than a bit embarrassed, but I had to listen, and was delighted when the crowd clapped when Davy had finished. Of course, they were probably clapping the singer, not the sentiments of his song. So the singing started, with man after man doing his bit, and the rest of us joining in. It was a great night, and we could have gone on a lot longer, but all too soon those dreaded words echoed round the bar: 'Time, Gentlemen, Please!' There was no arguing about it in those days, and no extensions. You were out in the street at closing time, and closing time was early. So we went home, relaxed and happy, and not too late.

It was a grand morning when we went off to work the next day. The birds were singing and the sky blue, and one was glad to be alive on such a lovely early morning. 'Good morning, lads,' I said as I reached the bus stop. 'It's a fine morning!' Old Davie the Grunt had his reply. 'What the hell's good about it?' he asked.

'Davie, man,' I told him, 'Look at the braw sky, and listen to the birds whistling.' 'Christ,' he replied, 'It's all they have to do! They are no going where we are going. We won't see much of your braw sky in the pit, will we?' But that was Davie all over.

I was not too pleased when I got to the pit because I was detailed to go and work on a driveage. The regular man on one of the teams was absent, so I had to replace him. I knew the work well enough, but it was the dust and the noise which I did not like. The work of driving the road was done with Blast Borers, and they created a hellish din, absolutely, and probably literally, deafening. I was classed as being on Special Duties, and so I knew I would not be long on the driveage, and I was glad of that.

The gang welcomed me, and I fitted into the team, and we worked away. I stuffed cotton wool taken from a face mask into my ears, but even so, when the borers and the scraper conveyor were switched off at the end of the shift and I pulled the wool out of my ears, I found that I could not hear anything that was said. I had experienced this before, and knew it was temporary, but I was always a bit uneasy about it. Normally, my hearing was very acute, and I wanted to keep it that way. I persuaded a number of other men in the team to try using the cotton wool, and told them I thought there was a danger of them turning stone deaf. They said they had got used to the noise, but I pointed out that the effects might be felt later. They could well be stone deaf. 'Well,' quipped one lad, 'That wouldn't be too bad. I wouldn't hear the wife narking at me!"

'No,' I told him, 'And you won't hear me asking if you want a pint in the pub!' I worked on that driveage for about a fortnight, and was glad when the regular man returned, and I could get back to my own work, the Special Duties. That was heavy and often dangerous, but I preferred it to mine driving. I raised that question of noise at the Safety Committee, and demanded that the men should be supplied with ear muffs. The Manager readily agreed to this, and I must say that Big Willie was always ready to do anything he could for safety in the mine. He would co-operate in all measures we suggested. He instructed the Safety Officer to investigate the supply of ear muffs, and in a short time they became available.

George Montgomery, our Union Inspector, had written an excellent article on the suppression of noise in the pits. He pointed out the dangers of excessive noise, especially in confined spaces, and called for noise suppressors to be fitted. The technology to do so was present. He saw noise as being a great hazard, and a growing one, as new machines and equipment were introduced to increase output. The new technology had to come, certainly, but it had to be recognised that the new technology introduced new dangers, and that amongst them was excessive noise. All the new machines needed to have noise abatement systems built in.

George also wrote about the necessity of better training and qualifications to work those new high powered machines. In the past, if a man fancied being a machine man, he would get a job as second man on a machine. This entailed such things as pulling up the cable and renewing the picks. He would watch the machineman, and soon enough, if there was a job on another machine going, he would apply for it and took over as Number One, so long as the Manager thought him qualified. George argued that such a system was not enough, and that there should be proper training and recognised qualifications.

George, our N.U.M. Permanent Inspector, gave me lots of information, advice and tips on what to look for when I did an inspection. When we worked together we always compared notes afterwards, and he was able to guide me in many ways. Dust and noise were the main problems, indeed, the great hazards, in modern mining, and they were a constant danger to the health of the men. There was hardly a meeting of the Safety Committee or the Consultative Committee at which I did not raise these matters, and some progress was made, because in those meetings we were all concerned with the health and safety of all the men in the pit.

There were other things than noise and dust, though. There was one occasion when I had to threaten Brian, the Safety Officer with a walk-out if he did not do something immediately about a plague of flies in one section. Shit flies, we called them, and indeed they bred on human ordure. Needless to say, there were no toilets down the mine, and when men had to answer a call of nature, it was a matter of going up the waste and dropping their trousers. This was a most unpleasant thing for those of us who had to work in the waste, and there was many a cursing delivered as we scooped up another shovelfull and dropped it into the middle of a pillar we were building. Sometimes flies started breeding, and when they did, it became most unpleasant. This had happened in one of our sections, and it got so bad that, as I told Brian when threatening to have a walk-out, that the men did not know whether they were eating Carluke steak (jam) or Fly pie at piece time. He got the message, and the next shift down was equipped with disinfectant sprays to clear the place up.

There were many more men working now in the mine than when we had started,but the mine still had the character imposed upon it by the original group from Bogside. We had a reputation for generosity and care. There were frequent collections for people in need of support, the nurses, old folk, striking seamen, cancer research — they all got help from the men of our mine at one time or another, and sometimes often. There were also deductions from wages for Dr Barnado's Homes, Miners' Welfare and other things. We had our disputes, certainly, but we found management reasonable, and disputes were usually settled quickly. Both sides believed in the settlement of disputes by discussions, and it was a rare issue that went to the length of a strike, and when it did, the strike was over quickly.

We took our safety inspections seriously, and once a fortnight the Safety Officer, a trainee Safety Officer, a tradesman and myself would inspect a section. There was one day I had to give a warning to a lad, a big burly youngster, about a dangerous practice he was using. He was not very pleased, but he saw the wisdom of my advice, and we left it at that. That night he and I happened to be together in the showers. He saw me looking over at him, and growled: 'Whit's wrang noo?' Nothing, I told him, I was just admiring his tattoos. They were really bonny, very unusual. He brightened and proudly displayed his arms and chest for my benefit. It seems he had been in the Navy, and had had a tattoo done at each port he touched. Certainly they were spectacular, and must have cost a pretty penny. There were birds and animals and flowers of all kinds. He was a friendly bloke really, and we had a good chat about his time in the Navy. As I was leaving, I asked if he was married. He told me he was, so I said if must be fun to be his wife: if she got tired of looking at his face, she could always look at his tattoos. He called me a cheeky wee bugger, and swiped with his towel.

When I got to the Union office I found Wullie and a few others in there discussing the so-called Incentive Scheme. This was something to which I was bitterly opposed, although it had been accepted by the Executive, and our President, Joe Gormley, was arguing for it. I believed it would split the unity of the men and pit man against man. In some areas coal was easy to get, and there the bonus would be high. In other places coal was difficult to win and the conditions more hazardous, so that the men would be working harder under worse conditions for less money. To me, that was grossly unfair. However, it had been accepted, and so we had to work it, whatever I thought about it. That was what happened in the Union. Now we had to explain it to the men at a meeting, and I was glad it was Wullie's job to do so, and not mine.

We discussed a strange smell that was pervading the Number One Mine. It had started in one place, but now was all over. None of us had met this before, and we had no explanation for it. Anything unexplained of this sort in a mine was worrying. It could be nothing or it could be dangerous. It could be the first intimation of a major disaster of some kind in the making, and we had to get to the bottom of it. Fortunately, a safety inspection was due the very next day, and in the meantime I was able to tell them that the men on the backshift would try to trace it. I had been down there myself, and agreed that indeed it was a manky stink, and I thought it might be coming from some old workings.

It was manky alright, agreed Tammy, so bloody manky that if something was not done about, then it would be a Home Go. Wullie stopped him, saying that nae doot the Workmen's Inspector (pointing at me) would investigate in the morning, along with the Safety Officer.

The next morning those of us doing the inspection met and decided what was to be done. Brian reported that the disinfectant had done the trick, and that the men would no longer have to eat Fly Pie. So that was one problem out of the way. We went down the mine, and when we arrived at the crossroads leading to different sections, we split up into two pairs. I went off with old Geordie, the Training Officer, while Brian and George, the Tradesman Inspector, went off in a different direction. I was leading the way, with my Glennie Safety lamp swinging at my waist, and my yardstick in my hand. That was useful both for measuring and as a walking stick, and I set a cracking pace, because there was a lot of ground to cover.

I was wondering about that strange smell which we had to investigate, and almost forgot about old Geordie. When I looked round, he was puffing and blowing, and I apologised and we sat down for a couple of minutes to let him get his breath back. I thought I could already smell the peculiar stink we were to investigate, but Geordie could detect nothing at first, then he caught it, very faint, but definite. We agreed that it had a faint tinge of sulphur. We went on, up and over an overcast, and I gave Geordie my stick to help him along, and we kept the pace down a bit.

The smell was definitely getting stronger, and we tested for gas with the Safety Lamp. We switched our headlamps off and I adjusted the lamp flame to the proper tip, and then moved it all round the area, up between the girders and low down at ground level. There was no sign of gas, but still the smell was strong. Geordie took the Safety Lamp and tried in other places, but with no result. The lamp showed no abnormalities. We switched our headlamps on again, and went further up the heading. Geordie was leading the way, and after a few more yards he dropped on his knees at a small opening. 'This is it,' he shouted. 'Hell, it's putrid! Smells like rotten eggs.' I dropped down beside him and took a good sniff. I felt my stomach turn over and thought I would vomit. We moved quickly away. I asked Geordie if he knew where that small opening was likely to lead to, and he said, thoughtfully, that it was probably Longannet. We got away from there as quickly as we could, but still pleased that we had found the source of the problem.

We worked our way over to the Longannet mine, and then back to where Geordie figured we were close to the source of that vile smell. There was no trace of it there, but there was evidence of an old heading, long closed up. Whatever was in there would have to stay: there was no way of getting any further. We went back and met the others, and made our reports. We were all baffled by this problem and really had no solution to it.

Various proposals were put forward, like putting dye in the water to try tracing its route and adding strong disinfectant to try killing off the smell. Different things were tried, and something must have worked, although we never did know what. In any case, the smell went away, and never returned, and we were very glad of that. It wasn't just that the smell was so overpowering and nauseating, but the fact that something was going on which we did not understand, and which might have been dangerous.

One of my more gruesome jobs as an inspector was to make a report on the circumstances of an electrician losing a leg in the pit. The man had been working above the belt, and had stepped back onto the moving belt. Unfortunately there was a slit in the belt just where he stepped, and his foot went straight through and he was trapped. He was dragged a considerable distance over the rollers, and the flesh was torn from his hands as he tried to reach the bell pull that would have automatically stopped the belt. He couldn't reach the bell, and was dragged up and over the gearhead, where his mates found him some time later. He lost his leg, and had dreadful injuries to his hands and arms, but he survived, although of course he could never work again.

Although I never got hardened to dealing with dreadful injuries and the causes of them, I had to develop a means of controlling my own feelings and emotions, otherwise I would never have survived in the job. There was the day that I went into the Union office and found a man there whom I did recognise, but only just, as a Fifer with whom I had worked, and whose claims I had handled. His jaw looked all agley, and his whole face was criss-crossed with scars. He spoke slowly and painfully of the number of operations he had had already, and of the number still to come. He had been so badly smashed up that only a small part could be treated at one time. And then he had to face the skin grafts. I knew what had happened to him. He had been working with a borer in a very confined space and the switch had jammed so that he could not turn it off. The borer had jumped, jamming his head against the roof. There had been help nearby, and the cable was quickly cut and the machine stopped, but he was in a bad way. His skull was smashed and his jaw broken. The lacerations on his neck had narrowly missed the jugular vein. They were dreadful injuries, and the First Aid men who helped him thought there was no chance of his survival. But survive he did, and with tremendous courage was able to make jokes about his condition.

As we talked, I had to make jokes, too, but only to hide the emotions I felt as I listened to his guttural and unnatural voice. I told him that when they were finished with him, we would have a new Clark Gable amongst us. All the girls would be after him, and he would be giving them a treat. His wife would think she had found a new man, and one looking better than the old one. He laughed at the crude humour, thanked me for what I had done for him, and went on his way. *He thanked me!* God Almighty! What I had done was not even a matter of doing my duty: it was simply a matter of doing what I could to help a fellow human being in trouble.

Sometimes we could not do anything to help. I was called out of the section one day by an oncost lad who breathlessly told me that I was wanted at once by Peter Fleming, the wee deputy. A man was dying. I sent the lad racing back to say that I was on my way, and told the lads in my team where I was going. They asked if there was anything they could do, but I said that at present there was nothing, and they should just carry on working. As I turned to leave the place, our own deputy stopped me, and told me I could not go. I was working in that place, and I had to stay and work. I told him in no gentle way just what he could do, and that I was going, and pushed past him. He threatened that I would be hearing more about this, but I could not even be bothered to gesture rudely at him as I walked off. When I got back to the belts, breathing heavily and sweating from hurrying, I found a cluster of men standing around mutely, looking down at their dying comrade. Peter Fleming was on his knees, applying mouth-to-mouth breathing, but as I knelt beside him to ask if I could do anything, Peter raised his head and shook it gently. The man was gone. Peter gently closed the staring eyes, and we stood for a few minutes in total silence, moved by the passing of this man, a friend, a respected and hardworking colleague. Then we lifted his body on to a stretcher and a squad of man bore him off on the strenuous climb to where a bogey was waiting to carry him up the mine for the last time.

He died from a heart attack, and he was not the first. We figured that about eight or nine men had died in a similar way, and wondered why it should be so. Was it the heavy work or the stress of climbing up and down the mine? We had no answer, but we all felt it was a situation that had to be watched.

We were not normally troubled by gas in this mine, but occasionally some would be reported. It was not always a popular measure to have the area cleared when there was gas. Some men took a lot of convincing that indeed there was gas, and that it was dangerous. I never lost the opportunity of drumming it into their heads. I had worked in pits where gas was present, and I knew its dangers. I once attended a safety conference at Strathclyde University when one of the lecturers astonished us with a practical test. We always used a safety lamp, a Glennie, to test for gas, and could detect its presence, and even estimate its percentage, we believed, by its effect on the flame of the lamp. This lecturer had a Glennie set in a glass container and asked us to examine it and decide whether gas was present, and what percentage, if any. I looked at it carefully, and saw no blue cap, the tell-tale sign of gas, so I said there was no gas present. The others agreed, although some suspected a trick. The lamp was taken out of the glass container, and then the lecturer exploded the gas that was there all the time. It proved beyond all doubt that the Glennie was not a certain way of testing for gas.

That lecturer also demonstrated how a piece of silver paper, tinfoil, could cause an explosion. Even experienced deputies did not believe me when I told them that. But I had seen it demonstrated, and I knew. If there was a rusty nail or a rusty girder and a piece of tin foil on it was given a smart smack with a hammer, there would be a spark sufficient to cause a gas explosion. Often I would be asked what was a safe percentage of gas, and I told them that the experts said two, two and a half, or even three percent was safe. Our Union Inspectors said, and I stressed that I absolutely agreed with them, that you get the hell out of a place if the percentage was one and a half. Get out, I told them, and report it.

Although obviously we had to watch for gas, because there was the very occasional pocket, dust was our real problem. The dust was made worse, in a way, by precautions which had to be taken against gas. One of the anti-gas measures was to spread stone dust along the roadways. The idea was to stop coal dust from filling the air as we walked along or as the hutches passed. Coal dust in the air was dangerous: it could explode, and if there had been a small explosion from a tiny gas pocket in a place where there was a lot of coal dust, you could have a major explosion. The stone dust kept the coal dust down alright, but it presented its own problems. As we walked or worked among it, it rose in clouds around us. Then at the face the coal dust rose in clouds. Altogether, we were enveloped in dust from the moment we entered the mine to the moment we left it, and there could be no surprise that lung troubles afflicted so many men. Noses and mouths were clogged with the stuff, and eyes irritated. The experts assured us that the stone dust was harmless, but the experts did not have to breathe it day after day, and stop breathing it only when they got to the faceline, where we breathed coal dust instead.

The mine experienced its setbacks and difficulties. There were hitches, or geological faults. There was an occasional flooding and other problems to be overcome, but we had entered a period of high output. Development was racing ahead and new areas being equipped with larger and better machines. It seemed that a long future was assured and there were good prospects for it. There was good co-operation between the workforce and Management, and this meant a more contented pit. Of course, we still had accidents. That was a reality we had to live with. Mining is dangerous, and always will be. There were still all the hazards that ruined health and left so many men crippled in their prime and their old age. Pneumoconiosis continued its dread attack, and far too many men did not realise it had struck them until it was too late. They died a dreadful death of slow strangulation.

Others found that their backs gave out, after years of handling heavy material — Dobson Props, girders, conveyor pans and heavy stones used in building packs. That was a Low Back Pain, and no damage or compensation claims were accepted for that. You simply worked on with it, taking time off when you had to, and eventually taking your bit of a pension, and getting what pleasure you could out of the rest of your life.

Industries in our area were beginning to run down. Indeed, they were everywhere in Scotland. As a Branch and as a Union we gave our support wherever workers were fighting for their future. With us, the textile industry suffered badly in an area where there had already been a big loss of jobs. It was proposed to close yet another factory, but the workers there decided to make a fight of it. It was mostly women employed in the factory, and they really did fight. They called a big protest meeting in Alloa Town Hall to be addressed by the M.P. George Reid. He was the S.N.P. man who had defeated Dick Douglas, as I had warned Dick he might, in the 1974 election. Various Trades Union officials were also on the platform, and everyone was determined to prevent the closure of the factory if possible.

Our Branch officials attended, and it was a lively meeting. Pledges of support were given by the various Unions, and George Reid vowed that no machines from the factory, nor any of the plant, would be taken south of the Border. That was a sentiment widely cheered. There was great enthusiasm and cheering that was almost deafening at times. 'Hear the howls of these women!' said Wullie. 'I wouldn't fancy getting on the wrong side of this lot. They would tear you to pieces!' There was an appeal from the platform for donations to a Fighting Fund, and our Treasurer, Wullie Graham, asked us what we intended to do. We had a brief discussion, and then Wullie Graham stood up and announced that our Union Branch was donating £50 immediately to the Fighting Fund, and that there would be a Branch Collection for more. The meeting went wild again, with cheers for us, and our example was promptly followed by donations from other Branches of the Miners Union, who all pledged to fight to keep that factory open with no loss of jobs.

The following Sunday there was our usual monthly Branch meeting, and after the normal business someone stood up and asked what action we would be taking to save that factory from closing. I prepared to answer the question, but Wullie MacDougall whispered that he would deal with it, because it could be a sticky one. He stood up and outlined what had been discussed and that we had agreed on their behalf to donate £50 immediately to the Fighting Fund. There was a howl of rage from the back of the hall. 'You had no right to do that! They were the bastards who chased our collectors away when we were on strike in '72 and '74!'

It was always a delight to watch Wullie controlling a meeting. He stood still and raised his hand. Quite calmly he said: 'Cool it, lad, simmer down! Two wrongs don't make a right! We're Trades Unionists and proud of our standing in the movement. It's our duty to help and support our fellow Trades Unionists in their struggle for better conditions, and in this case for their jobs. It's their livelihood that's at stake. As a Branch we must and we shall support them. On your behalf we have made a pledge and we will fulfil that pledge.' He was greeted with loud applause, and nothing more was heard from the dissenting voice. We continued our support for those strikers until the dispute was eventually settled, and by that time we had contributed a considerable sum of money towards their cause, just as we did for the sit-in at Clyde Shipbuilders, when another Reid, Jimmy Reid, led the struggle there.

There was no question that the leaders of our Branch were strong, capable and experienced. The leader, of course, was Wullie MacDougall. He had for a long time a position on the Executive of the

Union, as well as being our Chairman. George Bolton was our Delegate, and he was a competent leader, although at times I felt his attitude to the men was not good. He seemed to talk down to them when they were explaining a case to him, and were a bit unsure of themselves. But George was a man of great ability and intelligence that suggested he would eventually be deemed worthy of high office within our Union. George and I got on very well together, and it was very useful for me to be able to discuss matters with a man as able as him. As time went on, we saw less and less of him down the pit. We thought he should have spent more time with us, but he was always away at meetings, and only spent a few days with us to attend to our business, which, to his credit, he did superbly well.

I had a lot more work to do because of his absence, but fortunately there were two good Committee men who helped a great deal, John Millar and Frank Entwhistle. There was also Jimmy Hunter and big John Lee, and they were never slow in giving assistance and advice.

Frank Entwhistle had a very serious accident one day, and I was right there with him. We were on our way to a meeting, and were on the man-riding conveyor belts going up to the mine mouth. I was in front, and kneeling on the belt, which was wet. Frank was a little way behind me, but within earshot, and we were talking about the meeting we were going to attend. Suddenly I felt a slight shudder on the belt as we rode up the steep incline, then there was a trickle of small stones. This alerted us to trouble, and we were ready when there was a fall of some bigger pieces of stone. And then there was a really big one that fell onto the belt some way ahead. The belt was wet and slippery, and at a steep angle, and that stone slid down towards us at a tremendous speed. Somehow I managed to scream a warning, and grab the sides of the belt and lift my body up so that the stone passed underneath me. Frank called out in pain, and as I glanced round I saw him disappear off the belt. I grabbed the emergency bell pull and jerked at it, the wire burning into my fingers. Was the bloody thing not working? I jerked harder, and the conveyor stopped, leaving me with torn fingers. Jumping off the the belt, I raced back down the slope. There was no sign of Frank. I shouted and called his name and then I heard a faint cry. He was on the other side of the belt, curled up and clutching his chest and stomach. I crawled underneath the conveyor, knowing that my friend and colleague was seriously hurt. I lifted his arm away from his stomach, and saw a gaping wound. He groaned weakly, and I saw there was blood oozing from a wound in his chest. It was beyond me, and I told him I would have to get help. He nodded, and whispered to me to hurry. As quick as I could I went back under the conveyor and raced to the nearest Tannoy station. I pressed the button and called: 'Emergency, emergency. I need immediate assistance. I have seriously injured man here, at Top Belt Number Twenty One Manhole. I require a stretcher, First Aid men and stretcher bearers.' I repeated the message, and went back to Frank.

A few minutes later there were several lights bobbing in the distance from down the mine, and racing towards us. There was a loud clang from the steel door at the top of the mine, and more lights hurried down the slope. Matt McEwan, the oversman, was first on the scene with the gang from up the mine. He was a qualified First Aider, very competent and efficient. He sized up the situation, and issued his instructions. Peter Fleming, another First Aider, arrived from the bottom, puffing and blowing from the race up that slope. The two of them, with me, crawled under the belt where Frank lay. There was not much room under there, and Frank was on rubble that had fallen off the conveyor. I was, as usual, the smallest, and Matt asked if I could crawl through and hold Frank's head while they examined him and moved him. I managed to do that, and whispered to him that he was in good hands, and that we would soon have him out of that. He was in great pain, and moaning with it. The two First Aiders did what they could under there, and then gave instructions on how to get the injured man out. We carefully and gently manoevered him under the conveyor, and put him on a stretcher. The stretcher bearers, strong young chaps, set off up the steep slope at a fast pace, with others ready to take over and ensure the injured man was at the surface as quickly as possible.

Matt, Peter and I discussed Frank's injuries and how they had been caused. I told them what had happened, and they agreed that I had been very lucky. I was untouched, I thought, except for a bit cut on the hand where I had tugged at the signal wire. I looked at the hand, and to my astonishment found it crossed with a long and deep cut. I had not even known about it. Peter dressed it for me, and warned me to be careful with it. Matt assured me he would be making out a report as soon as he was washed, and said that if Frank was to make a claim for damages, he would have the best witness, me, in the pit.

We were nearly at the top of the slope when we saw where the stones and rubble had come from. There were broken straps there and the roof had fallen. It was all in dire need of repair, with the straps and cladding rotting away and giving no support to the roof. Further falls could be expected, and my report would certainly say that.

Frank was in hospital for a long time, and although he was his usual chirpy self whenever I visited him, I knew he was in pain, and he knew it would be a long time before he was back at work. Eventually he did get back, but only to light work on the surface, and I found that very useful, since he was always on hand to assist me when required.

There were changes made in our Branch Committee about this time. John Hixon joined us. He was a character, one who seemed to be able to sweet-talk himself out of any difficulty, and into any position where there was no work to do. Underground he was always wrapped up in a heavy duffle coat, which was not surprising, because he didn't do a lot of work. Jock and his duffle coat became famous, and jokes were made about it. It was said that you couldn't get the duffle coat off Jock with a Sylvester — a portable winch. There was one day a message came over the Tannoy: 'Hear this! Send for the Rescue Brigade! Jock Hixon is missing. We have found his duffle coat and he is not in it!' There were roars of laughter all along the section, but Jock just went on his way, oblivious to all the jokes.

A Minute Secretary was elected to assist me with the heavy workload that the Secretary had. He was Andy Law, a former Branch Secretary from another pit. He was very capable, and did excellent work for the Branch.

I was still on Special Work underground, and that suited me fine, since I had a variety of work, and was well acquainted with all the development roads and sections. I also knew most of the men, and where they worked and the problems they faced.

Although I was generally working with the same team all the time, there were occasions when one or another of us was taken off to work elsewhere. I remember one time when Matt, the oversman, sent me off to work with a bricklayer for a day or two. This man had never been down the pit before, and had to be shown everything about it. He had been working somewhere down south, and earning big money, but his wife had persuaded him to come back to Scotland, and the only job he could get at his trade was in the pit.

Jimmy and I did not get off to a very good start, because he thought I was a labourer to him, and expected me to carry in all his tools. He was disabused of that very quickly, but then I found that we had to rest several times going along the roadway to where he was to build up a doorway, with my help. Poor Jimmy was certainly not accustomed to hurrying along, bent double, and carrying a load of tools in almost total darkness. When we reached the place where we were to work, he was ready for a cup of tea.

The oncost lads had brought up sand and cement for us, and I found a steel plate that would do fine for mixing. Jimmy had pulled round a bit by this time, or at least he had got his breath back, and had stopped sweating. He was very nervous, though, and every new sound and creak made him start. Just after I had reassured him that the sound of distant shotfiring was neither a disastrous roof fall nor an earthquake, he asked where the toilets were! I told him there were no toilets down the pit. He had to take a shovel, go into the waste, dig a hole, do what he had to do, cover it up, and come back to work. He was not happy about going into the waste by himself, but that was one part of the pit and the job I was not going to hold his hand while he learned.

He had expected me to mix the cement for him, and was a bit put out when I rather curtly told him that was his job. I would go and bring some water. When I got back I found him mixing, but so slowly that I took the shovel from him, telling him that if he worked like that, 'the deid lice wad be drappin aff ye'. He worked away very slowly, and as it happened we had to go out into the main roadway twice that shift to get away from thick smoke from firings. By the end of the shift, Jimmy had laid two courses of bricks, and that was not much.

After I had showered at the end of the shift, Matt, the oversman, called me over and asked what the hell I had been doing all day, and did I think that was a day's work? I was about to answer and tell him what I thought of his new bricklayer, when I saw him start to grin. Jimmy had asked for his cards, and was already off down the road. He had lasted just the one day. As Matt said, it was the only time the Manager had to pay a day's wages to someone just visiting.

Another time I worked for a few weeks with a gang at the tail gate. They had not long finished their training, and were working in a difficult and dangerous place, so that it was better that at least one experienced man should be with them. They were young and strong and a bit headstrong, and it was a pleasure to show them some of the skills that they would have to develop as they went along in their time in the pit.

It was a few months after that that our team finally broke up, and I was the cause of it. I had finished my stint one day and was on my way outbye to a Safety Meeting. That was a bit ironic, as it happened, because when I was clambering over a wooden bridge across a conveyor, I fell about six feet. The bridge was wet and greasy, and a couple of rungs were missing from the ladder on the far side.

I landed on top of a rail and my self rescuer tin jabbed viciously into my back. There was a sharp pain and a blinding light, then all went black.

After that, I was dimly aware of voices and of hands lifting me. I shouted out with pain. There was something wrong with my back. The many hands helped me as I struggled to my feet and stood still. Muck was wiped off my face. The pain was still racking through my body, and I clutched at a support as I took a tentative step. Then blessed blackness engulfed me again, and took the pain away for a moment. Someone shouted for a stretcher, and I snarled that I wanted no fucking stretcher. I just wanted a couple of minutes to get my breath. I was still very dazed, and the pain got no better.

The deputy arrived and examined me where I lay. He hissed sharply when he saw my back where the battery and self rescuer had dug into me. He issued instructions for a stretcher, but again I refused, and said I would get up the pit on my own. By this time my old neighbour, Wullie MacGregor, had arrived, and he was the man I wanted to go with me.

They told me I was a crabbit wee bastard, and bloody stupid, but I still insisted that I was not going out on a stretcher. I really don't know what was in my mind: I had been injured often enough before, but had never been carried out, so perhaps it was just a determination to keep that record.

They got me on my feet again, and I set off for the boarding platform of the manriding belt. I had to struggle along holding to every support I could find. When I got to the platform, Wullie had already signalled "Man Riding". I struggled up the ramp, and tried to stand straight on the platform, but winced aloud as the pain caught me afresh. I was beginning to have serious doubts about my condition. Wullie would go first on the belt. He jumped on and looked back at me. I could not jump on, so I rolled on, with more pain chasing through my body. I cursed as every roller we passed over jerked and tore at me. I gritted my teeth, but that was a trip I never want to do again.

There was no way I could jump off at the top, where the sign said GET OFF, so Wullie signalled for the belt to stop, and I rolled over to the platform, where Wullie helped me to my feet. Together we got over to the baths, and I found the shower wonderfully easing and refeshing.

My friend, Tommy Gavin, the bath attendant, hastened over when I heard I had been injured. He examined my back, and told me what I already knew: I had had a bad knock. He insisted that I had to go to the hospital, and by that time I was really in no condition to do any more arguing. It was arranged that one of the lads would drive me to the hospital in my car (at long last we had managed to get a car of our own) and then take the car home for me. I wanted to drive myself, but even I finally had to admit that was not possible.

'Aye, man,' Tommy said, as he wrapped my ribs, 'You've buggered yourself up this time. We'll not see you for a while, and at least we'll have some peace! But I pity May, having to put up with a crabbit bastard like you all day. How that lassie puts up with you I'll never know, and what she saw in you in the first place, I'll never know!' Usually Tommy and I exchanged jokes and insults, but today, for once, he had it all his own way, because I was in no condition to respond.

Young Hendry, the other baths attendant, drove me to the hospital, and waited to see if he could do anything else. I was treated immediately, with X ray and examination. There was a good deal of damage done to the spine, but nothing internal except bruising. I was measured for a spinal support, and after a short wait was fitted with it, and sent home.

After a week I went back to the hospital and had a long talk with the orthopaedic surgeon. He was not comforting. There was quite serious damage to my spine, and quite certainly I would never work down the pit again. He wanted to operate, and thought there was a fifty-fifty chance of the operation being successful. Those odds were not good enough for me, so I declined the operation. I would have to be be very careful for the rest of my life, and avoid any further back injuries. In the meantime, I was still having to take painkiller tablets twice a day.

That was the report I carried back to my friends and fellow officials at the pit. I went up to the office, driven there by a friend who also happened to be off work, and collected a pile of forms and correspondence that was waiting for me. I told them the situation, and of course they commiserated. I was still able to do all the paper work, of course, and that was what I did for the next twelve months. I devoted all my time to the Union.

During those twelve months I saw several different doctors and medical boards, and gradually my back improved to the extent that I was able to think about going back to work. Not down the mine: that was over. I would never work down a pit again. That was a troubling thought. I had been a collier for forty six years, and now it was over. There would be no more of that life, with all its friendship and comradeship, in which I had spent all of my adult years, and some of my childhood. No more of the dust and the danger and the joking. No more of that strange way of life that had been mine and my father's before me. Well, it was not the end of the world, but it was the end of an era for me.

The year of "idleness" passed, with me still going to the Union office every Thursday and Friday to deal with anything that needed my attention, and still working for hours at the kitchen table most days, with reports and forms. Then one day I happened to meet the Manager in town, and he offered me a job on the surface, saying he needed a man like me. So it was back to work, and at least it was work around the pit, if not down under.

The job was to superintend a group of trainees who were working on the surface and learning something of what to expect when they went underground. There were other jobs to be done here and there, like a bit of painting or keeping the baths clean and tidy. It was fine so long as I did not try to lift anything too heavy. I still had a lot of pain at times, and lost a bit of work, but in general I was finding odd-jobbing on the surface was not too bad a life.

I got rather a shock, though, when it came to be Election time in the Union Branch. For the first time in twenty-one years I was being opposed. That was a blow to my ego. It was even worse when George Bolton, who was now a member of the Executive, warned me that it might not go well for me, because I had been losing a lot of time. My opponent was John Hixon, who almost beat Wullie MacDougall in a ballot, but I was sure I could beat him, even though he was popular and had a good line of patter.

Election day came, and I did beat him, by four to one. I had got almost seventy percent of the votes. I was triumphant as I shook hands with the men in the Office and heard their congratulations. So all the work I had done for so many years as Secretary was appreciated after all! That election victory put new life into me, and I went on with the Union activities with as much enthusiasm as ever.

Even working on the surface, painting or keeping the baths in order, or introducing trainees to their jobs, had its dangers. A group of youngsters and myself had just finished loading a lot of supplies on a rake one day, and I was turning away when I caught my foot on a steel plate that was lying half buried in the mud of the yard. I went down hard, and my back was again injured.

The lads helped me up as best they could, and stood me on my feet. Sweat poured down my face and body, and the pain was agonising. I told them I would be alright, and took some of the pain killing pills I always had with me.

But of course I was not alright. I told a couple of the lads to shift that bloody plate that had tripped me, and instructed the rest to carry on with what they had been doing. I went off to the baths, supporting myself with an old stemming rod, and with one of the lads holding me on the other side. Sitting in the attendants' room I began to recover a little, but was still in great pain. I must have been confused, too, because I swallowed another couple of pain killers, although I knew that I was supposed to have no more than two of them. After a while, it was arranged that one of the lads would drive me home. I had feared that perhaps I had done some more real damage to my back by that fall, but after a couple of weeks resting, I was able to get back to work again.

A gang of youngsters and I were busy one day unloading circle girders from a lorry when the Manager called me. He wanted the yard and all round about cleaned up. He wanted flower beds dug. He wanted a better environment all round, and I was the man to do it, with the help of one of the young trainees. Well, that was all right with me, and we set to work shifting a mass of rubbish, old cable, torn belting and the accumulated debris of years. We got a couple of barrows, and took it over to the bing, and we worked away quite happily. The weather was kind, warm and open, although it was January, and that was a great relief to me because I had been finding the cold and the wet of winter very hard to bear. I would much rather have been down in the warmth of the mine than up there in such miserable conditions.

Young John Logan and I worked away quite happily. I knew his father, and could tell the lad that if he became as good a miner as his father, he would do alright. I found myself telling the lad stories of my own youth as we worked, of what conditions used to be like in the pits, and of the games we played and the toys we had when I was a child.

I told him about Harry Dawson, who, a grown man, raced round the streets of the village where I was born with a gurr and cleek, honking on his motor horn. Young John laughed, but then I had to explain about the gurr and cleek, for he had never seen one. The gurr was a steel ring about the size of a bicycle wheel, and the cleek was a steel rod with a hooked end. You started running with the gurr rolling along beside you, and guided it with the cleek. We thought it was great fun, but I realised as I explained it to John, that I had not seen one for years. Of course Harry Dawson, with his gurr and his motor horn, was a harmless simpleton, but as children we were terrified of him, and ran to our mothers for shelter whenever he appeared.

As we worked away day after day I found that I was telling the young lad all kinds of stories about my youth and the characters I had known. It occurred to me one day — and it was a shock — that now I was the old timer who pottered about in the pit yard and told nostalgic tales. There was always one like that in every pit yard: now it was me, but apart from that hellish injury to my back, which still caused a lot of pain and for which I still wore a steel support, I felt that I was the same young man who had for so long been a faceworker, a proud member of the mining elite. I did not feel like the old man who pottered about the yard and told tall stories to the youngsters.

We certainly made a big difference to the appearance of the yard, and when the weather broke we had another job to keep us out of the worst of the cold and the rain. That was to clean up the mens' lockers in the baths. They were thick with grease and dirt, and that was not surprising, since they held dirty pit clothes. We worked at them with strong soda and brushes, and they soon began to look a lot better, to the pleasure of the men. They liked the new look in the yard, as well, and somebody suggested we should even get a couple of goldfish ponds going to set off the new flower beds we had built. That idea died, though, when I told them there were too many fishermen about, and that I didn't trust a single one of them.

We worked away for some months like that, in the yard, digging flower beds or loading rakes, and in the baths, cleaning up and working on the lockers. I was managing to cut down on the pain killers, but still had to take them sometimes, especially if I jerked or wrenched my back in any way. Still, I thought there was certainly progress. The Union work continued, and it seemed that it would be unending. There was always someone injured and with a claim for compensation. There were forms to fill in, witnesses to interview and reports to make. It was work I had done for a long time, and I was happy doing it. So long as I was doing that, then I was doing something useful. And then it happened — my last day at Bogside, my last day as a pitman.

I was working away in the locker room with young John one day. I was standing on the seat and reaching high with my brush when there was a sudden sharp pain racking through my body. The thought flashed through my mind that my back was away, and then I fell to the concrete floor, with my bucket of strong soda solution clattering down beside me. I still had the brush in my hand, and for several seconds I could not move at all. Was I paralysed? Finally I could move, but could not get up. I could hear John calling for help, and then John and the bath attendant were with me. They helped me to my feet and then to the seat. I couldn't stand straight, and the pain made me grit my teeth as the sweat poured down my body and I fumbled in a pocket for the pain killers.

They helped me off to the attendants' room and gave me tea, the universal treatment. As it happened, the Manager appeared just then, and he immediately insisted that I go off home, and that young Hendry, one of the bath attendants, would drive me. He had done it before, and joked that it was becoming a habit. It was not an easy journey, because every hole in the road made me groan with the pain of the jolt, and I was very glad to get to my door. May, of course, was out immediately she heard the car, full of worry and concern and love, and I had to walk into the house under my own steam, just to reassure her that I was really not all that bad. Hendry went off, glad to have had a short shift that day, and May helped me up to bed.

I was off work a long time again, and had a lot of pain. However, I did manage to get up to the Union office once a week to deal with affairs there. Usually someone drove me up, because I felt that I was still unfit to drive myself.

It was on one of the days I was in the Office that Wullie Graham broached a new subject. Wullie was now our Delegate, and Wullie MacDougall a member of the Executive. George Bolton, as I had long expected, had gone on to be Vice President of our Union. I dealt with all the correspondence, and we had our usual exchange of views, and then MacDougall told be that there was a scheme to offer some of the men redundancy. This was some of the older men, and others who had perhaps been injured. That could include me. They assured me that we were not giving up any jobs, and that there would be new starts to fill the numbers of those redundant. I was concerned about not giving up any jobs, but interested in the possibility of being redundant myself. It was something I had never considered. Now I had to consider it.

I thought about it, and talked about it with May, and finally decided that I would accept. It meant that not only would I give up my work in the pits, but necessarily also give up the work for the Union. Two big wrenches. But I faced up to it, largely because I knew that if I continued working there was a good chance that I would finish up crippled or disabled in some way. That was a chance I was not prepared to take.

So one afternoon I signed the papers, and walked out of the Manager's office, and then out of the Union office, for the last time. My Seven Steps In the Dark of the coal industry had brought me to this — a pittance of a "golden handshake", a bit of a pension and a back that was pretty well in ruins. No, there was more than that: my body was laced with blue scars, the miner's medals. And yet even that was not all, for there was the wonderful memory of the years of fellowship and comradeship, of the self-sacrifice and the heroism, of the solidarity of the miners and the warmth of the mining families. I was closing not just a chapter of life, but a book.

POSTSCRIPT

Some weeks later there was the annual Christmas dinner for the retired miners. Every man in the pit paid a certain amount each week towards this, and towards an annual outing to the Scottish Grand National. They were always happy and enjoyable occasions, and for the first time I was to attend as a retired miner, and not as Union Secretary. Those Christmas dinners were also the occasion for presenting men with their retiring presents, bought by a collection in the pit.

The Town Hall was crowded that night, and May and myself were ushered to our places by well-wishers who shook our hands and told us how much I was going to be missed. What a difference, I thought, from the beginning of these evenings for the retired men, when, twenty-one years ago, I had stood at the pit gate with a collection tin, and taken enough for a supper at the local hotel and a sing-song.

The evening began with presentations to the retiring men. Wullie Macdougall and the Manager, Tommy Rae, did the presenting, and I was the last to be called. There was no cheering as I went up to the platform in answer to Wullie's call, but people shook my hand and pressed my shoulder. I stood in front of Wullie, who shook me by the hand, very warmly, as did Tommy Rae. Wullie then spoke of the work I had done on behalf of the men. He recalled some incidents in which we had worked togther, and told the audience that many of them had received benefits from the unseen work I had done on their behalf. 'It is with sadness and regret we have to lose him, after the valuable contribution he has given to the men of Bogside and Meta. He is leaving us because of his injury, but will always be remembered as a valiant fighter for human rights and the rights of his fellow men. Good luck, comrade, and may you enjoy a long and happy retirement. You have earned our respect and our appreciation for the tremendous work you have done on our behalf. I thank you warmly on behalf of us all. Good Luck and Good Health.'

The Manager presented me with a wall clock, and said that I was one man who would be sadly missed. 'Thank you for everything you have done.'

The hall erupted with cheers and shouts. Feet stamped and hands clapped. The very plates rattled on the tables. I was overwhelmed and almost overcome with emotion. There was not much I wanted to say, but I thanked them all for the gift.

'It has been a privilege to have been elected as your Branch Secretary for twenty-one years. I have learned a great deal. We have fought together for better conditions and along the way have helped many other struggling Unions and organisations. That is a tribute to the generosity of the men here.

'I am sorry to be leaving you, but I cannot work underground any longer, because of injury. I have made my decision. A secretary, when he is dealing with accident claims should know how and where it happened and must be able to inspect the site. If he cannot, the result might be that a man's case is lost.

'I began work in the pits at fourteen, straight to the coalface with my father. I suppose I would be among the last to do so. How well I remember that first day. I felt I had become a man. They were the pick and shovel days, wooden props, ponies and hand drawing of the hutches. Then it was pans and belt conveyors along the faceline, and so up to the present day with the shearers and the Gullick supports.

'As Wullie MacDougall used to say, my workmates are a fine body of men, although there are some right buggers among them! But miners are the salt of the earth. I have worked alongside some men who have left the pits and prospered elsewhere. Two became Provosts, one a Minister and one a doctor. One became General Secretary of the Musicians' Union. I worked with Mick McGahey when we were young men together, living in a hostel, and planning to change the world. Mick is still there, working for humanity. Wullie MacDougall and George Bolton, our own Brothers, are on the Executive of our Union, and I wish them well. But my father had a saying that if you never reach the high life, you don't have far to fall, so here am I, still amang my ain folk.

'The very first resolution I wrote for Bogside was a claim for a substantial increase in miners' pensions. That was twenty-one years ago, and the pension was a pittance then, and it is still a pittance today. It is a disgrace, a despicable insult to men who have worked so hard in such deplorable conditions. It is an insult.

'To my successor as Branch Secretary, I say that you are in a position of great importance. Five minutes of your time can save a man a lot of misery. There is much to learn, and a lot you can do. I am saddened at leaving my workmates, and look back now at the happy times I spent working among you. Thank you, and Good Luck to every one of you.'

I don't think anyone heard my last words, for there was an eruption of cheering and a standing ovation. I was overwhelmed by it, and so was May when I eventually won back to our table.

It was a grand night, with singing and dancing and drinking, and we all enjoyed it very much. I was finished with the pits, and with Union work, but I could never be finished with my workmates, my comrades. They were as much part of me, part of my life, as my own body and the scars it bore. There was no way I could tell them how much I admired and loved them, so this book has to do that.

The year was 1979, and I was fifty-nine years old. They had given me a redundancy payment of £2100 and a promise of another £1000 in a few years time. And that was after working in the pits since I was fourteen years old. I had been a Union member for all those years, and an official for about thirty years. The General Secretary of the Union sent me a curt acknowledgement of my letter resigning from the Branch post. No more than that. The Compensation Officer, however, sent a long letter of thanks for the work I had done over so many years. Well, I suppose the General Secretary is a very busy man.

I left the industry before the final assault was made on it and our Union, and before it was disembowelled for political advantage. There is almost no mining now in Scotland, and few miners. There is no doubt where I would have been if I had still been working during that last disastrous strike. I would have been on those picket lines.

I am no politician, no economist, not an educated man, and certainly I have no crystal ball to see into the future. Yet I am totally convinced that some day the Scottish coal mines will be re-opened as a great national resource, perhaps the last one we have. There will be no miners then, and all the skills learned over the centuries will have been lost, and will have to be re-learned. Closing the mines, ripping the life out of that industry and so many others, will one day be seen as the greatest act of folly committed by any government this century.